TRANSCENDING ARCHITECTURE

TRANSCENDING ARCHITECTURE

Contemporary Views on Sacred Space

EDITED BY JULIO BERMUDEZ

Foreword by Randall Ott

THE CATHOLIC UNIVERSITY OF AMERICA PRESS 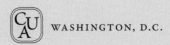 WASHINGTON, D.C.

Library of Congress Cataloging-in-Publication Data

Transcending architecture : contemporary views on sacred space / Edited by Julio

Bermudez ; Foreword by Randall Ott.

pages cm

Includes bibliographical references and index.

ISBN 978-0-8132-2679-8 (pbk. : alk. paper)   1. Architecture and religion.

2. Sacred space.   I. Bermúdez, Julio Cesar, editor.

NA4600.T73 2015

726.01—dc23   2014039452

For the invisible
yet always-present
and all-abiding
transcendent

CONTENTS

PART II. INTERDISCIPLINARY PERSPECTIVES

PART III. RESPONSE FROM ARCHITECTURAL PRACTICE

ILLUSTRATIONS

FOREWORD

Since the mid-1960s, skepticism about organized religion has largely eliminated discussion of the sacred from architectural curricula. This secular turn did not mean that all consideration of transcendence evaporated from our teaching and practice, but the operative program for such study decisively shifted. Despite orthodox modernism's wish for an architecture founded on "pure" utility (on efficiency, science, production, technology, forthrightness, and so forth), architects and architectural educators still intuitively recognized that buildings had to serve "other" needs. Humanity yearned beyond the pragmatic, mechanical, or biological. Instead of the temple, cathedral, mosque, or synagogue, the art museum became the alternate venue for this—a typology in which transcendent experience could be had without mention of literal faith. Nor did the architectural profession begrudge this necessity. We embraced artistic typologies with fervor, sensing or at least hoping that the aesthetical could address the same human craving that the spiritual once did. Art museums appeared on every design student's board—and often. A decade ago, I had an undergraduate at an institution where I was teaching tell me that for four consecutive semesters of design studio, the program choices made available were all art oriented: "House for a Collector," "Art School," "Museum of This-or-That Famed Artist," "The Photographer's Studio," and so on. The Guggenheim, Bilbao, and dozens of other prominent new art museums became the late twentieth century's cathedrals. Soon enough, no one could hope for fame in the discipline without a major facility for art in their professional portfolio (and we naïvely had thought it would be housing instead).

Even modest, mid-sized cities eagerly entered and competed in the contemporary museum wars, fielding ever more gorgeous, one-off, rather strident creations. If nothing else, this strange outcome of modernity's purported thrust toward pragmatism was to convince us, once and for all, that architecture cannot distill to budgets, footages, and building systems. Other profound needs cannot be addressed through those well-meaning areas. Pure utility as speechmaking led, remarkably, to pure aesthetics as a responding dream.

But in the end, did this swap of museum for temple still offer us transcendence? One senses we have already taken this transference as far as it can go, and come up short. Countertrends are becoming apparent. Why, though, doesn't the museum as social or ethical or personal "cathedral" still work—still convince us that we have had our weekly experience of transcendence? Is it a matter of simple boredom or overkill? Have we now built so many museums that they stand on every corner in every city (as is colloquially said of the hundreds of churches of Baroque Rome, for example) and offer not so much a respite from an environment founded on instrumental rationality but have become the surrounding environment itself, fostering a desire for a new upheaval or breakout? Or, alternatively, have we, after fifty years of museums as guides to the "other," perhaps simply discovered that aesthetics does not fully encapsulate that other? This seems closer to the truth. There is no dispute that aesthetics may open the door to an experience of transcendence, but in such a case it functions as a vehicle, not as the goal itself. The increasing hollowness of our ever more desperate museum-based pyrotechnics suggests such a realization. For millennia aesthetics and the sacred have had

a close if uneasy relationship—modernity's recent efforts are really just another reprise of the Platonic tradition's conflation of beauty with the holy. It seems we have begun to suspect that pleasing our eyes is not the same as pleasing our souls. Such thoughts drive us beyond the desire for aesthetic titillation and impel a search even among us blasé moderns for indelible meaning—perhaps the sacred's core constituent.

Even just a decade ago, it would have been hard to imagine transcendence as the subject for a conference at a school of architecture. "Transcending Architecture," a recent symposium organized at the School of Architecture and Planning at the Catholic University of America, highlights this emerging countertrend. This symposium brought together architects, theologians, philosophers, planners, scholars in anthropology, social work, and comparative religion, as well as critics and encouraged them to speculate about how the sublime ushering of built form into transcendent experience operates, and, crucially, what its meaning for humanity may be. How does architecture describe the indescribable and, in doing so, speak ably of things that are often considered most potent when left literally unsaid? The sessions explored how we create the architecturally transcendent today and how it can still exert an influence in our contemporary, highly secular lives.

Of course there is the danger, given our recent history as a profession, that we will simply substitute the study of artistic cathedrals for artistic museums and find ourselves right back where we started, staring into aestheticism from the pews instead of standing in a gallery. The symposium, and the chapters published here from it, addressed that concern by avoiding a focus on the rising trend toward recent, evocative religious spaces and instead stressed more elemental themes: the "groundedness" of home, nature as recovery, ethics, the holiness of life itself, the primacy of people over things, the power of empty but enabling nothingness, social justice, how reality always exceeds us, the processes of hermeneutics, and related ideas.

One would hope transcendence, of all topics, might evade hasty exploitation and subsequent boredom. The sacred retains inherent mystery, which may afford it unique resilience here. It has a profound grassroots allure for citizens. The increasing number of autonomous studies of the sacred in architectural curricula across the country today is an optimistic sign of such renewed interest. If the sacred eventually reestablishes itself as a primary force within architecture, that outcome will result more from these common, broadly based, grassroots efforts than from evocations of, and conversations about, the grandiose. Our profession's disdain for storefront epiphanies or megachurch mixers blinds us to this. History, of course, had its prestigious religious monuments that provoked architectural tourism, its sites of pilgrimage that bordered on consumerism. Yet what drove people toward such places was the honest belief in what they already experienced every day back home. The aesthetic power incumbent in history's great religious buildings had a role, but it was that of further consummating the visitor's prior experiences of life's daily profundity. One doubts that dynamic can function in reverse. Can an architectural pilgrimage to a new cathedral, if driven solely by its beguiling aesthetics, kindle anew a practical ethics offering meaning to one's day-to-day life? Truthfully, the process begins elsewhere, with the day-to-day itself.

The "Transcending Architecture" symposium was an outgrowth of our larger mission at the Catholic University of America, which stresses service to church and nation through the joint aegis of faith and reason, and our specific school mission of "building stewardship"—which we interpret as finding ways to create intersections between our role as stewards on this globe and our buildings. One outgrowth of that mission is our school's sacred space and cultural studies concentration in our MArch program—the only place in the country where an architecture student can spend several semesters studying the impacts of the sacred on our built environment. The graduate concentration is led by Associate Professor Julio Bermudez.

Our appreciation goes to Professor Bermudez for organizing the symposium and editing the resulting volume now in your hands, and to the Catholic University of America Press for publishing these important contents so they can reach a wider audience. We also deeply appreciate and acknowledge the support of the Walton Fund for Sacred Architecture, which has made possible so many initiatives related to the study of sacred placemaking at our school, including this one.

RANDALL OTT
Dean, School of Architecture and Planning, The Catholic University of America

ACKNOWLEDGMENTS

As I complete this project in late June 2013, I realize that it has been almost two years since the organization of the symposium "Transcending Architecture" got started. The result of this twenty-four-month journey, the book now in your hands, took much patience, time, effort, and help. And regarding the latter, now is the appropriate moment to acknowledge all the people without whom this publication would have been impossible. First, I would like to thank my dean, Randall Ott, who encouraged, trusted, and supported me in the organization of the event and later on in the production of this book. My appreciation also goes to the CUA architecture undergraduate students Kelly Corcoran, Matthew Kline, and Tyler Thurston and graduate students Gina Longo, Benjamin Norkin, Ashley Prince, Chloe Rice, and Mandira Sareen, who generously assisted me in a variety of ways before and during the symposium. In particular, I would like to show my indebtedness to graduate student Brandon Ro for his diligent, intelligent, and outstanding support in producing the final version of the manuscript for submission to CUA Press. I need to recognize several CUArch staff members for their various help as well: Associate Dean for Student and Academic Affairs Michelle A. Rinehart, past and present Assistants to the Dean Kathy Fayne and Patricia Dudley (respectively), Visual Resource Center Manager Bob Willis, Administrative Assistant Nora Petersen, and Systems Administrator Jerry Mosby. My thanks also go to all my faculty colleagues at CUArch for their honest interest, warm support, and active participation in the symposium. The Catholic University of America Office of Video Production and

News Media should be acknowledged for their video recording and webcasting of all the keynote speeches. The financial generosity of the Walton Family Distinguished Critic in Design and Catholic Stewardship program must be highlighted as it was instrumental in securing the event. Most generally, I want to publicly acknowledge and thank the Catholic University of America along with its School of Architecture and Planning for having the courage, intention, and passion to pursue matters of the spirit at the highest and most rigorous levels of inquiry.

It is with deep appreciation that I acknowledge all of the contributors to this book, adding that they were also instrumental in finding and securing the beautiful images illustrating these pages. It is the appropriate time for me to recognize photographer and artist Vivian Ronay for her inspiring photos of sacred spaces that were exhibited during the symposium and helped to create just the right atmosphere for formal and informal conversations. Dr. Michael Crosbie, editor-in-chief of *Faith & Form* magazine, deserves special credit for his generous advertising of the symposium in both print and web formats, as well as helping me select some of the symposium speakers. I don't want to forget to express my gratitude to the scholars that peer reviewed this book manuscript at the request of CUA Press. While I don't know their names, their criticism and advice were helpful in making this, I hope, a better text. Thanks should also go to the AIA-DC, AIA-Maryland, AIA-Virginia, the IFRAA (Interfaith Forum on Religion, Art and Architecture), the Embassy of Finland, and the ACS (Architecture, Culture and Spirituality) Forum for their active promotion of the symposium. And since no book can exist without a supportive, understanding, and yet critical publisher, I want to first thank CUA Press for undertaking a topic relatively new to its portfolio, and second acknowledge director Trevor C. Lipscombe for successfully overseeing the process of making the book. Various individuals at CUA Press deserve my recognition as well. This book would not have been possible without the committed and diligent work of Libby Newkumet, assistant to the director; Theresa Walker, managing editor; Tanjam Jacobson, editorial associate; Brian Roach, marketing manager; Nicole Wayland, copy editor; and Anne Kachergis, book designer.

Close to the end of these thanks, I want to tell Andrea Kalvesmaki, my life partner, how much I have appreciated her loving, accepting, and encouraging words and deeds that have enabled me to pursue and complete this project. In the end, however, the ultimate gratitude can only be directed toward the invisible yet always present and all-abiding transcendent to whom/which I wholeheartedly dedicate this humble effort.

PART I   DISCIPLINARY PERSPECTIVES

1 INTRODUCTION

If we ask professionals and scholars about the mission of architecture, most of them would agree that architecture is called to do a lot more than to guarantee the public health, safety, and welfare of building users. In fact, most would say that the promise of architecture begins fulfillment when such expectations have been met *and* transcended. But transcended into what? Will outstanding building functionality, economy, sustainability, formalism, or even symbolism do it? At first sight, any of these accomplishments would seem good enough, but, upon reflection, a majority of us would concede that "transcending" architecture insinuates something much deeper, bigger, and qualitatively different.

Seeking pointers for what this "transcendence" may entail, we find a variety of entries that, despite their secular or spiritual inter-

pretations, share strong commonalities. For there is little doubt that agnostic Le Corbusier's "ineffable," highly religious Rudolf Otto's "numinous," and philosophically minded Louis Kahn's "immeasurable" are indicating moments in which architecture is being transcended:[1] a building's geometric proportions turn into shivers, stone into tears, rituals into insights, light into joy, space into contemplation, and time into heightened presence (or absence). They are talking of an architecture that has removed the "opacity" hiding life's meanings so that we can catch a momentous and revelatory (even if unsettling) glimpse. We should also notice that these qualifiers are referring to something "other than" or "beyond" architecture. It is as if the experience of the building has exceeded the building, passing, as it were, through it into another realm that defies all words or gauging.[2] Here we are inevitably directed to pre-twentieth-century philosophical discussions on beauty.[3]

But there is more to transcending architecture than aesthetics, a path that, many would argue, is plagued with pitfalls leading to irresponsible hedonism, subjectivism, and escapism. Karsten Harries and Alberto Perez-Gomez remind us that transcending architecture in service of an ethical practice, while more horizontal and immanent than its sister aesthetics, may be a much wiser choice.[4] A building's layout, functionality, context, development, or construction may be strategically employed to advance social justice, environmental conservation, communal history or cohesion, moral causes, spiritual teaching, and more. In this perspective, doing good by or through architecture is the most direct and compassionate way not only to help people, other living beings, nature, or the world but, in so doing, to reach God and participate in his work, as Michael Benedikt claims.[5] The ethical pursuit of architecture leads to both its transcendence and transcendence itself.

Let us notice the difference in emphasis between aesthetic and ethical types of transcending. Whereas the former depends on the architectural artifact to induce the numinous (hence directing attention to the "object" or the beautiful), the latter occasions the transcending through architectural service (not the "object" but the "good"). In other words, the aesthetic interest tends to be formal, perceptual, and subjective (even though a building's beauty will have social and cultural impacts, no doubt), while the ethical attention leans to the functional, social, and intersubjective (even though their effects will be surely felt at a personal level). Obviously, this discrimination between ethics and aesthetics is only a rhetoric device to cast light

into the matter. In reality, ethics and aesthetics are irrevocably intertwined in architectural practice and experience, although one or the other may take the lead. What is clear from either form of architectural transcendence is that the building itself may be said to "disappear" or "spent" in the very act of revealing meaning, liberating being, provoking joy, and/or improving living conditions. Common to both is also the surrendering of architecture to something larger and better than itself, a movement beyond disciplinary partiality for the sake of the whole or holy. In this sense, transcending architecture depends on and/or brings forth the hypothesis, if not the intuitive certainty, that there is "something" so vast, profound, essential, or purposeful in life that architecture should actively study, seek, support, and even give itself up for. This "something" is transcendental.

This discussion naturally leads us to the intimate connection between transcending architecture and sacred space. After all, what else has been the goal of religious buildings but to facilitate the witnessing, advancement, or worship of transcendence? Long ago, we figured the real power of designed environments to quicken the metaphysical dimension of our humanity. Thus, talking of transcending architecture also refers to an entire class of buildings devoted to providing access to a transcending state, realm, or practice. However, we should quickly recognize that not all sacredness needs to be institutionally defined (i.e., be "religious") or be "spirituality" bound in the traditional sense of the word (e.g., God centered contemplation or worshiping). As mentioned earlier, architecture pursuing goodness (e.g., social justice, human dignity) probably could be considered "sacred" despite its immanent goal, service, or deployment. Its

FIGURE 1-1. AESTHETIC EXPERIENCES OF ARCHITEC-
TURE MAY CATAPULT US INTO A TRANSCENDENTAL
MOMENT FULL OF SPIRITUAL AND EXISTENTIAL
MEANING. THE PANTHEON IN ROME IS REPORTED
TO BE ONE PLACE WHERE SUCH EXTRAORDINARY
EVENTS MAY UNFOLD.

FIGURE 1-2. MAGGIE'S CENTRE AT NINEWELLS,
DUNDEE, UNITED KINGDOM, AN ARCHITECTURAL
WORK DEVOTED TO THE SUPPORT AND IMPROVE-
MENT OF HUMAN LIFE, THAT TRANSCENDS ORDINARY
BUILDING CONCERNS SUCH AS MARKET PROFIT,
GROSS FUNCTIONALITY, SUPERFICIAL AESTHETICS,
OR TECHNOLOGICAL EXPERIMENTATION, DESIGNED BY
ARCHITECT FRANK GEHRY.

sacredness would be found in supporting the care and development of other living beings, thus partaking in a larger, indeed transcending (religious or not), mission.

Despite the apparent importance of this topic, the architectural discipline has been hitherto too burdened by the ideological weight of modernity and postmodernity to pay close attention or care about it.[6] It is therefore heartening to notice a growing change in this attitude (as the surge of new groups, conferences, publications, and graduate programs addressing these matters suggest),[7] even when the discourse on anything transcendental stubbornly remains under the safe disciplinary confines of architectural history, building typology, and descriptive case studies. This means that the delicate and complex issues underscoring the phenomenology, culture, critical theory, and design of transcendence-seeking architectures continue to lag behind.

But let us not rush to respond to this disciplinary shortcoming too quickly. A project like this cannot afford naïveté, lest we fall into the traps and problems that made such pursuits something off limits to serious reflection, research, and work. We need to recognize that any study or practice aimed at transcending architecture will face difficult challenges. The first is likely to come from the architectural profession which, like any other expert organization, considers its area of expertise something of central importance not just to itself but to the society and culture it serves. Hence, the very idea of "transcending architecture" is poised to raise all kinds of fears and questions. Does "transcending" here mean a diminishing professional of competency or role? Does it signify to surrender architectural practice to the whims and desires of clients and society? Are the unselfish professionalism and altruist buildings that architectural transcendence suggests possible in our competitive economy and consumer society? How are we to engage these highly qualitative, esoteric, intangible dimensions of ethical/aesthetic transcendence so that we can accomplish the job? Are architects also called to be theologians, anthropologists, social workers, philosophers, and politicians?

A second set of difficulties will be presented by the astute intellectual who will object the very notion of "transcending" anything, architecture included. For hasn't poststructuralism irrefutably demonstrated that there is no possibility of breaking free (i.e., transcend) from embodied and cultural bondage? Transcendence is just an illusion built upon the myth of the given, ignorance of an over-

powering language and its inescapable representations, and/or blindness to monological consciousness. Human life cannot escape the always fluid, hermeneutically demanding, power-abuse-prone realm of "messy" inter-subjectivity. Since it is impossible to break the orbit of conditioned immanence, the very suggestion of accessing some metaphysical or holy realm is disingenuous, manipulative, a regression to premodernity, religious naïveté, if not worse.

A third challenge will simply point to the fact that architecture has been already transcended as a platform for advancing ethical or cultural agendas. Victor Hugo's nineteenth-century forecast of the obsolescence of architecture (i.e., its transcendence) as the prime cultural medium to synthesize and teach a people's understanding and zeitgeist[8] has been de facto enacted, not by the book but by the ubiquitous electronic-communication networks of the twenty-first century.[9] With the massive migration of social activities and individual practices to the media sphere, brick and mortars have little bearing in shaping contemporary discourse.[10] And, while the replacement of architectural space by cyberspace may not satisfy everybody, it is also obvious that any practice aimed at improving the world or cultivating our spirit would be best pursued by deploying means other than architecture, even if the ineffable is its ultimate goal.[11] Time, it would seem, has proven Hegel right: technology has replaced the arts as the main driver of conscious evolution.

A fourth critique will argue that gaining access to a holy realm ultimately necessitates no building at all. For example, as Kevin Seasoltz explains, not only did the origin of our Abrahamic traditions occur in the "undesigned" environment of the desert, but the Jews continued such a nonlocalized connection with God for centuries after (and forced by) the destruction of Herod's Temple in Jerusalem.[12] Christians picked up that tradition during their early days out of survival necessity. It was only after the institutionalization of the Christian faith in ancient Rome, the Islamization of the Middle East, and the establishment of relatively tolerant conditions for Jews in Europe that churches, mosques, and synagogues began to spring out. Still, as Jones convincingly proposes, the codification of religious practice (i.e., rituals and symbols) into special physical layouts (i.e., buildings) remains, to this day, largely a supportive and secondary method to access the divine.[13] It is religious practice itself and *not* architecture that engenders the phenomenon of transcendence.[14]

At a personal level, these challenges, however serious, do not compromise the value and reality of an architecture that seeks transcendence. They don't because nobody can intellectually, socially, or historically invalidate what someone has experienced firsthand at the most profound level of being.[15] In other words, the very phenomenology of transcending architecture guarantees its standing power. Yet this subjective position is far from being an acceptable argument for people who have never experienced or, at the very least, sensed a "transcending" goodness, truth, or beauty firsthand. It is even less convincing for a discipline committed to a secular, technological, and economical agenda. For them, we may need the assistance of science and impeccable rhetoric: today's only widely agreed systems to validate claims and hypotheses and a fifth area where a project investigating the transcendental nature of architecture

will find obstacles. Can empirical, logic, and hermeneutical methods be applied to demonstrate, describe, and perhaps elucidate events so immaterial, nonrational, and private as transcending architecture? If this sounds very hard to do, it is good to know that we are not the only ones facing these questions. Debate on the nature and reality of consciousness and "qualia" (as the qualitative "howness" or "raw feel" of subjective experience has been termed) as well as ways to technically and rationally explain them have been raging over the past decade in philosophy and science.[16] Suffice it to say that, although a transcending architecture may find empirical and argumentative backing in a number of trustable testimonies,[17] statistically significant survey results,[18] and a few books,[19] this evidence is hardly enough to command credibility.

This introduction clearly points to the promises and perils of architecture seeking transcendence. Certainly it makes the ambiguity of the title "transcending architecture" all the more nuanced and provocative. For who or what is doing the transcending? And exactly what is that being transcended? As many of the authors in this book recognize, I intentionally poised this interpretive uncertainty. There are good reasons for my doing so. The semantic vagueness of "transcending architecture" forbids closure, secures humility, and encourages new interpretations, even of the ones already concocted. In this sense, at least five general and different but potentially interrelated meanings are implicit. Transcending architecture may refer to a building type whose purpose is to (1) deliver users to a transcendental state (e.g., sacred architecture) or (2) support services, activities, and realizations that advance a transcending cause (e.g., human dignity). Transcending architecture

FIGURE 1-3. ÉTIENNE-LOUIS BOULLÉE'S "CENOTAPH TO
NEWTON," 1784, AN EXAMPLE OF A UTOPIAN WORK
AIMED AT TRANSCENDING THE SOCIOCULTURAL, EVEN
CIVILIZATIONAL, PARADIGMS OF ITS TIME. EFFORTS BY
THE ARCHIGRAM, METABOLISM, OR FUTURISM IN THE
TWENTIETH CENTURY FOLLOW THIS SAME PATH.

may also imply architectural practices and/
or results that go well beyond cultural, social,
or professional conventions. In this third
case, it is architects who are using the making
of architecture to enact the transcendence.
Fourth, it could also describe a psychological
state reached with (or without) architectural
assistance but which no longer pays attention
or depends on architecture. Such state may
(or may not) be ineffable. Lastly, the term may
be pointing to the act of moving past architecture (either as discipline or actual built

structure) due to its inability, irrelevance, or
being unnecessary to address transcendence—
or any other purpose, for that matter.

Having framed the discussion and acknowledged the indeterminate and disputed
nature of "transcending architecture," let
me now recognize the bias underscoring the
writing of this book: *a belief in the reality
and need for an architecture that advances the
cause of transcendence.* It is this conviction
along with the recognition of a world either
too resistant or too uncritically yielding to

such vision that motivated me to organize the interdisciplinary symposium "Transcending Architecture: Aesthetics and Ethics of the Numinous." This conference took place at the Catholic University of America School of Architecture and Planning during October 6–8, 2011, and its goal was to call attention, provoke reflection, facilitate discussion, promote action, and develop scholarship on the transcendental nature, function, and experience of architecture. Acknowledging that a serious consideration of the topic would demand many voices and disciplines, I invited an outstanding group of scholars and practitioners with recognized expertise in the relationship between architecture, culture, and spirituality, from fields as diverse as planning, philosophy, social work, theology, liturgy, anthropology, landscape architecture, comparative religion, and, of course, architecture. In order to avoid the loss of focus that typically plagues conferences, I expressly instructed the speakers (and kept reminding them throughout the time leading up to the symposium) to address only the transcending dimension of architecture. The result was one of the most direct, clear, interdisciplinary, and subtle conversations solely devoted to the lived relationship between the built and the numinous worlds to date—an event witnessed by over two hundred symposium registrants (not including students), some coming from as far as India, Argentina, and Denmark (and seventeen U.S. states). The success and uniqueness of this meeting, along with a lack of publications on the subject, naturally encouraged the making of this book. The lectures specially developed for the symposium were extended into a full-fledged manuscript, then edited and amended twice, followed by a peer-reviewed process

conducted by other nationally recognized scholars, and finally edited one last time in response to such evaluation before arriving to their present format in this volume. The whole process took time, patience, and effort from all the contributors who responded with enthusiasm and support for the project, never once complaining. Each author courageously stepped forward to make their case for transcending architecture even though they understood quite well that pointing or expressing the immeasurable nature of the built environment would inevitably fall short. Yet all of them, like me, did and do trust that the integration of all these perspectives will bring, on the one hand, understanding, relief, and growth to an architectural discipline that avoids transcendence and, on the other hand, a necessary dose of detail and reality to fields such as theological aesthetics, material anthropology, or philosophical phenomenology that too often fall trapped into unproductive generalizations and overintellectualizations. In this sense, one important contribution of this book is the authors' effort to bridge disciplines. In a very literal way, they are enacting the transcending (of their fields) and their chapters are all the more insightful and compelling for it. This effort is not common yet absolutely necessary in this day and age, especially in an area with transcending aspirations. The outcome is a coherent and wide-ranging text that confirms old wisdom and opens new vistas and depths.

This book is organized into three parts, presenting perspectives that scholars of the built environment (part I), scholars from outside the field of architecture (part II), and architectural practitioners (part III) have of transcending architecture.

Part I starts with Finnish architect Juhani

Pallasmaa offering an aesthetic and interfaith vision. His clear, soft, and evolving arguments build an atmospheric narrative that awakens our unconscious recesses to entertain his message: there exists a "non-devotional sacredness … [that] arises from the experiential holiness of life itself and a deep existential recognition of one's own being." Pallasmaa believes that transcending architecture turns us not toward the building or the world but rather toward ourselves, thus making our being opaque to realization. In other words, transcending architecture transcends itself by transferring all attention from itself to the visitor's own existence. In so doing, it is about silencing itself and needs to follow no particular liturgy, ritual, or typology to succeed. A lay building may very well induce transcending experiences and, for this reason, attain a sacred character albeit of a nonreligious kind (e.g., architect Louis Kahn's Salk Institute in La Jolla, California). For Pallasmaa, transcending architecture fundamentally necessitates the assistance of light and silence, phenomena that raise our ontological, existential, and spiritual sensibilities and, in so doing, call forth the sacred. He finishes by encouraging us to pursue transcending architecture because "more than ever before, the ethical and humane task of architecture and all art is … to reveal the existence of the transcendental realm, the domain of the sacred."

For sacred space scholar Thomas Barrie, transcending architecture naturally springs out of realizing, returning, or manifesting the holiness of home. He supports this conviction in a refreshing and nuanced study of domesticity that shows that the origin of all religious architecture may be found in the humble groundedness of human dwell-

ing. Barrie's argument makes perfect sense, although hardly anyone has articulated it this clearly before. For example, the experience and idea of home as the sacred place most intimately tied to understanding and striving for our original nature is at the center of the Christian notion of "paradise" and the Buddhist concept of "self." In a few pages, Barrie unpacks an impressive array of scholarship covering multiple cultures, religions, and epochs that opens transcending theoretical and practical opportunities for architecture. Barrie finishes his chapter by sharing two built examples. While not sacred buildings, these small houses designed and built by him illustrate the concrete possibilities that his reflections of home affords.

Rebecca Krinke brings attention to the healing, contemplative, and ethically awakening effects of experiencing a transcending nature. For landscape architect and artist Krinke, many of our most intractable problems come from being disconnected from our natural world. Grounded on this principle, she presents several provocative examples of how to bring us back into balance, focusing on the most dangerous symptom of today's unhealthy state: stress. Her four case studies properly transcend cataloguing: are they art installations, research projects, landscape architectural designs, psychosocial happenings, or political activism? The answer seems to be "yes" to all, but in different degrees. Most importantly, these creative interventions are trying to transform existing conditions of suffering and pain into transcending opportunities for personal, social, ethical, and spiritual growth and healing. It takes little time to realize that Krinke's arguments, while at first may appear secularly humanistic, actually point to the divine in subtle but nonetheless profound ways. Her position on the centrality of nature to recover (or be reminded) of the numinous resonates with those of several authors in the book, as the reader will certainly notice.

Can a transcending architecture become a transcending urbanism when asked to address the city? And if so, how? Urban planning researcher Maged Senbel approaches this challenge by presenting a timely, large scale, and spiritually sensitive view of sustainability. This perspective is essential to illuminate the forces pushing the progressive "green" agenda toward ever more technocratic strategies that are devoid of meaning and end up causing more harm than good. Senbel seamlessly intertwines ethics, aesthetics, symbolism, politics, economy, and culture in a discourse that keeps on pointing to the indefensible "cultural mythology" at play today: a blind consumerist and material civilization with an unlimited appetite for growth and deluded by an unquestionable faith in modernity. In exchange, he proposes what he calls "reverential urbanism," that is, "a form of urbanism that facilitates a deep sense of respect and awe for nature and for other human beings … a practice that requires the poetic cultivation of hope alongside empirical analysis and inductive reasoning." Going from the largest concept to concrete details of how it could be done, Senbel makes an impassionate case for establishing a model of city living that could encourage an "ethics of conservation over consumption [and of] spiritual growth over material growth." The reader will no doubt appreciate Senbel's sophisticated and heartfelt writing as well as the many references he deploys to substantiate his vision of a transcending urbanism.

Architectural historian and theoretician Karla Britton returns us to the challenging reality of pursuing a transcending architecture. How is one to determine and express what is sacred in the rapidly changing, ever more diverse, global, and materialistic milieu of today? The situation presents two great risks for architects, she tells us. The first one comes from trying to resuscitate a foregone era of spirituality and therefore going against the technoscientific and secular momentum of architectural and Western history. The second and far greater danger comes from brokering long-held yet slowly vanishing religious traditions and new, cutting edge, even controversial ways to address the divine. These difficulties may be tackled, Britton argues, by following Heidegger's teachings on building dwelling but illuminated by Vattimo's idea of "weak thought," that is, a humble recognition of the ultimate unavoidable uncertainty of all human positioning and action. Transcending architecture, Britton reminds us, cannot avoid indeterminacy and insecurity because it comes from and returns to us.

Since transcending architecture is fundamentally an action or event (not some esoteric, idealist construct deduced from dogma or philosophy), Julio Bermudez argues that understanding it demands a serious and detailed study of its experiential nature. And what better way to do this than by investigating one of the most well-known yet less probed transcending experiences of architecture ever recorded: the extraordinary encounter of Charles-Édouard Jeanneret (who was to become Le Corbusier a few years later) with the Parthenon in September 1911. Bermudez's phenomenological examination delivers an array of new insights on the psychological, physical, and spiritual dimensions of the architectural numinous. It also demonstrates the power that such extraordinary moments may have in one's life, not to mention the importance of this particular one in the architectural discipline given the stature of Le Corbusier—arguably the most influential architect of the twentieth century. Bermudez's focus on the receptive dimension of ineffable space (something about which Le Corbusier would talk quite often at the end of his life) highlights the central role of experience to a discipline that by training, tradition, and job description is vastly more interested in how buildings are produced.

Part II of the book, covering views from outside the discipline, opens up with theologian Kevin Seasoltz. He begins by acknowledging the Bible's teaching of "the primacy of people over places and things" while at the same time recognizing the ultimate sacramentality of all entities and spaces on Earth based on the principle of creation. Faced with this double condition, Seasoltz reaffirms the central role that incarnation plays in the Christian mystery: not only has God become immanent in all creation but particularly in Jesus Christ and his legacy in the body of the Christian Church. As a result, sacred architecture becomes a unique opportunity to observe and understand how divine transcendence turns into flesh. In other words, how the Church has been embodied in buildings throughout history is sacred teaching. Father Seasoltz thus embarks on a historical journey that only he, with decades of scholarship on this topic, is able to deliver at such a level of insight, synthesis, and clarity. At the end, we find ourselves back to the present where he considers the challenge of figuring out what constitutes Christian sacred space today. For Seasoltz, transcending architecture is about keeping a transcendent yet incarnated God

alive in the lives of His people. This chapter is of particular relevance not only because it illuminates other texts in this book, notably those of Wedig, Jones, Stroik, and Vosko, but also because it is Father Seasoltz's posthumous contribution. We were all saddened to learn of his passing in late April 2013. Besides praying for his gentle soul, we can find some comfort in knowing that through this writing effort, his voice, wisdom, and presence will continue to play a positive role in a world that surely needs his clarity and humble belief in transcendence.

Liturgical theologian Mark Wedig picks up where Seasoltz left off by zooming into our present postmodern condition. How should we look at sacred space and its transcending experiences today? His response is as simple as it is compelling: it is in the "opening and fractures created by the postmodern condition" that we will find transcendence and therefore our answer. Our contemporary civilization has exacerbated the feelings of existential emptiness and meaninglessness to such a point that, if properly approached, people may become all the more open to the absolute. Wedig calls for sacred rituals that admit and express the new social realities, namely diversity (of cultures, ethnicities, traditions, classes) and its challenges. Following Jean-Yves Lacoste's phenomenology of liturgy, Wedig proposes that today's transcending architecture should come out of a personal and communal practice of voluntary poverty and powerlessness that leads into the nonspace of prayer—a transcending moment characterized by "empty, but enabling nothingness." Postmodern holy places should be sanctuaries from the hazards of hypermodernity, centers for the formation and practice of religious identity from where a new redeeming force to heal our cities and era may spring forth. Wedig finishes by reviewing the directives guiding the design of contemporary Catholic environments and studying a successful postmodern example of Catholic sacred space: Steven Holl's Chapel of St. Ignatius in Seattle.

Social work scholar Michael Sheridan argues that transcending architecture must advance an ethical agenda of social justice. Quite simply, justice-seeking and spirit-growing architectures are one and the same. In her own words, sacred space emerges "when a deep and wide understanding of spirituality, a comprehensive view of social justice, and socially conscious architecture are joined." Sheridan goes through an insightful discussion on the meaning of spirituality, religion, and social justice in light of current theory and practice in social work. Her rational and compassionate arguments soon land us into a transcending architecture that is truthful, emancipatory, and inevitably beautiful. Knowing quite well that abstract ideas are not good enough, Sheridan moves on to three living examples of such transcending, spirit-growing architecture: the Rural Studio program of Auburn University in Alabama, the Hunts Point Riverside Park in New York City, and the Inner City Arts in Los Angeles. For Sheridan, transcending architecture means to move architecture beyond its traditional role of serving the status quo in order to heal the "wounds of injustice that permeate our human condition." Sheridan's socially progressive agenda is convincing, never dull, and while not easy to follow, it should be never forgotten by those practicing or teaching architecture.

Since transcending architecture implies to move beyond some given frame of ref-

erence, understanding what such displacement means could use some help from a discipline based on transcending frames of references: anthropology. Hence, I requested anthropologist Sue Ann Taylor to lay out an ethnographic view of sacred space and transcendence. In her chapter, Taylor takes us from early and limited one-dimensional understandings of religion to contemporary sophisticated cross-cultural studies able to define the common structures underlying most spiritual traditions. She also illuminates another essential consideration that must enter the serious analysis of any practice of beliefs today: hermeneutics. Having laid this foundation, Taylor then moves us to the function of space in the production of transcending places and situates this discussion in today's context of consumerism, tourism, transnational migration, multiple ethnicities, gender politics, and beyond. Here Taylor compels us to realize that a truly sacred space demands its visitors to transcend themselves in order to embrace the truly "other" but that in order to do so architecture must also be given up (i.e., transcended) for the sake of and in the act of finding transcendence—reminding us of Pallasmaa's position. This act of double transcendence is what constitutes great architecture and what creates true possibilities for a deeper understanding and experience of the metaphysical.

Comparative religion scholar Lindsay Jones dives into what he argues to be the three different modes in which built form and religious experience can relate: theater, sanctuary, and contemplation. The purpose is to address a disconcerting lack of contemplative functioning in religious buildings of pre-Columbian Mesoamerica according to existing scholarship. Deploying what he calls a "hermeneutics of suspicion," Jones advances a thorough, insightful, yet accessible investigation of each mode of embodying/experiencing transcendence via architecture using historical examples of Western and Eastern traditions vis-à-vis old Mesoamerica. The result of this long but rich inquiry is the confirmation of a strong bias of old and new scholars against recognizing any contemplative dimension in pre-Columbian sacred spaces. When the politics and prejudices behind even the most respected research become evident, when the suspicions are confirmed, we realize the inherent difficulty in any serious attempt at transcending architecture. Jones not only teaches us a great deal about the "hows" of transcending architecture but also the importance of keeping a skeptical eye to avoid falling into pitiful "provincialism" at the time of producing or receiving sacred spaces.

Philosopher Karsten Harries alerts us that aesthetics has become an obstacle to an appropriate understanding of architecture, especially of transcending architecture. He unfolds his thesis through a fascinating and novel investigation of Walter Benjamin's concept of "aura." The ensuing philosophical ping-pong among Benjamin, Kant, Heidegger, Descartes, Hegel, and other philosophers allows Harries to build his case: "all meaning is a gift" found in the fact that reality continuously, multidimensionally, and inevitably exceeds us. This transcending nature of the real is the origin and experience of the "aura" and the ineffable, and rooted in the union of matter and spirit—what Harries calls the "mystery of incarnation." He concludes by sharing his vision for a transcending, sacred architecture that "re-presents and thus recalls for us the aura of nature, especially our own nature," a nature or world which is given to us as a gift.

The third and last section of this book presents four responses from architectural practitioners that make, teach, consult, or critique transcending architecture. The first is from *Faith and Form* magazine editor Michael Crosbie who dives into Rudolf Otto's idea of the "numinous" with the purpose of clarifying the central role of phenomenology in sacred space. After a short and effective study of Otto's text, Crosbie arrives at the crux of the matter: the numinous is "not inside ourselves, but outside [although] it is sensed inside of us"—reminding us of Harries's discussion of the "aura." Consistent with this understanding, Crosbie reminds us that the "numinous" is a state phenomenologically encountered and not something "produced," "attached," or "added" to a building. Therefore transcending architecture can only invite, symbolize, host, or prepare for the holy. In other words, the desire, will, and effort invested in the design and building of an architecture devoted to transcendence in the end must transcend all that gave it origin, as it will depend on something other to become numinous. A transcending architecture permits the experience of transcendence, and in so doing it transcends itself and, paradoxically, makes itself all the more important—a conclusion that finds coincidence with arguments advanced by Pallasmaa and Taylor.

Architect Suzane Reatig puts forward a short but seductive narrative that takes the reader into a trance receptive to her simple yet seemingly flawless thesis: if architects heartily open themselves to nature and art and follow what they learn from them, they will be able to produce buildings that induce transcending experiences. Her image-driven argument grounded on a minimalist sensibility that highlights the essential makes evident the impossibility of using words to convey the sacred and reaffirms what many other authors in this book advance in their chapters. Reatig's visual-textual essay echoes sentiments presented by Pallasmaa, Krinke, and Harries.

Duncan Stroik shares his conviction that "transcendence," "procession," and "beauty" constitute the three essential dimensions of sacred architecture. Focusing on Christian holy spaces, he laments the poor performance of churches produced under the guidance of modernity and places the blame on their inability to awaken a sense of transcendence. According to architect Stroik, this failure is in no small measure due to a lack of proper attention to verticality and height and a resistance to working with typologies and imagery that have proven successful at communicating the divine mystery to ordinary folks. Stroik offers his own architectural work as an example of how we could approach the challenge of designing and building transcending architectures without feeling trapped in today's architectural ideology.

Calling forth the unity between man and nature and the intertwining of the physical and metaphysical as the drivers of all great sacred architecture, architect Travis Price presents a poetic and stimulating prose describing a pedagogic experiment that he has been leading for nearly twenty years at the Catholic University of America School of Architecture and Planning. This award-winning program consists of an intense design/build curriculum that selects, develops, and eventually erects a sacred structure in response to a foreign culture, belief, and land and in collaboration with the local population. Transcending architecture is thus studied, lived, built, and gifted away (i.e.,

transcended), producing transformative and lasting experiences in architectural students, local people, and visitors alike. Price's vision of a transcending architecture that brings together modern and premodern (or mythic, as he calls it) paradigms is as insightful as it is timely.

Sacred space planner Richard Vosko goes back to the biblical story of Jacob's Ladder as a productive metaphor for how to reach the numinous via transcending architecture. But let us not take this idea too literally, he advises us, unless we desire to concretize hierarchical orders that separate creator and creatures, and clergy and laity. Rather, transcending architecture necessarily invites us to move beyond established rules, existing biases, conventional practices, comfort zones, and so on. His argument dispels any hope that only certain architectural moves, types, or styles may deliver the experience of the holy. Consistent with this view, Vosko tells us that transcending architecture does not stop at churches, synagogues, and temples but is active in buildings that help the sick, the less fortunate, and the environment. In other words, a transcending architecture may also be a servant architecture that is advancing the ethical and spiritual causes of its time by transcending its era, its culture, its client, its architect, and itself indeed. After all, Vosko argues, transcending architecture is where human beings are invited to "elevate themselves, climb the ladder, [even] in face of dire circumstances." This chapter brings us back to Sheridan, Krinke, and Senbel's vision of architectural transcendence.

Thomas Walton ends the book with a review that reveals commonalities, indicates differences, suggests points of departure, considers missing opportunities, and highlights

FIGURE 1-4. THIS BEAUTIFUL WORK BY ARCHITECT ALBERTO CAMPO BAEZA DEMONSTRATES HOW ARCHITECTURE ALLOWS THE VISITOR TO LIVE, PONDER, AND ENJOY SOMETHING WELL BEYOND THE WORK ITSELF. BETWEEN CATHEDRALS, CADIZ, SPAIN, 2009.

the insights gained in this book. Instead of offering closing remarks, he turns our minds toward more subtle, focused, or unconsidered areas of transcending architecture. As a result, we leave the text with a fresh desire to continue exploring the always fascinating and full of potential transcendental dimension of our built world.

I cannot help concluding this introduction by pointing to the urgent need for the pursuit of a "transcending architecture." We only have to look at our world obsessed with speed, consumerism, technology, entertainment, and economic growth along with its mounting pile of overwhelming negative effects to realize the value and timing of an architecture that transcends. By providing us with a respite, environments intentionally designed to "reach beyond" afford us the rare opportunity to rediscover our bearings and, in so doing, frame our existential condition within the larger matters of life and the divine. They move forward responses that challenge unhealthy cultural practices by slowing or stopping mindless materialism, advancing the cause of justice, raising awareness, and so on. As such, they constitute a radical and risky act of love and compassion born out of a spiritual and cultural awakening. The effects of such architectural actions cannot be underestimated, even if they are small in scale or number. And for this very reason, in the end, far from undermining the discipline, a "transcending architecture" paradoxically reveals and restores the true and timeless power of architecture. Architects, through their work, may create the conditions that induce people to, paraphrasing Thoreau, awaken to the divinity of the present moment and, through it, to the deepest and widest meaning of the good, the true, and the beautiful.[20]

I sincerely and humbly hope that the following pages will provide the reader with ample opportunities for timely intellectual, spiritual, and disciplinary growth. After all, if ever there was a time when transcending architecture was necessary, it is undoubtedly today.

2 LIGHT, SILENCE, AND SPIRITUALITY IN ARCHITECTURE AND ART

I am not conscious of the miracle of faith, but I often live that of ineffable space, the consummation of plastic emotion.

LE CORBUSIER

Inspiration is the feeling of beginning at the threshold where silence and light meet. Silence, the unmeasurable, desire to be, desire to express, the source of new need, meets light, the measurable, giver of all presence, …

LOUIS I. KAHN

We tend to think of spirituality and sacredness in architecture in terms of specific building types, such as religious buildings and spaces, built especially for devotional purposes. Religious architecture and sites—churches, chapels, mausoleums, and cemeteries—intentionally express their spiritual purpose through deliberately evoking experiences of awe, devotion, piety, authority, mystery, ecstasy, timelessness, or afterlife. The experience of sacredness implies a feeling of transcendence beyond the conditions of commonplace and the normality of meanings. A sacred space projects experiences in which physical characteristics turn into metaphysically charged feelings of transcendental reality and spiritual meanings.

Yet we may ask whether the experience of sacredness is solely a consequence of the use of a specific symbolic language, distinct conventions, and architectural typologies or vocabularies. Is a distinct symbolic "language" a prerequisite for the experience of spirituality, sacredness, or the numinous? Is the sacred dimension in architecture a closed and precoded system of conventions and references, or is it an open experiential quality arising from situational, individual,

---

Epigraphs are from William J. Curtis, *Le Corbusier: Ideas and Forms* (London: Phaidon, 1986), 179; and John Lobell, *Between Silence and Light: Spirit in the Architecture of Louis I. Kahn* (Boston: Shambala, 1985), 20.

and unique artistic visions? What are the conditions and constituents of the experience of sacredness, and what is the role of the experiencing individual in the encounter of architectural spirituality?

THE TRANSCENDENTAL IN ARCHITECTURE

In addition to its practical purposes of providing shelter and enabling various activities, architecture establishes fundamental hierarchies and marks the domain of the ineffable and the numinous. Since the ancient cultures, architecture has mediated between the macrocosm of the universe and the microcosm of human life. It has simultaneously separated the gods from the mortals and mediated between these fundamental categories. Even the buildings of ageless tribal and vernacular cultures express cosmological beliefs and direct one's awareness to another reality. Aspects of the Dogon cosmology are mediated equally by their built structures, objects, and routines of daily work, whereas the nomadic Rendile in Kenya reconstruct their image of the world every evening in the circular configuration of their temporary settlement oriented in relation to the rising sun.

In the West, an experience of architectural sacredness may be arisen by the image of a Greek temple in the landscape as a worldly metaphor of the domain of Gods and cosmic order; the dramatic sense of materiality and gravity, light and shadow of a vaulted Romanesque space; the rising of the gaze to the heights of a Gothic cathedral; and the illusory space and movement evoked by the structures, sculptures, and paintings in a Baroque church. The extension of the interior of an ascetic modern chapel to the landscape makes us experience our connectedness with nature and cosmos and sense the pantheistic spirituality of existence itself. These are all architectural experiences that guide our attention and thoughts beyond the utilitarian realm of construction.

The experience of spirituality evoked by a nonreligious space or object is essentially a different category of experience than explicit religious sacredness. The latter is associated with specific places, events, phenomena, and objects which have been denominated as sacred in the Holy Word, or have otherwise been sanctified by a religious order. Thus, religious sacredness implies the encounter of a space, object, or ritual which has been specifically named or designated sacred beforehand. The spirituality invoked by a secular artistic work is a personal and individual existential experience which obtains its aura and impact through the inherent nature of human experience itself without any explicit religious symbolization, connotation, or designation. Such an experience may arise, for example, from an exceptional atmospheric character of place or space, expressiveness of form, immensity of scale, intense materiality or color, or a transcendent illumination. We could speak of "designated" and "ideated" experiences of sacredness. In the first experience, the subject encounters or confronts an explicit religious or spiritual representation or image, whereas in the latter case the experience of a spiritual dimension arises unintentionally from the special qualities of the individual experience itself. Ideated sacredness arises from the nature of the experience rather than its prescribed intentions.

The narrative and symbolic representation of mythical and sacred events has historically been one of the central themes of artistic works, yet even in the representations of

FIGURE 2-1. THE SACREDNESS OF NATURE. NORDIC FOREST AS THE BACKDROP OF A MODERN ECCLESIASTICAL SPACE. KAIJA AND HEIKKI SIREN, STUDENT CHAPEL, OTANIEMI, ESPOO, 1957.

explicit religious content, the actual experience of sacredness usually arises from artistic qualities, emotions, and associations, irrespective of canonical symbolization. The artistic and architectural experience of spirituality, detached from deliberate devotional purposes, seems to arise from a nameless and unintentional mental origin, the individual existential experience, which is initiated by a sensitized encounter of the self and the world through the artistic work. This experience arises from the experiential holiness of life itself and a deep existential recognition of one's own being.

Even natural scenes or landscapes can evoke a sacred experience through their exceptional scale, beauty, atmosphere, or illumination. This experience is often associated with the notion of the sublime which was a central notion in the Romantic art of nineteenth-century painting as well as European and American landscape painting of that period. The sublime experience was re-introduced in art through the large canvases of Abstract Expressionism and Minimalism as well as numerous examples of contemporary Land Art; the overpowering size of these works makes the viewer an insider and participant in the plastic event instead of merely viewing the work.

THE GROUND OF SACRED EXPERIENCE IN ART

Beauty invokes images of a utopian and spiritualized world, a "timeless reality," as Karsten Harries suggests.[1] The pure and perfected shapes of Constantin Brâncuşi's sculptures do not convey an explicit devotional content, but irrespective of their actual subject matter—a human figure, fish, bird, or a primordial egg shape suggestive of the beginning of the world—their radiant beauty makes them appear as harbingers of otherness, a more perfect and timeless world. Similarly, the contemporary works of Wolfgang Laib made of pollen, honey, and milk exude an air of fragility and holiness through their sense of purity and association with the origins of life; these works also appear as images of human innocence.

In the art form of architecture, even buildings constructed for earthly purposes can give rise to experiences of sacredness in the same way that an extraordinarily beautiful painting, devoid of deliberate religious subject matter, can evoke the air of holiness through the very purity of its intention. The paintings of Johannes Vermeer depict scenes of earthly life, but the precision and perfection of these paintings emanate an air of transcendence and holiness. These are images of

an untouchable and timeless world of beauty. The marble courtyard of Louis Kahn's Salk Institute in La Jolla, California, seen against the horizon line of the Pacific Ocean, turns the sky into the celestial ceiling of this ascetic but metaphysical outdoor space; this authoritative space confronts the individual with the universe and silences her/him to cosmic reflection. Luis Barragán's minute structures in Mexico designed for domestic and other mundane purposes, such as horse stables and drinking troughs, create dreamlike microcosms as images of transcendence. Although architecture operates in the world of concrete physical and human realities, such as climate, gravity, materials, technical means, and human skills, it always aspires for an ideal. Without the inner tendency for idealization and suggestion of a better world, architecture withers into banal construction.

A layered richness of association and openness to interpretation are crucial characteristics of all significant artistic works. They are not intellectual arguments or conventionalized symbols; they are existential objects, which place themselves directly in the observer's awareness and experience of being. As Merleau-Ponty states, "We come to see not the work of art, but the world according to the art work."[2] A profound piece of art is always about something other than its apparent subject matter or physical essence. "When a painter presents us an image of a field or a vase with flowers, his paintings are windows open to an entire world," Jean-Paul Sartre writes.[3] In other words, instead of mediating and communicating through symbolization, profound works of art make their impact directly on our existential sense through embodied association, identification, simulation, and empathy. Through art we encounter preconscious and preconceptual meanings through our existential sense. Sartre describes the magical "thingness" of the ambience of Jacopo Tintoretto's *Crucifixion* (1565): "Tintoretto did not choose the yellow rift in the sky above Golgotha to signify or evoke anguish. Not an anguish of the sky or the sky of grief; it is a materialized anguish and grief, which has turned into that yellow rift in the sky."[4]

Works of art open up channels of feeling, understanding, and empathy that would not be available for us without the authoritative and magical presence of the artistic imagery. These works present us with phenomena of beauty, spirituality, and transcendence that we could not otherwise confront, identify, and grasp. Artistic experience is an act of collaboration, compassion, and sharing that opens us toward the world. As Jean-Paul Sartre explains, "It is the joint effort of author and reader which brings upon the scene that concrete and imaginary object which is the work of the mind. There is no art except for and by others.[5] … Thus, reading is a pact of generosity between author and reader."[6] Reading calls for shared generosity, but so does experiencing of architecture.

After having deliberated generally upon the possibility of experiencing nondevotional sacredness, I would like to dedicate the rest of this chapter to two specific conditions that, in agreement with Louis Kahn, I consider central to architecture in general and existential sacredness in particular: light and silence.

EXPERIENCING SPACE: LIGHT, SHADOW, AND PLACE

Louis Kahn often spoke and wrote about light and silence as the deepest experiential qualities in architecture. Light and silence are also initiators and mediators of sacred and spiritual experiences. For Kahn, light is the "giver of all presence."[7] "[A]ll material in nature, the mountains and the streams and the air and we, are made of Light which has been spent, and this crumpled mass called material casts a shadow, and the shadow belongs to Light. So Light is really the source of all being."[8]

Every distinct landscape and setting, space and place, has its characteristic light, and it is often the experiential quality that most directly and forcefully conditions the spatial atmosphere and our mood. Light defines the atmosphere of the place, and it is usually the most comprehensive criteria of its emotive character. Light controls the processes of life and even many essential hormonal activities depend on light. As a consequence, it has a deep effect on our activeness and energy level in addition to conditioning our mood.

The interplay of light and shadow connects architectural spaces with the dynamics of the physical and natural world, the seasons, and hours of the day. Paul Valéry asks, "What is there more mysterious than clarity? … What more capricious than the way in which light and shade are distributed over hours and over men?"[9] Natural light connects us with cosmic dimensions and brings life into architecture. "Through vision we touch the sun and the stars";[10] light is the cosmic breathing of space and the universe.

Illumination is surely the most subtle and emotive of the means of architectural expression. No other medium in the art of building—spatial configuration, form, geometry, proportion, material, color, or detail—can express equally delicate and deep emotions, ranging from joy to melancholy, ecstasy to grief, bliss to sorrow. We experience light as a gift, and it obtains spiritual qualities. Through light we grasp our unity with the sublime grandeur of the universe.

Light and shadow articulate space into places and subspaces, and their interplay gives space its rhythm, sense of scale, and intimacy. Objects are separated by their shadows, and they dwell in the intimacy of their shadows. In order to touch our emotions, the work of art has to project a sense of authority and life. As Brancusi writes, "Art must give suddenly, all at once, the shock of life, the sensation of breathing."[11] In architecture, this sensation of life and breathing is most effectively mediated by light. Illumination directs our movements and attention creating hierarchies and points of foci and importance. The paintings of Rembrandt, Caravaggio, and Georges de la Tour demonstrate the power of illumination in defining hierarchy and dominance. In these paintings, human figures and objects are wrapped in a soothing embrace of soft light and merciful shadows. Focused light provides the human figures with a radiant halo, creating an air of significance and holiness. A mere candle suffices to create a drama. Due to its fluttering character, candle light is especially tactile; it seems to finger objects and surfaces like a gentle massage. It creates an entire universe of domestic intimacy. No wonder Gaston Bachelard wrote an entire book on the light of the candle.[12]

MIRACLES OF LIGHT: CONTAINED, LIQUEFIED, AND BLACK LIGHT

Light tends to be experientially and emotionally absent—we see objects rather than light. Light must be contained by space, or concretized by the surface or matter that it illuminates to be recognized. "Sun never knows how great it is until it hits the side of

FIGURE 2-2. DRAMATIC DAYLIGHT GIVES AN ECCLESIASTIC SPACE A COSMIC FEELING. JUHA LEIVISKÄ, MYYRMÄKI CHURCH, VANTAA, 1984.

a building or shines inside a room," as Louis Kahn suggests.[13] A mediating matter, such as fog, mist, smoke, rain, snow, or frost, turns light into a virtual illuminating substance. The emotive impact of illumination is remarkably intensified when light is perceived as a substance; this liquefied light feels like a moist veil on the skin and it even seems to penetrate into the pores of one's skin.

The paintings of J. M. W. Turner and Claude Monet exemplify this embracing atmospheric light made tangible by moist air. In his watercolours of Venice, Turner turns buildings into illuminated moisture, whereas Monet's façades of the Cathedral of Rouen appear to be weightless and immaterial radiance. Alvar Aalto's daylight arrangements frequently reflect light by means of curved white surfaces. The *chiaroscuro* created by these rounded surfaces gives light an experiential materiality, plasticity, and heightened presence. This light has a specific weight, temperature, touch, and feel. This is a moulded and slowed-down light that feels like matter.

The alchemy of light can also mediate sensations of weight or weightlessness. In Le Corbusier's Chapel at Ronchamp, the darkness and weight of the space under the hanging curved roof of concrete is heightened by the rich illumination through the punctured south wall, whereas the light sieved through the multiple layers of the complex illumination systems of Renzo Piano's museums bathes in a directionless light that seems to eliminate the force of gravity entirely.

Even more unexpected transformations and miracles of light take place in artistic works. The colored windows of the Matisse Chapel in Vence and many of James Turrell's architectural light works turn light into colored air invoking delicate sensations of skin contact, temperature, and oscillation; these spaces make one feel as if one is being submerged in a transparent, colored substance that turns light and color into haptic sensations. We can float in color in the way that we float in water, and feel its warmth or chill. Steven Holl's and Juha Leiviskä's use of reflected light and color creates the sensation of a pulsating mixture of color and light, a condition that paradoxically heightens both the immateriality and materiality of light. This is a caressing, breathing, and healing light that connects us with the constantly changing nature of daylight and its cosmic ambience. The delicacy of reflected color suggests a spiritualized existence.

Artists have created yet another paradox of illumination: black light. Certain paintings of Ad Reinhardt appear as mere black rectangles until our prolonged stare acknowledges a minute shade of light in the darkness of the painting, and a most subtle image gradually appears. At the moment that we are able to perceive the image, a weak dark light is projected by the apparently black surface. Yet we cannot quite decide whether the figure that our eyes barely detect really exists in the painting or whether it is a mere optical illusion on our retinas. Similarly, Mark Rothko's nearly black paintings in the Rothko Chapel in Houston invite us to take part in an experiential limit phenomenon; here we feel that we are witnessing the border zone between life and death, existence and nonexistence. Isn't this dark light the same harbinger of the other world that Victor Hugo, the French writer, witnessed; "I see dark light" were his last words.[14]

FIGURE 2-3. THE DARK INTERIOR OF A FINNISH
PEASANT SMOKE HUT TURNS INTO AN IMAGE OF
PURITY AND DOMESTIC BLISS. NIEMELÄ CROFT FROM
KONGINKANGAS AT THE SEURASAARI OUTDOOR
MUSEUM IN HELSINKI.

THE THINGNESS OF LIGHT

Light is understood as a purely optical phenomenon, but it can also be connected to haptic perception. James Turrell, the light artist, speaks appropriately about "the thing-ness of light".[15] "I basically make spaces that capture light and hold it for your physical sensing.... It is ... a realization that the eyes touch, that the eyes feel. And when the eyes are open and you allow for this sensation, touch goes out of the eyes like feel."[16] Turrell's light works are based on the experiential qualities of light and the properties of our perceptual mechanism, but they also give rise to spatial experiences that reorient our judgment of figure and ground, near and far, horizon and gravity. These works turn light into a substance that has a sense of oth-er-worldly mystery.

In some of his works, Turrell also concret-izes the age of light. We tend to think of light as a phenomenon of the present tense, in fact, the very definition of nowness. Yet Turrell's light devices sometimes select light from the firmament that is enormously old; he speaks appropriately of "old light." This light may have travelled through the silent darkness of the universe for thousands of years. In this context, we could appropriately speak of "an archaeology of light." Again, an artistic work puts us in connection with dizzying cosmic phenomena and makes us experience sensa-tions of the sacred. Turrell's works also reveal the phenomenal silence of the universe.

SILENCE

In his remarkable book *The World of Silence*, the Swiss philosopher Max Picard argues that "nothing has changed the nature of Man so much as the loss of silence."[17] The time that has passed since Picard's book was published,

more than half a century ago, has only made his concern more urgent. The oppressive thought that we are losing the silence of our souls is becoming increasingly evident. To-day, we even tend to escape silence and search privacy and intimacy in excessive noise. This pathological reversal reminds us of Erich Fromm's thought-provokingly paradoxical theme of "escape from freedom" in his book with this very title.[18]

"Silence no longer exists as a world but only in fragments, as the remains of a world. And as man is always frightened by remains, so he is frightened by the remains of silence," Picard reasons.[19] We are frightened by the remaining fragments of silence, because they reveal to us our loss of our spiritual home. In the world of increasing wealth, choice, and comfort, we are becoming homeless and un-certain of our destiny. The most authoritative voice for "biophilia," the ethics and science of defending life, Edward O. Wilson, gives our metaphysical homelessness a provocative explanation: "All of man's troubles may well arise ... from the fact that we do not know what we are and do not agree on what we want to become."[20] The remains of silence also make us conscious of our fundamental solitude. This is an experience in which we tend to escape into the temporary collective identity offered by mass communication, en-tertainment, fashion, and cultural noise. The primal stillness, or the ontological silence of the universe, is increasingly contaminated by cultural noise and clatter. This loss of silence reflects the disastrous secularization and materialization of human life.

THE SILENCE OF ART

Regardless of their overt radicality or sugges-tions of conflict and noise, great works of art safeguard the silence of the world. Whenever we are struck by a profound piece of art, architecture, painting, or music, the work silences us and we find ourselves listening to our own existence.

The significance of silence for music, poetry, and other arts is clear enough. "Poetry comes out of silence and yearns for silence,"[21] Picard writes. Great paintings and architecture also arise from and create tranquility. The paintings of Piero della Francesca, for instance, silence all sound; the events of these paintings take place as if carved into the solid matter of silence. Rainer Maria Rilke emphasizes the crucial importance of the conditions of silence and solitude in artistic work: "It must be immense, this silence, in which sounds and movements have room,"[22] and "what is necessary, after all, is only this: solitude, vast inner solitude."[23]

The greatest of modern and contemporary paintings are also impressive spaces of peace and calm. The subject matter of Giorgio Morandi's still-life paintings is eternal immobility and tranquility. These minute paintings of a few bottles and glasses on a tabletop are all meditations on the enigma of the verb "to be"—why is it that things and phenomena exist rather than not. These apparently simple and unproblematic paintings take us to the heart of our own existential mystery. The visual stillness in these images seems to draw the spectator into the vacuum of their melancholic but healing silence.

All great painters paint silence. In fact, all profound art deals with benevolent tranquility and quietness. Just look at the silence of the light in Mark Rothko's paintings. In fact, these embracing spaces of color, light, and shadow are not exactly silent. They whisper or caress our ears comfortingly; they seem to convey the original silence of the world. This stillness of the arts is not an absence of sound but an ontological sensory and mental state, an observing, receptive, listening, and knowing state. It is a mental state which evokes a feeling of melancholy as it reminds us of the transitoriness of our earthly existence.

SILENCE IN ARCHITECTURAL EXPERIENCE

A powerful architectural experience eliminates noise and turns our consciousness to ourselves, to our very being. In an impressive space, we hear only our own heartbeat. The innate silence of an experience of architecture results from the fact that it focuses our attention on our own existence; I find myself listening to my own being.

The interiors of Romanesque cloisters are cast in a benevolent silence that feels like matter. Additionally, profound modern and contemporary secular spaces from Adolf Loos's Kärntner Bar in Vienna (1907), to Luis Barragán's Mexican houses, and Peter Zumthor's Thermal Baths at Vals (1990–1996) silence the noise of the world as these spaces focus our attention on the mystery of existence. The mental task of architecture is to concretize our being in the world and to make us conscious of who we are. Instead of adding to the clatter and nervous speed of our lives, it has to create, safeguard, and maintain silence. We need to follow Søren Kierkegaard's advice: "Create silence! Bring men to silence!"[24]

The language of architecture is the drama of tranquility. Great architecture is petrified stillness, silence turned into matter. As the racket and clatter of construction work has faded, as the shouting of workers has ceased, the building turns into a timeless monument of soundlessness. "Just as ivy grows round a wall for centuries, so the cathedrals have grown around the silence. They are built around the silence."[25] Picard speaks of Greek statues as "vessels of silence," or "white islands of silence."[26] Alvar Aalto called his project for the Opera House at Lincoln Center in New York (1956), placed on an elevated plaza surrounded by high walls, "[a] Fortification of Silence."[27] And what a silent faithfulness and patience can be felt in ancient buildings! Experiencing architecture is not only looking at spaces, forms, and surfaces; it is also listening to their characteristic silences. Every great building has its unique voice of tranquility. Through these specific silences we experience the lifestyles and temporal rhythms of past cultures, and the entire depth of time resides in these silences constructed in stone.

LIGHT AND SILENCE

Light belongs to silence, whereas the stillness and darkness of night are a mere absence of sound; the quiet of the night is a sleeping sound. In the same way that light artists speak of the tactility and thingness of light, we can speak of the same materialized qualities of silence; silence turns into an embracing veil or soft matter. Paradoxically, every silence has its sound; Luis Barragán spoke of the "interior placid murmur of silence."[28] Silence and light create the innermost essence, the mental core, of architecture, but they are also constituents of the human soul. "Without an inner light, without a formative visual imagination, we are blind," Arthur Zajonc argues.[29] The same must be said of silence; without an inner silence, we are deaf.

Picard writes poetically of the significance of silence for architecture: "The colonnades of the Greek temples are like boundary lines

FIGURE 2-4. THE EXPERIENCE OF SACREDNESS CREATED BY THE INTERPLAY OF SCULPTURAL SPACE AND ILLUMINATION. ALVAR AALTO, THE THREE CROSSES CHURCH, IMATRA, 1955–1958.

along the silence. They become ever straighter and ever whiter as they lean against the silence…. Wandering amongst the Greek pillars is a wandering in a radiant silence."[30] For this philosopher of silence, "The forest is a great reservoir of silence out of which the silence trickles in a thin, slow stream and fills the air with its brightness."[31]

ART AND LIFE OF TRANQUILITY

The architecture of "The Society of the Spectacle" of today seeks striking images, speed, and immediate effects, but a resistance to this architecture of accelerated images and force is clearly growing.[32] We are, perhaps, rediscovering the virtue and expressive power of tranquility, subtlety, and restraint. The popularity of Andrei Tarkovsky's films, Mark Rothko's paintings, Tadao Ando's architecture, and Arvo Pärt's music seems to point toward the reemergence of a silent art which the American art critic Donald Kuspit forecast three decades ago: "A new inner need, a new vigor may be in the process of being born; an art that is not interested in direct communication, or any attempt to bring about an immediately observable significance. If the time of opera is on the wane, then the time of chamber music may be waxing. Where Opera externalizes, chamber music internalizes. Where the former appeals to the crowds, the latter appeals to the individual, offers only one experience, the feeling of being oneself."[33]

Perhaps the idea of turning life back to the unpretentious appropriateness and silent prestige that we admire in the peasant sphere of life, the Shaker culture, or in the most refined creations of modernity, proves to be a groundless nostalgia, but man has never mourned for a homecoming more than today. In the middle of today's digital, virtual, and instantaneous utopia, we desire to re-encounter the fundamental causalities and limits of life. Mankind has never yearned for silence as the focus of his being more than we do in our era of surreal and hysterical consumption and speed.

More than ever before, the ethical and humane task of architecture and all art is to defend the authenticity and autonomy of human experience, and to reveal the existence of the transcendental realm, the domain of the sacred. This calls for the identification of the spiritual and holy, not only in deliberate devotional contexts but in the ordinariness and humility of daily life.

The Finnish poet Bo Carpelan (1926–2011) evokes the nobility of restrained life and meditative tranquility in one of his poems in the collection appropriately titled *Homecoming*:

There are still houses with low ceilings,
window-splays where children climb up
and squatting, chin against knees,
watch the wet snow falling
peacefully over dark, narrow courtyards.
There are still rooms that speak of lives,
of cupboards of clean, hereditary linen.
There are quiet kitchens where someone sits
reading with the book propped against the
    loaf of bread.
The light falls there with the voice of a white
    blind.
If you shut your eyes you can see
that a morning, however fleeting, awaits
and that its warmth mingles with the warmth
    in here
and that each flake's fall
is a sign of homecoming.[34]

3 THE DOMESTIC AND THE NUMINOUS IN SACRED ARCHITECTURE

This chapter focuses on the domestic symbolism often incorporated in sacred architecture. A broad range of examples illustrate how home and temple were often conflated and how, paradoxically, the multifarious symbolic agendas of religious architecture often relied on symbols of home and dwelling—contravening and confirming it as the house of the deity. It will argue that understanding this particular lineage of sacred architecture can inform the materialization of the numinous and transcendent today, illustrated by two small houses designed by the author. It will conclude by suggesting that the history of architecture is ever-present in its capacity to inform the meaningful creation of architecture that both transcends and incorporates its contemporary settings.

INTRODUCTION

Ever since the earliest buildings, architecture has been asked to play many diverse, symbolic, and ritual roles. In Vitruvius's mythical account of the origins of the first "dwelling house," the creation of the house is conflated with the establishment of language, political discourse, and civilization.[1] In Vitruvius's brief exposition, home and house are not mere shelter but both emblematic and catalytic of culture, illustrating the enduring symbolism of home as the center from which civilization was conceived and born—and even as a symbol of civilization itself.

Examining architecture's and, in particular, sacred architecture's roots in, and references to, domestic structures can productively contextualize its various roles, agendas, and materializations. According to the historian

E. Baldwin Smith, "Architecture was on the way to becoming something more than mere construction when simple huts acquired in the imagination of men the significance of a type, an ideal, a concept, to which was associated meaning and importance."[2] According to Smith, the first sanctuaries evolved from the houses of the priests or rulers, who were often one and the same. As a place of consultation and judgment, power, prestige, and mystery, and the setting for rituals, large and small, enacted to ensure the health and longevity of the ruler (and by extension his subjects and their world), the house assumed significance as a primal and portentous place. Even religious rituals can be understood as emanating from the early domestic devotional acts of the serving the ruler-god.[3] The reciprocity of the sacred and secular in so-called primitive cultures suggests that the transition from the house of the ruler-god to that of the god-ruler was a logical and natural one.

The earliest sanctuaries were discrete places but, like religion itself, were also believed to be intermediate zones with the ability to join, connect, and unveil. The sanctuary represented a liminal zone that mediated between humans and that which they sought, revered, feared, or worshipped.[4] The house-sanctuary has assumed many forms and performed various roles, but can be essentially understood as serving to materialize a place believed to have the power and capacity to reveal what otherwise would be hidden and to connect with what otherwise would be inaccessible, a mediator between worlds.[5]

In the following sections, I will present a number of aspects and examples of the domestic in sacred architecture, including: conceptions of the first or primal dwellings;

the house of god; the house as a cosmogony or cosmology; the house as a symbol of power; the house as a portal to other worlds; and the house tomb. In a further discussion of the mythological and historical contexts of the primitive hut as an essential and portentous place, I will expand on the significance of domestic symbolism and lead to its potential relevance regarding the materialization of the domestic today.

DOMESTIC SYMBOLS IN SACRED ARCHITECTURE

It has been suggested that the earliest of domestic structures were circular in plan and covered by expediency by curved roofs of whatever light and flexible materials were available. According to this argument, the dome emerged from the earliest domestic architecture and eventually (or inevitably) came to potently conflate home as center and the domed sanctuary as the center of the cosmos.[6] According to Norman Crowe (referencing Eliade), religious architecture can be understood as having evolved from domestic architecture. To illustrate, he outlines a lineage that begins with the Mycenaean megaron and results in the classical Greek temple.[7] The house of the deity (a statue of which was typically enshrined in the cella) was a replication and elaboration of domestic models, and wooden construction was eventually replaced by stone as a further materialization of the enduring house of god. Similarly, early Christian "House Churches" (e.g., the well-known Dura Europos, Salhijeh, Syria, third century CE), appropriated and transformed domestic architecture to facilitate the nascent rituals of the formative faith. According to Crowe, one can trace a lineage from the first "*domus ecclesia*" to early atrium churches.

The sacred structures of the Shinto Naiku Shrine of Ise Jingu, the first buildings which date from seventh century CE, offer another example of the appropriation of domestic archetypes as a means to both replicate the divine "first dwelling" and valorize its special powers. At Naiku, wooden domestic structures are meticulously rebuilt every twenty years according to precise, prescribed site, material, and construction methods. The Naiku Shrine is not the only site of its type, but it is the one most closely associated with the gods and royal family and is the preeminent pilgrimage destination for the Japanese. The result recreates and represents ancient Japanese dwellings associated with the founding of the nation, where the past is ever-present through the mediating agency of the architecture.

Symbolisms and descriptions of home enjoy an extensive lineage in religion and sacred scripture. The Jewish temple is often described as the "house of god," continuing a long tradition of an earthy habitation for the divine—and Christian cathedrals were called "*domus dei*" or "God's house."[8] In the Christian gospels, the parable of "the Wise and Foolish Builders" equates a house built with firm foundations "upon rock" with the security only offered by adherence to the faith.[9] In I Kings, Solomon's Temple is presented as the "house of the Lord," a specific place for God to "dwell in forever,"[10] and its descriptions in both the visions of Ezekiel and in I Kings have provided inspirations and aspirations for church building ever since.[11] Abbott Suger apparently expressed his admiration for and aspiration to the Solomonic Temple in his building programs at St. Denis,[12] and there is Justinian's famous proclamation, "*Nenikika se Solomon* [I have surpassed thee Solomon]," on the completion of Saint Sophia.

The Hindu temple is called the "house of god" (*devagriham*), and great care is taken in choosing its site and groundbreaking rituals and in its design and proportioning—all to ensure that the deity will "dwell" there.[13] Temples are commonly referred to as "vamara" or "well proportioned,"[14] and whether the deity dwelled there (or not) depended on strict adherence to proportioning systems outlined in detailed manuals. The ability of the deities housed in the temple (and the temple itself) to mediate between humans and the "world" depended on these systems and established their authority by means of the *vastu-purusha mandala*—the primordial ordering of the cosmos by Brahma. Consequently, the Hindu temple, in one aspect, materializes both a cosmogony (a formative birth of the universe) and a cosmology (a form of the universe or, according to George Michell, a "microscopic image of the universe.")[15] Similar to the priests and the gods themselves, the Hindu house of god serves as a medium that reflects the order of the world while also maintaining that order.

Domestic symbolism materialized religious and political agendas at the Third Dynasty Funerary Complex of King Zoser in Saqqara (Egypt 2750 BCE), where the tomb for a deified king (Zoser was known as "The Holy") not only symbolized his cosmic status but also served as his eternal domicile. At this early walled necropolis, crenelated temenos walls replicated elements of the Royal ("White") Palace of Memphis. Throughout, domestic forms and materials were immortalized in stone, testament to the primacy of domestic symbolism (as well as the fundamental conservatism of Egyptian architecture).[16] At the entry hall, often cited as a prototypical hypostyle hall of pylon temples, two open wooden doors are rendered in stone and lead to the central passage. Here forty-two engaged, stone columns appear as the bundled reeds of traditional house structures and support a stone roof that imitates the round beams of timbered construction.[17] The chapels of the Heb-Sed Court similarly reproduced traditional domestic architecture, as did the paired "red" and "white" palaces, which also served to concretize the political union of the north and south for which Zoser's reign was known. According to Joseph Rykwert, "The temple was among other things a stone model of the creation landscape."[18] All of which was further concretized by the periodic renewal and rebirth festival of the Heb-Sed, where the pharaoh symbolically visited the chapels, palaces, and the entry hall (where the bundled columns symbolized the forty-two *nomes* or provinces of the Egyptian world). And so the *pharaoh*, a term that meant "great house," both represented and was immortalized by the multiple roles and meanings of the architecture (in a manner, perhaps, that centuries later the church would be believed to mystically embody Christ).

The domestic architecture of American Indians offers many examples of dwellings serving multiple ontological and symbolic roles. According to Nabakov and Easton, "The buildings of Native Americans encoded not only their social order, but often their tribal view of the cosmos. Many Indian narratives tell of a "Distant Time" or a "Myth Age" when a "First House" was bestowed upon a tribe as a container for their emerging culture. Some tribes have likened the creation of the world itself to the creation of a house, strengthening the metaphoric correspondence between dwelling and cosmos. Thereafter

Indian peoples held the ritual power to renew their cosmos through rebuilding, remodeling, or reconsecrating their architecture."[19] According to Nabakov and Easton, the Hidatsa of North Dakota conceptualized their world as a colossal earth lodge, with the sky held up by four posts, a structure replicated in their wooden domiciles. Often, the houses of American Indians symbolized the center of the world and served to co-join the multiple tiers of the cosmos. Sweat lodges were often believed to embody the animal gods that these rituals sought connection with, and houses were similarly viewed as animated. The hogan, or "house place," of the Navaho was such a living entity, with its origins positioned in the beginning of time. According to their "Blessingway" myth, the gods presented hogans to them as representations of significant landmarks in the Navaho world and as models to be replicated. The cosmic and ceremonial orientations and dispositions of the hogan communicated and facilitated its roles as an amalgam of the cosmos and the setting for rituals to ensure its continuity.

The Iroquois longhouses were similarly described in origin myths and offer a particular example of the multifarious roles often assigned to American Indian domestic architecture. Originally they were rectangular, wooden structures, longitudinally expendable to accommodate additional families over time—domestic structures built at a colossal scale, which served as the ritual and spiritual centers of their world. Each family group occupied a section, with their own hearth and smoke hole, but all were the "people of the longhouse" (as they often referred to themselves).[20] However, with the advent of the Iroquois Confederacy they came to symbolize the political unity of the League of Five

Nations as well as a cosmogram of the territory they claimed as their own.[21] The council that created the League of Five Nations was described as the building of a longhouse, and subsequently symbolically represented the boundaries of their amalgamated territory (with the Seneca guarding the "western door" and the Mohawk the eastern one).[22]

The Hopewell Era mound-builders of the American Midwest built wooden charnel houses, homes for the dead that echoed those of the living, and which were ultimately transformed into the massive mounds for which they are known. At Hopewell Era mortuary sites, wooden charnel houses, some with multiple rooms, served as ritual centers and repositories for cremations and talismanic artifacts. They were eventually covered by an earthen mound, sometimes burned beforehand, replacing impermanent flesh and materials subject to rot and decay with the permanence of earth, sand, and gravel. Christopher Carr and D. Troy Case describe various functions regarding the extensive use of charnel houses by tribes of southeastern North America[23] and outline multistage funerary rites, which may have included participants from diverse geographical locations (similar to the periodic rites of the Huron and the Algonquian tribes).[24] According to William Romain, charnel house funerary practices were widespread throughout the native peoples of eastern North America, and in many instances they were referred to as "temples."[25] He suggests that many were aligned with positions of the moon—the nocturnal celestial object most closely associated with death and even the "mirror world" of the land of eternal spirits, which served to reinforce their roles as portals to the land of the dead and the spirits of dead ancestors.[26]

And, of course, there is the lengthy history of house tombs, where domestic images symbolize the eternal house of the dead—a place often built not only to house the dead but to materialize their lives and provide portentous bridges to the land of the dead and revered ancestors. Ancient Egyptians referred to tombs as "eternal habitations" or as "residences for eternity" and, as is well known, included many of the accouterments of living within their sepulchral domiciles. In a related fashion, Etruscan tombs explicitly recreated the house in stone, their underground chambers including stone doors, staircases, servants quarters, beds with pillows, kitchen implements, and pitched roofs[27]—and Lycian rock-cut tombs were rendered in a manner that replicated the wooden construction of homes for the living. All of which suggest the enduring ontological symbolism of home and its multifarious symbolisms in the sacred.

THE PRIMITIVE HUT

Beginning perhaps with Vitruvius, the so-called primitive hut has enjoyed a lengthy lineage as a place of birth and renewal, perhaps most provocatively (and famously) in the eighteenth-century *An Essay on Architecture* by the Jesuit priest Marc-Antoine Laugier, who extols the virtues of the "little rustic hut." This interest, according to Joseph Rykwert, is "displayed by practically all peoples at all times," and he postulates that "Adam's house in paradise" was an "exposition of the paradisal plan, and therefore established him at the center of it."[28] Often misappropriated (as in the case of Laugier, who cited the foundations of the rustic hut to lend authority to his argument for the revivification of Classicism), and narrowly interpreted as a symbol of formal perfection, the primitive hut, or essential dwelling, actually enjoys a much more diverse and substantial lineage.

An enduring (and endearing) subject of myths, folktales, and literature from around the world, "home" is a word that has assumed a particular significance and meaning. The myth of Philemon and Baucis (made famous by Goethe's *Faust*), symbolically presents the propitious setting of simple domesticity, where the pious old couple welcomes into their simple hut the gods Jupiter and Mercury, disguised as wayfarers, after all of the other inhabitants of Phrygia had turned them away.[29] Even though they are very poor, the couple generously feeds the gods who eventually reveal themselves and punish their neighbors by flooding the valley. At Philemon and Baucis's request, their primitive hut becomes a temple that they tend until their death—the simple hut now a sacred setting.

In Zen Buddhism, the simple hermit scholar's retreat, celebrated in landscape paintings of the Southern Sung period, was both a place to live an authentic life and a threshold to the unconditioned realms of enlightenment.[30] These prototypical dwellings are also situated in myth, often described as the first monasteries founded by enlightened teachers as spiritual retreats, but eventually expanding as acolytes joined and built their own dwellings. The twelfth-century "An Account of My Hut" describes the virtues of the primitive and portentous abode:

The present hut is of no ordinary appearance. It is a bare ten feet square and less than seven feet high.... Since I hid my traces here in the heart of Mount Hino, I have added a lean-to on the south and a porch of bamboo. On the west I have built a shelf for holy water, and inside the hut, along the west wall, I have installed an image of the Amida.... Above the sliding door that faces north I have built a little shelf on which I keep three or four black leather baskets that contain books of poetry and music and extracts from the sacred writings.[31]

The pilgrimage to the sacred abode of an enlightened being was symbolically recalled in the *hojo*, or abbot's quarters, of Japanese Zen Buddhist temples, particularly in their intrinsic entry paths and gardens. Akin to the poetic "dewy path" of Medieval Era teahouses, it elongated the experience of entry—marking sacred thresholds and providing a sequence of spaces that served as a means of spiritual preparation through the kinesthetic and haptic experiences they provided, reinforced by its references to formative models. At Koto-in (1601 CE), a subtemple of the culturally important Rinzai Zen Buddhist monastery of Daitoku-ji (founded as a hermitage by Daito-kokushi in 1319 CE, Kyoto, Japan), a skillfully choreographed path sequence traverses a series of articulate spaces, gateways, and thresholds, before attaining the *hojo* itself.[32] *Hojo* translates as "one jo" (tatami) square, a reference to the prototypical teahouse, but also to a legendary mythical space where a Buddhist sage was said to have accommodated thousands of disciples. The simple hut, carefully positioned and ritually attained, marks a sacred center while establishing connections to the vast cosmologies central to Mahayana beliefs.[33]

Similarly, Henry David Thoreau's philosophical discussions regarding the building and inhabitation of his simple hut on Lake Walden occupy a broad territory, encompassing practical, economic, social, political, psychic, spiritual, sensual, quotidian, metaphysical, and cosmic realms. Thoreau argues that "every man is tasked to make his life, even in its details, worthy of the contemplation of his most elevated and critical hour"[34] and systematically describes the virtues of an authentic life—facilitated, materialized, and symbolized by his self-built simple dwelling. The primitive hut in this case is both a means to shed the encumbrances of material life while providing the means to do so. Throughout his extended essay, even though anchored to a specific place delineated by essential architecture, he looks both inward and outward. The parable of the artist of Kouroo that appears toward the end of *Walden* illustrates how simple acts of creation lead to vast cosmologies and ontological understandings.

And lastly here is the strange and provocative house that the Swiss psychiatrist Carl G. Jung built for himself (and his family) in Bollingen on Lake Zurich. During a period of over thirty years, Jung employed the media of architecture to explore and materialize the inner work he was engaged in, especially during the formative time he characterized as his "confrontation with the unconscious." The house was built in stages, a sequence that aligned with major periods of Jung's life. The first building was a primitive hut of sorts, a single, circular room, quartered like its primitive predecessors (and, in particular, the African huts Jung would synchronistically visit later). This "maternal hearth," begun shortly after the death of his mother, was the first of a series of buildings that Jung used to "achieve a kind of representation in stone of [his] innermost thoughts and of the knowledge [he] had acquired." The first stage of construction aligned with the stage of his life where "words and paper did not seem enough," and he needed to make a "confession of faith in stone," which eventually included carvings and sculpture. The last tower, completed after the death of his wife, signified for Jung "the extension of consciousness achieved in old

age" and materialized a "symbol of psychic wholeness."[35]

For Jung, the practice of architecture (as well as painting and sculpture) was a means of reconciliation and connection. The simple dwelling, the essential house in this case, demonstrates the power of architecture to materialize the immaterial and to embody the numinous. It was the means by which Jung "carved out rough answers" to life's questions. And so for Jung, the media of architecture through a simple dwelling became a medium of personal and psychological transformation. In the end, his house, similar to the simple dwelling of Philomon and Baucis (a myth that held much importance to him), was transformed into a sacred place (and remains one, though contested, for devotees of his work and life).

Home in all of these contexts is a sacred realm, which comprises broader ontological territories that transcend the common assignation of home to the secular. It bears noting that the profane in the Ancient Greek world was the place outside the temple where offerings were made to the goddess or god within (from the Latin, *profanes*, meaning "before the temple"). Simple acts of building, of making a home in an inherently unstable world, serve to connect us with ourselves and our place in the cosmos while simultaneously revealing the vast contexts of which we are a part. This double mediation—individual to architecture and architecture to the world—speaks of the essential roles that architecture has been asked to play generally, and has often materialized specifically, through the domestic.

OBLIQUE AND OCCLUDED REFERRALS AND APPLICATIONS: TWO EXAMPLES

So what might all this have to do with how we conceptualize and materialize architecture today? Does the background of the domestic and transcendental in sacred architecture provide useful and provocative positions that may help us to articulate our contemporary milieu? The past, I contend, like some of the dwellings previously cited, can be understood as alive, an ever-present dynamic ground

FIGURE 3-2. THE GATEWAY MARKS A THRESHOLD AND INITIATES A PATH SEQUENCE. HOUSE FOR TWO ARTISTS, THE BERKSHIRES, MASSACHUSETTS.

nections between the built works and their sources are oblique but may be understood as interpretations and translations materialized through the language of architecture.

House for Two Artists, the Berkshires, Massachusetts

A number of years ago, I designed a small house for two artists and their children located in the lake-dotted and mountainous terrain of the Berkshires in western Massachusetts.[36] The project focused on the broader context of its rural setting and explored ideas about site, orientation, center and path, spatial sequence, geometry, materials, and time. A forty-foot long, ten-foot high concrete block wall, aligned precisely to geographic north, marks and transforms the site and serves as a giant sundial (figure 3-1). The studio, clad in rough-sawn western red cedar, rests on top of this wall and is capped by a bright, galvanized steel roof. In this manner, the architecture recreates and expresses a fundamental act of architecture—the mediation between earth and sky—with the wall firmly grounded in the earth, the roof reflecting the sky, and the living spaces located in between (a triad that recalls the formal organization of traditional New England barns, which typically have a stone foundation, a rough wooden building, and a metal roof).

upon which we may figure architecture in authentic and meaningful ways.

To illustrate in an incomplete but hopefully useful manner, I now turn to two small houses I have designed. They are not presented as sacred places but to illustrate particular interpretations and applications of the environmental orientations, path sequences, geometry and proportion, and material expressions, including perhaps most importantly the experience and feeling of places that have touched, affected, and even changed me. The con-

A small gateway is aligned with a lake to the east and a mountain to the west and marks the threshold to the private domain of the house. It initiates a spatial sequence: a journey from west to east; earth to sky; outside to inside; public to private (figure 3-2). The owners have watched the sun rise over the lake during the vernal and autumnal equinoxes and observed its alignments with the wall, threshold, and path as it circled the horizon to set behind the mountain. The wall mediates between the earth, the sun, the mountain, and the water in a manner that establishes a broader context for the architecture (and its inhabitants) and dissolves the confines of the site.[37]

Geometry and proportion were applied to further articulate this simple dwelling, while suggesting its relationship to the larger orders of the world. The materials have aged naturally, an authentic rendering of their inherent qualities, in the spirit described by Mostafavi and Leatherbarrow where "weathering is a process that can productively modify a building over time."[38] Thus, the studio also aims to transcend the confines of time, changing and maturing as it ages: the wall carrying vines, the roof dulling to a variegated patina, the cedar turning shades of gray and ocher. All change as the seasons come and go, as the sunlight illumines different walls and different aspects of the architecture. Its specific places also speak about time and seasons: the marking of the equinoxes; rooms oriented to the mornings and evenings; the upper deck directed to the moon as it rises over the lake (inspired by the Moon Viewing Deck at the Old Shoin of the Imperial Palace at Katsura).

I have imagined the studio, and in particular the wall, as a ruin similar to the walls of long collapsed barns and abandoned farms that dot the New England countryside; bare, exposed, but still standing. In this way, though the studio was carefully designed in response to the client's needs, it also transcends these and occupies a broader historical context. Hundreds of years from now, when the house has long-since been eaten by insects and its dust blown away, perhaps part of the wall will still remain—casting a shadow as midday turns to dusk.

Mountain Retreat, Boone, North Carolina

The contemporary philosopher Thomas Moore invokes Heidegger when he characterizes the earth as our home and argues, "[We are always making a house for the heart and always looking for the house of divinity."[39] This small house (800 sq. ft., with a 250 sq. ft. loft), built for myself and my family, attempts to maximize its limited spaces by incorporating its larger environmental and cosmic settings. Similar to the previous example, it begins by consecrating the cardinal directions, this time with an L-shaped concrete block wall. An entry sequence includes a series of vistas, constrictions, and expansions as it descends to a small entry space, enters a double-story living room, and ascends to a loft, culminating in a dormer that overlooks the beginning of the path—the end becoming a beginning. A south-facing courtyard and eastern-facing windows frame the space of nature and a vista of a distant mountain, as well as marking the transit of the sun throughout the day (and on certain nights, the moon) (figures 3-3, 3-4, and 3-5).

Geometry and proportion govern the plan and volumes of the house in a manner that both delimits and expands its contexts. The house is planned according to a four-foot square module reminiscent of the planning grids of Japanese Shoin-style residences of the Medieval Period. The footprint outlines a thirty-six-foot square, which was then subdivided to create a series of proportionally interrelated spaces (a methodology inspired by the proportioning practices of the Ottoman court architect Mimar Sinan).

In the spirit of Alberto Perez-Gomez's assertion that architecture is a "poetic representation of significant human action,"[40] the house is imagined as only complete when the quotidian rituals and periodic celebrations inhabit and animate its spaces. This small retreat was conceptualized with an Epicurean sensibility, as a soulful, sensual place. Its cypress walls, inside and out, invite our caresses, their hues and textures changing throughout the day as the sun charts its course. Similar to Jung's house in Bollingen, the house may be rooted in symbolism, but the rituals of meals, baths, fires, repose, and sleep complete it. And like Jung's experiences at Bollingen, the house may simply offer a setting where whatever emotions arise or events occur—joy, comfort, ecstasy, fear, sadness, confusion—may have a place to be authentically experienced, offering perhaps moments such as this one described by Thoreau:

Sometimes, in a summer morning, having taken my accustomed bath, I sat in my sunny doorway from sunrise till noon, rapt in a revery, amidst the pines and hickories and sumachs, in undisturbed solitude and stillness, while the birds sang around or flitted noiseless through the house, until by the sun falling in at my west window, or the noise of some traveller's wagon on the distant highway, I was reminded of the lapse of time. I grew in those seasons like corn in the night, and they were far better than any work of the hands would have been. They were not subtracted from my life, but so much over and above my usual allowance, I realized what the Orientals mean by contemplation and the forsaking of works.[41]

In most of the previous sacred examples, home is the place of stability, often symbolizing the endurance of the gods, the power of rulers, the people that built them, or even the cosmos itself. The primitive hut, in its most diverse interpretations, depended on its identification as a primal place—first in time and importance—to establish its ontological

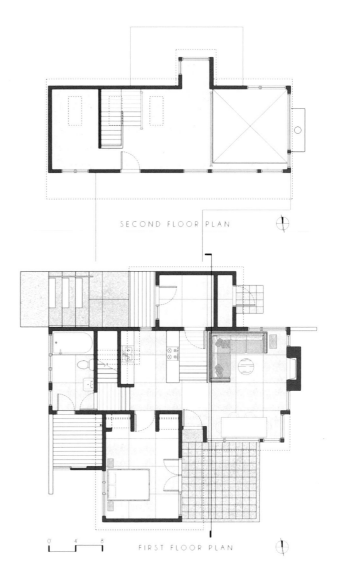

SECOND FLOOR PLAN

FIRST FLOOR PLAN

FIGURE 3-3. FIRST- AND SECOND-FLOOR PLANS, MOUNTAIN RETREAT. BOONE, NORTH CAROLINA.

FIGURE 3-4. ENTRANCE AND VISTA, MOUNTAIN RETREAT.
BOONE, NORTH CAROLINA.

FIGURE 3-5. THE SOUTH-FACING COURTYARD, MOUN-
TAIN RETREAT. BOONE, NORTH CAROLINA.

authority. In this context, architecture can be understood as "arche-tecture," or a "form of origin." The two houses aimed to interpret what might be understood as fundamental elements and orientations, to both reveal some essential qualities of their environmental settings and express that understanding through the timeless language of architecture. I realize this is an ambitious claim, and that only time and experience will indicate its veracity (or not), but it also states a position regarding the larger task of architecture to materialize our (albeit limited) understandings of the world and our place in it.

CONCLUSIONS

We all want to make a home in the world—a place of comfort and stability from which we may depart but always return. To structure his ontological argument, Thomas Moore defines "home" in three ways: as the psychic interior that houses our soul, the place of intimate and sensual domesticity, and as the broader home of our culture, homeland, and even universe. In this context, I would like to suggest three fundamental notions of home, which may serve in further reconsiderations of the previous historical examples and provide expanded and helpful definitions. First, there is the home of our bodies and the inner realms of our psyche and soul, the vast mysterious territories of our memories, dreams, and self-definition. Secondly, there is the domestic home—the place of comfort, rest, and ease of family, meals, and intimacy, the setting for the dramas, passages, pains, and joys of our lives. And lastly, there is the home of the world, a condition of interconnection with others and the natural environment of which we are an intrinsic part, of being at home in the universe.

Our home is not only a refuge that protects us from the world but also a place that connects us. According to Moore, the root word of "inhabit" means "to give *and* receive." Home satisfies our phenomenological and psychological needs for comfort and security, while also providing the threshold for our departures to the broader world. Symbolically, it is a place that looks both inward and outward, and thus its significance to the broader tasks of architecture is general. As stated by Gaston Bachelard, "All really inhabited space bears the essence of the notion of home."[42] Consequently, we may understand home in more diverse and multifarious ways, from inner psychic realms to vast cosmic perspectives, which may serve to inform the housing of the psyche and the incorporation of sacrality in the places we design. In this context, architecture may participate in the enduring human need to come home to themselves, others, and the universe.

4 NATURE, HEALING, AND THE NUMINOUS

INTRODUCTION

"Transcending Architecture: The Aesthetics and Ethics of the Numinous" was the title of the symposium that gave birth to this book—and it was this subtitle that was the catalyst for this chapter. The numinous has been described as a "direct encounter with the wholly other,"[1] and "what we sense when we bow to what seems not to be on human scale."[2] Certainly nature has been seen and experienced in this way across cultures and throughout time. Take a moment to imagine a forest, perhaps a redwood grove, with sunlight slanting through the trees. If you have ever stood among the redwoods, it is hard not to feel a sense of the numinous. Landscape scholar Christopher Thacker states, "No doubt about it. The first gardens were not made, but discovered .... In the oldest accounts, such spots

[natural features felt to possess a mysterious quality of difference from their surroundings, such as a clearing in the forest, a valley or island] are the gardens of the gods."[3]

Redwood trees exude a sense of the primordial; they can live thousands of years and have existed on Earth as a species since long before humans. It is easy to forget that vegetation is key to life on Earth: plants provide the oxygen that we breathe, and plants, in turn, need carbon dioxide. This relationship is now out of balance as humans are producing vast quantities of carbon dioxide, too much for the Earth's vegetation to use or sequester. As a result, the Earth is heating up, creating change to the planet's climate, and deforestation is a major result.

The idea that humans and the Earth live in a reciprocal relationship, and that contact with nature is beneficial or healing to humans, has long been an intuitive understanding. But in the last twenty-five years or so, a growing body of empirical evidence supports that contact with nature, especially vegetation, has a beneficial effect on human physical and psychological health. This includes lower blood pressure, reduced muscle tension, and elevated mood. These are many of the same beneficial effects of a meditative or contemplative practice.[4]

Scholars from both the natural sciences and social sciences have put forth different theories about why contact with vegetation is beneficial. Research by Roger S. Ulrich and others is focused on the involuntary responses of the human body, suggesting "that the parasympathetic nervous system—that is the component of the nervous system thought not to be under conscious control—must be involved in the calming effects experienced in response to nature."[5] Evolutionary theories developed by Jay Appleton, E. O. Wilson, and others focus on the premise that humans evolved in reciprocity with nature—especially in environments with water and vegetation—that would favor survival, therefore the theory suggests that we would unconsciously associate nature with survival (health). Environmental psychologists Rachel and Stephen Kaplan have developed a theory of "directed and non-directed attention" inspired by the work of psychologist William James. Their idea is that all day long we use directed attention to manage our lives and do the work of the intellect, but engaging nondirected attention throughout the day is essential to our heath, as it provides the ability to recover from overuse of our directed attention. The Kaplans cite contact with nature as a primary way to engage nondirected attention. For example, watching sunlight flicker across

leaves or observing waves at a beach can quiet discursive thought and allow for the recovery of directed attention. Their research also shows that sleep is not the complete answer; we need opportunities to engage our nondirected attention several times throughout the day for optimum health.[6]

Another link in the relationship between contact with nature and human health is the ongoing research into "green exercise" done over the last ten years at the University of Essex in the United Kingdom. The benefits of exercise to health, including reducing stress, are well known. The Essex research shows that if you exercise with vegetation present, the benefits of exercise are enhanced. For example, participants were evaluated after walking with vegetation present compared to no vegetation present; the presence of vegetation measurably enhanced health benefits for a majority of participants (including lower blood pressure, less depression, less anger, and elevated self esteem) compared to those who walked without vegetation present.[7]

"Forest bathing" is a relatively new concept and area of research that is investigating the health benefits of contact with forests, but it has its roots in research done over a hundred years ago. In 1903 Dr. Svante August Arrhenius, a Swedish chemist who received the Nobel Prize in Chemistry, discovered that pine forests are a key producer of negative ions, which have many positive health benefits, including increasing the flow of oxygen to the brain resulting in higher alertness and more mental energy, balancing the opposing sympathetic and parasympathetic branches of the autonomic nervous system (promoting calm). Pine forests carry around 4,000 negative ions per cubic centimeter whereas city air during rush hour has around 100–120 ions per cubic centimeter.[8] Since 1982, research done primarily at Chiba University in Japan has found that forest walks dramatically increased white blood cell activity—the "natural killer" cells (cancer fighting cells). There is research that supports that the phytoncides (wood essential oils) that plants emit in order to protect themselves from insects is inhaled by humans and produces a positive effect on our immune systems.[9] I cannot help but wonder: when we have contact with nature, and gain the beneficial effects to our body and mind described earlier, does this enhance the opportunity to feel a sense of nature as numinous?

I would like to now turn to investigating how the aesthetics and ethics of the numinous have been engaged and manifested in designed landscapes. My entry point for this study is the archetypal dialectic of forest and clearing. Forests evoke the primordial—and, as such, have been seen in strong terms in human history—as places both alluring and terrifying. As humans found or made clearings in the forests, cultivation of the land and dwelling in one place became possible.

FOREST AND CLEARING: AN AESTHETIC OF THE NUMINOUS

The forest-clearing archetype is found in some of the world's most powerful designed landscapes and is often used to move us toward a feeling of the numinous. For example, think about the impact of encountering the emptiness of the clearing and its opening to the sky after the dark, dense, and often almost claustrophobic nature of the forest. The dark-light dialectic exemplified by forest-clearing can be a catalyst to thoughts of other pairings such as the subconscious-conscious, pain-healing, and life-death. I'll

briefly discuss four case studies, two situated within religions (the Ise Grand Shrine and the Woodland Cemetery) and two found in secular settings (the Reflection Garden at the Bloedel Reserve and the National Library of France). Richard Haag, designer of the Reflection Garden, and Dominique Perrault, designer of the National Library of France, have both stated that it was their intention to create a contemplative realm. Their definitions for a contemplative landscape coalesced around the idea of a setting that removes us from the everyday world and its concerns, quieting the mind and subsequently fostering the potential for new insights.

The two-thousand-year-old Ise Grand Shrine (Ise Jingu) in Japan is considered the most sacred place in Shinto, a religion where all of nature is seen as divine. Originally, there were no shrine buildings; instead a tree, forest, or a large boulder or a mountain, marked with rope, would be the focus of worship. This is still part of the religion today. A vast sacred forest of ancient cypress trees surrounds the Ise Grand Shrine. One walks through the forest to find that most of the shrine buildings are hidden from view. The design of the shrine complex is composed of two adjacent clearings in the forest, covered with pebbles. Both the Inner and Outer Shrine buildings are constructed of wood, and every twenty years both are totally rebuilt on the empty adjacent site. The only building on the empty site, which retains its sacredness for the intervening twenty years, is a small wooden enclosure inside of which is the sacred central post. The new shrine will be erected over and around this post, which is the holiest and most mysterious object in the Ise Shrine.[10]

In another religious tradition, Christianity, the Woodland Cemetery near Stockholm provides an additional example of the archetypal power of forest and clearing for contemplative, even numinous, space. Architects Gunnar Asplund and Sigurd Lewerentz integrated Woodland Cemetery (design and construction 1915–1940) into an existing pine forest. The Central Clearing is the symbolic "heart of the cemetery, and [the architects] elevated it above the site's periphery, creating a physical void where key elements of the cemetery emerge."[11] In the clearing, one pauses to observe earth and sky, but not graves. A profound sense of quiet ensues. It is when one enters the forest that the tombs are found. The architects' sensitive use of the forest-clearing archetype is both healing and provocative as it moves one to reflect on fundamental questions of existence.

The Reflection Garden (final design, Richard Haag, 1984) is the last garden in a series of linked gardens at the Bloedel Reserve on Bainbridge Island, near Seattle, Washington). The 150-acre reserve is the former estate of Prentice and Virginia Bloedel, who were also pioneers in the research on plant-people relationships, hosting symposia and publishing research. The Reflection Garden is deceptively simple: a clearing in the forest containing a long pool of water in a vivid green rectangle of lawn—all bounded by clipped yew hedges with the forest trees reflecting in the water. I spent a long time here, and I noticed that most people were startled as they entered this garden, oftentimes literally stopping short: attention arrested, voices stilled, and (seemingly) minds quieted down, as they encountered this transcendent space.

The National Library of France in Paris by Dominique Perrault (completed in 1995) is an innovative experience of forest and clearing.

FIGURE 4-1. SUBTEMPLE AT THE ISE GRAND SHRINE. THE GRAND SHRINE ITSELF CANNOT BE ENTERED OR PHOTOGRAPHED.

FIGURE 4-2. WOODLAND CEMETERY NEAR STOCKHOLM, SWEDEN. CENTRAL CLEARING.

FIGURE 4-3. THE REFLECTION GARDEN, BLOEDEL RESERVE, NEAR SEATTLE.

The library surrounds a gigantic transplanted forest, a forest open to the air. The trees were going to be removed due to road construction, but instead they were brought into the library. The forest is physically inaccessible, reminding us that many contemplative gardens throughout time are inaccessible. For example, think of the traditional Japanese raked sand garden that you do not enter but instead view from the veranda. At the National Library, there are views into the forest from a glassed walkway that rings the building, but where the forest really comes alive is on the top level, where an outdoor wooden deck surrounds the forest at treetop height. This vast deck functions as a clearing surrounding the forest, in the reverse application of the clearing-forest archetype.

I found both of these contemporary projects to be very successful at creating a contemplative experience. They are both enclosed gardens employing a minimalist sensibility. Overload or arousal theories posit that very complex spaces overstimulate both eye and mind, making relaxation difficult. This may reveal why so many contemplative spaces have a minimal aesthetic, but it is also important that the space not be too empty. It is important that the participant not be bored or alienated. It is a balance between minimalism and too much minimalism. Here it is instructive to consider the new 9/11 Memorial in New York. Michael Arad's original proposal, called "Reflecting Absence," is all clearing. The footprints of the Twin Towers became pools in his proposal, but everything else is depicted as pavement. The response was that it was too empty and too much about the void. Arad began working with landscape architect Peter Walker to investigate potential solutions. They have employed

FIGURE 4-4. THE NATIONAL LIBRARY OF FRANCE, PARIS.

the ancient archetype of forest and clearing, as four hundred oak trees have been added to the design. In the 9/11 Memorial's forest, the pools are clearings, but there are also smaller areas of clearing within the now forested site.

FOREST, CLEARING, GARDEN: AESTHETICS AND ETHICS OF THE NUMINOUS IN THE WORK OF MICHAEL SINGER

Michael Singer's life and work provide another window into the aesthetics *and* ethics of the numinous. In 1971 Singer was selected for the Ten Young Artists Exhibition at New York's Guggenheim Museum; he was only twenty-five years old when he won this award. Singer has discussed how it raised an important question for him: should he invest himself in the art world or should he invest in himself and his own development? "It seemed to me that one way to understand this better would be to leave the city, to leave the environment where all the issues of the contemporary art world were happening and go somewhere where it really didn't matter."[12] Singer rented a primitive cabin in rural Vermont and stayed there for five years. He unplugged from the art world and focused on the natural world. He read extensively on environmental issues, indigenous cultures, and ways of living lightly on the land.

In the Vermont woods, Singer continued to explore the themes of balance and tension that he had expressed in the minimal wood and steel sculptures he showed at the Guggenheim. But with the forest as his studio, his artistic practice was to work directly in and with nature, positioning and arranging fallen trees and branches. This work was not for exhibition, nor did he take visitors to see it. Working in the woods was a contemplative act for him, and he has described it to me as having a profoundly transformative effect on him. Toward the end of this five-year period of time in Vermont, Singer created the work *Ritual Series 5-79* in a dark hemlock and spruce forest. He began this work—which he considers the pivotal piece in his development—by breaking off the dead lower branches of trees, opening up a space in the woods. He felt that after five years he had earned the right to intervene. He collected these branches, arranged them to make a level platform, and stacked branches to create low walls on three sides. Singer and this work have some interesting things to say about the fundamental, ongoing power of forest and clearing: "I thought the first thing a human being would desire and need is a level place in these woods.... I realized I built a human place; this is clearly a human intervention: it's rectilinear and level.... There's no mystery how it was made. After studying this for a time I decided to place a sculptural structure into it, as if I'd been working there."[13] This

piece, *Ritual Series 5-79,* is primordial and fundamental and evokes the presence of dwelling and living lightly on the Earth.

Singer began to bring these ideas indoors to his studio practice and to move back and forth from indoors to the outdoors in his work. He began to reenter the art world and expand his work to commissions and collaborations. On the Wellesley College campus near Boston, he created an outdoor contemplative space that is a subtle room in the woods—creating a clearing in the forest. The Becton Dickinson Atrium is an example of his work moving inside architecture—and one could argue that this building, with its repeating columns, echoes the forest—and the atrium is a kind of clearing where Singer designed a below-grade garden of water, stone, and moss. At the Denver airport, Singer has created a visually accessible but physically inaccessible sculptural garden space that grows, lives, changes, and decays, highlighting his intention to insert contemplative space into places they typically haven't existed.

Singer has been increasingly collaborating with, or leading, large interdisciplinary teams on a range of architecture, landscape, engineering, and infrastructure projects. For his work with the Alterra Institute for Environmental Research (Wageningen, Netherlands), Singer's overarching agenda was to question fundamental assumptions; this perspective was instrumental in creating a building and site designed as one—with their systems designed together. The interior and exterior gardens clean the air, cleanse graywater, and provide climate control without air conditioning. Stormwater is cleansed on all parking lots outside and graywater is cleansed and recycled through the pools in the building's

FIGURE 4-5. *RITUAL SERIES 5-79* BY MICHAEL SINGER

exterior constructed wetlands and into the interior atrium pools. As Alterra is a research institute, these systems also function as sites of research. The sculptural, planted water pools also contain pavilions and decks to provide meeting and social space. These gardens are visible from surrounding offices, providing a contemplative respite for researchers.

Singer's work takes as its starting point that the relationship of humans to the Earth has to be reciprocal and balanced. He has been talking about and manifesting ideas of sustainability since long before the word was in common use. Michael Singer's work in and with nature creates a human designed nature that is aesthetically compelling, restores ecological function, and conjures the numinous. His innovative contemplative spaces encourage us to ponder our place in the larger scheme of things—and speak to Singer's ethical purpose. And he still lives in Vermont.

EXPERIMENTS: TWO RECENT WORKS

My own work is primarily an experimental art-design practice, a practice that is informed and inspired by research. My studies and publications on contemporary contemplative landscapes have their origin in a question raised in practice: a colleague and I were commissioned to design a "contemplative landscape," necessitating research into definitions, precedents, and principles. Our site was forested land adjacent to a small cedar-clad chapel. While the chapel had a Christian background, the landscape was to be a secular, contemplative space. Our design response resulted in a minimal intervention that amplified the clearing found in the forest.

After writing about contemporary contemplative landscapes, with an emphasis

on how contact with nature is beneficial to human health, I found that I wanted to experiment with this idea in my practice. What are innovative ways to connect with nature—and especially with nature indoors? Research reveals that Americans spend 90 percent of their lives indoors.[14] While many homes and offices contain the languishing houseplant, is this really a nature we can see anymore? I also wanted to address the high levels of stress in contemporary life and the especially high stress levels of college students. Rather than a new stress reduction program or special meditation room, my approach asked: What are the possibilities for objects and/or spaces that provide the health benefits of contact with nature (and an opportunity for stress reduction) as overlays to spaces we already have? This led to a new body of work, including my project *The Table for Contemplation and Action* (*A Place to Share Beauty and Fear*).

The Table for Contemplation and Action (A Place to Share Beauty and Fear)

I designed this table in 2008; it was brought into the interior public courtyard of Rapson Hall (home to architecture and landscape architecture students and their 24/7 studio culture) on the University of Minnesota campus in 2009, and it has been in use ever since. The table is a six-foot square of wood with a central (flush) copper box containing a changing, single, unusual element from nature. The table also provides participants with the opportunity to write about their fear/stress/hopes/wishes and to deposit these writings into the table's attached handmade glass vessel. When the vessel is full, the papers are emptied and burned without reading. Writing is completely voluntary; you learn about this aspect of the table via a small book on

FIGURE 4-6. *THE TABLE FOR CONTEMPLATION AND ACTION* BY REBECCA KRINKE.

the tabletop that also functions as a comment book. Anyone is invited to use the table: for studying, meeting, and eating.

The unusual table and the changing innovative element of nature brought to the table make it a unique object and cause people to notice it, come over, sit down, and engage. Writing, especially writing that expresses emotions, has also been linked to stress reduction and benefit to health.[15] This project has been extremely successful, meaning that participants understand, use, and benefit from the table as I had intended. Some of the many positive responses written in the comment book at the table include: "A wonderful place to sit and study. Sight, texture, smell, lovely. The opportunity to write something down and let it go is very freeing and I am thankful for it." What I didn't expect was that the comment book began to collect some writings referencing religions/religious faith, as well as quotes by Camus and Thoreau.

Recently, someone was inspired to leave a small vase of flowers at the table. A book of Psalms was also left.

After reading the comment book, seeing the table "in action," discussing the table at an open forum event, and after a trip to Japan, I began to see my table project in a new light. Could any correlations be made between the ritual-like writing at *The Table for Contemplation and Action* and ritualized writing found within religions? Shinto, Zen Buddhism, and Judaism all contain methodologies to facilitate writing to the transcendent at sacred settings that are open to all. In these three religions, writing may be done directly by the worshipper to the transcendent (with varying degrees of officiating). In Shinto, one can write on wooden prayer plaques and hang them on prayer racks at a shrine, left for as long as the writer desires. In Zen Buddhism, prayer sticks can or must be written, depending on the temple. They are left at the temple and ritually burned. At Jerusalem's Western Wall, Judaism's most holy site, written prayers are placed into cracks in the walls by worshippers and collected twice a year and ritually buried—as they are seen as sacred writings. Although *The Table for Contemplation and Action* was conceived of as a secular activity in a secular setting, the participant may choose to (and indications are that some do) address their writing toward the transcendent.

Writings collected from the table's glass vessel are burned at a public event, advertised in advance; this has been done three times and each time has been attended by several people. Several of the students in attendance said that the act of watching their writings burn was important to them. The way *The Table for Contemplation and Action* has been embraced on campus raises provocative questions about the role of private contemplation and action in a shared public space.

Unseen/Seen: The Mapping of Joy and Pain

Unseen/Seen: The Mapping of Joy and Pain was a temporary, traveling, participatory work of public art that I created in the summer of 2010. The project traveled to several Minneapolis and St. Paul parks and other public spaces, creating the setting and the opportunity for the public to map where in Minneapolis/St. Paul they have experienced joy and pain. The project's sculptural setting included a unique table-like object that contained a custom, wooden map of Minneapolis-St. Paul. The map was laser cut and is to scale with streets clearly labeled to provide easy orientation for mapping; visitors had the opportunity to literally add color to this map—gold where they have felt joy and gray for pain. But obviously there's a gradient/ dialogue between joy and pain, and people mapped by coloring both colors in the same place and creating their own symbols or expressive coloring. Each individual defined joy or pain for themselves. Using the setting/ map was free and open to everyone, and participating in mapping was entirely voluntary. Members of my student team and I were on hand in each location to talk with anyone interested about the project and invite them to add their experiences to the map.

This project was unlike other work I had done, but after *The Table for Contemplation and Action* (*A Place to Share Beauty and Fear*), I continued to be interested in the table as a device to gather people—and mapping beauty and fear was an initial thought. I also wanted the opportunity to interact

FIGURE 4-7. *UNSEEN/SEEN: THE MAPPING OF JOY AND PAIN* BY REBECCA KRINKE.

more with participants. (I rarely actually see someone put messages into the table's vessel.) These were the starting points for what became *The Mapping of Joy and Pain*. I thought of mapping as a rather silent, contemplative process, but, instead, most people talked as they mapped, oftentimes as soon as they picked up a pencil. Sometimes someone else's mapping triggered a response from another. A powerful example of this was when a participant was mapping/talking about where he overdosed on heroin and almost died were it not for a certain kind of shot the paramedics gave him right away. Then another participant named the lifesaving drug and said, "That same thing happened to me." And they looked at each other with a kind of "we made it" and a "not alone, no shame" shared moment. A dozen people witnessed this exchange.

The map is sculptural/physical (in opposition to the digital/virtual world) and emphasizes face-to-face interaction. As the mapping was advertised in advance, some people came to the map almost like an appointment—with their locations figured out ahead of time—but many people just happened upon it and participated. I did not expect to hear the stories I heard while people mapped; I had no idea so many people held such intense experiences. This map and mapping process created a shared temporary space for emotional engagement and catharsis, and was transformative for me as well. I have a much broader sense of warmth, compassion, and respect for my fellow citizens. This project has changed me and my art practice.

FOREST, CLEAR-CUT, FOREST: ETHICS OF THE NUMINOUS IN THE WORK OF WANGARI MAATHAI

To conclude this chapter, I would like to change scale, and even change continents. Dr. Wangari Maathai (1940–2010) was a professor, scientist, environmentalist, activist, and parliamentarian who started the Kenyan Green Belt Movement in 1977. This was an outgrowth of her work on the National Council of Women, where she introduced the idea of community-based tree planting as a way to both empower women and begin to address Kenya's massive deforestation. Kenya's forests were and still are declining due to several interrelated issues including: clear cutting and intentionally set fires to create land for agriculture and new settlements, and policies that do not do enough to protect forests. Deforestation exacerbates the effects of climate change such as desertification and drought, and this, in turn, cripples economies.

Maathai saw that women's lives especially were deeply affected by the loss of trees. Kenyan women are often the leaders in producing food for the family through farming and cooking (often with firewood); trees were being cut for farmland and firewood and not being replaced, in turn causing soil erosion and degraded water supplies. Maathai began to see that all of the root causes of environmental destruction have social, political, and economic roots. She developed her tree planting idea into a broad-based grassroots, nonprofit organization whose main focus is poverty reduction and environmental conservation through tree planting. Grants were secured to pay women a tiny stipend to plant a tree. Tree nurseries were started. Her work enlarged to teaching and advocacy for social and environmental justice. And 40 million trees have since been planted in Kenya.

Her last book, *Replenishing the Earth: Spiritual Values for Healing Ourselves and the World*, outlines the four core values of the Green Belt Movement which Maathai sees as spiritual values: 1) love for the environment, 2) gratitude and respect for the Earth's resources, 3) self empowerment and self betterment, and 4) the spirit of service and volunteerism. She has stated that her work could not have succeeded without these values.[16] Maathai describes her Kikuyu upbringing as an example of living sustainably and as a framework for seeing nature, and especially the forests, as sacred. She also draws inspiration from other faiths and belief systems, including her Catholic education, the Jewish mandate *tikkun olam* ("repair the world"), and her interpretation of the Japanese term *mottainai* ("don't waste"). Through the "simple" entry point of planting a tree, forests and communities are nurtured. Wangari Maathai won the Nobel Peace Prize in 2004 and the Green Belt Movement is now worldwide.

FOREST, GARDEN: CULTIVATING AN AESTHETIC AND ETHIC OF THE NUMINOUS IN EVERYDAY LIFE

Community forests and community gardens are burgeoning typologies of space in the United States and many other countries worldwide. Community gardens at their most fundamental level are "any piece of land gardened by a group of people"[17] and can include vegetable gardens, flower gardens, and urban agriculture gardens where produce is grown to be sold. Community forests may be less well known but they are an old/new idea that speaks to the importance of forests to communities—and of protecting them, planting them, and managing them for ecological, spiritual, ethical, aesthetic, social, and often economic reasons. A community forest exists when: 1) residents have access to the forest and its resources, 2) residents participate in decisions concerning the forest, and 3) the community begins by protecting and restoring the forest.[18]

The act of gardening, including planting and cultivating plants from vegetables to forest trees, is a therapeutic activity and it has wide appeal, from kids to elders. "Cultivation activities trigger both illness protection and healing responses. Community forests and gardens benefit both individuals and neighborhoods, contributing to overall community health."[19]

Cultivation, care, and service are ethics of community gardens and forests. There are many ecological and social benefits to these gardens and forests, but questions are often raised about their aesthetics, especially in urban settings. What could these new gardens and forests look like? For example, I noticed a church near the University of Minnesota campus with a large vegetable garden on its grounds where there used to be only lawn, and schools are increasingly home to "edible schoolyards." I found myself imagining place typologies becoming increasingly hybridized and more and more settings starting to include the garden or forest. What would our cities look like if they all had (new/more) community forests? And what might be the benefits for our ecological and spiritual health?

As important as it is to cultivate gardens and forests, I would like to argue that protecting the forests we have, especially the oldest growth forests most untouched by human hands, is essential on many levels but fundamental to our sense of the numinous, or sense of the "wholly other." In his book *Forests: The Shadow of Civilization*, Robert Pogue Harrison argues that when we think about deforestation, we are affected

> not only in the enormity of the scale but also because in the depths of cultural memory forests remain the correlate of human transcendence. We call it the loss of nature, or the loss of wildlife habitat, or the loss of biodiversity, but underlying the ecological concern is perhaps a much deeper appreciation about the disappearance of boundaries, without which the human abode loses its grounding. Somewhere we still sense—who knows for how much longer?—that we make ourselves at home only in our estrangement, or in the logos of the finite. In the cultural memory of the West, forests 'correspond' to the exteriority of the logos. The outlaws, the heroes, the wanderers, the lovers, the saints, the persecuted, the outcasts, the bewildered, the ecstatic—these are among those who have sought out the forest's asylum.... Without such outside domains, there is no inside in which to dwell.[20]

Walter De Maria's *New York Earth Room* is an artwork that helps to make Harrison's words tangible. The artwork is located in a SoHo brownstone; climbing a flight of stairs visitors are startled to see three feet of black dirt covering the entire floor of a former apartment. It is an inaccessible place of contemplation, it is a garden about the soil. Soil is millions of years old, and, again, it is easy to forget, but soil sustains life and all gardens and forests. De Maria said of this work, "The earth is not only there to be seen, but also to force people to think about it," adding, "God has given us the earth, but we have ignored it."[21] While it is very rare for a contemporary artist to speak so directly to the transcendent (giving the project and his words a great deal of revelatory power), the garden has often been seen as the meeting point between "Heaven and Earth." German writer and philosopher Rudolf Borchardt wrote, "The human being embodies a tension between a nature which has since been lost and an unreachable Divine Creator. The garden stands at precisely the center of this tension."[22]

To garden is to cultivate a relationship with the self, Earth, community, and, for many, the divine: "The gardens that have graced this mortal Eden of ours are the best evidence of humanity's reasons for being on Earth. Where history unleashes its destructive and annihilating forces, we must, if we are to preserve our sanity, to say nothing of our humanity, work against and in spite of them. We must seek out healing or redemptive forces and allow them to grow in us. That is what it means to tend our garden."[23]

CONCLUSION

Through my own practice, through projects ("gardens"?) such as *The Table for Contemplation and Action* and *The Mapping of Joy and Pain*, I realized—as the participants shared

their stories of trauma and healing with me —that there is a powerful opportunity for new objects and new spaces in our world to address and transform pain. And these can be overlays to the spaces we already have.

A rarified space like Walter De Maria's *New York Earth Room* and more ordinary spaces like community gardens remind us that the soil of our Earth is worthy of our attention and even reverence. Ancient archetypes of forest and clearing continue to resonate qualities of healing and the numinous to us in settings both sacred and secular. The works of Michael Singer and Wangari Maathai offer two compelling examples of the ongoing power of forest and garden to engage the emotional, psychological, ecological, and spiritual issues of contemporary life. And this contact with garden or forest can be as simple as seeing the ones in our everyday lives.

5 FROM BIOREGIONAL TO REVERENTIAL URBANISM

The state of the world's ecological systems is both tragic and catastrophic. It is tragic that through our machinations as a growing civilization we have managed to remain blissfully oblivious to the negative impact that our urban development has had on the world's ecosystems. It is catastrophic because we seem equally oblivious to the fact that our own health is inextricably tied to the well-being of other forms of life on Earth. We have also been unjust in our exploitation of our celestial home. A privileged minority have benefited while the majority teeter between vulnerability and despair. The urgency of our predicament has been well documented and well argued in countless spheres of inquiry, and has led to a number of calls to broaden the scope and nature of environmental scholarship and action. From professional proclamations by psychologists to vocational imperatives by theologians, the need for rapid, widespread, and comprehensive action is acknowledged across diverse contexts. As a result, the role of spirituality and religion in cultivating an ethic of responsibility, stewardship, and charity among various faith communities has accelerated. This chapter contributes to this discourse by introducing "reverential urbanism" as an approach to city building that is conceptually and practically imbedded in the realities of the ecological crisis. I argue that reverential urbanism is a transcendence of architecture in its expansion of the demands that we place upon buildings and cities in fulfilling our spiritual, social, and ecological needs.

ECOLOGICAL IMPERATIVES

A critical appraisal of our ecological accounts gives us a strong normative position. The work of William Rees and his students on the ecological footprint has systematically and consistently demonstrated how much ecological deficit we are in as a global economy.[1] We can endure in this state of deficit for a short while as we pollute our own water and air,[2] but long-term sustainability requires that we would generate only as much waste and pollution as can be safely neutralized by the natural cycles of the global ecosystem. Quite aside from the utilitarian ethics of pausing to consider the long-term viability of our world to support our populations of urban habitat, we have a moral position to consider. Can we legitimately justify using up the wealth and finite resources of our planet to give a global minority lives of luxury simply because we discovered efficient ways of exploiting resources. The fact that not all humans, not even a majority of humans, can live at the same standard of consumption that many of us in the global North currently enjoy should be cause enough for pause.

While the dual practices of concentrating human settlements and sheltering humans from the elements have gone through numerous stages of evolution, the last four decades have added a growing set of responsibilities to the city-building professions. Research on the impact of building and urban design on consumption, particularly energy consumption, has inspired new approaches to building. Before the modern movement, it was in the nature of architecture to strictly adhere to the constraints of local site and climate. We now know that when we deviated from this vernacular architecture, we lost a great deal more than just a local aesthetic and local craft. We lost an intrinsic awareness of our place in the web of life. Instead, we thought ourselves invincible in our ability to overcome environ-

mental constraints and the ebbs and flows of climatic conditions.

Our buildings symbolized our attitude of subjugating nature. The first shock to this attitude was the oil crisis of the 1970s, when gas shortfalls crippled the US economy. While it spun off important architectural innovations, like trombe walls, and revitalized traditional passive solar design, the historical moment produced the wrong lesson: that oil is a strategic resource worthy of securing politically and militarily. The notion that it is a finite resource did not seem to enter our collective mythology. However, as concerns about the sustainability of global growth emerged in the late 80s and 90s, an earnest critique of contemporary urban settlements began. The so-called "green design" movement was born and is now entrenched with the institutionalization of smart growth practices and LEED building rating systems. However, even this mainstreaming of the green agenda is problematic. William Rees, who invented ecological footprint analysis, writes: "Mainstream 'solutions'—hybrid cars, green buildings, smart growth, the new urbanism—are thus rooted in denial and delusional. These approaches do not address the fundamental problem of 'overshoot', but rather attempt to maintain the growth-bound status quo through efficiency gains and related technological 'fixes'. This might actually worsen the situation. Achieving sustainability requires that such marginal reform give way to a complete rethink of society's relationship with nature. Developed societies need a new, more adaptive cultural mythology. The building sector arguably has greater material leverage in reducing the human ecological footprint than any other major industrial sector."[3]

On the margins of mainstream movements, a new generation of design has emerged to answer precisely this call for a paradigmatic shift in the way we build. Buildings and clusters of buildings are envisioned as net ecological producers rather than consumers. In doing so, they would contribute to their neighbors who may be in deficit. This bold new generation of sustainable design is articulated under a number of different banners including *biotic architecture*, *living architecture*, and *regenerative design*.[4] Each has a slightly different focus; for example, regenerative design takes a systems approach to building whereby buildings attempt to repair the damage done to the environments and ecosystems they inhabit, whereas biotic architecture attempts to encapsulate ecological services such as water filtration and microclimate mediation within the boundaries of building sites. The living building challenge, which is now the threshold of achievement for the Green Building Council in Cascadia, requires the built environment to have net zero water and energy impacts and to meet exacting standards of health, beauty, and equity. The living building challenge seems radical because of its geographical boundary, which privileges bioregional territory over political boundaries, and because of its attempt to include difficult-to-quantify subjective indicators such as beauty.

These movements hint at the kind of epistemological shifts that we should consider as we cast our gaze outward beyond the confines of the urban parcel to include the systems that comprise the contemporary city. As we begin to aggregate buildings in our conceptual constructs of desirable communities, we begin to face common questions about transportation infrastructure, regional resources, and regional distributions of jobs

and homes. We also begin to face difficult questions about the sustainability of our growth and consumerism paradigm. The seeming disposability and replicability of natural resources seem to be compounding our problems. Instead, we need normative positions that are rooted in the biological world in ways that uphold its sanctity rather than its rapid commodification and demise. Ecological philosophy or, according to Arnae Naess, ecosophy, is derived from a fundamental awareness of the finite nature of ecological resources, the interdependence and intrinsic equality of all forms of life.[5] By contrast, through the Modern project we had somehow incorrectly assumed that we could transcend the need to pay attention to living within our ecological means.

While it is the macro-scale analysis of ecological limits that renders our ontological transformation urgent, and it is at the macro scale that our political and policy action will need to challenge the unfettered exploitation of ecosystems by financial capital, our personal epistemology and interaction with the material world occurs at the local scale. It is here, in our home environment, that we touch the soil and drink the water and cook our food. It is here that we shelter from the sun and the cold and the rain. It is here that we walk and sit and reflect and talk and rejoice. It is here that our bodies learn to drum with the rhythm of day and night and summer and fall and winter and spring. It is here that we can articulate our dreams of a healthier tomorrow and it is here that bioregionalism begins.

BIOREGIONAL URBANISM

Bioregionalism is rooted in place. At its essence, it is about nesting the local environment in a territorial hierarchy of increasing scales defined by ecosystem boundaries.[6] For most ecosystems, these boundaries are defined by the flow of water. Where does the rain gather when it falls and how does it flow once it gathers? It is therefore not unusual to think of bioregions as watersheds. A bioregional approach to building would serve to facilitate our functioning as biological beings in more ways than to simply ensure shelter. It would require us to consider the context beyond urban infrastructure to include the watershed and system of ecosystems in which we live. This is the essence of the new movements in architecture exemplified by the living building challenge and biotic architecture, both of which allow for performance to be measured at the scale of a block or neighborhood rather than just individual buildings. For example, a neighborhood scale–constructed wetland that filters wastewater is much more efficient and effective than a building scale system. The same is true for a large wind turbine but may not be true for photovoltaic panels. Constructing the ecological service at the appropriate scale is critical in the urban interpretation of bioregionalism. The intent is to always work within the parameters of natural systems to achieve a locally robust, resilient, and low- or no-impact human settlement.

As attractive a theory and methodological approach as bioregionalism may be, it has not been applied or tested in urban settings. One of the challenges of local self-reliance as promoted by bioregionalism, for example, is that some watersheds are simply not hospitable to water self-reliance, and most urban watersheds are not capable of food self-reliance. Most cities are ecological deserts and have not been structured to interface let alone intertwine with local ecosystems. Can

a bioregional approach still guide us toward a path of reduced material consumption? The answer lies in evidence-based empirical research that requires testing prototypical projects. Such research linking the design of the built environment to environmental consciousness is in its infancy. However we can postulate that, by structuring or restructuring our cities to help protect, reveal, and celebrate urban water systems as the lifeline of urban life, we begin to symbolically shift what we as a society deem to be important.

How might we retrofit the urban regions that we conceived during times when the ethos of the day had nothing to do with revering nature and everything to do with subjugating it. We have examples of streams being day lit and rivers being brought back to life. Parks and greenways are being reimagined as important habitat for birds and frogs and other keystone species. There are enough built examples of these projects that we can begin to string together a vision of a city comprised of living buildings adjoining streams and parks. In some places, this fabric may be cohesive enough that we can begin testing its effect on its human inhabitants. We would ask if the presence of ecological systems comprised of plants, animals, water, energy, food, and organic waste in neighborhoods alters the attitudes and consumptive habits of the human inhabitants of those neighborhoods. Can the symbolism or meaning creation of those environments begin to transform our urban mythology?

The form, orientation, and arrangement of buildings have embodied varying degrees of symbolic significance from the beginning of human settlements. From the powerful geometry and cardinal alignment of the pyramids of Giza, indicating a clear cosmology; to the hierarchical arrangement of the tribesmen's huts around the chief's hut in the Serengeti; to the awe-inspiring grand symmetry of Versailles; symbolic meaning has been integral to human settlement. But it is not only the geometrically powerful that carries meaning. The 7-Eleven on the corner lot with a few parking stalls in front, the freeway exit, and vinyl siding all carry meaning. They may not be poetic or compelling, but they mean something to those who experience them. If we were to attempt to articulate the meaning that our contemporary cities exude what would we conclude? Robert Venturi's *Learning from Las Vegas*[7] may be considered fatalistic in its acceptance of perverse consumerism, but it is methodologically helpful in its interpretation of the hegemony of consumer culture. The work exemplifies just how subjective the derivation of meaning can be. To one observer, converging freeways may seem beautifully ordered in their graceful adherence to the radius at which trucks can safely travel without having to slow down. Yet the same artifact could seem abhorrent to another observer who sees it as a monument to the billions of dollars spent subsidizing auto travel at the expense of other social projects.

As Almquist and Lipton (2010) argue, Christopher Alexander's Pattern Language is an aspiration for a form of universality that carries commonly appreciable meaning and fosters generalizable functionality.[8] We will consider the problem of generalizable functionality later, but here let us consider the notion of meaning. The work of photographer Edward Burtynsky (2003) attempts to capture the often unseen social and environmental impacts that our cities generate. His photographs are striking in their beauty and remarkable in their meaning. Burtynsky's body

of work is similar to the ecological footprint in that it makes tangible the impacts of industrialized urban societies on the hinterland. The abandoned oil towns of Azerbaijan with thousands of derelict wells and the glowing bright red rivers of mine tailings in Ontario are particularly disturbing. Burtynsky's film *Manufactured Landscapes* includes a more probing social commentary on the enormous scale of manufacturing and waste operations feeding our consumption and coping with our waste. Beyond this aesthetically provocative work are the more pervasive and egregious impacts of climate change that have made coastal regions throughout the world vulnerable to catastrophic loss.[9] The fact that carbon emissions caused by our various transportation, industrial, and agricultural systems can potentially create close to a billion international refugees escaping sea-level rise is clearly meaningful; and that meaning is indefensible. The cumulative meaning that emerges is that consumption and material growth are the primary values that we uphold as a global culture. We have come to value consumption, it would appear, over everything else.

Architecture as it is currently practiced has, at best, failed to challenge the centrality of this basal practice and at worst has been complicit in its ascendancy. The design of the built environment has failed to capture the public's imagination. It fuels intellectual and disciplinary discourse but does not engage citizens in their hopes and aspirations for a better future. It may presume to do so, but whether it succeeds is contestable.[10] What is needed is an architecture that transcends the intellectual exclusivity of conceptual creativity to engage people in mutually reinforcing acts of engagement. In other words, architecture that facilitates public engagement by enabling community residents to co-create an aspirational objective and to share in the magic of design can become a catalyst for cultural transformation. Theories of social learning and communities of practice all suggest that shifting behavior comes with social co-creation. What if the built form facilitated co-creation? It would necessarily be procedurally different, programmatically different, and also different in its prioritization of an aesthetic that cultivates aspirational meaning. This fundamental role of design makes explicit what is often implicit, the profundity of design quality. Every addition to the built environment is a compositional addition to our world: an experiential artifact that contributes to its collective meaning. As Nas and Samuels (2006) demonstrate, there is a powerful symbolic element to a city that gives meaning to its residents. The question for us is what meaning do we want to uphold and how do we manifest it through our built environment.

REVERENTIAL URBANISM

Having arrived at an interpretation of the cultural mythology at work today, it is perhaps worthwhile to posit a meaning that we ought to uphold and cast backward toward an urban design and architectural condition that might foster it. Let us name this aspiration "reverential urbanism," whereby the meaning it cultivates is the antithesis of disposable material consumerism. It is a form of urbanism that facilitates a deep sense of respect and awe for nature and for other human beings. Let us consider how we might apply it to different cultural traditions. First of all, we must recognize that the capacity to implement such a vision cannot be exclusively the domain of urban design, and that we

must ask ourselves: what is it about our cities that can foster a more reverential relationship to others and to nature? At the level of corporeal reality, we would shift from conceiving of ourselves as material beings devoted to measuring success through the acquisition of material wealth, to seeing ourselves as biological beings aspiring to feel secure through the health of the ecosystems we inhabit and the bonds we have in our immediate surroundings. As our palette of considerations begins to include aspirations and fundamental values, we move into the territory of core beliefs. As we consider that the majority of the world's population subscribes to some form of faith, or religious belief, it behooves us to consider how religious narratives might intersect with social and environmental ethics to shape our built environment.

Deductive reasoning based on scriptural interpretation, as well as inductive ethical imperatives based on ecological reflection, are well developed in religious scholarship of every persuasion. The role of the built environment in perpetuating material and energy consumption is equally well developed. What appears less developed is the dialogical relationship between spiritual reflection and an urbanity that seeks to do less harm to life on earth. How might the built environment facilitate an ethic of conservation over consumption, spiritual growth over material growth? In exploring these questions, I advance that bioregionalism provides the necessary foundation for organizing a more responsible form of human habitat. It articulates a biosocial normativity that sees social systems intertwined with ecological ones. Watersheds are divisible into walksheds whereby daily amenities and destinations are within walking distance or within walking distance to transit. However, unlike its cousin smart growth, reverential urbanism would draw on the work of Timothy Beatley (2011) to uphold the primacy of the watershed as a functional and experiential feature of urban design. Buildings and neighborhoods would collect, filter, and store rainwater; filter and treat wastewater; harness and generate power; and they would compost our waste and would grow a portion of our food. Significantly, they would do all of this in a way that is visible and interactive so that we may be constantly reminded of our biological selves. This may be the easy part.

In celebrating the presence of our biophysical needs in symbolically meaningful ways, we would also create opportunities for reflection and pause, meditation and prayer. The health benefits of personal rejuvenation are well documented and the capacity of flora to catalyze such an effect is likewise well documented.[11] Connecting human rejuvenation to ecological processes further emphasizes the symbolic significance of such processes. A continuous physical connection to ecosystem services would become integral to our evolving urban ontology. We would come to see ourselves as integrally connected to processes that are precious and vulnerable. Our way of knowing about the world might shift toward the corporeal, social, and spiritual and away from the material.

More difficult still is helping to foster community bonds across cultural differences so that we may begin to see the *Other* as an independent actor and not a parasite threatening our own ideology and livelihood. How might we foster social cohesion? There is a strong need to directly address the conflicts and tensions that consume so much of our energy. If resources are at the heart of our

conflicts, then we must be careful not to expend more resources perpetuating the conflicts than we set out to secure in the first place. For peace to replace conflict, parties must look toward their fundamental aspirations and not their positions on specific issues. Eschatologies and end-of-the-world mythologies will never be homogeneous, but short-term life goals such as raising children in a world of calm, and eating, drinking, and breathing sustenance that is devoid of poison are possible starting points.

Considering utopian thinking might help elucidate the outlines of a symbolic and functional common ground for a pluralistic nature-based urbanism. Thomas More's *Utopia* included some degree of religious pluralism in a context of communal ownership and trade-based self-sustenance. Ecological utopianism focused more on self-sustenance and a strong ethic of living within the carrying capacity of the land upon which a community resides. Similar to other models of utopia, it articulates a strong critique of capitalist consumer culture.[12] Bioregional philosophy shares this ethic. It seemed to hold greater promise, however, because it included a systematic method of engaging the notion of place and the unique ecological conditions of each place nested in the larger region. These ideologically driven theories all share a common limitation in that they cannot be readily applied to cities or to urban environments with high concentrations of people. The density threshold of their application has not been tested, but judging by the density of partially self-sustaining eco-villages, two people per acre might be the maximum number of people that a highly productive ecosystem can support. This, of course, depends on the lifestyle, travel, and consumption habits of residents, but in terms of day-to-day ecological needs it is important to acknowledge that cities are ecological parasites, living off the functioning of other systems without contributing to them ecologically.[13]

While the strong opposition to capitalism is an important critique relevant to the issue of rampant consumerism, utopia is criticized for being a static idealization of a fleeting interpretation of justice and harmony. It seems indifferent to the messy realities of the human condition.[14] From dystopian thinking, we gain an appreciation of the chaos that is human interaction and it is that tension that perhaps illuminates the calm that so many movements have aspired to achieve. The sacred is therefore all the more so because in our imperfect messy lives, it is juxtaposed against the profane. What is compelling about utopian and bioregional movements, however, is not the model itself, because it simply will not work for the majority of the earth's urban dwellers. What is compelling is the simple idea of ethical aspiration.

From utopian thinking we draw an ethic of distributed resources and mutually beneficial coexistence. Skinner's *Walden II* imagines a complete nesting and integration of natural, social, and cultural systems whereby each individual is elevated to unprecedented heights of excellence, achievement, and creativity. All species are equally empowered to flourish. Herbert Marcuse (1978) would take it further in his discussion of the artist as an agent of society whose expressions invoke a longing for a utopian vision and the promise of an enlightened happy, peaceful, and beautiful future. The artist, according to Marcuse (1978), has a channel for capturing truth, and it is that truth that can awaken in us a quest for deeper meaning and fulfillment.

For Bruno Latour, there is no privileged actor in the network of relationships that constitute society. We are all imperfect actors, which gives each of us, designer of the built environment and mere inhabitant alike, the opportunity to help shape a collectively derived and meaning-rich future. Harman (2009) builds on this to conceive of all actors as objects with an essential quality. At a metaphysical level, this essential quality resonates with mystics whereby we all have access to divine knowledge should we seek it. We see from the popular poetry of Rumi and Hafiz that this quest for the divine is an aspiration for both internal and relational harmony. It encompasses what Latour would characterize as the actors—human, animal, plant, and inanimate—and the network. Latour does not add a metaphysical dimension beyond the basic supposition that all things are actors.[15] Harman, however, suggests that each of those actors, or what he would call objects, has an essence, or an essential quality, which is unique in its relationship to others. In other words, every essence is distinguishable from the essence of the smaller parts of which it is comprised or the essence of the larger objects to which it contributes. This perspective would draw some sympathy from Arne Naess's notion of deep ecology: that while hierarchies are essential for understanding the functioning of systems, they do not suggest significance within the system. However, while Naess might choose to "promote" all living things to the status of the human, he would not go so far as to say that a rock or a cliff deserves the same levels of citizenship as do butterflies, snakes, and leaches. Bioregionalists would not disagree with this basic hierarchical distinction but would insist on a sense of place that is intimately connected to the characteristics of geology and hydrology in addition to flora and fauna.

Beyond the general notion of revering all varieties of parts and wholes, if reverential urbanism is to become relevant it must have the capacity to adapt to different cultural contexts. This is where it expands beyond the scope and framework of bioregionalism. As Goodwin and Taylor indicate when referring to the ecology movement, "[I]t may be that ecology will remain a relatively small, intellectual, fringe group."[16] Reverential urbanism would need to find a conduit for mass appeal and would uphold the valuation of nature in an eclectic way that recognizes the fundamental diversity of belief systems and traditions that comprise contemporary society. While bioregionalism espouses an earth-based spirituality grounded in environmental paganism to "resacralise" nature,[17] reverential urbanism would require urban dwellers to resacralize nature drawing on their own varied spiritual traditions. That kind of pluralistic accommodation is critical if the objective is a transformation of society rather than an oppositional adversarial stance against the mainstream majority. It also follows that reverential urbanism has to find a way to mediate between different and sometimes clashing cultures. In doing so, it has to appeal to a common higher order aspiration that can have broader appeal and that can help cultivate an ethic of simplicity, efficiency, austerity, and conservation over ostentation, materialism, and conspicuous consumption.

TRANSCENDENT ENGAGEMENT

Drawing on both traditional and contemporary religious scholarship, we could argue that urbanism must attempt to both symbolize and support compassion, humility, and fairness that are so deeply venerated in every religious tradition. Not only is such an urbanism theoretically defensible, it is also morally imperative given the urgency of our ecological crises. The sense of humility and awe that reverence eschews is akin to the kind of mindfulness and presence that mystical practices attempt to cultivate. Meditation has the capacity to create a state of consciousness and awareness of the self-connected-to-others and not in opposition to others.

The form of reverential urbanism I outline here can be derived from any number of mystic traditions or philosophies of simplicity and nonconsumption. In this chapter, I write about Islam for two interrelated reasons. First, it will become increasingly important to engage all of our various intelligences, all of our emotional states, and all of our spiritual inclinations in the struggle to transform our societies into less consumptive facsimiles of their current states. As antithetical as spirituality may be to the secular academic enterprise, it cannot be excluded from visions of the city that attempt to inspire a sense of deep respect and wonder for all forms of life. The spiritual dimension is deliberate. It allows us to draw insight from meditative and contemplative rituals so that they may be integral to urban design. Related to this aspiration is the realization that to engage people in shaping the built environment in ways that might influence cultural norms of consumption, we must engage them about values and worldviews that matter to them. Like every other cultural, religious, or ethnic group, Muslims have to come to terms with the indefensibility of current patterns of urban consumption and have to seek internally resonant arguments to guide their future actions.

In attempting to reach any group, it is incumbent upon the designer to capture the group's imaginations and aspirations by acknowledging the belief systems that are central to the lives of its members. If the group's belief system is rooted in religion, then that religion must be integral to any meaningful public engagement with the group.

Let us briefly explore how the Muslim worldview can nest its aspirations within a bioregional sensibility. Sufism, the mystical branch of Islam, has a long tradition of cultivating a sense of transcendence of self in the quest of longing for the divine. For ascetics, this is the adoption of a life certainly devoid of luxuries but also devoid of what most of us would consider necessities. Etymologically, *Sufism* is derived from the Arabic word *suf* meaning "wool" and is thought by some scholars to refer to the utilitarian use of a simple wool garment that is rough in its texture and bereft of ostentation. An essential characteristic of the Sufi is humility, simplicity, and austerity in attire, in shelter, and in the consumption of food and drink. Another central attribute of Sufis is encapsulated in the name by which they refer to one another, *mureed*, which translates from Arabic as "seeker." The Sufi is in a state of yearning and seeking union with the divine, a union with the creator and the source of all life. This is a yearning that does not cease until the soul that harbors it returns to its origin, the maker, the divine. Finally, Sufis would posit that there is a certain harmonic or reverberation within all objects that has the capacity to be in a state of remembrance and *tasbeeh* to the divine. This is the final attribute of the Sufi—to be in a state of hyperconsciousness of the divine.

Aside from being a curious way of living,

how does this inform us about our lives, those of us who are non-Sufis and those of us who might aspire to the ideals of Sufism but are encumbered by our attachments to our sprawling houses, Armani suits, lobster bisque, and SUVs? Despite our habits, austerity, contemplation, and a state of seeking unity with other beings may serve to reinforce our ecological position as individuals and as a species. An ontology of simplicity might help suppress the modern unquenchable thirst for material acquisition and replace it with a perpetual quest for love and connection to creation. Islamic discourse on contemplation cultivates a relationship to natural processes and systems in two distinct ways. The most direct and most cited in Muslim environmental writings is the edict of reflection on the majestic wonder of natural phenomena at every scale, from the cellular, to the ecological, to the cosmological. Humans are invited to exercise their intellect in pondering the complexity, precision, and beauty of the universe. Such a state of reflection clearly requires pause from the hectic pace of contemporary lifestyles and our functioning as biological and social beings seeking physical fulfillment. It additionally redirects our search for psychological fulfillment.

A second, less discussed relationship to nature in Muslim scholarship is much more utilitarian and has to do with harnessing resources. According to Petruccioli (2003), the tradition of ecological consciousness in Islam is less about wild nature and distant vistas and more about the art of agriculture. I use the term *art* because it combines function with aesthetic beauty and symbolic meaning. There is a long tradition in Islamic landscape architecture of treating the garden as a reflection of paradise and a precious worldly reminder of the bounty of creation and the sanctity of life.[18] Muslim philosophy does not consider nature as profane, vulgar, and wild. Rather, it sees nature as a web of signs that point to the majesty and divinity of creation.[19]

This begins to suggest a continuation of the traditional focus on the garden as a central-organizing and meaning-making feature of urban design found in Islamic architecture. The garden provides a simple organizing feature that is the symbolic if not geometric heart of urban design and architecture. Symbolically, it is more important than any other space, be it market or home, and is a constant reminder of that essential Muslim ideology of seeking the divine and that life is but a journey of returning to the divine. This conceptual priorization of the garden suggests a slightly different function to the park that we commonly consider in urban neighborhoods. The garden would serve as a symbolic meaning and would be a physical reminder of the preciousness of life and the cosmic cycles of life, death, and rebirth. The garden would add meaning and focus and a sense of awe to our daily habitation of the city.[20] Deriving a physical urban design out of deeply held spiritual values is the kind of public engagement in the built environment discourse that is both missing and sorely needed in empowering citizens toward aspirational behavior.[21]

The notion of the garden as a rejuvenated source of cultural mythology is a theoretical exploration of transformations inspired by the values of reverence, humility, and contemplation illustrated by Muslim spiritual praxis and facilitated by urban design. The inspirational core would vary across cultures and across religions, but as I have argued here, this core has to be rooted in place and in ecology and in people's interaction with place and ecology. It is not that cities would foster a sense of awe, or perpetually trigger numinous experiences in all who inhabit them, but they would support such experiences, should people seek them, and would programmatically and aesthetically symbolize their significance. This work is neither a call for religiosity nor an attack on secularism. Nor is it a proclamation of the relative superiority of any particular dogma, Muslim or otherwise. Rather, it is an acknowledgment of the urgency of the human predicament relative to the health of the planet and the necessity for urban patterns and systems to undergo radical transformations in concert with broader ontological transformations.

Reverential urbanism is an approach to urban design that expresses and embodies qualities of humility, awe, respect, and adoration. It points at a practice that is necessarily grounded in the quest for flourishing human societies comprised of mutually respectful communities nested in healthy and thriving ecosystems. It is a practice that requires the poetic cultivation of hope alongside empirical analysis and inductive reasoning. As fantastical as it may be, it is no less extraordinary than the challenges we face as a global community of communities whose destinies are necessarily intertwined. I argue that achieving specific ecological functionality as well as symbolic gestures in urban design are necessary catalysts, exemplars, and holders of meaning for our evolving sense of who we are as a society and as a civilization.

6 THE RISK OF THE INEFFABLE

What do we consider sacred today? How do we express it in built form? How do we address these questions within our own religious traditions? How do we address these questions within the pluralism of the public sphere?

These are arguably the key issues at the heart of "transcending architecture," the topic of this book. The difficulties of such questions are acute. To readdress such foundational questions is, however, perhaps crucial today—especially within a school of architecture. For in academic fields all around us there is increasing recognition that religious conviction, or at least the search for recognizable patterns of meaning, persists as a potent force in our contemporary lives. The active role of religious thought and experience in our societies is central not only to contemporary debates in moral philosophy and theology. Disciplines such as law, medicine, and environmental studies are engaged as well in how religion as a significant social fact is shaping today's cultural and personal identities in surprisingly complex and powerful ways.

As the title of this volume reminds us, the discipline of architecture also has a role within these debates. And it is my intention in this chapter to develop what I perceive to be the risks that an architect takes by entering into a discussion of the relationship between transcendence and architecture.

Questions of aesthetics and ethics are, of course, bound up with religious affiliation—whose most material expression is the religious building. The major traditions have different narratives for the stages of life and for life's purpose and meaning—for birth, youth, old age, and death; for the plight of the poor, the imprisoned, and the sick. Throughout history, houses of worship and sacred grounds have traditionally been the focal points around which these narratives evolved and were represented. For this reason scholars up through the period of the Second World War would continue to draw lessons from the relationship between sacred forms and societal values—one thinks, for example, of the German architect-planner Karl Gruber's illustrative documentation of the relationship of European urban form to religious building;[1] or Rudolf Wittkower, who used the geometric forms of the centrally planned church as a summary of the hierarchy of values of Renaissance humanism;[2] or Erwin Panofsky who aligned the narrative of medieval Scholasticism with its manifestation in the artistry of the Gothic cathedral.[3]

Augustus Welby Pugin's commitment to the moralizing force of the Christian Gothic is perhaps one of the most concentrated paradigmatic expressions of this alignment of architectural practice with religious thought, and its consequences for ethical and aesthetical choices. Pugin famously posited a direct causal relationship between architecture and the ethical values of society. Construing fifteenth-century Christian medieval England as a vision of social harmony, Pugin depicted in the well-known illustration from the second edition of his book *Contrasts* (1840) a preindustrial, prescientific age, when religious structures were organically integrated into the urban fabric.[4] As a consequence of industrialization, Pugin presented the accompanying dissolution of collective faith brought on by the demise of both the Gothic cathedral and the traditional medieval city.

There are, of course, other paradigmatic moments in the history of modern architecture when religious form served as a reflexive response to the technological project. Following the Second World War, for example, many prominent writers on architecture sought a return to the deeper impulses of culture, looking to the religious rituals and myths of an ancient or primitive past. In this vein, one might point to Sigfried Giedion's last work, *The Eternal Present*, published in 1962, which addresses a "trans-avantgardist" modernist impulse to return to the timelessness of a prehistoric moment.[5] In the same year, Vincent Scully published the dominant theme of his life's work in the book *The Earth, the Temple, and the Gods.*[6] Scully communicated to generations of students how cities have been shaped since the time of the Ancients by holy precincts which served as anchors around which all else revolved—from pyramids and temples to spires and minarets. Joseph Rykwert, too, in *The Idea of a Town* (1976), used ancient religious rites for getting at his larger point that a town's walls and gates, central shrines and public spaces, are all part of important generative myths, rituals, and beliefs that continue to define the cities in which we live.[7]

We may now be entering into a new paradigmatic moment of engagement with the relationship between matter and spirit, between architecture and religious thought. We may be more open than previous generations in our acknowledgment of modern life's religious roots. Following Jürgen Habermas, we may recognize today that in spite of the homogenizing forces of globalization, the distinctiveness fostered by religious commitments seems only to have strengthened in recent decades. Such a societal phenomenon has called into question what Habermas terms "the secularization hypothesis"—that increasing material wealth and modernization would necessarily diminish the role of religious identity.[8] One might think, for example, of the rise of the "unofficial church" or "house churches" of China. Indeed, Habermas himself now speaks of a "post-secular age" in which political and social movements are powerfully shaped by religious conviction, in part as a means of resistance to the ubiquity of market capitalism. In light of these changed circumstances, Habermas argues that the idea of secularization has to be nuanced to take into account the continuing influence of religious convictions in social discourse, albeit at a more individualized level. (I am thinking here, for example, of the recent decodings of the Egyptian Revolution of 2011 in light of discussions of secularization and the public sphere.)

At the same time, there is little common ground in a shared narrative of religious meaning across cultural and social boundaries. There obviously remains a startling variety of religious voices and dissonant worldviews that are often not bound together by common objects or themes of debate—hence, the work of organizations such as the "Coexist" movement which seeks to promote understanding between religious traditions. In the changing social composition of many regions around the world, we realize the necessity to rethink architecture's relationship to the plural dimension of religion as well.

Since late Roman times in the West, however, ecclesiastical form has traditionally emanated from the shared cultural narrative of Augustine's concept of the *civitas dei*—an intermingling of historical reality with spatial metaphor in the conception of two cities. This framework provided a cosmological synthesis for human history guaranteeing its ultimate meaning, providing a stable communal vision for patrons, artists, and architects seeking to meet the challenge of evoking the promise of the heavenly city. The great patrons to whom we attribute so much of the history of ecclesiastical form—figures such as the medieval Abbot Suger of the Basilica of Saint Denis, the Renaissance Lorenzo de Medici and Leo X, or the Baroque Julius II and the great cardinals of the seventeenth century—shared this communal and inherited narrative of the world with their architects. Today, however, we can no longer assume such a commonly held ideal, either within the Christian tradition or certainly within a pluralistic society which emphasizes the priority of the individual rather than communal experience of the sacred. How, then, is one to build a religiously meaningful work of architecture?

The Catalan architect Rafael Moneo has expressed well the challenge of this dilemma for an architect. Reflecting on his own approach to these questions in building the Cathedral of Our Lady of the Angels in Los Angeles, commissioned in 2006, he wrote, "What are the architectural implications of this shift from an understanding of the world as the civitas dei to a perception of religion as an individual, private matter? This change implies that an architect of a church cannot appeal to society as a whole, but rather quite the opposite: society is actually asking the architect to take the risk of offering others his vision of what constitutes a sacred space."[9]

Moneo's perspective suggests a framework for the challenges of the production of ecclesiastical form. In a more individualistic and pluralistic age, in place of a unifying vision to which the architect can appeal, there is now an underlying ambivalence about what religious buildings can communicate. Such ambivalence establishes the parameters within which the contemporary architect of sacred works must seek to maneuver. Without a foundational metanarrative, there is no assurance that a built form can convey a cohesive communal vision of humanity's relationship to God. Thus, rather than conceiving of the religious building as capable of speaking from a center of reference drawn from the longer beliefs and commitments of ecclesial communities, the architect today (as Moneo suggests) is actually asked by society "to take the risk of offering others his [or her] vision of what constitutes sacred space."

DIMENSIONS OF RISK

So taking as a starting point Moneo's very self-revelatory statement, I now want to broach two interrelated factors that get at the risk an architect takes in venturing to build a sacred work. While not exhaustive, these factors contribute to an understanding of the working reality of the architect who is faced with fusing together in built form the oppositions of materiality and transcendence, community and individual.

First, working by way of historical analogy, I want to suggest moments in the history of modern architecture in which questions of faith or the spirit were privileged over structures of rationality. Collectively, these cultural moments produce what might be described as a *marginal counterhistory*—that is, a trajectory that often stands outside of, or is resistant to, the normative techno-scientific drive which has governed much of the momentum of the evolution of modern architecture. This trajectory inevitably invokes "the other reason"—that which is often expelled from the world of the useful, calculable, and

manipulable. Such a counterhistory is not a new phenomenon but may consistently be seen to characterize the problematic condition of religious thought within the evolution of the history of modern and contemporary architecture.

Secondly, I want to address the role which sacred architecture now plays in the public sphere and the resulting challenges of identity and identity formation. In a pluralistic society such as ours, religious works are inevitably active, even provocative, presences in the public sphere. We have evidence of this, for example, in the recent attention paid in the press to the urban and civic roles of such proposals as the building of a mosque near Ground Zero,[10] or the referendum on the minaret in Switzerland.[11] In such politically and culturally charged environments, an architect of a sacred building must be especially attuned to mediating between both private, sectarian commitments and convictions and the public, communal role that such works play. The resultant risk for the architect is twofold: on the one hand, he or she can risk a reliance on traditionally recognizable forms that retreat from an active authentic engagement with the diversity of the public sphere; or the architect can risk challenging the assumptions of what religious building ought to be, in order to suggest forms that are open to a wider range of projected meaning.

THE BACKGROUND: CONSTRUCTING THE INEFFABLE

Before exploring these dimensions of risk more thoroughly, however, I first want to identify more overtly the antecedent background from which they emerge. These themes are in part derived from what I learned from editing the book *Constructing* the Ineffable: Contemporary Sacred Architecture.[12] Recognizing that the topic of religious building was worth reexploring through a contemporary lens, the Yale School of Architecture convened in 2007 an interdisciplinary symposium to begin the discussion that lies behind the essays in the book. It was our contention that while religion is a central motivating force behind many political and social movements in the world today, the religious building type is seldom discussed in a critical manner within most American schools of architecture. The intention was to draw together theologians, philosophers, historians, and leading architects to engage in discussion of the role religious space has to play in contemporary civic life, and the concretization of that interest in the design and construction of religious spaces.

We especially felt it was important to remind students of architecture that the design of sacred buildings (including not only mosques, synagogues, churches, and temples but also monuments and memorials) has consistently engaged the most prominent modern and late modern architects. Over the last two decades alone, there have been numerous examples of notable new sacred spaces and religious buildings that have received wide public attention. Indeed, the religious building type has often been a locus for advancement and innovation in modern architectural design. This fact remains true today: many recent religious works have creatively addressed architecture's contemporary concern with technology and material by engaging these factors in relation to the heightened challenges of historical tradition, cultural identity, social memory, and spiritual and symbolic form which are often typical characteristics of the religious building type.

The title of the symposium and the resultant book, *Constructing the Ineffable*, is intentionally reminiscent of Le Corbusier's famous characterization of the experience of *l'espace indicible*, or ineffable space. The term *indicible*, meaning "indescribable, incommunicable, or incapable of being spoken in words" was first used by Le Corbusier in an article published in 1946 and translated into English in 1948 as the opening of *New World of Space*.[13] Le Corbusier would return repeatedly to the theme of "l'espace indicible" throughout the 1950s and into the 1960s, republishing his earlier essay in *Modulor* (1950) and *Modulor 2* (1955) as well as leaving notes for a book by this title which he thought of writing as late as 1959. "L'Espace Indicible" emerges in his thinking as a concept exploring the living being's foundational need to control space and the "aesthetic emotion" that is the potential outcome of such control.

The occupation of space, Le Corbusier argues, is a proof of existence and a fundamental manifestation of the human search for "equilibrium and duration." Architecture, sculpture, and painting, he asserts, are those disciplines bound up with a fuller understanding of this fundamental need for spatial control. When perfected, the "action of the work" of the architect, sculptor, or painter produces a "phenomenon of concordance" as exact as mathematics, which can be a conveyor either of joy (e.g., music) or of oppression (such as undifferentiated racket). Le Corbusier describes such a carefully controlled spatial experience as a mathematical "fourth dimension," where the construction of such space is capable of providing a human experience beyond real time and space: "The fourth dimension is the moment of limitless escape evoked by an exceptionally just consonance of the plastic means employed.... Then a boundless depth opens up, effaces walls, drives away contingent presences, *accomplishes the miracle of ineffable space*."[14]

Le Corbusier's own engagement with the concept of ineffable space, along with his religious architecture itself, has at times confounded historians who have seen it as an abrupt and sometimes even disappointing departure from the rationalist themes of his early and middle career. Likewise, his association with the Cistercian abbey of Le Thoronet, with the Dominican monk Marie-Alain Couturier, and with the French journal *L'Art Sacré*, represented for some a peculiar deviation.

Yet the term "ineffable" is associated not only with his iconic Notre Dame-du-Haut at Ronchamp (1950) and the monastery of La Tourette (1953), but it also evokes his 1948 project for the legendary site of the retreat of Mary Magdalene, known as La Sainte-Baume near Aix-en-Provence; the cosmological Philips Pavilion for the Brussels World Exhibition of 1958; and St-Pierre at Firminy-Vert, begun in 1960 and left unfinished at the time of his death. The connection between these ecclesiastical buildings and the concept of ineffable space is perhaps best summed up by Le Corbusier's own description of his working intentions in regards to his religious works: "I am not conscious of the miracle of faith, but I often live that of ineffable space, the consummation of plastic emotion."[15]

My point here, however, is simply to register the fact that one of the lessons of the "Constructing the Ineffable" conference was the degree to which modernist reflections such as Le Corbusier's "ineffable space" continue to stand in the background of—and might be said to have been recently rediscov-ered by—many recent architectural explorations of the sacred. A significant outcome of the book, therefore, leads to the historical trajectory that speaks of this larger context of engagement and experimentation with sacred space in modern architecture—a level of engagement that has typically been sidelined or even overlooked in canonical readings of the history of modern architecture.

THE MARGINAL COUNTERHISTORY

Le Corbusier's identification with the ineffable may be said to lead us into the first factor of risk that an architect faces in considering the task of building a sacred space: that is, in regards to the practice of the profession of architecture, the building of sacred space aligns one with a marginal counterhistory. A key moment within this counterhistory turns around Mies van der Rohe's engagement with the idea of the "spirit" in relation to the art of building. Shaped by his close association with architect/theologian Rudolf Schwarz and the Catholic intellectual Romano Guardini, Mies demonstrated a strong philosophical concern for the spiritual foundations of architecture in an age of technology. Arguing that building could not be viewed as merely a matter of function and technology, Mies stated that "the building art is always the spatial expression of spiritual decisions."[16] As the historian Fritz Neumeyer has written, "For Mies 'the question as to the nature of the built art' was of decisive significance. It led him to search for the truth 'in the quarries of ancient and medieval philosophy.' From this question came the search for a spiritual orientation of architectural truth, without which there could be no clarity in the relationship between essence and appearance, necessity and possibility, construction and form. The problem of the building art cannot be viewed apart from the problems of being."[17]

Schwarz's 1938 book *Vom Bau der Kirche* (On the building of churches), translated into English in 1958 as *The Church Incarnate*, provided Mies with the theoretical framework for addressing architecture as a spiritual concern.[18] The book is a rethinking of the typological organization of the Christian church, and Schwarz was above all concerned with the theological issues of building the church itself, "the building and people, body and soul, the human beings and Christ, a whole spiritual universe." Based on a system of seven diagrams, such as the Cathedral for All Times, Schwarz posits various patterns for the arrangement of sacred space and the symbolic and metaphysical manifestations that lie behind this spatial ordering.

In Schwarz's Corpus Christi Church in Aachen (1930), for example, clear natural light is used to play off the white-faced interior walls, underscoring the architect's understanding of architecture as bound up with the idea of the spirituality of the body as it is connected to the world, as it experiences light, and as it is brought into relationship with the Other. Schwarz is concerned with creating a space of "emptiness and silence"—the physical and psychological space necessary to create a sacred bond to the body of the whole. Through an identification with the essential universal proportions of the human form and the human ability to respond to light, Schwarz sought to create buildings which he described as "inhabitable pictures." This way of understanding the human body within the body of the Church as a whole is the canon that governs the theoretical intent of Schwarz's plans.

The trajectory represented by the com-

FIGURE 6-1. CHURCH CORPUS CHRISTI IN AACHEN BY RUDOLF SCHWARZ, MAIN ENTRANCE, 1930.

mon concern of Le Corbusier, Schwarz, and Mies for the spiritual indicates in brief the contours of the marginal counterhistory of sacred works within the history of modern architecture. One could, of course, amplify that history to include numerous other examples—one thinks, for example, of Frank Lloyd Wright's Unity Temple (1905); or his later work such as the Synagogue in Elkins Park (1954); or of Auguste Perret's Notre Dame du Raincy (1922) and his later church of St. Joseph at Le Havre (1951); or of Karl Moser's Church of St. Anthony in Basil (1927); or Dominikus Bohm's St. Engelbert in Cologne (1932); the list could go on and on. In each case, what is striking is that while the architect was concerned with the issues of the spiritual, he utilized the opportunity of engaging with the typology of sacred building to venture some bold new experiment in architectural form, always in dialogue with the techno-scientific yet also seeking to transcend it. The ultimate question, as Mies put it, was to give the spirit opportunity for existence—and it is this very challenge that the contemporary architect continues to enter into in choosing to become a part of this marginal counterhistory of the spirit. It is a lineage that is as identifiably consistent as it is diverse.

POSTSECULARIZATION AND THE PUBLIC SPHERE

Let me go on, then, to the second major risk I see for the architect of sacred buildings, namely, the challenge of building in a postsecular age in which we are once again more aware of the powerful role religion plays in the public sphere in general, and of the influence of religious buildings in their built environments in particular.

Seeking to engage these themes more directly, I convened in January 2011 a second conference at Yale as a sequel to "Constructing the Ineffable," this time on the theme "Middle Ground/Middle East: Religious Sites in Urban Contexts." This discussion addressed the manner in which religious building and sacred sites have come to play an increasingly important role in contemporary urbanistic discussions around the issues of cultural heritage, conservation, preservation, and identity.

There are in the Middle East any number of state-sponsored projects which represent the urban scale of sacred building. One thinks, for example, of the Great Mosque of Riyadh, designed by Rasem Badran in the 1990s, which is intended to be the focal point of the redevelopment of the old city quarter. Or there is the reconstruction of the city center of Beirut, which has one of the densest configurations of religious sites anywhere in the world. But the importance of religious buildings as anchors of urban environments is not limited to the Middle East: one thinks also of such recent projects as the new cathedrals in Los Angeles and Oakland, California, which play similar roles in addressing the redevelopment of their respective contexts. Such religiously motivated urban interventions—on a scale that shapes the configuration of whole cities—point toward the importance of our taking into account the ways that a resurgence of religious identity is playing itself out in the built environment, and the risk that an architect takes on in being asked to execute such works laden not only with specific religious and denominational values but also the cultural and economic values of the public sphere as well.

In his 1995 essay "Spirituality and Architecture," the influential Islamic scholar Mohammed Arkoun addressed what he called the "critical confrontation of spirituality and architecture."[19] All important architectural achievements, Arkoun argued, contribute either to strengthening the dominant ideology in any historical tradition and political order, or to creating a breakthrough in the inherited system of values and beliefs. Following Arkoun's point, one could say that by addressing such an expansive challenge as constructing a religious site (which is exacerbated all the more in the gap between Islamic and Western contexts) the architect is forced to become responsible for negotiating the tensions between competing and often conflicting sets of cultural and historical convictions. Either way, the architect of religious buildings takes on a significant risk: if the emphasis is too much on strengthening a dominant ideology by replicating received patterns of meaning, the risk is of a detachment from the complex cultural matrices of contemporary global society. If the emphasis is too much on creating a breakthrough in inherited values and beliefs, then the risk is of a disconnectedness from a received system of meaning that lends intelligibility and coherence.

The evidence for Arkoun's analysis of the tension between these two poles may be seen in recent work at both ends of the spectrum. On the one hand—at the more conservative end—is the controversial, stubborn, and even idiosyncratic position of the architecture of Abdel-Wahed El-Wakil. His work might be characterized as being grounded by a belief that the construction and physical presence of sacred buildings must be an overt expression and bearer of cultural life. Having built more than fifteen mosques largely in the Middle East—the Quba Mosque in Medina,

the Miqat Mosque in Dhul Halayfa, and the King Saud Mosque in Jeddah—Wakil emphasizes traditional building methods, often deployed with considerable skill and subtlety.[20] His stance might be read as betraying an exemplary philosophical dignity closely allied with the work itself—a sacred geometry that is quietly and heroically subversive in an extraordinary relationship with both the craft and expressive power of architecture.

At the other end of the spectrum are the discourses that characterized many of the architects included in the *Constructing the Ineffable* book, namely, a cultural predilection for more ambiguous or indeterminate forms of representation. Some of these architects speak openly about their doubts that architecture can represent any coherent message or set of beliefs. Moshe Safdie, for example, in his Yad Vashem Holocaust Museum built in Jerusalem in 2005, overtly addressed the inability of the building to communicate a coherent meaning. Peter Eisenman, too, in designing the Berlin Memorial to the Murdered Jews in Europe (completed in 2008), openly asserted that his work seeks to avoid any form of representation whatsoever—and subsequently asked the question whether there is a religious space for the twenty-first century.

In a comparative vein, the revered Japanese architect Tadao Ando orients his sacred architecture not to a specific religious symbolic system but to an appeal to the natural world. Kenneth Frampton describes Ando's work in *Constructing the Ineffable* as evoking a tautological "secular spirituality." Using Ando's work as a backdrop, Frampton raises a focal issue that runs throughout the volume: how can architecture be unequivocally modern, yet in the face of relentlessness modernization

FIGURE 6-3. BERLIN MEMORIAL. MEMORIAL TO THE
MURDERED JEWS IN EUROPE. BERLIN, 2005, PETER
EISENMAN, ARCHITECT.

also be informed by modes of beholding that
are more primordial and historically layered?

Architects of religious spaces may therefore have to see themselves as the interme-
diaries between the needs of the client and
the more indeterminate expressions of the
sacred that are apposite in a multicultural,
multifaith, and multiethnic context. They
may thus return to an ethos like that of the
Mexican master Luis Barragán, who asserted
emphatically that to design for serenity is
the primary duty of the architect. "Serenity
is the great and true antidote against anguish

FIGURE 6-2. KING SAUD MOSQUE, THE SAHN OF THE
MOSQUE. JEDDAH, 1987, ABDEL EL-WAKIL, ARCHITECT.

and fear," Barragán said, "and it is the architect's duty to make of it a permanent guest … no matter how sumptuous or how humble."[21]

To attempt to construct a sacred space today stands as a provocative—some would say anachronistic—assertion of meaning. Yet the distinctive narrative that sacred building has historically provided within modern architecture suggests that, even in environments that are essentially determined economically and technologically, sacred building can take a critical yet precarious stance that says more, even, than the architect may at first intend. And that perhaps is the ultimate risk the architect of sacred architecture undertakes: to say more even than the architect intended to say by saying less than anyone would initially understand.

THE INDETERMINATE

By way of conclusion, then, I would offer the following thoughts. The indeterminacy suggested by the aforementioned examples may indeed result in an indefinite and even provisional language for sacred architecture. Yet this does not mean that the messages conveyed by these works are without meaning. For as the Italian postmodernist Gianni Vattimo would have it, provisionality may be truthful precisely because it is neither definitive nor ultimate. Vattimo's notion of "weak thought" is a manner of thinking about how one can continue to assert claims to some form of truth (religious or otherwise) within a pluralism of competing values and commitments. These claims can no longer be asserted with the force or absoluteness of "enlightened" reason; rather, they must be posited with a certain caution and uncertainty, recognizing that they will run headlong

into other perspectives that will call into question their validity and coherence.

Like Hans Gadamer, Vattimo remains deeply aware of the importance of historical tradition in shaping our thought and experience. Although the convictions of the past can no longer necessarily be held to be as true, we must nevertheless continue to engage them with an attitude of respectful attentiveness, even while seeking to overcome their limitations. This respectful attentiveness is what Vattimo calls the attitude of *pietas*: "We must keep in mind that it is the dissolution of metaphysics that liberates us for *pietas*.… Once we discover that all the systems of values are nothing but human, all too human productions, what is left for us to do? Do we dismiss them as lies and errors? No, we hold them even dearer because they are all we have in the world, they are the only density, thickness, richness of our experience, they are the only "Being."[22]

For the purposes of this volume, it is perhaps significant that Vattimo directly connects his attitude of *pietas* with Heidegger's notion of dwelling. By binding the idea of building to the meaning of dwelling, Heidegger addresses "the manner in which mortals are on the earth." To dwell, Heidegger insists, means more than simply to occupy a territory. Rather, it is related to a sense of rootedness in the earth. He imagines this dwelling as taking place within a fourfold matrix of earth and sky, gods and mortals: dwelling, then, is the formation of presencing through the creation of space within identifiable boundaries. Echoing Heidegger's essay "Building Dwelling Thinking,"[23] Vattimo writes in his 1996 book *Belief* that the complexity of a pious reflectiveness is what allows us to dwell with some sense of poise in our multifarious world.[24] Heidegger's concept of dwelling and Vattimo's attitude of *pietas* are ways of allowing ourselves to inhabit a world without having to control it—to exist with the provisional and indeterminate without paralysis.

If one thinks of Heidegger's idea of dwelling as related to inhabiting a certain bounded space on the earth, and Vattimo's idea of dwelling as an intellectual habitation of an indeterminate terrain of thought, one perhaps comes close to understanding the "risk" of which Moneo speaks. An architect, choosing to build a sacred building, must both seek to ground the work, in the Heideggerian sense, in its site and location so that it has the permanence, presence, and peace of dwelling, and at the same time communicate something of the provisionality, contingency, and indeterminacy of Vattimo's *pietas*.

JULIO BERMUDEZ

7 LE CORBUSIER AT THE PARTHENON

According to Rudolf Otto, one of the most influential theologians and philosophers of religion of the twentieth century, the experience of beauty in art and architecture may afford us, however momentarily, a glimpse of the Holy or numinous.[1] He explains that these aesthetic occasions are rare, difficult to facilitate, and involve a phenomenology of "tremendous mystery." More precisely, he describes the experience as a blissful mix of exhilaration, joy, insight, and peace, although it sometimes manifests itself as awful, depressing, and even horrific because, for the most part, we are not ready for an encounter with the "Other." Put differently, for Otto, pleasing and dreadful sublimes may possibly arise and coexist in a given aesthetic experience of the Holy not unlike, perhaps, when we see the Gestalt vase-face shape and see either figure or ground but never both at

once.[2] For certain, arriving at the numinous means to have transcended our ordinary state of consciousness and, not surprisingly, the ensuing experience is so powerful and profound as to cause an enduring transformation—like Dante after his epic journey in the Divine Comedy—since those who have tasted the transcendent are never quite the same again. Although Otto's way of relating beauty and metaphysics is arguably one of the most phenomenologically sophisticated, it belongs to a long-evolving, premodern, and Western philosophical (and sometimes theological) tradition that goes all the way to Plato via (going backward in time) Schopenhauer, Kant, Thomas Aquinas, Saint Augustine, and Plotinus (to name a few illustrious examples).

At first sight, these few lines about the numinous seem fantasy or sheer exaggeration geared to gullible people of a bygone era.

For, can an educated and rational citizen of the twenty-first century really believe that immediate, sensorial experience is able to deliver the most profound understandings and delights available to humanity? As said in the introduction of this book, modern and postmodern perspectives have repeatedly pointed out the fundamental flaws behind such skewed thinking and its erroneous arguments and conclusions. Most reasonable people would heed to today's zeitgeist, turn the page, and forget the matter altogether.

But not the open-minded. There is too much at stake. What if reaching the transcendent through architecture was truly possible, even partially? After all, Le Corbusier and Louis Kahn, two towering figures in architecture, made no secret of their lifelong commitment to invite the ineffable and immeasurable through architecture (arguably their own way to call the numinous, respectively). And there is more backing. For example, recognized contemporary practitioners such as Alberto Campo Baeza, Steven Holl, Juhani Pallasmaa, and Claudio Silvestrin affirm the possibility of the transcendent in architecture.[3] Additionally, highly respected scholars support the serious consideration of the "architecturally numinous." For instance, comparative religion expert Lindsay Jones says that sacred structures may "lift one to higher levels of consciousness and spiritual awareness in ways that the ordinary acquisition of knowledge cannot ... [causing] transformations that entail not simply new ways of thinking but even new ways of being."[4] In the same fashion, phenomenologist Alberto Pérez-Gómez argues that architecture holds the promise of a "radical orientation in experience, beyond words ... [that] has the power to change one's life in the present, like magic

or an erotic encounter."[5] In short, there seems to be some good reasons to delay a swift denial of the transcendent in architecture.

A fair examination of this matter would demand a close inspection of transcending experiences of the built environment. Given the nature and power of the numinous (not to mention the recognized figures supporting its reality), we would expect plenty of examples in the disciplinary record. However, the opposite is true. A three-year-long extensive search for first-person accounts only found a handful of samples.[6] It is hard to make apathy the culprit for this silence considering the (supposedly) highly passionate quality of the event. A better explanation would certainly be the long-standing "professionalist" attitude that privileges the technical, productive, material, and intellectual over the experiential, receptive, immaterial, and emotional—a tendency that finds insidious complicity in a contemporary culture that depreciates the subjective, unscientific, immeasurable, slow, and unprofitable.[7] Or perhaps, as Pérez-Gómez argues, the lack of interest (or taboo?) is endemic to all institutions that must confront something at the core of their concerns that is mystical, graceful, and ungraspable.[8] Regardless of the causes and even the likelihood of a censoring and narrow-minded profession, the fact is that having few examples of transcending architectural experiences in the public record casts a large and damaging shadow of doubt on the phenomenon. In our era of scientific empiricism and rationality, lack of data means no evidence and constitutes a legitimate reason for swift hypothesis rejection—especially if the claim is controversial and qualitative.

Given this situation, the logical step forward is to undertake a phenomenological

FIGURE 7-1. CHARLES-ÉDOUARD JEANNERET (WHO WOULD CALL HIMSELF LE CORBUSIER AFTER 1920) AT THE ACROPOLIS, SEPTEMBER 1911.

study of an actual architectural experience of the numinous. But since the stakes are high, not just any example will do. We need a case that offers a good, detailed, and highly trustable account. This presents a large challenge because, as explained previously, our choices are limited. Worse still, most of the available testimonies are short and lack descriptive specificity. Two exceptions are the experiences reported by architects Steven Holl at the Pantheon and Bruno Taut at Katsura. But even these are no match for what remains to this day the most accessible, complete, and in-depth published account of the extraordinary in architecture: Le Corbusier's experience of the Acropolis and Parthenon in 1911.[9]

This example may come as a surprise to many because although it is public knowledge that young Le Corbusier had a momentous time at the Acropolis, it is a whole other story to claim that the event had a transcendent dimensionality. In fact, if anything remotely numinous actually happened in 1911, we would have surely heard about it by now, given the large amount of scholarship covering Le Corbusier's life. Since we have not, most of us assume that nothing occurred, or if it did, it was just an overreaction of an impressionable youth. Besides, we have been repeatedly told that Le Corbusier was not a religious person, making any spiritual encounter out of character with the man. Yet, despite these seemingly established "facts," a more careful observation would show that all these assertions rest on shaky ground as the actual phenomenology of the 1911 episode remains largely unaddressed in the available scholarship. Indeed, the few studies covering Le Corbusier's experience of the Parthenon offer only descriptive[10] or, as I will show later, misleading interpretations of the occasion.[11] This is puzzling considering that most scholars agree on the important role that his first visit to the Acropolis played on Le Corbusier's professional trajectory.[12] This major oversight can be partially explained by yet another (and related to the one discussed earlier) disciplinary prejudice against anything religious or sacred,[13] a position that finds justification in the little interest that modern and postmodern historians, critics, and philosophers have for issues covering beauty, spirituality, or phenomenology.[14] But the greatest reason for the lack of a serious examination of the 1911 episode is that important challenges to the authenticity and accuracy of Le Corbusier's account remain without proper response. The net result is that our "knowledge" of Le Corbusier's remarkable encounter with the Parthenon is "thin," inadequate, and/or misleading and can therefore use a deeper phenomenological examination. Such a study would benefit from the existing wealth of scholarship on Le Corbusier. This rich knowledge base would allow us to confirm the lifelong influence of this episode—thus verifying the lasting and transformative effect that a numinous experience is said to have.[15] However, before we engage in our phenomenological inquiry, it is imperative to address the legitimate concerns that have kept our discipline from considering this event beyond an anecdotic tale. The next two sections are devoted to such a task. Those wanting to move directly into the study of the experience should skip to the section entitled "The Testimony: Jeanneret at the Parthenon in September 1911."

THE IMPORTANCE OF THE EXPERIENCE OF THE PARTHENON ON LE CORBUSIER'S LIFE

During the last years of his life, Charles-Édouard Jeanneret, known as Le Corbusier after 1920 (from now on, I will use Jeanneret to refer to Le Corbusier before 1920), often reflected on his youth.[16] Thus, a few weeks before his death, Le Corbusier found himself reviewing and only mildly amending the travel notes and observations he made during his journey to the East fifty-four years earlier.[17] The fact that this was his last publishing decision is a remarkable testament considering the profound and life-changing role that one particular chapter of that trip had on his life: the experience of the Acropolis and Parthenon. There is no secret in this matter, an elderly Le Corbusier would say: "Over the years I have become a man of the world, crossing continents as if they were fields. I have only one deep attachment: the Mediterranean. I am Mediterranean Man, in the strongest sense of the term. O Inland Sea! Queen of form and light. Light and space. The essential moment came for me at Athens in 1910 [sic]. Decisive light. Decisive volume: the Acropolis. My first picture, painted in 1918 was of the Acropolis. My Unité d'Habitation in Marseille? Merely the extension."[18] Ivan Zaknic, editor of the 1987 English translation of Le Corbusier's *Le Voyage d'Orient*—the book containing the notes of his 1911 trip, including his experience of the Parthenon—agrees: "There was, it seems, a pre-Parthenon Jeanneret and a post-Parthenon Le Corbusier. It was after the experience of Mount Athos and the Parthenon that he decided to be an architect."[19]

The power of his 1911 experience was such that from then on Le Corbusier would

often come back to the Greek temple as the fundamental compass to guide his professional (and, perhaps, personal) life. And he started right away by writing the 1921 article "Architecture: Pure Creation of the Spirit" in *L'Esprit Nouveau* and then populating his first and most influential book *Vers une Architecture* (1923) with an unordinary number of pictures and references to the Parthenon. It is impossible to read *Vers une Architecture* and not concede that Le Corbusier thought of the Parthenon as the ultimate exemplar of architectural beauty and related it to something much larger, possibly transcendent or numinous. In the text, he tells us that the strong aesthetic response to the temple is due to the building's capacity to induce a harmonic alignment between ourselves and an "absolute" or natural order. This is because, in his own words, harmony is "a moment of accord with the axis that lies within man, and thus with the laws of the universe—a return to the general order." He applies this to the Greek temple immediately thereafter: "If we stop in front of the Parthenon, that is because the sight of it makes the inner chord sound; the axis is touched."[20]

If this sounds mystical or cosmological, well, it is. Later on, during his speech to the Fourth CIAM congress in Athens in 1933, Le Corbusier would return to the importance of his 1911 experience (and later reaffirm its significance by publishing it in his 1948 book *New World of Space*):

I came to Athens twenty-three years ago; I spent twenty-one days on the Acropolis working ceaselessly and nourished myself with the admirable spectacle. What was I able to do during those twenty-one days, I ask myself. What I know is that I acquired there the idea of irreducible truth. I left, crushed by the superhuman aspect to the things on the Acropolis, crushed by a truth which is neither smiling nor light, but which is strong, which is one, which is implacable. I was not yet a man and, in the face of the life that was opening, it remained for me to develop character. I have tried to act and to create harmonious and human work.... I have done it with the image of this Acropolis in the depth of my spirit.... The Acropolis made me a rebel.... I have kept this certitude: "Remember the clear, clean, intense, economical, violent Parthenon—that cry hurled into a landscape made of grace and terror. That monument to strength and purity."[21]

The supreme and lasting power of his 1911 experience on the Acropolis is not only acknowledged by the man himself but confirmed by many scholars.[22] Indeed, the strong influence of the Acropolis-Parthenon is readily noticeable in Le Corbusier's most important works, namely Villa Savoye, Chandigarh, and Ron-

champ, as researchers often point out[23] and any careful analytical observation attests. For this reason, "one is not surprised by the legend which states that the ageing Le Corbusier kept a picture of the Domino on his wall next to a photograph of the Parthenon: both were central to his lifelong production, and both embodied notions he regarded as fundamental."[24] Thus, it is not a far-stretched suggestion to propose that Jeanneret's encounter with the Parthenon was so extraordinary that it transformed him forever. Perhaps, as Le Corbusier says in *Vers une Architecture*, the experience of the Parthenon did produce a fundamental alignment between an absolute realm and his inner self—an alignment that, we can hypothesize for now, delivered him into some type of transcendent experience. For certain, we can say that this event had a lifelong impact in the master's career and, given his great influence in the discipline, to architecture at large.

THE AUTHENTICITY OF THE EXPERIENCE

A main reason why Jeanneret's 1911 experience of the Parthenon has not received proper analysis or consideration is because its veracity and accuracy remain contested. There are four challenges to the testimony that we need to address if we intend to accept the narrative as authentic.

The first challenge points to the lack of freshness (if not plagiarism) of the testimony. Most scholars agree that Jeanneret's story has been directly influenced by French philosopher Ernest Renan's pamphlet *Prière sur l'Acropole*.[25] This is based on evidence that Jeanneret had read or was reading this short text at the time of his visit to the Parthenon—something customarily done by educated French-speaking travelers to Greece at the time. Indeed, anyone who reads Renan's piece would concur that it probably inspired Jeanneret both when visiting the Acropolis and his later writing of the chapter "The Parthenon."[26] However, Renan's short text is a philosophical and emotional writing, more poetic than factual, and lacks architectural detail and logic. It is in the compounded reality of Jeanneret's architectural narrative; his careful writing; his committed autodidactic education prior to the situation;[27] the months-long effort to reach the Acropolis, including his taking the risk of contracting cholera (see the following discussion); and the lifelong bearing of the experience where we can confidently ground the authenticity of his intention, experience, and therefore testimony, aside from whatever (real) influence Renan may have had.

A second challenge to the account's genuineness comes from Jeanneret's writing it in 1914, that is, three years after the actual occurrence.[28] This raises doubts not only about its accuracy but also, more insidiously, about whether or not the whole experience was fabricated for other, less noble purposes—perhaps Le Corbusier's relentless ideological agenda and/or campaign of self-promotion. However, since his writing happened before Jeanneret became Le Corbusier in 1920 (and before the publication of *Vers Une Architecture* in 1923), the suggestion of a 1914 fabrication of the account for its later utilization in something that Jeanneret had not even thought about is hard to defend. The fact remains that no scholar proposes that the chapter "The Parthenon" was significantly altered after 1914, not even in 1965 when Le Corbusier revisited it in preparation for its publication, which rebuts any "tampering" with the actual text. And since the piece was

by and large unknown until its first publication in 1966, it is impossible to claim its utilization for propaganda purposes. Regarding the fabrication of a "general" rapture at the Acropolis to advance an ideological agenda, we can only point to Le Corbusier's continuous return to the Parthenon throughout his life to indicate that, if anything, his 1911 visit to the Acropolis and Parthenon was effectively an authentic event in his life, not a forgery, lest the man himself be a liar. This argument also responds to scholar Allen Brooks's assertion that Jeanneret's experience of the Acropolis was exaggerated to cover up his real but shameful motive for shifting his architectural position to classicism: his bigotry toward anything German. By inventing a fundamental change of heart based on an extraordinary aesthetic experience, Brooks argues, Jeanneret is able to avoid being cast as Germanophobe.[29] On the contrary, a case could be made that the experience of the Parthenon clarifies for Jeanneret that the German (modern, rational, industrial, materialist) view of architecture was incomplete and that emotion, spirit, and beauty were necessary for any thick understanding and practice of architecture.[30] Information supporting this interpretation is offered in the section "Interlude One."

Regarding mnemonic loss and a consequent invention of the story, recent research on extraordinary architectural experiences has found that these remarkable aesthetic events do produce memories that last a very long time without much loss of vividness.[31] Hence, writing about the experience of the Parthenon "only" three years after the event would have caused only very minor recollection errors in a young and (very likely) still impressed Jeanneret. Besides, any such mistake would be irrelevant to the matter under consideration: a transcending experience of architecture.

A third possible contention to the truth of the story comes from Jeanneret being sick during his stay in Athens. This may suggest that the powerful experience could have been an artifact of such illness, the medicine he was ingesting, or both acting on a body already exhausted by a nonstop, six-month-long trip. In his testimony, Jeanneret tells us three times that he is suffering an illness that is affecting his experiences. For instance, "I must have drunk too much resin wine to hold at bay the cholera of 1911 that was sweeping all the East.... My illness made me weak.... Again today I imbibed too much resin wine."[32] Scholars do agree that Jeanneret was ill. For example, Weber says that Jeanneret had been "extremely sick for ten days" with intestinal attacks and endless diarrhea while at Mount Athos (his stop prior to Athens) and continued with digestive problems when he was in Athens.[33] Geoffrey Baker goes further (but wrongly), claiming that Jeanneret got sick with cholera and was taking absinthe throughout his whole time in Athens.

While it is true that Jeanneret was not completely healthy, it is a different story to state he was not "sober" enough to have an authentic experience. His continuation of the trip into Italy and back home for another few weeks after Athens suggests that he could not have been that ill after all. Additionally, let us not forget that we are talking about a twenty-three-year-old man who, despite looking a bit thin in the picture (see figure 7-1), was likely to withstand a debilitating but certainly not invalidating sickness. A better interpretation of the role that his ailment played in the experience would posit that it weakened Jean-neret's strong intellect and will, thus allowing an already existentially intense moment to penetrate deep enough to become the heart wrenching, physically shaking, and mentally enlightening experience that it was.

The last challenge to the integrity of the testimony focuses on sex. Although this argument has not yet been advanced, it is better to address it than leave it untouched. According to Weber, Jeanneret remains a virgin at least until his trip to the orient and possibly still practicing abstinence at the time of his visit to Athens.[34] Since some schools of psychoanalysis argue that such sexual conduct is due to repression or other psychological traumas and leads to anxiety, frustration, and erratic mood/behavior, some may understand Jeanneret's aesthetic experiences on top of the Acropolis as the effects of libido sublimation and not of his encounter with architecture or, much less likely, the numinous. However, we have come a long way since Freud to know that many other dimensions besides sex influence our psychological and physical well-being. In other words, while sexual tension or repression does impact one's life, it would be a reductionism to assign it enough power to shape Jeanneret's extraordinary experience. This, however, does not diminish the role that the erotic may have played in Jeanneret's moment. In fact, Pérez-Gómez has given us very compelling phenomenological arguments showing that at the root of architectural aesthetics and ethics lies the erotic, updating something that Plato first argued 2,500 years ago. This erotic "quality" may manifest in a variety of ways, ranging from shallow (i.e., physical or sensual) attraction to profound and all-encompassing transcending love and grace.[35] Jeanneret's sexual abstinence may have actually accentuated, however superficially or deeply, the erotic encounter with architectural beauty and, maybe, the transcendent. After all, Rudolf Otto acknowledges that erotic experiences have several similarities and relationships with religious experiences of the numinous.[36]

I hope that this short response to four important challenges to the authenticity of the extraordinary experience of the Greek temple depicted in the chapter "The Parthenon" of Le Corbusier's *Journey to the East* are compelling enough to approach Jeanneret's remarkable story with an open mind.

THE TESTIMONY: JEANNERET AT THE PARTHENON IN SEPTEMBER 1911

Jeanneret's extraordinary experience of the Parthenon occurs close to the end of his four-month-long voyage to the East (or six months if we add his actual starting point from Germany in April 1911).[37] It is clear that he considers this trip educational, perhaps modeled (in reverse) after the "Grand Tour," a rite of passage that upper-class and educated young European men used to take.[38] He was twenty-three years old and traveling with his friend August Klipstein, an art history student. By the time he arrived to Athens, Jeanneret had gone through a rich variety of experiences, building up a momentum toward his visit to the Parthenon. Scholars say that he had planned his itinerary with Athens at the end given the high place the Acropolis occupied in his mind and heart.[39] Jeanneret reveals that much at the very beginning of his testimony: "To see the Acropolis is a dream one treasures without even dreaming to realize it…. A long time ago I accepted the fact that this place should be like a repository of a sacred standard, the basis of all measurement in art."[40]

Interlude One

How come Jeanneret at twenty-three already had such a strong viewpoint about the Acropolis? What else did he believe? In other words, what was in his mind as he reached Athens that September morning of 1911? No phenomenological study can proceed without accounting at some level for an individual's beliefs, knowledge, and expectations even if, in the "moment of truth," they succumb to the experience. Considering Jeanneret's autodidactic education, answering this question demands us to review, however briefly, the influence that early mentors, books he read, people he acquainted or worked for, and other special experiences may have played in shaping his mind and attitude.

Scholarship covering his early life points at two particularly decisive forces that were going to build Jeanneret's philosophical/ideological foundation: the teachings of his first art and design teacher Charles L'Eplattenier[41] and the writings of Provensal.[42] L'Eplattenier passed on to Jeanneret an idealist, informed, and aesthetic view of the visual arts and design, with nature at the center of creative inspiration and accessible through formal analysis. He is likely to have recommended that Jeanneret read Henry Provensal's book *L'art de Demain*. Scholars (e.g., Frampton, and particularly Turner) argue that this Hegelian text taught Jeanneret the existence of a spiritual realm underlying and giving meaning to the material world along with the importance of art (and architecture) to express one's zeitgeist. More poignantly, Provensal's essential theme that "the artist's role is to connect Man with the eternal principles of the 'Absolute'"[43]—based on an aesthetics of "ideal beauty" that embodies mind and spirit and not simply delivers pleasurable physical sensations—would clearly influence him as we briefly saw in the short discussion about harmony that Le Corbusier's advances in *Vers une Architecture* about a decade after his encounter with the Parthenon. Notice that Provensal and Hegel follow in their own way the same philosophical tradition assigning beauty the ability to call forth the transcendent that we saw at the beginning of this chapter.

Turner makes a very compelling case (accepted by other scholars such as Baker and Richards) that so strong was the idealism that Jeanneret constructed upon Provensal's book and L'Eplattenier's teachings that no matter how much rationalism, materialism, functionalism, and industrial logic he found later on (some through renowned architects Perret and Behrens), Jeanneret was not going to be fundamentally affected by them. Instead, he adapted all such learning within his already-gained idealist vision. Another relevant piece of information is that Jeanneret becomes involved in spirituality during his autodidactic years as is evident in his intense reading and marking of *Thus Spoke Zarathustra* by Nietzsche and *Vie de Jèsus* by Ernest Renan.[44] These two books present the tragedy and effort involved in any radical attempt to turn the world toward spirituality which, in the context of Provensal's central role of the artist in transforming society, resonated with young Jeanneret (and may have led Le Corbusier to believe in his messianic role in modern architecture later on). At the same time, these readings may have also reignited some of his own spiritual beliefs—a product of a very religious upbringing within a Swiss region with a strong heritage in religious activism.[45] Jeanneret would not become a self-acknowledged agnostic until later in his life.

A second wave of influences completed the education of Jeanneret prior to his trek to the orient. They can be traced to his year-long stay in Germany in 1910 (while working for architect Peter Behrens and others). As scholars note, Jeanneret went to Germany as a committed medievalist and returned home a convinced classicist, a substantial change associated with two sources: William Ritter and Alexandre Cingria-Vaneyre's book *Entretiens de la Villa du Rouet*.[46] William Ritter, a Swiss novelist and poet, was one of the people who would affect Jeanneret the most. For certain, he was to replace L'Eplattenier as Jeanneret's main mentor and whom he would frequently communicate with and request advice from, especially around the time of his trip. Ritter gave Jeanneret a romantic introduction to the East, vernacular architecture, and the spiritual dimension of the ancient Greek world. Regarding Cingria-Vaneyre's book *Entretiens de la Villa du Rouet*, it provided Jeanneret with reasons to subsume his home region and culture of Jura (Switzerland) under the sphere of classicism. Le Corbusier would later say that this book unlocked the "German vice" in him, meaning a revalorization of the Mediterranean Classicism and the arts over the utilitarian, standardizing, and invasive drive behind German culture.[47] Reading *Entretiens de la Villa du Rouet* apparently exerted strong weight in deciding to include Greece and Turkey in his trip to the orient (which originally only included Eastern Europe).

As a convinced Hegelian idealist converted to classism, twenty-three-year-old Jeanneret started his journey to the East, not so much to verify his views but to find examples that embodied his beliefs.[48] His search was anything but superficial or practical but rather spiritual and idealist, and filled with the same devotion, intensity, and reflectivity that he had engaged his autodidactic study of architecture. Since the Acropolis/Parthenon is figured as "the" example of classical architecture and ideal beauty, we can see that he carried heavy expectations as he was approaching Athens that September of 1911.

Continuation of Testimony

Let us return to the moment when Jeanneret was arriving at Athens' harbor. He had been at sea since leaving Mount Athos (North-East Greece) and could not wait to get to the Acropolis. In fact, before leaving for Athens, Jeanneret admitted to be "haunted by a dream, a yearning, a madness," strongly hinting that he had yet to fulfill his trip's mission. Not surprising, the night before arriving, and in company of his friend Auguste, he recorded: "We feel a true excitement to think that by this evening we shall have seen the immortal marbles." The next morning, as the boat approached the harbor, he saw his destination for the first time: "Very far away in the center of the harbor, at the bosom of some hills forming an arch, a strange rock stands out, flat at the top and secured on its right by a yellow cube. The Parthenon and the Acropolis!"[49] His excitement turned first into dismay upon realizing that the ship would continue course avoiding the harbor, and then into anger when he and other passengers were escorted to a small island and put on a cholera quarantine for four long days. This unexpected and frustrating delay in conjunction with the high hopes for the Acropolis explains Jeanneret's total exhilarating yet stressful mood upon being released and getting to the city on September 12:[50] "Fever shook my heart. We had arrived at Athens at eleven in the morning, but I made up a thousand excuses not to climb 'up there' right away. Finally I explained to my good friend Auguste that I would not go up with him. That anxiety gripped me, that I was in a state of extreme excitement, and would he 'please' leave me alone."[51] He decided to wait until later in the afternoon to visit the Acropolis in order to "finish the day 'up there' so that once [he came] down again, [he] could only go to bed."[52] He confessed to be still trying to pacify himself from his anxiety as he approached the Acropolis later that day. He told himself to lower his expectations as he passed through the Propylaea while, at the same time, acknowledged to himself to have the "deliberate skepticism of someone who inevitably expects the most bitter disillusion."[53]

Interlude Two

It is relevant to consider the nature of Jeanneret's anxiety prior to his ascension to the Acropolis because it may affect our interpretation of his experience. In his book *Warped Space*, Vidler approaches Jeanneret's anxiety by first considering Freud's well-known psychoanalytical account of his own anxiety at the Acropolis.[54] While Vidler doesn't equate the experience of Freud to Jeanneret's, it is hard to avoid the drift that some type of psychological "disturbance" or "malfunction" is at play. Vidler explains Jeanneret's anxiety as a psychological defense "against the terrifying thought that it [the Parthenon] might never be surpassed … replicable … captured … reproduced."[55] He backs his analysis in worrisome comments that Jeanneret makes later on in his testimony about his (or any architect's) ability to match what he has encountered at the Acropolis: "Painstaking hours spent in the revealing light of the Acropolis. Perilous hours, provoking heartrending

FIGURE 7-3. CHARLES-ÉDOUARD JEANNERET,
"L'ACROPOLE, ATHÈNES," CARNET DU VOYAGE D'ORIENT
N°3, 103, 1911.

doubt in the strength of our strength, in the art of our art. Very often, I left the Acropolis burdened by a heavy premonition not daring to imagine that one day I would have to create."[56] While Jeanneret does make these statements, they cover experiences that took place after September 12. In other words, Vidler's diagnosis cannot explain the anxiety *before* Jeanneret's first experience of the Parthenon unless we think that he was already imagining this outcome (i.e., a "pre"-preoccupation of what might have happened if what he was to experience was really as good

as he hoped). In fact, the opposite is true. The anxiety is caused by Jeanneret's fear that the actual building will *not* match the high expectations that he had been amassing for so long and which was covered in section "Interlude One." Indeed, he is expecting disillusion and says so.[57] Vidler's narrow and pessimist understanding comes under fire from other scholars as well.[58]

CONTINUATION OF TESTIMONY

We left a very anxious Jeanneret worrying about the likelihood of being disappointed by what he is about to experience. He is crossing the Propylaea and entering the Acropolis esplanade when he tells us:

As by the violence of a combat, I was stupefied by this gigantic apparition. Beyond the peristyle of the sacred hill, the Parthenon appeared alone and square holding high up above the thrust of its bronze-colored shafts, its entablature, its stone brow. The steps below served as its support and increased its height by their twenty risers. *Nothing existed but the temple, the sky, and the surface of paving stones damaged by centuries of plundering.* And no other external sign of life was evident here, except, far off in the distance, Pentelicus, creditor of these stones, bearing in its side a marble wound, and Hymettus, colored the most opulent purple.

Having climbed steps that were too high, not cut to human scale, I entered the temple on the axis, between the fourth and the fifth fluted shafts. And turning back all at once from this spot once reserved for the gods and the priest, I took in at a glance the entire blazing sea and the already obscure mountains of the Peloponnesus, soon to be bitten by the disc of the sun. The steep slope of the hill and the higher elevation of the temple above the stone slabs of the Propylaea conceal from view all traces of modern life, *and all of a sudden, two thousand years are obliterated, a harsh poetry seizes you. Dropping down onto one of those steps of time, head sunk in the hollow of your hand, you are stunned and shaken.*[59]

He continues his account with entries on the behavior of sunlight and shadows in the temples, the landscape as seen through the temple's colonnade, and some other architectural details. He concludes, "At the very moment the sun touches the earth, a shrill whistle drives the visitor away, and the four or five people who have made the pilgrimage to Athens cross again over the white threshold of the Propylaea and pass through the

three portals. Pausing before the stairwell and impressed by this abyss of darkness, they hunch their shoulders as *they sense, sparkling and elusive above the sea, a spectral past, and ineluctable presence.*"[60] Jeanneret's personal, profound, and lifelong relationship with the Parthenon starts with this very first encounter. Everything else is a commentary or deepening of what has been opened here. In other words, this part of the story is the most important and helpful to assess whether or not Jeanneret witnessed the transcendent. Therefore, let us study it in more detail.

It would be hard to find a more illuminating first sentence in a testimony. It depicts an awareness "violently" (i.e., involuntarily, forcefully) collapsed to its most fundamental and nonintellectual functioning. At the "apparition" of the Parthenon, Jeanneret's anxiety disappears and his attention completely shifts outward. A good deal of architectural detail starts to flow right afterward and without any trace of mind wandering. He leaves no doubt of the sudden onset of the experience, which evidently occurs without his conscious anticipation. In other words, it just happens. Even though he certainly "knew" the Parthenon from prior reading and study, the actual event takes him totally by surprise and proves him as utterly unprepared and ignorant.[61] He is bewildered precisely because all his posturing, planning, and expectations are rendered useless, transcended. Unable to deploy ordinary intelligence and knowledge (i.e., being "stupefied"), he is abandoned to live the moment as it unfolds. Although his analogy to combat may seem gruesome, it does point to phenomenological situations with similarities: impossible to avoid external, dramatic, sudden, and life-changing conditions that demand the immediate

FIGURE 7-4. THE PARTHENON AS SEEN FROM THE PRO-
PYLAE. CHARLES-ÉDOUARD JEANNERET, "LE PARTHÉNON,
ATHÈNES," CARNET DU VOYAGE D'ORIENT N°3, 115, 1911.

rerouting of all cognitive, emotional, and physical resources toward it. The result is a "reversion," or perhaps evolution, to an instinctive or intuitive functioning in tune with the emerging circumstances (see "peak states" in the following discussion). The net effect is that the architectural experience "seizes" Jeanneret to the point that "nothing exists" except the building, the earth, and the heavens. It is a very physical, perceptual, and embodied moment—definitely not intellectual. No critical, speculative, or analytical reasoning underlies the account. He has

already reached a very high state of aesthetic contemplation when, again abruptly, poetry takes the experience one step further, causing "involuntary" corporal reactions: he "drops down," "sinks his head on his hand," and gets "stunned" and "shaken."[62]

This powerful set of responses casts light into an otherwise odd passage at the end of Jeanneret's testimony when, referring to this first encounter with the Parthenon, he says: "The first shock was the strongest. Admiration, adoration, and then annihilation."[63] This short but poignant statement (to which we shall return) reveals several other traits of the experience. First, Jeanneret confirms that the first encounter with the Parthenon was indeed "the one" and that it was a "shock," that is, something very powerful that took him unprepared and astonished him. The terms "shock" and "annihilation" continue to play along the combat analogy which, despite its valid (albeit uncomfortable) parallels to the encounter, may also have to do with the time when he wrote his testimony, and perhaps his age and gender.[64] Still, it offers another fitting meaning: it prefigures the impact that Jeanneret's first experience of the Parthenon is going to have in his entire life—like a soldier who never forgets the experience of battle. Additionally, his use of the word "shock" is consistent with the short duration of the event. Some simple calculations confidently clock Jeanneret's total time at the Acropolis to no more than 2.5 hours—most likely 1.5 hours.[65] The magic of the first time must have certainly had a role in the extraordinary experience, but also solitude, a mostly empty and silent Acropolis (there were very few visitors due to the cholera outbreak), and the inspiring time of the day that is sunset (dawn and dusk are threshold periods used by all religions to invite divine contemplation).

The quote also discloses a process of progressive intimacy between Jeanneret and the Parthenon: first "admiration," then "adoration," and last "annihilation." Admiration describes a personal, friendly relationship strongly tilted toward one party: the loved "other." Adoration is a step closer and involves an emotional surrendering of the lover to the loved one and conjures up images of religious devotion (if not adulation and infatuation). Notice that these two initial relationships are about love, which reminds us of our earlier reference to this erotic relationship to beauty and, probably, the numinous. Yet, despite the progressive closeness that they imply, there remains a difference or separation between the two entities. In contrast, the third stage—annihilation—implies the loss of one party, namely the subject (Jeanneret) at the hands of the object (the Parthenon). Here, we could no doubt speak of the self being transcended, although the method employed seems far from caring and desirable. For this reason, an initial interpretation of the term "annihilation" may direct us to a negative, Burkean sublime—especially when we consider that Jeanneret makes this statement late in his testimony, while undergoing a depressing period in his visit to Athens. But this segment may be best understood if we contextualize it to his first and shocking experience of the Parthenon—a more fair reading because it is what Jeanneret is referring to. In this case, the word "annihilation" would allude to the collapse of the spatial boundary separating self and other. After all, Jeanneret does say "nothing existed but the temple, the sky, and the surface of paving stones damaged by centuries of plundering." His "nothing" here means that even his "I" (reflective self-consciousness) is no longer present in awareness, only the Parthenon, the ground, and the firmament. Jeanneret's object of love has displaced the last distraction keeping him from the supreme erotic embrace: his ego. In other words, subject and object have become undifferentiated in the lovemaking act of unwavering aesthetic appreciation. The two lovers are one. Jeanneret's statement that "all of a sudden, two thousand years are obliterated" along with "dropping down onto one of those steps of time" hint to yet another major phenomenological turn: the arrival of a timeless present. With Jeanneret's ordinary sense of space, time, and self gone, a nondual state of consciousness ensues.[66] Such heightened state of awareness, characterized by an atemporal and nonreflective wholeness or oneness with the situation, is a condition that many spiritual traditions associate with meeting the Holy. For example, in *Varieties of Religious Experiences*, American philosopher-psychologist William James speaks of "*unio mystica*" as the moment when a believer and his/her God enter in synchrony and the ultimate reach and bliss of a religious experience.[67] Notably, Rudolf Otto uses the same exact wording as Jeanneret, "annihilation of the self," to describe the fundamental step to open the gates of transcendence: nonduality—a common demand of mysticism of all forms, he adds.[68] Needless to say, all his gained experiential state feels quite perplexing to Jeanneret who, coming from a rational and intellectual sensibility, initially associates it with stupidity! Not surprising, and despite his misplaced labeling, the experience delivers everything Jeanneret hoped for (and stressed him so much) and a great deal more. The truth and power of the occurrence manifest, he writes, "with the formidable strength of trumpets blasting from a hundred mouths like the noise of a waterfall."[69] Thus, when scholar Papapetros speaks of Jeanneret attaining "heroic self-fulfillment" in the experience of the Parthenon, I believe he is referring to the ecstasy found when dualism is transcended—possibly indicating an access to the numinous.[70] Richard Etlin, another scholar covering this episode, adds that Jeanneret's sublime moment at the Acropolis transports him "to a place and to a condition 'beyond and above us,'" making expressed reference to the sublime.[71] It goes without saying that how we respond to the possibility of nonduality

defines the type of sublime experience we encounter.[72]

It is obvious that Jeanneret's first experience of the Parthenon is hardly terrifying, awful, or depressing. To the contrary, the account narrates a "peak" or "flow" experience, that is, one of the highest examples of "positive psychology."[73] In this state, a person is so engaged and tuned in to the unfolding moment that awareness and action become merged, our temporal sense of time is distorted, and reflective self-consciousness vanishes. Paraphrasing American philosopher and educator John Dewey, the experience *becomes* the experience. The result is a nondual, highly intense, and rewarding event that enables the highest levels of performance, insight, empathy, perception, or whatever the particular circumstance calls forth or is about. In the case of aesthetic encounters, a flow experience may be so potent and absorbing as to cause us to weep, kneel, shiver, get goose bumps, and so on without our consent or even notice—similar to what Jeanneret reports. Also consistent with flow experiences, Jeanneret's story possesses a high level of vividness as if the moment occurs in a superconscious yet relaxed mode not unlike one of intense meditation or, as we will view shortly, lucid dreaming. While the building receives a great deal of attention and creates the condition for the peak state, nature still plays an important and integral part of the whole experience. As such, the text reminds us of German philosopher Martin Heidegger's discussion of how the sheer presence of an ancient Greek temple uncovers the fundamental conditions of being-in-the-world (his untranslatable "Dasein").[74] Nondual states describing the highest levels of artistic or architectural experiences have been discussed by some scholars.[75]

FIGURE 7-5. CHARLES-ÉDOUARD JEANNERET. ACROPOLIS OF ATHENS, STEPS AND COLONNADE. WATERCOLOR (SEPTEMBER 1911).

The fact that Jeanneret stayed in Athens and visited the Acropolis almost every day for another three weeks provides further evidence of how much he was affected by his first experience. Nobody displays such sustained devotion out of intellectual curiosity or stubborn will alone. Naturally, not all that transpired during the weeks following Jeanneret's first magnificent encounter involved transcendent phenomenologies. Much of the remaining testimony is filled with commentaries, arguments, and details that cover relatively ordinary experiences which, given the focus of this inquiry, we will skip. Still, there are a couple of occasions when Jeanneret registers other moments that point to the numinous. On one such occasion, Jeanneret recognizes the pleasing nature of the transcending experience by pointing at strong positive emotions and their bodily correlates: "Physically, the impression is that of a most profound inspiration that expands your chest. It is like ecstasy that pushes you onto the bare rock devoid of its old slab paving, and out of joy and admiration, throws you from the Temple of Minerva to the Temple of Erechtheum, and from there to the Propylaea."[76] In a different part of the testimony, when summarizing his whole experience, Jeanneret defines his being transcended: "Never in my life have I experienced the subtleties of such monochromy [referring to the color of the temples' marble under the light]. The body, the mind, the heart gasp, suddenly overpowered."[77] He continues, "Here … the strong spirit triumphs…. The feeling of a superhuman fatality seizes you. The Parthenon, a terrible machine, grinds and dominates; seen from as far as a four-hour walk and one hour by boat, alone it is a sovereign cube facing the sea."[78]

We should notice that the three main dimensions of his humanity (body, mind, and heart) are transcended (i.e., "overpowered") by beauty (the "monochromy"). He tells us that a "strong spirit" emotionally takes over his destiny by means of some superhuman power acting, as it were, via a dominating other (i.e., a "sovereign" architecture). This part goes hand in hand with Jeanneret's conclusion of his first visit to the Acropolis when he tells us that, as he is leaving the ruins, he senses "sparkling and elusive above the sea, a spectral past, and ineluctable presence." All these references give indication that Jeanneret perceived something uncanny, "other-worldly," nonhuman, beyond reality, perhaps transcendent. This is consistent with Otto's argument that the numinous is sensed as Something-Other outside the self, a superpresence that fascinates and attracts us by its "over-abundance" or "surplus of meaning" yet terrifies and repels us by its overpowering might and fundamental alienness.

In another section, toward the middle of the testimony, Jeanneret describes his many visits to the Acropolis as if lived under some altered state of consciousness: "Days and weeks passed in this dream and nightmare, from a bright morning, through intoxicating noon, until evening, when the sudden whistle of the guards would tear us away from all this, and cast us out, beyond the wall pierced by three huge portals which, as I have said, overlook a growing darkness."[79] As Vidler, in this case, rightly points out, Jeanneret appears to be under a "feeling of disbelief, of unreality": the real not only matches but surpasses the dreamed. In other words, it is a dream come true but more real and conscious than any dream without losing its illusory feel. Every day, while at the ruins, Jeanneret is living in two realities at once until being abruptly returned to ordinary consciousness by a whistle only to start all over again the next day. All this is relevant to our phenomenological inquiry because several esoteric teachings compare lucid oneiric states with subtle or mystical states of consciousness.[80] The fact that Jeanneret is somewhat sick (as we saw in an earlier section) makes him more susceptible to enter in such trance-like states that are, given their nonrational and subtle quality, more sensible to "something-other"—perhaps transcendent. Although this type of psychophysical condition may seem strange, eerie, and cultish, Otto—a Lutheran theologian—assures us that the "blissful excitement, rapture, and exaltation" of numinous experiences may often verge "on the bizarre and the abnormal" but that such expressions are genuine and make sense given the unutterable nonrationality of its tremendous mystery.[81]

If for most of the testimony, the blessing and awful sublimes (dream and nightmare) seem to coexist, Jeanneret's mood decidedly turns toward the dark at the very end of his stay in Athens. He says, "Every hour it grows more deadly up there. *The first shock was the strongest. Admiration, adoration, and then annihilation. But it disappears and escapes me*; I slip in front of the columns and the cruel entablature; I don't like going there anymore. When I see it from afar it is like a corpse. The feeling of compassion is over. It is a prophetic art from which one cannot escape. As insentient as an immense and unalterable truth."[82] In this telling quote, Jeanneret confesses his unfulfilled desire to repeat the "magic" of his first encounter with the temple. Instead, he gets an indifferent and implacable "it" that, despite his best wishes (and, one would suspect, efforts) remains "compassionlessly" away. Hence, when Jeanneret speaks of the cruel, inhuman, uncaring, and even "evil" and "crushing" Parthenon here or elsewhere, he is possibly voicing his enormous frustration, resentment, and/or anger—another probable indication of the likelihood of his witnessing the transcendent. Those who have directly "felt" the Holy but are unable to reestablish connection show this type of affliction.[83] That fact is that Jeanneret can no longer deal with this situation and a Burkean, dreadful sublime takes over. Weber refers to a letter that Jeanneret writes to his teacher on October 25, 1911, where he explicitly says so: "But for three weeks I've seen the Acropolis. God Almighty! I had too much of it by then—it crushed you until you're ground to dust.[84] This quote raises an interesting question: Can we have "too much" beauty, perhaps transcendence? The experience of Jeanneret suggests an affirmative answer for two reasons. First, the (cognitively, emotionally, and physically) strenuous nature of holding an extraordinary aesthetic (or any other) state for any extended period of time is

unsustainable. For all their might, peak experiences are very taxing and therefore cannot and do not last long: a few moments in such heightened states will exhaust us. Second, as said, we can easily fall in despair and anger if unable to reestablish the blissful "paradise" that has been lost. Jeanneret's fatigue and illness make his situation all the more difficult—not to mention that by this time his travel companion, August Klipstein, has left Athens and he is now for the first time in six months truly alone, perhaps adding to his depressed mood.

Unfortunately, Jeanneret's heavy feelings voiced at the end of his stay have made a few scholars lose perspective and interpret the whole experience as negative. For instance, after a quick recognition of the awe that Jeanneret felt initially, Vidler chooses to dwell only on the gloomy effects presented in the testimony and other statements made by Le Corbusier elsewhere: terror, fear, violence, and sacrifice.[85] Baker also implies a negative situation by saying that Jeanneret's experience "can best be described as an ongoing battle between himself and the building."[86] Although there is no question that Jeanneret feels terror-sublimity a few times, his testimony also and unmistakably presents an enlightening and awesome experience. In fact, despite the depressing final part of his account, Jeanneret finishes his story quite upbeat and not only reassures himself that the "Acropolis … fulfills … exalts!" but also recognizes that a profound change has operated in him: "It is uplifting to carry away the sight of such things as a new part of my being, hereafter inseparable."[87]

I don't want to finish this section without recognizing that many a skeptical reader may object to my literal reading of Jeanneret's testimony. They will say that his two-plus-year delay in writing it makes it more a piece of fiction than a record of what occurred at the Acropolis and that, therefore, cannot be taken factually. They will point at the moments in the story when writemanship takes over strict accuracy to cement their case. My response to such observations is simple. Jeanneret, especially when writing the parts we are interested in (e.g., his first encounter with the Parthenon), had to make use of metaphoric and analogical wording to express the ineffable. Let us remember that we are considering whether or not Jeanneret experienced the transcendent. If he did, choosing a poetic prose and not a documentary style was the right decision. For, as Otto reminds us, the true nature of the numinous can be "neither proclaim[ed] in speech nor conceive[d] in thought, but may [be] know[n] only by a direct and living experience.... Only from afar, by metaphor and analogies, do we come to apprehend what it is in itself, and even so our notion is but inadequate and confused."[88] This would make any "literal" reading of Jeanneret's testimony impossible even if we tried. Still, of course, it would be misleading to depart altogether from the text as it offers, regardless of its inevitable inadequacies, a framework or pointer toward what did happen. I therefore strictly limited myself to the wording while, at the same time, attempted to discern the spirit of the message. In the end, Le Corbusier's lifelong continuous return to the Parthenon as a reference and inspiration to his work and message affirms (as argued earlier on) the authenticity and accuracy, however metaphoric or belatedly written, of his account and, in so doing, provides my hermeneutic effort, I would hope, some validity.[89]

CONCLUSION

Jeanneret's extraordinary encounter with the Parthenon cannot be understood unless we assign some spiritual dimension to it. How else can we understand Jeanneret's experiences of shocking awe, profound nondual intimacy, sublime beauty, timelessness, high emotionality, "automatic" corporal reactions, references to an uncanny and overpowering presence, back and forth swings between fascination-attraction and fear-rejection, and anger toward the inability to repeat the ecstasy that caused a lifelong transformation—all conditions reported by Rudolf Otto as characterizing a numinous experience? For certain, there is sufficient evidence to claim that Jeanneret had a peak aesthetic experience involving a blissful, moving, and penetrating realization that resolved in that instant his long-sought questions, ideas, knowledge, and more about architecture (an "Aha! moment"). Naturally, Jeanneret has a hard time making sense of all this, something he acknowledges in his testimony: "In the face of the unexplainable intensity of this ruin, increasingly an abyss separates the soul which feels from the mind which measures."[90] Not only is he recognizing the inscrutable nature of the experience but also, and significantly, a spiritual being (the "soul") that uses feelings to sense the immeasurable. There is little doubt that he is referring to something transcending rational grasp or empirical gauging. This discernment goes hand in hand with his realization of the limitations of language to depict not only his rapture but all his travel experiences. About a month after his setting foot in the Acropolis, he confesses in a letter to a friend: "These notes are lifeless: the beauties I have seen always break down under my pen."[91]

It is not farfetched to say that Jeanneret's insight on the ultimate incommunicability of the lived experience[92] along with his 1911 breakthrough at the Parthenon laid the foundation upon which Le Corbusier started building his phrase "ineffable space": the inexpressible, "miraculous," and emotionally sensed "fourth dimension" of space that, if reached, "effaces the walls, drives away contingent presences," and opens up "a boundless depth."[93] Le Corbusier was well on his way toward coining the term when he confidently wrote in 1923 that good buildings (and he explicitly points at the Parthenon) provoke us to align ourselves with an "absolute" order—likely to be transcendent given the influence that Provensal's aesthetics had in Jeanneret.[94] From here, there is only a short distance to "ineffable space," an aesthetic event of the highest caliber possible, comparable only to a spiritual experience. For, in light of all that we have investigated, how else can we understand his always-cited statement? "I am not conscious of the miracle of faith, but I often live that of ineffable space, the consummation of plastic emotion."[95]

"Consummation" is not a light word to use in this context. It implies the "perfect completion" of a task to the point of utter satisfaction. In our case, we are speaking of reaching the highest possible end of aesthetic contemplation and, along with it, the attainment of complete emotional fulfillment—one reached, presumably by aligning oneself fully and thus gaining total (nondual) unity with (in his own words) an "absolute." In this sense, "consummation of plastic emotion" finds commonalities with the beautiful sublime including, no doubt, its inevitable numinous dimension. Daniel Naegele's scholarship supports this reading. According to Naegele,

Le Corbusier's ineffable space is neither the horrifying vacuum that Kandinsky refers to when he is approaching total abstraction[96] nor the phobia-stricken and warped space described by Vidler but instead a pleasing, mind-heart expanding "transcendent event"[97] that has to be thought of (at least partially) as spiritual—though not necessarily religious.

Assigning a transcendent dimension to Le Corbusier's "ineffable space" is not an exaggeration although (and as far as I know) it seems that the master architect never publically spoke of such possibility (except for the cited quote). But this silence could have more to do with the rational, secular, and pragmatic pressures of his zeitgeist than to his heart of hearts. In this sense, too much has been made of Le Corbusier's agnostic positioning. As a growing number of scholars have begun to show, he was a lot more involved with the spiritual world than his contemporary fellows either knew or gave him credit for.[98] This is hardly surprising in light of what we reviewed about Jeanneret's early interests, his religious upbringing, and the idealist aesthetic position he had adopted. Or perhaps it was the other way around. The elderly and "spiritual" Le Corbusier is likely to have been present in some embryonic shape in the young Jeanneret during his three-week-long stay in Athens. Either way, we can confidently say that Jeanneret's 1911 experience of the Parthenon would have been called one of ineffable space by Le Corbusier and thus be considered, as Kenneth Frampton says, "a spiritual encounter."[99]

If Jeanneret's 1911 rapture at the Acropolis catapulted him into a transcendent state that transformed him forever, then when Le Corbusier ends *Vers une Architecture* with his famous "Architecture or revolution… Revolution can be avoided," he is possibly

FIGURE 7-6. CHARLES-ÉDOUARD JEANNERET AT THE
ACROPOLIS, SEPTEMBER 1911.

calling not only for a massive, gross, egalitarian, and technological transformation of our civilization through architecture as it is stereotypically (and to some extent correctly) believed but also for a deeper, higher, and subtle human revolution, one of the spirit, done one person at a time through the power of architectural beauty. A lifelong conviction gained during an unforgettable sunset of September 12, 1911.

My hope is that instead of shying away with a postmodern nod, architects, artists, and others use this reappraisal of an extraordinary century-old event as leverage to continue to strive for beauty, seeking transcendence with and within architecture.

PART II   INTERDISCIPLINARY PERSPECTIVES

8 THE CHRISTIAN CHURCH BUILDING

The Christian church building, as a place or a house for a Christian worshipping community, is certainly a sacred space; therefore, some preliminary remarks about sacred space in general should be helpful before moving into a more detailed discussion of the Christian church building.

Because of the creative work of Mircea Eliade and others in the comparative study of world religions, sacred space has become a common category used to interpret diverse religious traditions. Those authors usually affirm that sacred space is something given with creation; hence, they agree that in order to appreciate the natural world as sacred one must always read and interpret it in the light of what the major religious traditions describe as divine revelation.[1] Alexander Schmemann, the distinguished Orthodox theologian, in an important book called *The World as Sacra-*

ment, maintained that the world only has meaning and value when viewed as a sacrament, the revelation of God's living presence everywhere and always.[2] Of course, atheists, holding that there is nothing beyond the here and now, beyond the material world, will strongly reject Schmemann's conviction.

Given the sacramentality of all of creation, authors have maintained that some places are especially sacred and become so because of the use to which they are put or because of the religious memories, reverence, and awe commonly associated with those particular places. Therefore, a place may be sacred and nonsacred at the same time, depending on the interpretation given to it. The significance of sacred space is grounded in the fact that the divine has intervened or continues to intervene in a particular way at such a place. The transcendent divine has become immanent in creation. Hence a sacred space is a symbol or revelation of divine presence and mystery.[3]

A space is sacred because it fulfills a religious role, not because it has special aesthetic or physical qualities. It is customary to identity three functions of space considered to be sacred. First, it is a place of communion with the divine, with the transcendent Other. The three Abrahamic religions—Jewish, Christian, and Islamic—as well as the Hindu tradition, abound with stories of theophanies, visions, and auditory experiences wherein the divine presence has been believed to have made itself felt in a special way. Hence a sacred space is often marked by a special symbol, such as an altar, a statue, a mandala, or a pillar, which represents the presence of the divine in an intense way. Second, sacred space is a special place where divine power manifests itself. The effect the power of divine presence has on human life varies from one religion to another. In some traditions, the transformation is described as salvation, in others as healing or illumination. For example, Lourdes has often been the location of miraculous cures. Third, a sacred place is often regarded as a mirror of what the human world should look like as it relates to the divine. It provides an orientation for human life and focuses attention on what is thought to be significant for human transformation. Consequently, in some religious traditions, sacred places face in a certain direction.[4]

It is generally recognized that many contemporary people are deeply interested in spirituality, even though they have little commitment to any organized religion. Many of these people espouse a creation-based spirituality; they look upon the whole earth as somehow sacramental. A renewed understanding of the whole earth as sacramental and imbued with divine presence from its very beginning should encourage us to rethink what we mean when we talk about "fallen nature" and "original sin." There has also been a renewed interest in the biblical understanding of place and how we understand the creation narratives in Genesis, as well as the place of land, temple, exile, and pilgrimage in the Old Testament.[5] There are serious efforts by Protestant, Anglican, and Roman Catholic liturgical theologians to rethink the role of sacred places in the celebration of the liturgy. Additionally, there have been interdenominational dialogues among Christians as well as dialogues with the major world and tribal religions in an effort to understand how the world's diverse people relate to the physical world and in particular to those spaces that are designated as especially sacred.

There are theological difficulties or at least questions that should be confronted if our understanding of sacred space is to be deeply rooted. Unfortunately, there has been little rigorous treatment of the topic by systematic or dogmatic theologians. As a result, much of the discussion has been confined to liturgical scholars, specialists in ritual behavior, art and architectural historians, and historians of religion. The latter tend to base their reflections on how sacred space functions in Eastern or tribal religions; at times, their work is intertwined with the findings of depth psychology and semiotics. Liturgical theologians have been concerned with how sacred places function in the celebration of liturgical rites. The result has been that the theology of sacred places has often not been very theological, nor has it been profoundly Christian. Art and architectural historians who have an interest in Christian theology have tended to focus on how the theology of a given time and place has been translated into worship spaces; they have shown how shifts in ecclesiology, Christology, and sacramental theology have affected architectural plans and the artistic representation of Christ and the communion of saints. We have had some excellent histories of church architecture and to some extent some histories of sacred art, but we have not witnessed a careful and detailed correlation between those histories and the history of theology. Finally, the discussions of sacred space and the construction of sacred places have been complicated by the challenges that have come from the serious issues raised by the defenders of social justice, mission, evangelization, and ethics. The renovation of extant churches and the building of new ones in recent years have regularly been challenged by those who object to the expenditure of large sums on religious buildings when so many in the world are unemployed and countless people go hungry.

Contemporary disciples of Jesus Christ, who call themselves Christians, need a place to gather as God's people, to recall their blessings and to grieve over their failures and pain, and then to move on to penitence, forgiveness, thanksgiving, adoration, and praise. In a sense, the Christian liturgy in its diverse sacramental forms simply expresses basic human needs.[6] God in Jesus Christ and through the power of the Holy Spirit responds to those basic needs in liturgical rites that are known by different names in our various churches. God, through the simultaneous missions of Word and Spirit, invites us to embark on a journey which is meant to last a lifetime. We are called to cross a threshold that gathers us into communities seeking to allow God to displace idols so the reign of God and all God's blessings might be realized in our personal lives and the lives of those in our communities.[7]

All Christians regularly accept the teachings of the Bible as normative in their practice of religion; however, the interpretation of biblical texts varies considerably from one Christian community or individual Christian to another. Nevertheless, the biblical text has a privileged position in communities of Christian faith, since the Bible is the normative witness to the Christ-event in Jesus of Nazareth and the living mooring of contemporary believers to its foundational past. Unfortunately, the Bible is often sadly neglected in contemporary discussions of Christian church building and renovation. The Bible, both in the Old Testament and the New, clearly affirms the primacy of people over places and things. An overview of that teaching should be foundational for any contemporary discussion of Christian church building or renovation.

DIVINE PRESENCE IN THE OLD TESTAMENT

The Israelites experienced God in space, but unlike most of the ancient gods, their God traveled from place to place as a nomad with the people. The Lord guided Abraham in the Promised Land, liberated Hebrews from Egypt, wandered with them in the wilderness, dwelt with them in Jerusalem, and accompanied them as exiles into Babylon. In his study of sacred space, Mircea Eliade analyzed various images that he described as "symbols of the center."[8] The ladder, mountain, and tree each symbolize a link between heaven, earth, and the underworld; they constitute the places where the divine presence has manifested itself in a special way. Above all, mountains captured the religious imagination of the Israelites as places where God intervened in the human sphere. Mount

Sinai and Mount Zion were the two most important pivots in their sacred history.[9] It must, however, be emphasized that the sacred places and objects were secondary; God had not made a covenant with a place but with a chosen people, for God had assured them: "I will be your God and you will be my chosen people."[10]

As their history progressed, the Ark of the Covenant and the Temple at Jerusalem became the dominant symbols of God's intervention in the lives of the Israelites. Certainly, the building of the temple modified the relationship between God and the people, for God no longer appeared as a nomad in the midst of nomads but rather as a sovereign in a palace, a king whom no one sees except his special servants. The temple was the great place for prayer, and it was there that the people assembled in a special way as God's chosen people.[11] In 586 BCE Jerusalem was captured, the temple was razed, and the Israelites went into exile in a foreign land. The glory of the Lord left the temple because false idols had invaded the lives of the people. The prophets proclaimed that in the future the lives of the chosen people would be founded not simply on religious cult but on the principles of justice and righteousness, above all on the interior dispositions of the covenanted people.[12]

Although synagogues are not mentioned in the Old Testament, they were actually one of the most important religious institutions in the centuries immediately preceding the birth of Jesus. The synagogue services were nonsacrificial and based on readings and prayers. Above all, they were places for the gathering of the faithful people.[13]

In addition to the temple and the synagogue, the home was also a special place for Israelite worship. The Sabbath celebrations really began there, just as it was in the home that the family gathered each year to celebrate the Passover meal. The Jews also gathered outdoors in order to pray together. There were then five special places of worship in the life of the Old Testament Jews: the temple, the synagogue, the outdoors, homes, and sites of monuments. It was, however, the people who were sacred; it was their presence and activity as they related to God that made the places sacred.

DIVINE PRESENCE IN THE NEW TESTAMENT

Jesus and his disciples worshipped in the tradition of the chosen people. But the coming of Christ and the mission of the Holy Spirit inaugurated a new religious regime. The followers of Jesus lived in every place where the Gospel was proclaimed. In the church of Christ, there were neither Jews nor Greeks, neither barbarians nor free people (Acts 2:5–11). The church was made up of men and women of every race, language, and nation. The unity attained by the presence and power of the Holy Spirit was a true organism in spite of widespread dispersion. The people of God formed one body (1 Cor. 12:12).

Certainly, in the New Testament and in the early Christian period, the emphasis was on the community of God's people. Paul developed the image of the church as a body; he was also accustomed to employing the figures of the temple and a building. But the temple of which the New Testament speaks is not built of inert stones but rather of all those who are members of Christ through baptism (1 Pet. 2:4–10). What surfaces with great clarity in the New Testament is the primacy of the community over any material edifice.

First of all, the temple of God is the body of Jesus Christ; and then through the outpouring of the Holy Spirit, the temple of God is the community of the faithful disciples of Jesus Christ. If material edifices have any intrinsic Christian meaning, it is because of the community assembled there and what they do when they are gathered—namely, hear the Word of God proclaimed, break that Word for one another, and celebrate the life, death, and resurrection of Jesus Christ in their various liturgical rites. Christianity is an incarnational religion. That means that the transcendent God who is everywhere and always has, in fact, become immanent in creation—above all in the humanity of Jesus, and then in his body which is the Christian church.

Initially, the early Christians would have gathered and worshipped in private homes, since households constituted the basic organizational structure in the early church. In the Acts of the Apostles, Luke depicts the apostles, Mary, and others gathered for prayer in an upper room, which must have been spacious enough to hold a large group (Acts 1:13–14). Early Christians would also have celebrated baptism. There are several explicit references in the Acts of the Apostles, including the baptism of the three thousand believers (2:41), the baptism of the Ethiopian eunuch (8:36–38), and the baptism of the centurion Cornelius along with his whole household (10:34–42). Presumably, these were all baptisms by immersion in a river or other natural body of water. Christianity was nurtured in its early days in what would be described as secular places; it developed in the ordinary transactions of daily life; and it was localized in small communities.

POST-APOSTOLIC PERIOD

In the third century, Christians began to hold church property in common, a practice facilitated by the peaceful existence of the church, the increased number of Christians, and legal developments that allowed property to be held in common. Some of the larger houses were converted into house churches so as to accommodate the liturgical needs of the Christian communities.[14] The most famous of those house churches would be the one excavated at Dura Europos.[15]

During the fourth century, the term "basilica" was regularly applied to church buildings, above all in the Mediterranean world.[16] With Constantine's victory over Maxentius in 312 and the consequent freedom from persecution that was extended to Christians, the number of Christians rapidly increased, thus necessitating larger buildings for worshipping assemblies. They naturally took over the basilica as a place where the Lord convoked his people so he could share his Word with them in the sacred Scriptures, welcome them into the Christian community through Baptism, and nourish them at the Eucharistic table.[17]

In the secular world, basilicas were large meeting halls used for public gatherings and the transaction of official business.[18] Such buildings could conveniently accommodate the various needs of the early Christians. From an architectural point of view, the early Christian basilica manifested a profoundly symbolic interpretation of the Christian life in the world. An emphasis on interiority was common to all early Christian churches. They were conceived as interior worlds representing the eternal city of God. A simple treatment of the exterior served to emphasize the inward thrust.[19]

The center of the Christian world was

more than a geographic place. Jesus Christ was the center, for he was the mediator between God and the people; he was Savior and Lord. His presence was symbolized above all by the Christian community, the assembly of persons who were all initiated into the paschal mystery of Christ through baptism and who, as a result, formed the church as the body of Christ and the people of God. All were equal in God's sight through baptism. It was the whole assembly that celebrated the liturgy. As the church grew in size, various ministerial roles developed, but those ministers did not lord it over the people; they were above all servants who functioned in the name of the Lord, fulfilling the Lord's command at the Last Supper to wash the feet of the disciples. The bishop eventually was looked upon as the leader of the local church. His seat was ordinarily placed in the apse of the church facing the people and became a focus and symbol of unity among the people in the same way as the altar and ambo were unifying symbols of Christ who nourishes his body the church by means of the Word of Wisdom, the Bread of Life, and the Cup of Salvation.

ROMANESQUE CHURCHES

With the death of Justinian in 565, the Roman Empire withered. Church architecture also declined until stability was restored in the middle of the ninth century, and a second phase of church building, the Romanesque style, emerged in which the structures were both more modest in dimensions and more monastic than imperial in character. Countless Romanesque churches, monasteries, and castles still dot the European landscape, manifesting a strong cultural unity in spite of much political unrest and divisions.[20] Throughout the interior of the churches, the iconography portrayed the divine hierarchy in descending order from the image of Christ Pantocrator in the dome down through the choirs of angels and bands of patriarchs and apostles, ending with the local saints appearing in the church calendars.[21]

The most obvious characteristic of Romanesque churches was their combination of massive enclosure and strong verticality. Whereas early Christian architecture represented the human tendency to turn inward to find God, the Romanesque style was the creation of people who wanted to bring God to the world. Throughout the middle ages, there was a major shift in Christian ecclesiology. The church was no longer the community of the baptized who were all equal in the eyes of God. Rather, the church was a hierarchical structure, clearly divided between the ordained bishops and priests and the lay people. The ordained alone governed, taught, and sanctified the people. The lay people were no longer considered the primary celebrants of the liturgy. As a result, the church was no longer thought of as a communion of the redeemed people of God united to the risen Christ, the head of his body the church, all gathered together by the power of the Holy Spirit. Instead, great emphasis was placed on a pyramidal understanding of the church with the clergy at the top representing Christ as head, ruler, sanctifier, and teacher of the lay folk.[22] In the sanctuary, the clergy presided over the people and were clearly separated from the laity in the nave, often by steps and eventually by a rood screen and a communion rail.

In Spain and France, the fight against Arianism so accentuated the divinity of Christ that his humanity in general and his role as mediator in particular were overshadowed, resulting in a changed understanding of the Eucharist.[23] The early church had appreciated the Eucharist as the great ritual prayer of thanksgiving, which the whole community celebrated in union with Christ. The Romanesque church, however, emphasized the significance of the Eucharist as the great gift of divinity which God grants men and women and which descends on the altar at the consecration of the Mass through the words of the ordained priest. The eucharistic prayer became veiled in mystery, since the priest recited it in a quiet voice. He alone was deemed worthy to enter into the mystery, while the rest of the people were left to pray silently at a distance from the sanctuary. The altar was moved to the rear of the apse, seemingly as far from the lay people as possible. This necessitated moving the presider's chair from a central place near the rear wall to a place at the side of the altar. The benches for the clergy, which had formed a half circle around the altar in many of the early Christian basilicas, were set in rows facing one another on either side and in front of the altar. This arrangement prepared the way for the development of a screen between the sanctuary and the nave.[24] Since the people then could not see what was taking place in the sanctuary, their attention was centered on their own private devotions.

Monasteries played an important role in the development of Romanesque architecture. Certainly, one of the most significant monasteries of the Middle Ages was the foundation at Cluny in 909/910. The splendor of that monastery was given expression above all in the third abbey church built in the late eleventh and early twelfth century.[25] The Cistercian order also played an important role in the history of sacred architecture. Their buildings were originally distinguished by their simplicity and absence of ornamenta-

tion. The monks felt that the life of God was manifested in the material world. Their practice of *lectio divina* resulted in a careful pondering of their structures and decoration. The mysterious quality of spaces that were open and closed, with clean lines, shadows, and shafts of light, all invited the eye to behold the beauty of God, just as the play of sounds in their churches invited the ear to hear the Word of God. The monks were convinced that the human mind and heart should be drawn beyond what it sees and hears. Their spirituality was one that emphasized the importance of place, light, and word, but they wanted all to sustain and foster the contemplative dimensions of their lives.[26]

The Cistercians wanted to be poor with Christ who was poor. Consequently, they sought to reject anything that might appear to be luxurious, whether in their worship, their clothing, or their food. In architecture, they rejected the construction of bell towers, paintings, and sculptures. These commitments were vigorously set out by St. Bernard in his famous *Apologia* addressed to his friend William, the Benedictine abbot of Saint-Thierry. He protested against the splendor of Cluniac churches and their grand size, as well as the decoration and ornamentation of the capitals in both the churches and cloisters.[27]

GOTHIC CHURCHES

In the twelfth century, Romanesque architecture gave way to the development of the Gothic. Gothic architecture symbolized Western culture in a period that has been described as a great age of Christian faith, for it expressed the human understanding of divine revelation and God's relation to everyday life. Romanesque architecture had created the strongholds people needed to receive God's revelation, but in the Gothic church God came especially close to the people. The church itself became a mirror reflecting God, especially as God was present in Christ, his mother, and the saints, but also present in the world and its inhabitants. The iconography of the Gothic church, expressed above all through the stained glass windows and the numerous sculptures, brought the heavenly and earthly spheres together. It told the tale of the creation, fall, and redemption of the world so that even illiterate people could grasp the history of the world as well as the basic teachings of Christianity. Both the community as a whole and individuals were able to see their place in a totality that was divinely arranged in a structured order descending from God through Christ and the church to the simplest aspects of creation.[28]

The Gothic church related effectively to its surroundings, since the walls of the building more or less dissolved and became transparent, thus offering a fresh interpretation of light. Stained glass magically transformed natural light into a mysterious medium that seemed to communicate the immediate presence of a transcendent God who sought not only to illuminate minds but also to share the divine life and love with people so they, in turn, could learn to love one another. Gothic people had a keen appreciation for the material world, as is evidenced by the details of their stained glass windows, their sculptures, and their illuminated manuscripts, but they felt that the beauty of the material universe was simply a foretaste of the divine beauty that they would enjoy in heaven. Appreciating the Gothic world involves seeing it as an icon and a bearer of the divine mystery. Romanesque architecture prepared the way for the Gothic; there was certainly

continuity in the church's understanding of itself as a pyramidal institution in which the ordained presided at the top of the pyramid and the laity at the bottom.[29] In practice, the actual celebration of the liturgy was usually not a source of deep piety for the ordinary people, for they were no longer the principal celebrants of the liturgy. Their religious lives were sustained above all by their popular and private devotions; many of which concentrated on the Eucharist, on Mary, the mother of God, and on the saints.

ITALIAN RENAISSANCE

The full realization of humanism that originated in the high Gothic period appeared in the succeeding epoch known as the Italian Renaissance, which extended approximately from the early fifteenth century to the end of the sixteenth and was characterized by a recovery of the ancient Roman and Greek world, its ruins, and its writings.[30] The new spirit concentrated on the world here and now; it valued above all the world of human individuality and personality. It took a keen interest in all aspects of human life—mind, body, social relationships, economic conditions, politics, and religious experience. Much of modern historiography, especially that rooted in nineteenth-century scholarship, has asserted that the Renaissance, which established a new understanding of humanity, art, literature, and scholarship, arose in opposition to the Christian religion; however, other scholars today maintain that it developed out of the full vitality of a deeply religious spirit that was characteristic of the Gothic period. They see much of the culture as embodying an authentic incarnational theology and many of its artistic representations as genuine expressions of that theology. The spirit of the age was reflected especially in the art and architecture of the period. The spiritualized understanding of space, so significant in the Gothic period, gave way in the Renaissance to a conception of space as a concrete container. This represented a return to the classical, especially Roman, world. Architecture was regarded as a mathematical science entrusted with making the cosmic world visible. Perspective was stressed as a means of describing space, and proportion was given special importance as a way of relating the building to the human body. In this way, architecture was experienced as both cosmic and human. Naturally, it departed from and, in fact, rejected the Gothic emphasis on verticality.

The institutional church was still important in the life of the city, but as an institution it often adapted to its surrounding secular culture. Hence the churches constructed during the period were often modeled on pagan temples in that they followed a centralized plan and contained various side chapels. The content of the decorative forms, however, was often more pagan than specifically Christian. It was fashionable to use the mythology of the Greco-Roman era as a literary and artistic medium. The Renaissance was an age when artists would paint a Bacchus and a St. John, or a Venus and a Blessed Virgin that were almost indistinguishable from each other.[31] What was most unfortunate from a Christian point of view was the oblivion of biblical imagery from the minds of ordinary people. During the Renaissance, the world of Christian symbols was often displaced by pagan figures entirely foreign to the rites of the liturgy.

Christian Norberg-Schulz sums up that basic characteristic of the Renaissance when he writes: "During the Gothic age, God was envisaged as close to humanity. Only a small step was needed to change the image of the human God into the image of the divine human being, and in the Renaissance divine perfection no longer consisted in the transcendence of nature, but was found in nature itself."[32]

SIXTEENTH-CENTURY REFORMS

The sixteenth century saw the culmination of the Renaissance, but it also witnessed the assertion of older traditions. Three movements coalesced to produce radical changes in both society and the church: conciliarism in matters of ecclesiology,[33] nominalism in academic thought,[34] and humanistic scholarship as a basis for religious piety[35] facilitated radical changes in both society and the church. On the part of those looking for reform in the structure and operation of the church, there was severe criticism of the arrogance and corruption that had, in fact, made their way into various aspects of church life in the high Middle Ages, a criticism that eventually manifested itself in the Protestant Reformation. With the Protestant Reformation, the spirit of independent thought active in the arts, letters, and architecture was expressed in theology and liturgy as well.

The Protestant reforms and the Catholic response to those Protestant assertions introduced fundamental changes in the worship patterns of many European Christians. Easy generalizations must be avoided because they would disregard the variety of local practices and exaggerate the rapidity with which changes were introduced. However, it was in many ways the engagement of the visual and auditory senses that became a focus of both the Protestant and Catholic reform movements.[36]

Martin Luther was adamant that no one can merit or earn God's grace. He felt that all religious answers were to conform to the norm of the Word of God as found in the scriptures.[37] Ulrich Zwingli carried the reform measures much further by stressing that all concrete manifestations of the church, whether sacramental, institutional, ascetical, or artistic, were irrelevant to the inner life of the believer. Hence he was intensely iconoclastic and even limited the celebration of the Eucharist to several times a year.[38] John Calvin sought to reconstitute Christianity by imitating what he thought were the practices and structures of the early church. Hence he sought to institutionalize what he thought was the authentic Christian tradition.[39]

Protestants were committed to the primacy of the Word of God and the human responsibility to listen whenever God speaks. They felt that the relationship between God and human beings should be as pure as possible and should be distanced from anybody or anything that might hinder or add to that essential relationship. Hence they strongly affirmed the basic equality of all Christians through baptism; they rejected the pyramidal image of the church and the ordination of bishops and priests. They stressed that the primary means by which God's Word comes to people is by preaching and the sacraments of baptism and the Lord's Supper. Because of the emphasis on preaching the Word, pulpits were given a prominent place in Protestant churches; the people were gathered around the preacher, whose sermon was meant to bring the faithful together through the power of the Word so as to build up the church.

The Protestant Reformers also maintained that God's presence was not to be found in either monuments or images, for between the utter transcendence of God and the immanence of the world there exists an abyss that only God can bridge in order to approach humanity. The emphasis was on the fallen nature of the human race. Certainly, Martin Luther fought passionately against human efforts to contain the divine within any persons, places, or things. For him, God was not located in a church or temple any more than in any other place.

In the long run, the Protestant Reformation generally rejected sacred images in places of worship because it was felt that preaching was the most suitable means to fulfill the church's prophetic mission. The plastic arts were thought to be the least suited to express the tension between the present and the future, since architecture, painting, and sculpture produced works that were static, whereas speech and music were more mobile. Because sacred images threatened to become idols, they were generally eliminated or confined to catechetical materials. The Protestant Reformation, however, made a very important contribution to the development of church music. It was felt that one of the best ways to proclaim the Word of God was to set theological and biblical texts to hymn tunes which could be sung by the whole congregation.

As a result of these developments, in many of the Protestant churches the chancel or sanctuary was often abandoned altogether so that the nave, as the place for hearing the Word of God, was looked upon as the only necessary place for worship. When Holy Communion was celebrated, a rather rare event in most churches, a small table was placed at the head of the central aisle in the nave.[40]

BAROQUE PERIOD

In response to the Protestant Reformation, the Roman Catholic Church convoked the Council of Trent, which sought not to set out a complete Roman Catholic theology but simply to respond to specific charges made by the Protestant reformers. Many of its decrees and canons were so critical of the Protestant reformers' positions that they assured that the division would almost be irreparable. Whereas the Protestant reformers focused attention on the religious literacy of ordinary Christians, Trent gave its attention to the reform of clerics and religious. In many ways, the council was a classical response to the emerging modern or scientific culture spreading throughout the Western world. The teachings of Trent, however, were unfortunately cast primarily in scholastic theology rather than in biblical or patristic terms.

In architectural matters, the Catholic reform stimulated the development of baroque architecture and art, an exuberant proclamation among Roman Catholics of traditional Roman Catholic beliefs. The prototype was no longer the temple, as had been the case during the Renaissance, but rather the theater, which through the opera became a cultural focus for people, at least for those who were better off economically. For Roman Catholics, the focus of their worship was not so much on the celebration of the Eucharist as the exposition of the Blessed Sacrament, which was reserved in a large tabernacle on the main altar. In the presence of the sacrament, a kind of grand opera was performed, with the high altar, profusely decorated with candles and flowers, as the centerpiece. Worship by the lay people was frequently focused on devotions rather than on the basics of the liturgy itself. The liturgy was celebrated by the ordained clergy, but the lay people celebrated with great devotion processions in honor of the Blessed Sacrament, especially on the feast of Corpus Christi; they had deep devotion to the Blessed Mother and various saints and took part in popular rituals during Advent and Holy Week. These devotions were often held in the squares outside the church and through the streets of the towns and villages, especially in Germany, Austria, Italy, and Spain.[41]

In the baroque churches, emphasis was on both visual and aural experience. Worshippers were concentrated in the large central areas of the churches, made possible by the width of the nave; there they could both see and hear. Pulpits were usually placed a third to halfway down the nave, where the preacher's voice would be better projected among the people. The choir, which traditionally separated the clergy from the other worshippers in medieval churches, was placed in another part of the church, often in galleries when they became architecturally available. In the liturgy of the baroque church, words, spoken or sung and heard, were meant to balance the elaborate visual symbols.

The Council of Trent refused to allow the liturgy in the vernacular, so the language of the rites continued to be foreign to ordinary people, who were left to their own devotional devices during the liturgical celebrations. The liturgy naturally became increasingly unrelated to the daily lives of ordinary Roman Catholics.

Devotional images of figures in ecstasy as well as in death were prominent in baroque churches. In many ways, the use and popularity of these images affirmed those aspects of traditional piety and belief that were severely criticized and rejected by Protestants. There was certainly an air of triumphalism about the way Catholics used religious images.

POST-REFORMATION PERIOD

The seventeenth century was an era of much intellectual ferment and scientific discovery; consequently, religion was more or less marginalized and so settled comfortably into Protestant and Catholic camps, each intensely antagonistic to the other. Toward the end of the century, orthodox Christianity was challenged by pietism, a personalized "religion of the heart," as well as by the spirit of rationalism. It was inevitable that the various scientific discoveries would raise serious questions about the reliability of the Bible, that a much more positive understanding of the human person would champion free will over predestination, and that a new natural theology would be developed on the foundation of a fresh understanding of the cosmos. Those clergy who were influenced by rationalism found the traditional worship books and sacramental practices objectionable, since they had no sympathy for any worship based on a faith they no longer embraced. The worship books of Roman Catholic and Anglican churches were generally not affected by rationalism, but the Reformed and free churches were more vulnerable because they often depended on outlines of worship developed by the minister rather than formally approved rituals.[42] Sadly, the ideal of the church as a eucharistic community was lost in much of Protestantism, so the preaching of the Word became the general focus of Protestant worship, including Anglican worship. Strong voices objected to these developments, including that of John Wesley, the founder of the Methodist Church.[43]

In the Roman Catholic Church of the seventeenth and eighteenth centuries, worshippers were concerned with their obligation to hear Mass but did not feel obliged to receive Communion. In practice, the Mass was the priest's Mass. The altar was not so much the table for the sacrificial meal as a pedestal for the Eucharist reserved and venerated in the tabernacle. Consequently, the basic interior arrangement of Roman Catholic churches did not change much from the time of the Council of Trent until the Second Vatican Council.

A rebirth of liturgical community and a renewal of eucharistic worship among Roman Catholics, Anglicans, and Lutherans began in the nineteenth century as part of a response to the industrial revolution.[44] Among many Christians, however, religion was generally looked upon as a strictly private affair to be kept to oneself. Naturally, the experience of community declined steadily in the industrialized world. Distinguished ecclesiastical voices, including those of John Keeble, Edwin Pusey, John Henry Newman, Nikolai Grundtvig, and Wilhelm Löhe, were raised in defense of the poor working people as well as in opposition to the dismal quality of liturgical celebrations in the mainline Christian churches.

TWENTIETH-CENTURY DEVELOPMENTS

What has come to be known as the Liturgical Movement made steady progress in the twentieth century, reaching a peak in the years following World War II. Most of all, contemporary attention in the mainline Christian churches (Protestant and Catholic) was placed above all on the primary importance of the assembly of celebrants. Though not mentioned in Vatican II's *Constitution on the Sacred Liturgy*, liturgical/architectural consultants emphasized the importance of a place for the assembly to gather before it moves into the church proper. Although many Roman Catholic churches were renovated in haste, often by pastors and architects who simply attended to adjustments in the sanctuary—such as installing a poorly designed altar facing the people—more enlightened bishops, priests, and parish committees concentrated on three basic issues that must still be faced by all Christian communities, Protestant and Catholic alike, engaged in church building or renovation. First of all, they must ask major theological/liturgical questions: Who are we as Christians? What do we believe, and by what moral standards do we live? Who are we as members of a particular denomination? What do we attempt to do when we gather for worship? Where have we come from? Where are we now? Who do we hope to be in the future? As we all know, our ecclesial communities are often highly polarized these days with the result that our liturgical celebrations are often reflections of our divisions rather than our Christian unity. How much doctrinal and moral diversity can we sustain in our communities and still call ourselves communities of faithful disciples of the Lord Jesus Christ? The liturgical/theological judgment, then, is of major importance.

Secondly, Christian communities need to make a sound pastoral judgment. Our churches are very often culturally diverse these days, sometimes even multicultural—which means that complex pastoral decisions must be made. In our larger cities especially, ecclesial communities are often made up of members coming from very diverse ethnic, racial, and linguistic backgrounds. Unfor-

tunately, minority groups in the community are often simply marginalized and their basic cultural differences are in no way taken into account by the larger dominant community.

Finally, ecclesial communities are called to make an aesthetic judgment. People today are often bombarded with both aural and visual images that are, in fact, violent and ugly, sometimes even pornographic. We all have a deep need to see and hear what is beautiful and what can challenge us to respond to the need for justice and peace in our world. Certainly, beautiful art and music are precious but also priceless, enabling people to grow more and more into a holy temple where God can dwell and set out the work of transforming the world. What the poor often suffer from most is the absence of anything beautiful to enrich their human spirits. However, ethnic and racial groups today often have very different concepts of what is beautiful and devotional. That is certainly a challenge that needs to be confronted in the building and renovation of churches.

In any liturgical space there are three different rhythms that need to be properly orchestrated: a visual rhythm (what we see), an aural rhythm (what we hear), and a kinetic or motor rhythm (how we move about or act). In some spaces, the community might suffer from a visual overload, so little attention is given to the quality of the kinetic rhythms. In another space, the aural rhythm might be so overpowering that the assembly is reduced simply to an audience. Often, it is the motor rhythm that is neglected—the community is simply immobile during most of the celebrations, since there is little encouragement or permission to engage in gestures or dignified processions. As already noted, Roman Catholics, especially in European countries, have often found an outlet for the kinetic rhythm in processions and devotional practices outside the church proper.

Guerric DeBona gives an interesting example of how the visual, aural, and motor rhythms have been effectively orchestrated in the Los Angeles Cathedral of Our Lady of the Angels. The communion of saints has been depicted in warm, earth-toned tapestries by John Nava on both sides of the cathedral walls, suggesting a space that is far from static. DeBona tells of his presence at a Eucharist, which focused on the ministries of the Igbo community in the cathedral. The interior of the church seemed to shift as the liturgical dancers from Nigeria, dressed in blazing orange, yellow, and blue vesture, moved down the aisle with bowls of incense, all the while swaying to the music sung by the assembly; the whole congregation swayed along with the dancers. DeBona notes that few church buildings could have absorbed so effectively such a striking array of diversity.[45]

The years after Vatican II witnessed emphasis in many of the Christian churches on the basic importance of baptism and the design of the font, so that it facilitates baptism of both infants and adults by immersion. It is the water in the font that is important, for it is the living water through which we die to sin and rise to new life in Christ and through the power of the Spirit. Since it is baptism that initiates one into the community, the ideal place seems to be at the entrance to the nave. However, we need to note that what might be liturgically and theologically ideal in theory is not always ideal in practice.[46]

The baptistry should lead to the altar, which is the holy table where the Eucharist, the sacrificial meal, is celebrated. It should be emphasized that it is sacrificial in the sense that God in Jesus Christ and through the power of the Spirit is the sacrificing one—the one who does something that is holy.[47] For that reason, the altar is a very special symbol of Christ in the midst of the assembly, as the rites for the consecration of an altar make eminently clear.[48] Because of its symbolic importance, the altar should have a strong sense of presence, not because of its grand size but because of the materials out of which it is made and the design of its construction.

The experience of God's mystery is discovered above all when we are conscious of God's presence and have centered our lives on God. That experience flourishes in a climate of hospitality, of welcome, in which people are present to one another as the body persons they are, as members of the body of Christ, comfortable with one another, gathered together with one another, able to relate to one another as well as to the ministers, capable of seeing and hearing all that is enacted within the worshiping assembly. Besides seeing what is done, because good liturgy is a ritual action, it is important that worship spaces allow for movement.

Chairs or benches for the presider and other ministers should be so constructed and arranged that they are clearly united with the one assembly and should facilitate the exercise of various ministerial roles. The chair of the presider and the cathedra of the bishop should be in a presiding position facing the assembly, but they should not suggest either triumphalism or remoteness.

Overlooking the whole assembly is the ambo or pulpit from which the Word of God is proclaimed, thus showing the essential relationship between the Word and Sacrament. Like the altar, it should be handsomely designed, constructed of excellent materials, and proportioned carefully so it fulfills its important function, since it represents the dignity and uniqueness of the Word of God and reflection on that Word. The books from which the Word is proclaimed should be beautifully designed and produced. Certainly, the use of loose-leaf binders and pamphlets detracts from the visual integrity of the liturgical action.

No architectural or artistic forms have a legitimate place in our liturgical celebrations if they are not honest and appropriate in form. Good quality, of course, is perceived and appreciated only by those who are able and willing to assume a contemplative distance from experience and to see, hear, touch, and taste symbols for what they truly are. Images should never intrude their presence or distract us from the primary symbols in the church: the assembly of the faithful, the baptistry, the altar, the ambo, and the presider's chair.

CONTEMPORARY CHALLENGES

Not only are the mainline Christian churches highly polarized these days, but there is also an extensive growth in evangelical and Pentecostal churches at the same time that there is a significant shift of the center of Christianity to the southern hemisphere—to South America, Africa, and Asia.[49] Furthermore, many migrants and immigrants who are frequently baptized Christians are moving from the southern hemisphere to the north, thus constituting numerous multicultural communities. Many traditional Protestants and Catholics are leaving their church of origin; some cease to be affiliated with any church, others become evangelicals or Pentecostals, and others frequent the so-called seeker-service churches, which attract hundreds of people each weekend. In such churches, it is often not the liturgy that is celebrated, but what might be called pejoratively an entertainment experience is laid out for the people with emphasis on dynamic preaching and rousing music by a band. Unfortunately, various mainline Protestant churches are abandoning their distinctive liturgical books and pursuing the seeker-service model of worship in order to attract larger congregations.

One of the challenges that contemporary congregations face is how to incorporate new developments of media into a space.[50] Certainly, all in the liturgical assembly have a basic right to see and hear what takes place in the church building. Many new developments in media surely facilitate that experience. But the installation of such equipment is often very expensive; older buildings frequently do not lend themselves easily to the incorporation of such media. Furthermore, the effective operation of such media necessitates training and competence. Another of today's demand comes from addressing the growing environmental awareness of the challenges confronting us. In this sense, church clergy or lay people involved in a project must see that there is serious concern for environmental responsibility.[51] And while budgetary planning is essential for communities desiring to renovate their church plans or to build new ones, monetary limitations should not necessarily be the primary determining factors. It is important that parishes and congregations have a master plan so changes do not happen haphazardly and future developments can effectively take place.

Clearly, church leadership plays a vital role in either planning the building of new structures or renovating old ones. One of their roles is to encourage and commission competent architects and artists. It is likely that the most competent architects and artists will design and adorn the most effective church buildings. It is important that the architect of a church building thinks of himself or herself as a minister, as a servant of God and God's people, rather than as a master. The architect is simply one of several very important players in a church project. The bishop and the pastor have a role, the building committee has a role, the artists who will work on the project have a role, the engineers have a role, the architect has a role, and the whole community has a role. It is hoped that all will bring distinctive competencies to a project and that all will be capable of intelligent and sincere dialogue and, if need be, express a willingness to compromise, if that seems to be the right solution to a problem. If appropriate competencies are lacking in the group involved in a project, a competent liturgical/architectural consultant should be hired and become seriously involved in the project from the beginning.

It should be clear that it is the paschal mystery of Jesus Christ celebrated by the Christian assembly through the power of the Holy Spirit that provides the foundational meaning for all places of worship. Their meaning is always derivative. Apart from the centrality of the paschal mystery and the assembly which is the body of Christ, they easily degenerate into mere monuments, often very impressive monuments, but monuments nonetheless. We do well to remember that no liturgical spaces, no artistic images, no symbols or ritual practices, even those that are an integral part of the liturgy itself, exhaust the infinite riches of God's real presence everywhere and always in Jesus Christ and through the power of the Holy Spirit. God's presence is inexhaustible; it is irreducible to any single ritual or symbol.

Vatican II's *Constitution on the Sacred Liturgy* notes that "the Church has not adopted any particular style of art [or architecture] as its own, but guided by people's temperaments and circumstances, it has admitted styles from every period. Thus, in the course of the centuries it has brought into existence a treasury of art [and architecture] which must be very carefully preserved. The art of our own times from every race and country should also be given free scope in the church, provided it bring to the task that reverence and honor due to the sacred buildings and rites" (art. 123). However, not all styles can effectively be accommodated to the demands of the liturgy and facilitate the active and intelligent participation of the whole assembly in the ritual actions. The *Constitution on the Sacred Liturgy* insists that "when churches are to be built [or renovated], let great care be taken that they are suitable for the celebration of the liturgical services and the active participation of the faithful" (art. 124).

Speaking at a symposium on environment and art in Christian worship several decades ago, Archbishop Rembert Weakland warned that "the further church art, architecture, and music are removed from the contemporary idioms and styles of our time, the more likely it is that they will be sterile and artificial."[52] As Gustave Mahler, the distinguished musician, is reputed to have once noted, tradition does not consist in adoration of dead ashes; it rather consists in keeping the fire alive. The fire in the celebration of the Christian liturgy is the Holy Spirit given generously by the Lord Jesus so that his disciples may relate to God and to one another as members of God's people, all called to live as God lives—in unity and peace.

The challenge that confronts our contemporary churches was put in a very provocative way by Armand Veilleux, a distinguished Canadian Cistercian: "The only way to belong to a community, a church, a civilization is to help build it."[53] Are we going to be part of a new humanity, or shall we be found cultural runaways once more one revolution behind? In a world in evolution, one assists in every epoch of in-depth change at the emergence of new species but at the same time at the forming of vast fields of fossils. The questions facing every community at this turning point in human and ecclesial history are as follows: Shall we choose to be members of the new species or shall we rather go to enrich the collection of fossils? The latter alternative is not wanting in attractiveness, for fossils are sought after and marveled at. May we at least have the courage to make our choice in full cognizance rather than let ourselves be passively pigeonholed by history.

MARK E. WEDIG

9 ECCLESIAL ARCHITECTURE AND IMAGE IN A POSTMODERN AGE

One encounters many pitfalls when attempting to comprehend contemporary religious experience. Understanding present-day religious concepts and practices often necessitates examining religion from the inside out or upside down. Moreover, interpreting the contemporary religious aesthetic landscape is even more complex due to the plurality of postmodern rituals and aesthetic praxes. And yet, despite the decentering challenges of contemporary global culture, religion continues to assert ritual encounters and seek environments to house it. The malleability of religion to culture enables people to enact their morality and belief often in spite of the barriers that thwart certain institutionalized religious participation and the confusion of meaning brought about by the smorgasbord of religious options.

This chapter will first examine some of the basic contours of contemporary religion and the ritual actions and spaces that mediate those inclinations in a postmodern context. It will focus particularly on those who seek transcendence from hypermodern experience in environments that permit a critical realism to stand forth amidst the onslaught of simulated existence. This part of the chapter will explore a new typology for religious communities that has characterized the postmodern religious encounter. Here we will explore the makeup, disposition, and character of communities born out of new realisms and resistance. These characteristics will be tied to both ritual performance and sacred space.

Even though this chapter explores religious encounters from a cultural and theological perspective named as postmodern, it does not endorse any particular architectural style or movement with the same nomenclature. In other words, it does not attempt to sanction or support what has been identified as postmodern architecture. Nevertheless, this chapter will explore what it deems as sacred space that has welcomed and advanced postmodern religious experience. In doing so, Steven Holl's St. Ignatius Chapel at Seattle University will be examined in terms of accommodating the postmodern pilgrim by providing refuge and sacramental sustenance.

The chapter concludes by critiquing some of the norms that have guided the Catholic Church in late modernity for interpreting and constructing ritual environments and art. The two USCCB (U.S. Catholic Conference of Bishops) documents *Environment and Art in Catholic Worship* (1978) and *Built of Living Stones* (2000) will be analyzed in terms of the relative success and failure to both decode and form religious edifice and image in light of postmodern religious concerns. It will emphasize that the highly prescriptive norms (especially of the document *Built of Living Stones*) tend to obstruct and hinder, for better and for worse, certain contemporary religious sensibilities and inclinations. Insofar as this project puts forward Steven Holl's St. Ignatius Chapel as an authentic expression of religious architecture for our time, this work will demonstrate that the earlier 1978 Bishops' document still remains an important, and perhaps better, aesthetic guide for the contemporary religious pilgrim.

INTERPRETING RELIGION THROUGH A POSTMODERN LENS

Encountering the postmodern condition is socially, philosophically, and religiously daunting. Facing the surge of hypermodern social and economic forces can leave us dismayed, exhausted, and overwhelmed. Albert Borgmann illustrates that dilemma: "Commodities, glamorous ones especially, are alluring, but they are not sustaining. A highly interactive hyperreality may provide you with fitness and coordination. Totally disburdening hyperrealities can keep emptiness at bay through ever more refined and aggressive stimulation. But since the realm of commodity is not yet total, we must sooner or later step out of it into the real world. It is typically a resentful and defeated return, resentful because reality compares so poorly with hyperreal glamour, defeated because reality with its poverty inescapably asserts its claims on us."[1] The problem is that, in postmodernity, the traditional theories of reality fail to elucidate the difference between the real and the hyperreal. New ontologies, moralities, aesthetics, and theologies are needed in order to rethink some of the fundamental categories and methods that undergird our most cherished claims.

Theological interpretations have resisted grappling with these forces. And yet, despite such resistance, there have emerged an increasing number of theologians that have found a common ground in consistently ordering their concerns in response to the postmodern condition.[2] These thinkers are attentive to the driving forces of the hypermodern world charted by cyberspace and global markets. They understand the postmodern condition as a social construct that has undermined the worldview of modernity, especially as it has imploded into the exhaustion of simulated and hypermodern madness. Philosophically, their project questions and reconceives the solutions of modernity by attempting to assert new realisms against the tides of nihilism and positivism that often have characterized late modern thinking. Utilizing continental critical theory and post-Heideggerian French philosophy, these theologians rethink the fundamental discourses of religion. In the words of Graham Ward, theology "must subsume postmodernism's cyberspace, writing through and beyond it, in order to establish its own orders."[3]

In their effort to assert new theological discourses about divine presence, postmodern theologians especially look for where the persuasiveness and eloquence of symbol, ritual, and language occasion meaningful and poignant truths that are revealed aside from or even through the din and pandemonium of hyperreal display. It is precisely in the openings and fractures created by the postmodern condition itself that give rise to things that in themselves focus a human life. Powerful presences that speak for themselves and assure what they signify often lie at the breaking point of hypermodern discourse. It is at the breach of postmodernity that we now turn to ponder the new religious communities characteristic of the age in order to fathom the arrangement of space to house them.

COMMUNITIES BORN OUT OF NEW REALISMS AND RESISTANCE TO THE HYPERMODERN

Christian essayist Rosemary Haughton suggests that overarching structures of the hypermodern environment have created clefts and fissures that provide access to religious transformation.[4] Effective environments in the contemporary period help ritual participants to identify the new persuasive reality that the hypermodern superstructure has unintentionally created. Globalization and postmodern critiques have generated unusual and unique associations of persons, ideas, and

things. The juxtaposition of these unlikely associates makes for a new social realism. People encounter one another under new circumstances.

The fissures, crevices, and clefts created by the hypermodern environment provide opening and access that become the bases for new communities. People meet under the duress of the hyperreal, hyperactive, and hyperintelligent global village, giving them ways to fashion a new inclusive communal order.[5] The excitement and entertainment generated by technology impinges on the realization of public life in festive celebration. But there must be real reasons to celebrate. Eloquence must emerge from communities of resistance to dominant cultural forces.

This chapter claims that the churches, synagogues, and other sacred temples need to organize themselves so that new social realisms can come forth. Commanding ritual spaces shape new typologies whereby connections are made between curious and even daunting social forces and the mysteries of religious faith. Examples of such sacred spaces fostering these new realisms abound often in urban culture where refugees from hypermodern fatigue find welcome and opportunities for repose. Philosopher Albert Borgmann suggests that the Episcopal cathedral of St. John the Divine in New York serves as a fine example of space collecting and enabling a rare assortment of peoples to experience these new social realisms.[6] In this chapter, the Chapel of St. Ignatius at Seattle University will serve as another pristine example for what can be seen as a sacred environment that welcomes a plurality of religious perspectives through its unique realisms.

But what are the realisms experienced by communities of resistance for which this chapter addresses? Often the mysteries of the faith, the moral life, and the sacred spaces reveal the contrast and underside of a human life. The assurance and confidence in correlating sign and reality are born out of a communal imaginative realism that sees a commanding presence of God's work in the negations that the global world emits. Moreover, the underlying reality is often the residue of the environment. Here, this analysis will borrow from the work of Jean-Yves Lacoste and his ideas about liturgy and space.[7] In particular, Lacoste's concept about liturgical encounter as nonspace serves as a way to conceive the divine-human relation in communities centered on new realisms and resistance. Lacoste's phenomenology of the liturgy provides a philosophical construct that challenges Heidegger's classical idea of *being-in-the-world*, providing an alternative metaphysics for religious experience. His idea that liturgy creates a fundamental restlessness and discontent with the world as ordinarily experienced disposes the subject to the "nonspace" of prayer, interrupting place burdened by history. In this chapter, Lacoste's philosophy substantiates interpretations of liturgical space.

RITUAL AND LITURGY AS NONSPACE

Lacoste envisions religion in the postmodern context born out of asceticism and ethics derived from the constraints, not the excesses, of a human life before the divine. This is portrayed particularly in his construct of the fool's liturgical act of subversion, where the human subject stands before the divine as lunatic to the rational world. The only way in which true nothingness can be seen is in the shadow of the overwhelming plenitude of God; pure darkness can only be perceived

when one has first encountered absolute light. He concludes that "liturgy is non-place." He further claims that with the liturgy there exists a "will to powerlessness," which is "deprived of any hold over the absolute" and instead "totally submits itself to the will of another"; this will to powerlessness thus opens up the space of liturgy as "nothing but an empty space."[8] Lacoste concludes that this nonevent, or nothingness, found in liturgy thus acts as an "empty, but enabling, nothingness." In this way, the nonevent of liturgy is like an empty canvas, such that the empty canvas is the necessary precondition for the creation of something new.

Lacoste's construct of ritual "nonspace" is significant to those who ponder the hermeneutics of ritual environments in the postmodern context because of his emphasis on the far-reaching role that the worshipper plays in the fuller consideration of architecture. Here, the religious ritual and liturgical act plays a primary function in the interpretation and mediation of the space. Moreover, the radical subjective poverty of the ones who place themselves before the divine must be taken into consideration of the environment itself. The exalted status of the human rational subject as guided by modernity's social and intellectual project is replaced by a humiliated fool.

In other words, according to Lacoste, postmodernity teaches us about the religious communities that are born out of humility and "will to powerlessness," that is, associations originated in nonspatial ritual. Hence religious formation is found in places where reality, community, and divinity are joined in an unusual configuration; where the most unlikely associations of people gather for religious purposes; where their humanity is

FIGURE 9-1. EXTERIOR VIEW OF CHAPEL OF ST. IGNATIUS
WITH REFLECTING POOL, SEATTLE UNIVERSITY.

opened to the absolute and sacred by means of having been emptied out meaning by postmodern life.

This chapter attends to the face of a new religious Diaspora where religious identities are formed by environments that serve as the refuge for those wearied by hyperreal, hyperactive, and hyperintelligent solutions to contemporary life. Those of us who sensitize ourselves to such people and their environments are aware that these pilgrims often defy the social, economic, and religious barriers that once defined religious communities. As the global U.S. society undergoes radical shifts in the fundamental linguistic, ethnic, and religious makeup of our land, we brace ourselves for the challenges of more radical inculturations of religious subjectivity.

STEVEN HOLL'S CHAPEL OF ST. IGNATIUS

The design of American architect Steven Holl for the Chapel of St. Ignatius at Seattle University can be seen as creating a ritual and liturgical space open to the social and religious phenomena characterized by Borgmann and Lacoste. Holl purposely and intentionally creates what he calls a "phenomenology" to build perceptual bridges in order to open the space for a multitude of religious pilgrims.[9] Holl's religious architecture elicits the human imagination to become a viaduct of perception. It is precisely through the condensation and compression of light, architectural shapes and forms, and interior-exterior relations of the edifice itself that permits the religious architectural construct to elicit a variety of religious realisms. In addition, how the space designed by Holl has been received and extended in its interpretation by religious subjects since its 1997 construction also war-

rants consideration as architecture uniquely sensitive to the contemporary religious pilgrim.

As mentioned previously, this chapter reflects on the postmodern social and religious context but does not set out to endorse a movement or style of architecture, postmodern or otherwise. In fact, Holl's designs can be understood as defiant to a particular architectural movement. He incorporates modernism's forms and sensibilities while integrating more complex social and cultural concerns of the contemporary religious person into his approach to architecture. Even though Holl himself has expressed a strong aversion to postmodernism as an architectural movement,[10] in this chapter it will be demonstrated that the Chapel of St. Ignatius is an edifice receptive to postmodern religious subjects.

LIGHT AND NONSPACE

The overall thematic of the chapel at Seattle University can be distinguished as bottles of light tightened by the compression of space. Light, understood as an invisible form, shapes the global plan of the edifice and its environs. From the writings of Ignatius of Loyola, the image of the divine is arranged through the metaphor of light from above. Seven crucial parts of the edifice are organized as containers of different colors, projecting arrays of light through various angles in a stone receptacle. Light from above can be sensed as a powerful autonomous force moving throughout the structure and constantly changing the volume of its presence. Nevertheless, the sovereignty of the light overwhelms the space and its inhabitants.

It is precisely light and its condensation into various capacities that characterizes the sacredness of the chapel. The singularity of this dominant metaphor organizes the space so that the human agent cannot assume control over it no matter what religious perspective or tradition to which they belong. Light as a single phenomenon preoccupying the design is multidirectional shifting from west to east, south to north, and orchestrating and uniting worshippers and pilgrims. The colors, tones, and intensity of light embody Ignatius's vision of the many inner lights and darknesses that encompass the spiritual life.

Light as conceived, projected, and encountered can be understood as nonspace similar to Jean-Yves Lacoste's metaphysics of human ritual experience itself. The presence of light as encountered in the Chapel of St. Ignatius is close to how Lacoste defines sacramental presence. Light in that conception is "much less a place than a non-place ... and encountered is only here and there as putting aside the logic which governs experience, and the conceptual organization of all which is "there."[11] From this perspective, the sacramentality of light bathes both subject and space in reality that renders architecture nonexistent.

COMPRESSION OF LIGHT, COLOR, AND SPACE

The chapel at Seattle University was designed and constructed with compression as another overall metaphor of the religious space. Compactness and density crescendo in the building and at its site. "Condensation of a multiplicity of things into something confined"[12] was an accidental *and* an intentional approach taken by Holl. Some of the compression of the space was accidental when the original budget for the chapel construction necessitated reducing the square footage of the space from 10,000 to 6,100. As a result,

FIGURE 9-2. CLERESTORY, CHAPEL OF ST. IGNATIUS, SEATTLE UNIVERSITY.

rooflines intensified in terms of greater verticality, condensing the original conception. And yet, compression was intentional from the onset because the sacred space fits into a compact urban university environment. Design, site, space, and even fixtures of the chapel were interlaced and entwined to create a purposeful compactness to fit its urban setting. As a result, curving and titling rooflines, elongated casements, and the campanile reach up from their heavy foundations.

The compression, especially of light, color, and space, also is intricately related to the particular effect of what this chapter has referred to as its nonspace. A spiritual and emotional intensity of the chapel is achieved through the compressed interplay of elements of light and color inside and looking out from a thick-walled box. One experiences views as if one were within a box camera where the intensity of light is compressed by the positioning of the lens. Moreover, the use of light with color, especially complementary color, affixes a stratum of vibrant emotional power to the overall spatial experience. As a result, the worshipper and religious pilgrim are overwhelmed by the epiphany of divine presence in light revealed through a particular vessel.

COMPOUNDING METAPHORS

As one moves from the entrance into the chapel, ushered by shifting displays of light, the religious subject is forced to juxtapose interior/exterior, religious/secular, and action/meditation. The mixing and compounding of metaphors are extended and protracted through sinuous space. For instance, through projected shadows and refracted light, the polished and cracked concrete floors become like a new form of stained glass. The interplay and juxtaposition of light, color, shadow, window view, opacity, and surface combine to produce a symphony of subjective responses.

It is precisely the metaphor of light and the compounding of additional related effects that open the space so as to create multiple axes of the sacred for manifold religious groups. Even though the space was conceived for and is used primarily as a Roman Catholic worship environment, the chapel actively has become a place of sacred worship and devotion to diverse religious groups that make up the Seattle University faculty and student bodies, along with the religious diversity of the Seattle urban area.[13] The metaphors open the space so as to invite and include a diversity of religious traditions into it so that they may appropriate it as their own. As a result of this, the space has become a home for regular prayer for Buddhist, Muslim, and a variety of Christian groups. Instead of it serving as an *axis mundi*, it has become *axes mundi*, engendering and compounding multiple religious dynamics in the same space.

SACRED SPACE AND THE POSTMODERN CITY

In Catherine Pickstock's musings about Plato's ideas concerning the formation of the soul and the establishment of the just city, she says, "The city which goes beyond itself is the only actual city; the ethic which goes beyond itself into the tragic is the only true ethic; and the philosophy which exceeds itself into the religious is the only true philosophy."[14] At the heart of the postmodern theological project is the retrieval of the city's religious center that modernity hijacked for its own purposes. In its identification of new religious realisms arising from the destructions of cyberspace, postmodern theology posits a religious locus at the center of any new view of urbanism.

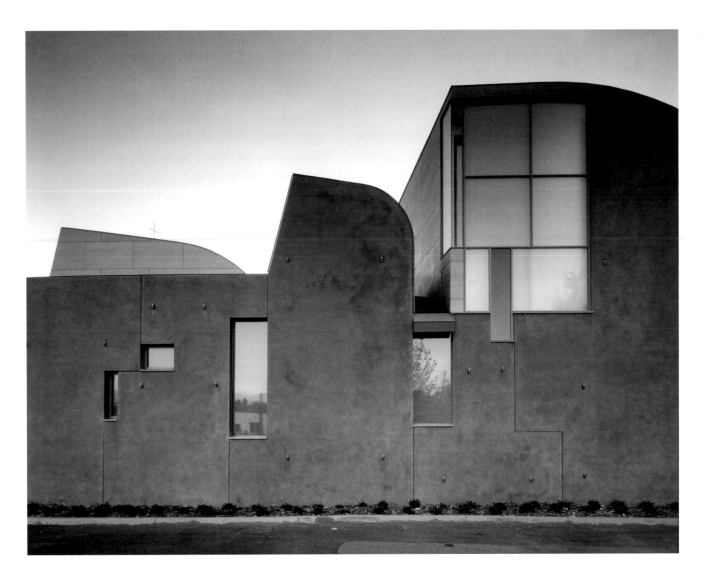

FIGURE 9-3. EXTERIOR WALL AND CLERESTORY, CHAPEL
OF ST. IGNATIUS, SEATTLE UNIVERSITY.

This theology envisions new *axes mundi* for the city. This chapter suggests that the Chapel of St. Ignatius at Seattle University is an example of an effective religious space for the postmodern religious context, particularly because of the way it negotiates those axes to generate a new type of city and urbanity.

As envisioned in postmodern theological thinking, a novel urbanism will redeem the city by providing spaces that collect and engender transcendent realisms for those seeking refuge from the perils of "hypermodernity."[15] It imagines environments that assemble communities nurtured by ordinary, unpretentious, yet eloquent experiences that make claims to totality. The Chapel of St. Ignatius is a wonderful example of a place that permits what Albert Borgmann calls "focal realism." Borgmann defines what he means by that as "an orientation that accepts the lessons of the postmodernist critique and resolves the ambiguities of the postmodern condition in an attitude of patient vigor for a common order centered on communal celebrations. What can invigorate the attitude and provide a center for celebration is reality."[16] His idea of focal realism can become a fulcrum for how certain architecture works in the postmodern age.

The realisms occasioned by the chapel at Seattle University are modest, unpretentious, and ordinary compared to the simulated reality of cyberspace or the glamour of hyper consumerism, and yet its unassuming discourses mediate truths for religious subjects that no technology or material product can render. In that sense, the understated genres of the chapel possess a dynamism and vitality for making community that no artificial need or mechanism can induce. Furthermore, the communities that the space gathers and sustains are composed of authentic persons engaged in religious rituals that only the city and new urbanism can produce. Diverse and unlikely partners bowing before their gods through the compressed metaphors of light, color, shadows, and shapes are projected on roughhewn floors and walls. Muslims, Buddhists, Jews, and Christians who find no offense in a common space profess uncommon traditions. Pilgrims discover mutual resonances through metaphors and abstractions that only postmodern urbanism can provide.

NORMS FOR CONTEMPORARY CATHOLIC RITUAL ENVIRONMENTS

I would like to briefly bring these reflections on the postmodern condition and theology to the context of liturgical environment and

art in the Catholic Church. The liturgical reforms of the Roman Catholic Church in the twentieth century brought about new ideas and practices concerning the worship environment.[17] In order to fully understand these developments, one must employ a religious hermeneutics to them. In other words, a complex set of ideas and practices embedded in an evolving history remains the most adequate way to decipher the aesthetic meaning of what transpired in the Catholic Church as part of its liturgical movement.[18] That being said, ultimately one cannot judge the norms without examining theological, liturgical, and ethical factors that affected them. One need apply a synoptic interdisciplinary lens to fathom the architectural and artistic principles set by twentieth-century reform.

The reforms of this past century nevertheless culminated in guidelines and principles for church environment and art set forth especially by *Sacrosanctum Concilium*[19] and the subsequent *General Instructions of the Roman Missal*.[20] Each of these documents articulated key principles and guidelines that apply to the arrangement and furnishing of the liturgical setting. Accompanying those reforms, further work by conferences of local bishops was accomplished to guide both the renovation of already-existing sanctuaries and churches and the design and creation of new ones. For the purposes of this chapter, the two documents produced by the United States Conference of Catholic Bishops (USCCB), *Environment and Art in Catholic Worship* (1978) and *Built of Living Stones: Art, Architecture, and Worship* (2000), need examination in terms of how they relate to the postmodern religious context.

Ascertaining a single or uniform aesthetics from any or all of these documents is very difficult or near to impossible to do. The documents are careful not to overtly advocate for a particular style or genre of art or architecture. Mostly in understanding the Catholic Church's inheritance of worship spaces that span hundreds—and in Europe well over a thousand—of years, no one epoch or genre of art or architecture could be advocated for over another. That being said, the task of *Environment and Art in Catholic Worship* and *Built of Living Stones* has been to reflect on the liturgical and ecclesiological principles of Vatican II reforms and to particularly translate the principles of those reforms into the renovation and design of ritual spaces, images, and furnishings that adorn them. Moreover, these documents also present guidelines and processes for dioceses, parishes, and other religious communities to carry out renovation, design, and construction. Given the tasks of the USCCB documents, how do their guidelines and principles stand in relationship to the enculturation of postmodern religious sensibilities as articulated in this chapter?

As discussed previously, while there is a purposeful attempt to avoid supporting a particular aesthetics for contemporary ritual environments, one must highlight the strong value for the contemplative, transparent, and modest nature of forms at a human scale that is the hallmark especially of the 1978 document. In that sense, the strong incarnational quality of forms is sought by the opening of symbols against the backdrop of an uncluttered and simple space. These values especially override other aesthetic considerations in *Environment and Art in Catholic Worship*. The 1978 document is explicitly concerned with a postindustrial and multicultural church that can only communicate the mystery revealed through simple, symbolic discourse.

Both the 1978 and the 2000 documents strongly emphasize the absolute centrality of the liturgy in the overall schemata of design. Ritual space must be organized according to the contours of the church's official rituals that mediate its public prayer. Any other considerations for the space are secondary. That being said, *Environment and Art* views the liturgical action as being directed from and by the assembly at prayer. The church at prayer is characterized as the full congregation at worship. The subject of the liturgical action is clearly the church assembled with its many functions. *Built of Living Stones* nuances or even corrects that view by emphasizing that the altar area or sanctuary is the source and summit of worship in coordination with the assembly as a separate axis. From its standpoint, design must keep both orientations in mind. One can surmise that the 2000 document breaks down the ecclesiological ordering of the liturgical space, emphasizing the hierarchy of ministries.

Another discrepancy that exists between *Environment and Art* and *Built of Living Stones* concerns the placing of the reserved Eucharist in relation to the worshipping body and how devotional prayer is conceived of in the overall schemata of church design. The 1978 document finds little room for the reserved sacrament within the church proper. A separate chapel or room designed apart from the place of the liturgical action is preferred so that there is no confusion between the action of liturgy and the stasis of devotion. The 2000 document emphasizes that the reserved sacrament need be in view of the main assembly at prayer and does not solely advocate for a separate chapel or room for devotion. *Built of Living Stones* directs that the bishop should determine the design and placement of the tabernacle. Moreover, the 2000 document gives greater credence to the role of devotional images in the church itself. It acknowledges that devotional practices do not interfere with the fuller liturgical action.

The 1978 and 2000 documents both recognize the importance of the originality, imagination, and inventiveness of the artist and architect in creating and designing sacred images and edifices. In addition, both documents strongly underscore the significance of the relationship between the congregation and the architect and liturgical design consultant. As conceived, they work together as a team and learn from each other in the process of building a house for the local church. Without a dialogical process, the structure will not serve those for whom it is constructed. And yet *Built of Living Stones* unambiguously delineates the role of the bishop and diocesan structures in regulating, directing, and approving designs and plans for church buildings. Overall, the 2000 document is much more prescriptive in its approach to designing, renovating, and building sacred environments. The guidelines themselves are organized in a way that clearly outline processes based on the sole authority of the local ordinary in the ultimate sanctioning of the space.

CONCLUSION: DESIGNING SACRED ENVIRONMENTS FOR THE POSTMODERN WORLD

This chapter has delineated some of the dominant forces that characterize the postmodern social and religious condition. It has shown that encountering postmodernity can be socially, philosophically, and religiously daunting. Facing the surge of hypermodern social and economic forces can result in exhaustion and dismay. Conversely, postmodern theology offers alternative praxes to the social sway. In the words of Graham Ward, theology "must subsume postmodernism's cyberspace, writing through and beyond it, in order to establish its own orders."[21] As presented, new urban environments will redeem the city by providing spaces that collect and engender transcendent realisms for those seeking refuge from the perils of the hypermodern world. Environments are imagined that assemble communities nurtured by ordinary, unpretentious, yet eloquent experiences that make claims to totality. The Chapel of St. Ignatius at Seattle University is understood as one of those places that has opened symbol and metaphor to postmodern religious pilgrims.

Criteria for the renovation, design, and construction of sacred space need to keep these social and religious factors in mind. How to draw and plan through and beyond hypermodern intrusion is no simple charge. How to conceive new urban oases through and beyond the lure of simulated reality is no easy undertaking. And yet the answer lies in incarnational forms against the backdrop of unpretentious and even austere space as presented in the criteria of *Environment and Art in Catholic Worship* and by Steven Holl's design. Humility in design, not hubris, is the religious and architectural answer to the frightening and overwhelming forces of contemporary culture. It is suggested here that the seeds of courage, ingenuity, and faith to design through and beyond hypermodernity can still be seen in a document like *Environment and Art*. Incarnational realisms, assemblies unified by a common ministry, all housed against condensed rough-hewn beauty, sound like a good idea.

MICHAEL J. SHERIDAN

10 SPIRITUALITY, SOCIAL JUSTICE, AND THE BUILT ENVIRONMENT

This chapter on spirituality, social justice, and the built environment is grounded in the conceptual frameworks, values, and ethics of social work, as this is the world I inhabit—a discipline and profession that differs in many ways from the world of architecture. As such, it is important to clarify both the worldview and language reflected here so that, hopefully, this offering can be part of a dialogue that allows both of us—writer and reader—to be standing on similar ground. Important signposts in this terrain are the key concepts of *spirituality* and *social justice*. Each has a particular meaning within social work, even as they are continually debated and fine-honed. This chapter begins with an overview of these two concepts and then discusses their relevance to the goal of "transcending architecture." It concludes with examples of what I

am calling a "justice-seeking, spirit-growing" architecture. Hopefully, this discussion will illuminate my overall premise, which is the following. When a deep and wide understanding of spirituality, a comprehensive view of social justice, and socially conscious architecture are joined, sacred space emerges.

AN EVOLVING UNDERSTANDING OF SPIRITUALITY

Central to the focus of this book is the concept of *spirituality*, an arena that has garnered increased attention in social work and other helping professions over the past twenty to thirty years. Although early human services, institutions, and social welfare policy were significantly influenced by Judeo-Christian worldviews on charity, communal responsibility, and social justice,[1] social work began to distance itself from these sectarian roots in the 1920s in pursuit of professionalization—striving to attain the status accorded to law, medicine, and other professions.[2] The means to this desired end was allegiance to scientific empiricism and secular humanism as the major foundation for the profession's values, ethics, and practice approaches. This stage has been described as one in which "religion and spirituality were increasingly viewed, at best, as unnecessary and irrelevant, and, at worst, as illogical and pathological."[3] Beginning in the 1980s, we witnessed a resurgence of interest in spirituality within social work, which continues to evolve in the present day.[4] This period has been marked by an explosion of publications and presentations, the development of a national Society for Spirituality and Social Work, and re-admittance of the terms "religion" and "spirituality" within the profession's educational accreditation standards after an absence of over thirty years.[5] Some scholars say that we are currently in a period of "transcending boundaries," characterized by continued expansion and exploration across divides of "spiritual perspectives, academic disciplines, nations, governmental and religious institutions, and between humans and nature."[6]

This renewed attention to spirituality differs from the earlier sectarian era in that it emphasizes the importance of recognizing and valuing diverse spiritual traditions and respecting personal self-determination.[7] A major challenge has been defining spirituality in such a way that truly honors these principles, requiring inclusion of both sectarian and nonsectarian perspectives and traditions, as well as distinguishing the terms "religion" and "spirituality." Although conversation

and debate concerning definitional issues continue, the general consensus within the field today is that "spirituality" is the broader term, with "religion" falling within this larger construct. I hasten to add that we teach our social work students that the most important definition of these terms is what the client or community considers them to be. For some, religion encompasses spirituality and is the larger construct, for others the two terms are inseparable, for still others they are quite distinct. Regarding social work practice, the message to students is to honor "where the client is." But for scholars in the field of spirituality and social work today, the following definitions by Canda and Furman capture the current understanding of these two terms. Spirituality is defined as "a process of human life and development focusing on the *search* for a sense of meaning, purpose, morality, and well-being; in *relationship* with oneself, other people, other beings, the universe, and the ultimate reality however understood (e.g., animistic, atheistic, nontheistic, polytheistic, theistic, or other ways); orienting around centrally *significant priorities*; and engaging a sense of the *transcendence* (experienced as deeply profound, sacred, or transpersonal)."[8] As a related concept, religion is defined as "an *institutionalized* (i.e., systematic and organized) *pattern* of values, beliefs, symbols, behaviors, and experiences that involves spirituality, a *community of adherents, transmissions of traditions* over time, and *community support functions* (e.g., organizational structure, material assistance, emotional support, or political advocacy) that are directly or indirectly related to *spirituality*."[9] Given this broad understanding of spirituality, most social work scholars writing on the topic take the stance that spirituality is an innate and fundamental part of the human condition, albeit experienced and expressed in myriad ways.

Canda and Furman offer a holistic model of spirituality that addresses both the universal and innate quality of spirituality while allowing for its diversity. This model is diagrammed as three concentric circles, each reflecting a different metaphor of spirituality: spirituality as the *wholeness* of the person (outer circle), spirituality as the *center* of the person (inner circle), and spirituality as one of four fundamental *aspects* of the person (middle circle).

As "aspect," spirituality is part of a quaternity that also includes the biological, psychological, and social aspects, which each have their necessary functions. The spiritual aspect is said to orient persons and groups "toward meaning, purpose, connectedness, and transcendence."[10] Spirituality as *wholeness* refers to that quality of being human that is not reducible to any part or that which is "sacred and transcendent" or the "divine nature within humanity."[11] Spirituality as the *center* of the person can be described as the "soul or seat of consciousness (providing) the connection and orientation point between all aspects of the person."[12] Canda and Furman suggest that the metaphors of the center and the wholeness of the person are actually different ways of coming to the same place: "By going within, we find unity with others. By going without, we find a scope of consciousness that embraces all."[13] When all three vantage points are considered (aspect, wholeness, and center), a more complex and rich understanding of spirituality emerges.

This multifaceted understanding of spirituality is important for the current discussion, as it has implications for every area of human life, including our experiences with the built environment. What types of built environments support and nurture positive growth and development, addressing the spiritual aspects of people, as well as their physical, psychological, and social needs? What qualities of structures and surrounding environments provide pathways to both the expansive, transcendent experience of spirit (wholeness), as well the more inner-focused, immanent nature of spirituality (center)? Equally important, how does architecture negatively impinge upon spiritual development or stifle spiritual experiences and expression, producing deleterious effects for both the individual and the community? In other words, beyond concerns for public health, safety, and welfare, what is the role of architecture in lifting and nurturing the human spirit in all of its manifestations? And most salient to the focus of this chapter, what are the consequences within any society of having widely disparate opportunities to inhabit spiritually supportive environments, whether it be where people live, work, go to school, gather in community, or come to for solitary refuge and reflection? Consider these questions as you place yourself in the environs pictured in figures 10-1 and 10-2. What messages do these architectural "places and spaces" transmit—about your worth and capacities as a human being; about your place among the human family and within the encompassing universe; about your connection to the Divine?

THE CHALLENGE OF PROMOTING SOCIAL JUSTICE

Concern for disparities in every facet of human life is a major focus of social work's commitment to *social justice*, which has been heralded as the characteristic that distinguishes it

FIGURE 10-1. A RESIDENT LOOKS OUT OF A STAIRWELL WINDOW IN IDA B. WELL HOMES, A HOUSING PROJECT IN CHICAGO, ILLINOIS, 2005.

from other helping professions.[14] From its beginnings, the profession recognized that personal troubles were at least, in part, connected to public ills. As C. F. Weller, head of the Charity Organization Society of Washington, D.C., said in 1902: "For, although we are not inclined to forget that poor people make poor homes, we are beginning to appreciate, also, that poor homes make poor people."[15] This dual focus on both individual change and societal reform has been consistent within the profession, although tension between the "micro" and the "macro" approach to social work has been a continuous challenge.[16] So what does social justice entail? At a very basic level, social justice can be defined as all citizens sharing in both the benefits and burdens of a society. A major challenge in defining a just society is delineating a way to achieve a fair distribution of societal goods—both tangible and intangible.

RAWLSIAN DISTRIBUTIVE JUSTICE

For much of the twentieth century, utilitarian arguments were embraced as the best approach for dealing with problems of distribution. Utilitarianism, grounded in the "Greatest-Happiness Principle,"[17] has been generally characterized as doing the greatest good for the greatest number of people. It was assumed that this would naturally occur through processes that were equally accessible to all members of a society in an atmosphere of general benevolence. John Rawls challenged this perspective in his classic book *A Theory of Justice* (1971), stating that utilitarianism provided no imperative for social justice as it can be used to justify the state violating the rights of or ignoring the needs of some people in order to attain a greater overall benefit for others. Thus, the

FIGURE 10-2. ABANDONED HOUSING ON BROAD STREET,
NORTH PHILADELVANIA, PENNSYLVANIA, 2009.

inherent respect due to each individual is not guaranteed. He argued that social justice demands the fair distribution of what he called "primary goods," or those resources needed for living a decent life.

Rawls bases his theory of justice on two principles.[18] The first is known as the *equal liberty principle*, which guarantees basic political and civil liberties such as freedom of speech, assembly, religion, property ownership, and political participation to all. The second principle has two parts. The first part is known as the *fair equality of opportunity principle*, and it guarantees fair access to education and work for all citizens with equal ability and talent, irrespective of socioeconomic background, gender, and race. The second part of the second principle is known as the *difference principle*, which states that a just society may accept some inequalities in social and economic institutions as fair but requires that these inequalities benefit the least advantaged citizens to the greatest extent possible. Rawls further stated that

undeserved inequalities call for redress; and since inequalities of birth and natural endowments are undeserved, these inequalities are to be somehow compensated for. Thus, the principle holds that in order to treat all persons equally, to provide genuine equality of opportunity, society must give more attention to those with fewer native assets and to those born into the less favorable social positions. The idea is to redress the bias of contingencies in the direction of equality.[19]

Furthermore, citizens are expected to contribute to society through capital, labor, or both, and when this is not possible through conscientious effort (e.g., people unable to work because of ill-health or because of the seasonal or temporary nature of their jobs, or when their work fails to provide a living wage), they may have "claims of need"[20] and the government is required to pay a "social minimum" or public assistance.[21]

Social workers have long recognized that definitions of "fair" and "the greatest good" have been skewed toward those who hold positions of power and privilege, while leaving out the voices and needs of those most marginalized. The opening sentence of the profession's *Code of Ethics* declares that the twofold mission of the profession is "to enhance human well-being and help meet the basic human needs of all people, with *particular attention to the needs and empowerment of people who are vulnerable, oppressed, and living in poverty.*"[22] Thus, social workers have historically embraced Rawls's conception of distributive justice as it seems congruent with

the profession's goal of meeting basic human needs and eliminating racial, gender, economic, and other inequalities.[23] This egalitarian approach to social justice has served as a foundation for the modern social welfare system, which attempts to ensure a "safety net" or "social minimum of primary goods below which nobody is allowed to fall."[24]

THE CAPABILITIES APPROACH TO JUSTICE

However, the second focus of social work's mission—*enhancing human well-being*—is not directly addressed by Rawlsian notions of justice. An alternative model of social justice is currently being identified in social work as better addressing the profession's dual commitments to both human need and human well-being, known as the "capabilities approach."[25] This approach has also been assessed as being more congruent with "spiritually sensitive social work practice" in that it better addresses four core principles of this approach: 1) supporting full human development, 2) prioritizing the vulnerable, 3) addressing global/ecological interrelation, and 4) respecting spiritual diversity.[26]

Initially developed by the 1998 Nobel Prize winner in economics Amartya Sen, the capabilities approach is more focused on enhancing social justice and removing injustice than proposing an idealized model of justice. As Sen states, "Justice cannot be indifferent to the lives that people can actually live."[27] Thus, the capabilities approach goes beyond the distribution of resources to focus on the fair distribution of *capabilities*—or the resources and power essential for exercising true self-determination.

While recognizing the importance of "primary goods" as essential for well-being, the capabilities perspective sees them as a means to an end, not an end unto themselves. Sen reasons that "as a direction to go, concentration on the possession of vital commodities seems fair enough. The more exacting question is not whether this is the right direction to go, but whether taking stock of commodity possession is the right place to *stop*."[28] He reasons that focusing solely on resources tells us nothing about what a person is able to do with them; that justice should be concerned with what resources do to or for people—how they affect people's freedom to function in valuable ways. He offers the example of a person who uses a wheelchair needing more resources in order to fully participate in community life.

Sen describes "functionings" as valuable activities that impact people's lives and well- being, such as being safe, being healthy, becoming educated, and participating in public life. Capabilities are "the various combinations of functionings (beings and doings) that a person can achieve. Capability is, thus, a set of vectors of functionings, reflecting the person's freedom to lead one type of life or another ... to choose from possible livings."[29] Simply put, capabilities lead to functionings, which then lead to well-being. Thus, Sen's vision of a just society is one that supports people's freedoms to develop capabilities in order to achieve valuable functioning because this greatly impacts "what life we lead and what we can and cannot do, can and cannot be."[30]

Martha Nussbaum, a contemporary philosopher and collaborator with Sen, has further developed the capabilities perspective. Nussbaum emphasizes the interactive nature of social justice, stressing that capabilities are "not just abilities residing inside a person, but also the freedoms or opportunities created by a combination of personal abilities and the political, social, and economic environment."[31] She explains that a society that "does well at producing internal capabilities but [that] cut[s] off the avenues through which people actually have the opportunity to function in accordance with those capabilities"[32] cannot be considered a just or decent society. For example, people receiving education may be capable of free speech, but this capability does not represent true functioning if free expression of speech is repressed. Nussbaum also stresses human dignity and respect as integral to her theory, stating that "some living conditions deliver to people a life that is worthy of the human dignity that they possess, and others do not."[33]

Another central notion discussed by Nussbaum is that of "threshold"—the starting point for every person in a just society—which she links to ten central capabilities required for anyone to be able to pursue a dignified and minimally flourishing life. These capabilities include:

- life
- bodily health
- bodily integrity
- senses, imagination, and thought
- emotions
- practical reason
- affiliation
- relationship with other species and the natural world
- play
- control over one's environment

The basic claim of Nussbaum's view of social justice is that respect for human dignity requires that "citizens be placed above an ample threshold of capability, in all ten of those areas."[34] Furthermore, she asserts that it is fundamentally wrong to subordinate the "ends of some individuals to those of others … [stating that] to treat a person as a mere object for the use of others" is the essence of exploitation.[35] This notion of an "ample threshold" differs greatly from the "safety net" metaphor of social justice inherent to Rawls's distributive justice perspective.

SOCIAL JUSTICE, SPIRITUALITY, AND ARCHITECTURE

What is the connection between this "ample threshold of central capabilities" framework of social justice, delineated by the capabilities approach, and the discipline and profession of architecture? As someone with no expertise in the field, architecture's contributions to human capability are readily apparent to me in addressing four of the ten central capabilities advanced by Nussbaum: *life*, *bodily health*, *bodily integrity*, and *control over one's environment*. Quite simply, adequate shelter and safe environs are essential for optimal functioning in each of these areas. But I would like to focus on the six remaining capabilities that I believe could be most amplified by the transcendent or spiritual potentials of architecture. These potentials were described so eloquently in the program materials of the interdisciplinary symposium "Transcending Architecture: Aesthetics and Ethics of the Numinous": "At its highest, architecture has the ability to turn geometric proportions into shivers, stone into tears, rituals into revelation, light into grace, space into contemplation, and time into divine presence."[36] It is through this creation of sacred space that architecture holds the most promise for uniting social justice and spirituality and supports the development of capacities needed for living a fully human life.

First, the capability of *senses, imagination, and thought* refers to "being able to use the senses, to imagine, think, and reason—and to do these things in a 'truly human' way," including being able to "experience and produce works and events of one's own choice, religious, literary, musical, and so forth."[37] All of these come alive within structures that stimulate us and stir our own creativity—and all of these are deadened when buildings are constructed paying attention only to issues of structural soundness, utility, and economic expediency. Most apparent in the construction of prisons, confining elements are also evident in other kinds of institutional settings, such as schools, hospitals, elder care residences, and even whole neighborhoods, when they do not take into account the transformative power of fully engaging the senses, the imagination, and free and open thought. Environmental design scholars are beginning to integrate recent advances in neuroscience research regarding how people's brains respond to different physical environments, highlighting empirical findings on the effect of the built environment on alertness, concentration, and creativity.[38]

The second central capability addresses *emotions*, which Nussbaum defines as "being able to have attachments to things and people outside ourselves; to love those who love and care for us, to grieve at their absence … [and to not] have one's emotional development blighted by fear and anxiety."[39] The capacity for embracing the full range of human emotions also includes deep-felt responsiveness to whatever is present—another person's tears; a beautiful sunset; the last breath of a dying animal; the thrill of dancing through space; the soft, quiet comfort of evening. Whatever the experience, architecture has long recognized that the built environment can be incredibly powerful in evoking emotions. In Nussbaum's terms, planned environments can provide safe spaces conducive to feeling all of our feelings, to honoring whatever emotional challenges we face, to having a sense of connection to people and things beyond the self—including the sacred. We know it intuitively when we enter these spaces and our bodies, minds, and spirits respond by opening to the fullness of our own humanity and to that of others. And we also know immediately when we enter places that are not welcoming of our deepest feelings and we respond to this, too, by shutting down and by tuning out. As with senses, imagination, and thought, research is also demonstrating the impacts of physical space on both positive and negative emotions at the neurological level.[40]

The third central capability of *practical reason* involves the ability to "form a conception of the good and to engage in critical reflection about the planning of one's life," which includes "protection for the liberty of conscience and religious observation."[41] In our modern times, time and space for such reflection is not easily found. Often, our environs offer up unceasing distractions that make it extremely difficult to think at all, much less find space to listen to the "small voice within" so necessary for making deeply considered decisions and determining our most cherished life commitments. As an educator, I long for an academic physical setting that is supportive of this kind of practical reasoning that honors contemplation as well as critical thinking. I am talking about learning spaces where instructor and student alike are invited to slow down, to breathe, to notice what arises, and to engage in discernment. Huebner addresses these elements when he

argues that education should be concerned with and attend to the journey of the self and avoid reducing this passage to merely a technical process, thereby ignoring its sacred nature.[42] Architecture and design can offer a holding environment for this kind of contemplative learning, or practice reason in Nussbaum's terms, or work against it.

The fourth central capability of *affiliation* focuses on being able to "live with and toward others; to recognize and show concern for other human beings; to engage in various forms of social interaction; to be able to imagine the situation of another."[43] Nussbaum also states that this capability involves "having the social bases of self-respect and nonhumiliation; being able to be treated as a dignified being whose worth is equal to that of others."[44] The built environment can either encourage these aspects of affiliation or create barriers to such connections. This, of course, includes issues of accessibility for older persons and people with disabilities—addressed by universal design as coined by architect Ronald Mace.[45] It also addresses what urban designers call "nodes of human activity." But it goes beyond these considerations to create a space that is truly welcoming and facilitates authentic encounters with others. Architectural design that fosters affiliation addresses the universal human need for connection— with self, with others, and with the sacred, however this is defined.

The fifth central capability, relationship with *other species and the natural world*, addresses our ability to "live with concern for and in relation to animals, plants, and the world of nature."[46] Sociobiologists affirm the importance of this capability, proposing that human beings have a genetically based need to affiliate with nature, calling it *biophilia*.[47]

Consideration of the nonhuman or natural world is certainly evident in the push toward green, sustainable design today, but I think Nussbaum would envision an architecture that paid attention to more than efficient heating and cooling systems and the use of green building materials. Truly honoring and relating with other species and the natural environment is a value central to Indigenous spiritual traditions worldwide. From this view, human beings are recognized as part of nature and the web of life, not separate from or above it—and both the human and nonhuman world are considered to be imbued with spirit. The power of nature to help us access the spiritual is also increasingly recognized within industrialized societies, providing an antidote to the often dispirited and disconnected rhythms of modern life.[48] Built environments that mindfully find ways to "re-member" us with the natural world, in line with what Joye calls "biophillic architecture,"[49] also help reconnect us with the world of Spirit.

Finally, the remaining central capability identified by Nussbaum as essential for living a fully human life is *play*, defined simply as "being able to laugh, to play, to enjoy recreational activities."[50] Organized recreation programs emerged in the United States from the settlement house and playground movements of the late nineteenth and early twentieth centuries. Progressive reformers at the time spurred civic attention on developing safe spaces where children could be "protected from vice and prepared for citizenship,"[51] noting the positive effects on both physical and spiritual health. Architecture has long been involved in creating recreational spaces for children, increasingly moving toward principles of participatory design, where children are directly involved in the design of play areas versus being the passive recipients of adult notions of what a playground should be.[52] The need for play has increasingly been seen as central to the well-being of adults as well, demonstrated by the explosion of adult recreation, sports, and physical fitness centers. However, as with all social goods in our society, equal access to such resources for all citizens remains an unrealized ideal. A social justice-seeking architecture would advocate for environments supportive of play, not only for those with a certain level of financial resources and leisure time, not just for the young, not just those with certain physical or mental abilities, but for all people. And a spiritually attuned architecture would recognize the importance of creating space for recreation—or re-creation—that is truly restorative of the human body, mind, and spirit. Spirit-filled, replenishing elements can be integrated into any planned space or structure—not just those designed for the purpose of exercise or leisure. A window that calls us to view the world a little differently, a special nook that bids us to enter and daydream, an open space that tempts us to lie or tumble on the grass—there are many ways to offer an invitation to step out of the ordinary and venture into the contemplative or mystical. Entering therein provides a door to the spirit.

JUSTICE-SEEKING, SPIRIT-GROWING ARCHITECTURE

There is a growing emphasis on socially conscious architecture within the field of architecture today, which I believe exemplifies a capabilities approach to issues of social justice. These endeavors go beyond ensuring public health, safety, and welfare to address the six capabilities described previously, representing what I am calling a "justice-seeking, spirit-growing architecture." There are numerous examples of this movement occurring all over the globe. Architects for Humanity's website (http://architectureforhumanity.org/) is a wonderful source for discovering what is happening worldwide, but I want to highlight three initiatives that have taken place in the United States, as concern for Nussbaum's central capabilities is easily identifiable in these projects: the Rural Studio in Alabama, Hunts Point Riverside Park in New York, and Inner-City Arts in California.

THE RURAL STUDIO

In 1993 Samuel "Sambo" Mockbee and his colleague and friend Dennis K. Ruth established the Rural Studio within the School of Architecture at Auburn University.[53] It was created as a design-build program aimed at improving living conditions in rural Alabama while providing real-world, hands-on experience to students. Mockbee consistently challenged his students to ask themselves: "Do I have the courage to make my gift count for something?"[54]

Using salvaged lumber and bricks, discarded tires, hay and waste cardboard bales, concrete rubble, colored bottles, old licensed plates, and other kinds of innovative building materials, the Rural Studio first focused on providing houses to people in need.

The first house was completed in Mason's Bend, Alabama, in 1994. It was built for elderly Shepard and Alberta Bryant, who were living with their three grandchildren in a "rickety shack with neither heat nor plumbing but with abundant holes that admitted reptile visitors and the elements."[55] It was called the Hay Bale house because of its use of eighty-pound hay bales wrapped in polyurethane, secured with wires, and coated with stucco

to provide inexpensive, super-insulated walls. The Bryants told Mockbee and his students that they wanted a front porch where they could entertain neighbors and family. The goal, according to Mockbee, was "not to have a warm, dry house, but to have a warm, dry house with a spirit to it."[56] This ethic of providing a "shelter for the soul" became a recurrent theme in Rural Studio projects.

In addition to private homes, Mockbee and his students also took on community projects, including a chapel built in Sawyerville, Alabama.[57] Located on a bluff, the chapel opens to an open field and wetlands. Use of innovative building materials allowed the structure to be built for $15,000. The chapel's walls are composed of donated tires, which were packed with soil until they were rock hard, reinforced with reinforcing bars, and then wrapped in wire mesh and coated with stucco. You enter the chapel through a narrow, dark entry, which leads to a pulpit made of recycled metal materials. Nature joins you via a little stream that comes through a break in the back wall and flows through the front of the space, eventually cascading into the wetlands beyond. These features invite you to enter a slower, contemplative space. As Mockbee put it, "You want to keep the mystery going—you don't want to give your secrets up too soon."[58]

Over the first few years, the Rural Studio completed a variety of individual homes and community projects, including a center for abused and neglected children, a baseball field, a farmer's market, a community center, and a boys and girls club—all with input and involvement from the people who would inhabit them. Following Mockbee's untimely death of leukemia in 2001, the program came under the direction of Andrew Freear, who

FIGURE 10-3. JOANNE'S HOUSE, FAUNSDALE, ALABAMA, 2011. BUILT BY STUDENT TEAM JACOB BEEBE, ERIKA HENRIKSSON, ERIC SCHMID, AND SANDRA YUBERO; PROJECT INSTRUCTORS ANDREW FREERAR, DANNY WICKE, AND MACKENZIE STAGG.

was teaching at the studio. Under his directorship, the studio has embarked on a series of larger, community-based projects. Many of these span several years and are built in phases. Freear says that the projects are more academically challenging and allow them to help more people. The Rural Studio has completed around 120 private and public projects to date, still steeped in the vision of students becoming what Mockbee called "citizen architects." As Freear says, "I love and respect greatly the fact that Sambo [i.e., Mockbee] thought going to school was not only about yourself, but about making the world a better place."[59]

HUNTS POINT RIVERSIDE PARK

The South Bronx is a community overburdened with a variety of polluting industries, including food processing plants, public waste treatment facilities, and heavy diesel truck traffic. Plagued by having the highest rates of asthma and diabetes in New York City, while having one of the lowest ratios of parks to people, this community was in desperate need of open, green space.[60] "Collective efficacy" is a term that speaks to a community's belief that they can accomplish something together. Not surprisingly, this area was deemed as having low collective efficacy, demonstrated through high crime rates, chronic health problems, and general environmental and social degradation. A serendipitous discovery of an open access point to the Bronx River offered an opportunity for engagement in collective efficacy for this community.

In the late 1990s, Majora Carter was on staff at the Point CDC—a nonprofit organization focused on youth development and cultural and economic revitalization. While out jogging one day, Majora's dog, Xena, dragged her into an illegal garbage dumping area that led to the Bronx River. Inspired by actually seeing that there was an access to the river, she wrote a $10,000 seed grant to fund what would eventually become the multimillion dollar Hunts Point Riverside Park project. Situated along the Bronx River, the park opened in the spring of 2007 and transformed a degraded industrial area into a natural retreat for a variety of family and community activities. It represented the first recreational access to the Bronx River, while connecting several South Bronx communities.[61]

Community residents were very much involved during all phases of the project and made their desires known through several public forums and participation on various committees. Among the requested elements were "a green lawn to lie down on, a place for kids to play, an amphitheater, access to the river, and a water feature in which children could splash on a hot day."[62] There is also a place to barbecue and have picnics as well as places to store and launch boats. In the end, landscape architect Jenny Hoffner notes that community members definitely saw the park as "our design."[63] The ability to be involved in conceptualizing, planning, and completing this park has created a feeling of competence and empowerment—or the aforementioned "collective efficacy"—that has carried over to other projects and allowed residents to imagine other options for their community.

INNER-CITY ARTS

Every year, the Inner-City Arts complex provides education in ceramics, visual arts, theater, dance, and animation to ten thousand K–12 Los Angeles public school students and art educator training to their teachers. Their programs serve students who primarily come from very poor families, some of them homeless. According to Cynthia Harnisch, president and CEO, the overall goal is to "increase graduation rates and keep kids in school,"[64] noting how art can have a significant impact on children's lives. Findings from a five-year study by the U.S. Department of Education reveals that the program has indeed increased graduation rates and improved overall academic performance.

After occupying small, temporary spaces for several years, Inner-City Arts teamed up with architect Michael Maltzan to retrofit and repurpose an abandoned garage in Los Angeles's Skid Row neighborhood. Maltzan

states that "the idea was to craft an urban village with a series of indoor and outdoor spaces."[65] The Inner-City Arts complex certainly stands out amid its surroundings—an oasis for at-risk kids surrounded by the dull gray boxes of Los Angeles's Skid Row. Its gleaming white color marks the complex as "a place of hope, a clean slate for troubled kids."[66] Although treated with an anti-graffiti coating, the buildings have rarely been defaced. Harnisch says that local people have embraced the campus as a valued part of the community, and homeless men often act as volunteer crossing guards and tour guides.

The finished project, a one-acre campus built in three phases as demands for space grew, uses simple, geometric lines and bright accents of color to provide an environment that stimulates students' creativity. Both interior and exterior features are designed for adaptability, providing spaces to foster contemplation, intimate connection, and open movement. The complex includes many professionally equipped studios, a state-of-the-art black box theater, a resource library, and several gardens designed by landscape architect Nancy Goslee Power and Associates. There is also a main courtyard for children to gather, play, and explore, providing a haven in a community where outdoor space is often unsafe. As *Los Angeles Times* architecture critic Christopher Hawthorne points out, the Inner-City Arts campus "make[s] up a small-scale essay on the power of architecture to create community, and even a sense of wonder, not with formal fireworks but simply by shaping space."[67]

The Rural Studio, Hunts Point Riverside Park, and Inner-City Arts are just three examples of the transcendent potential of archi-

FIGURE 10-4. HUNTS POINT RIVERSIDE PARK, 2009, TRELLISED SEATING AREA.

FIGURE 10-5. HUNTS POINT RIVERSIDE PARK, 2009, BOAT DOCK ON BRONX RIVER.

FIGURE 10-6. CHILDREN PLAYING IN THE INNER-CITY ARTS COURTYARD.

tecture to unite spirituality and social justice for marginalized and vulnerable populations in our society. There are numerous other projects emerging in the field, all in some way "creating sacred space for all peoples."

CONCLUSION

I have offered this discussion on spirituality, social justice, and the built environment from the vantage point of a different kind of architect. Social workers endeavor to help people build their lives—not their houses, or public squares, or places of worship. As such, my interpretation of "transcending architecture" leans more heavily on the *ethics* of creating sacred space versus a focus on the aesthetic or technical or economic aspects. Such ethics require that architects make structures and spaces of beauty, inspiration, respite, and encounters with the numinous accessible to *all peoples—especially* those who are most marginalized by society.

This, for me, is the essence of creating sacred space, whether this space stems from the efforts of architects or social workers. Whenever we provide such space for souls who have not been granted (as the old spiritual saying goes) a seat "at the welcome table," we enrich the souls of all who take their place for granted. Sacred space emerges when we do this not from any misguided sense of noblesse oblige or charity but from a simple recognition that we are all connected, all members of the same human family. Both architects and social workers need to remember this universal, spiritual truth, which has been voiced by every religious tradition across time.

Can either profession repair all of the wounds of injustice that permeate the human condition? No, but each can participate in the healing that arises when we share our particular gifts with intention and purpose and humbly receive the gifts that come back to us. Borrowing Samuel Mockbee's words, "having the courage to *make your gift count* for something" may just provide a "shelter for your *own* soul."[68]

SUE ANN TAYLOR

11 RITUAL, BELIEF, AND MEANING IN THE PRODUCTION OF SACRED SPACE

An anthropological perspective on the production of sacred space starts with an understanding of religion as a cultural phenomenon. Edward B. Tylor (1871) called the earliest form of religion "animism," or the belief in spiritual beings. Based on the nineteenth-century unilineal evolutionary paradigm, the beliefs and practices changed as humans moved from this original state of what was viewed at that time as "primitive" religion to forms of polytheism (i.e., belief in multiple deities) and later emerging as monotheism (i.e., the belief in one Supreme Being).[1] Tylor's ideas about the origins of religion are basically nontheistic as he concentrated on the concept of the souls and spirits as a major part of religious philosophy. Yet he influenced others to continue the study of religion, such as Sir James Frazer's *The Golden Bough* (1911–15). This twelve-volume

work—abridged into one volume in 1922—was the earliest comparative study of this scope to make a distinction between magic, religion, and science. Frazer also influenced Bronislaw Malinowski (1948), whose fieldwork in the Trobriand Islands of Melanesia revealed a relationship between magic and religion in the way people satisfied their basic needs and relieved stress and fear. Both Tylor and Frazer were criticized as "armchair anthropologists," because their writings relied on the reports of missionaries and travelers rather than their own fieldwork. Their own beliefs, along with general Eurocentric biases toward nonliterate peoples of the world, may have affected their thinking about religion or, more appropriately, belief systems.

As anthropologists engaged in ethnographic fieldwork with participant observation as a primary method of gathering data, it was evident that belief systems have always been a part of everyday experiences. Even though there may be no special word that matches our concept of "religion" or "belief," it is a part of the worldview of nonliterate people and the understanding they hold of themselves.[2] Both "religion" and "belief system" are the terms used here and they are at times interchangeable. However, as an explanatory concept, it may be preferable to refer to belief systems rather than religion and avoid the Western view that religion "means first and foremost *theism* even *monotheism*, the belief in some kind of, but definitely a single, god."[3] Lang (1901), a critic of Tylor, suggested that some "primitive" people did believe in a supreme moral being even though he offers no hypothesis and has no evidence of proof. Yet throughout history, most belief systems have not been monotheistic. Wheeler-Barclay (2010) critiques the study of religion by British social anthropologists 1860–1915, including the writings of Frederick Max Müller, Edward Tylor, Andrew Lang, James Frazer, and others.

Social theories continued to emerge by expanding beyond the search for origins and definitions of religion. Durkheim focused on religion as a way of increasing social solidarity as expressed through collective beliefs. He described religion as "a unified system of beliefs and practices relative to sacred things, that is to say, thing set apart and forbidden—beliefs and practices which unite into one single moral community called a Church, all those who adhere to them."[4]

Following the methods of Durkheim, Guy Swanson (1964) examined a world sample[5] of fifty societies using a statistical analysis to show an association between belief systems and social structure. He found that belief in high gods and ancestral spirits stems from experiences and varies among sovereign groups according to kinship structure, social classes, and other factors including a link between supernatural sanctions and moral behavior among simpler people. Even with Swanson's study, differences appear in what has been viewed as homogenous societies, and this makes defining religion problematic. In an attempt to produce a workable definition across time and cultures, Bonvillain says religion refers to: "Thoughts, actions, and feelings based on belief in the existence of spirit beings and supranormal (or superhuman) forces."[6] The defining elements of a religion or belief system encompass an array of symbols, artifacts, texts, sacred edifices, and religious leaders from shamans to priests and other official practitioners that validate beliefs and activities. Wallace (1966) described four types of religion: (1) shamanic with a part-time religious figure with power of mediating between the people and supernatural forces, (2) communal religions based on community rituals with adherence to multiple deities with some control over nature, (3) Olympian with full-time religious professionals in state level societies, and (4) monotheistic religions with a belief in one Supreme Being.[7] Each type functions in a way that supports the needs of people at a particular time and place.

Bonvillain describes the functions of religion in five ways: (1) explains the world and provides answers for the unknown, (2) provides solace and healing for the exigencies of daily life, (3) motivates and supports societal cohesion, (4) attempts to maintain social control through a system of rewards or punishments reinforced by moral and ethical beliefs, and (5) offers a means of adapting to the environment through regularized, sanctioned practices.[8] Rappaport (1967, 1968) provides an excellent example of the relationship between the natural environment and belief in his studies of the Tsembagas of New Guinea. For additional readings, edited works include a survey of the classic writings on the anthropology of religion.[9]

This brief outline of the anthropology of religion creates an opening to focus on the various beliefs that delineate what is sacred, the role of ritual, and the meanings that have guided the creation of sacred objects and places. The key to cross-cultural insight starts with contextualizing these beliefs within the larger framework of history and contemporary social, political, and economic interventions that have an impact on human interaction and responses to unforeseen events or circumstances. Today, globalization, transnational migration, and the conflicts inherent in religious territoriality are issues worthy of critical consideration. Furthermore, old and new religious movements contribute to new patterns of behavior and different meanings of the sacred perhaps creating new challenges in the production of sacred space.

THE SACRED AND THE PROFANE

Rudolf Otto (1923) used the term "numinous" to describe the "wholly other" or the sacred as being something extraordinary or *mysterium tremendum* (i.e., mysterious or awe-inspiring). Contemporary anthropologists understand the numinous, or what is sacred, as part of a cognitive process associated with individual and collective beliefs and practices and with only a tangential connection to a formalized view of religion. What is sacred is not a supernatural occurrence but a social construct created within the context of what people view as their reality. Consequently, the sacred and sacred space is not limited to the physical environment but embraces the capability of objects, animals, plants, people, and spirits to become a part of what is considered holy.

The conceptualization of religious order stems from the separation of the natural from the supernatural and the division of the world into two domains—the sacred and the profane—one containing all that is sacred and the other everything else. Although such dualist construct creates disagreement among today's scholars over the simplistic apportionment of the universe, it is responsible for advancing our understanding of religion and related practices. For example, Eliade (1959) provides a detailed description of the sacred and the profane by drawing examples from around the world to explicate different meanings of the cosmos, nature, time, and history. Knott (2008) credits Eliade with making sacred space an important subject for critical enquiry saying: "Eliade's axioms—of sacred space as other or set apart from ordinary, profane space, as the 'Center' or *axis mundi*—have become foundational for scholarly articulations of the meaning and the power of the sacred in space and time."[10] Mugerauer refers to Eliade as "a consummate scholar of the phenomenology and hermeneutics of religion" in order to explain myth and ritual.[11] According to Segal, "The ultimate payoff of myth is experiential: encountering divinity. No theory of myth could be more rooted in religion than Eliade's."[12]

RITUAL AND MYTH IN THE PRACTICE OF BELIEF

Thomas Barrie explains that "religion, mythology, and ritual are fundamental elements of human consciousness and society and have long served as a measure to explain the world and humans' place within it."[13] Drawing on earlier writings and building on the premise that supernatural things exist, Wallace explored the way human action—prayer, music, magic, witchcraft, use of hallucinogens, taboos, sacrifice, and special forces (i.e., *mana*)—work through ritual as "the primary phenomenon of religion."[14] French sociologists Hubert and Mauss (1898) were the first to make the distinction between the sacred and profane in describing ritual as a process through which one passes from the ordinary to an extraordinary space. Arnold van Gennep (1960) identifies three phases to the ritual celebrations as individuals move through stages of life recognized in some way in all societies (i.e., birth, puberty, marriage, and death). These phases are presented as separation (*liminality* or an in-between state), transition (a transformational ritual), and incorporation (welcoming the person into the community in this new state). The idea reiterated by Victor Turner (1969) is that rituals mark "liminal" moments when individuals are not firmly anchored in social structural positions, and he uses the term *communitas* rather than community to incorporate social relationships rather than an area common to a group of people. Both van Gennep and Turner move beyond the distinction of sacred versus profane to suggest a broader conceptualization of belief, ritual, and the sacred.

Myths are stories or fables of an allegorical nature about occurrences in the distant past to provide explanations about the cosmos, destiny, identity, and provide purpose in life. The writings of Joseph Campbell (1988) brought about a renewed interest in the importance of myth in everyday life. Anthro-pologists understand that when members of a society believe myths come from ancestors, the fable is felt to be true and continues to be passed down through generations. Paraphrasing Campbell, a myth is never a myth for those who believe in it. According to Claude Lévi-Strauss, a French structural anthropologist, myths express cultural values as humans assign meaning to their experiences. He says, "Mythical stories are, or seem, arbitrary, meaningless, absurd, yet nevertheless they seem to reappear all over the world."[15] His ideas were to find order out of disorder, meaning out of absurdity, and myths provided one way of doing this. Influenced by Saussure's linguistics, he attempts to derive a link between myth and the mind believing that the common mental structures of all humans lead people to think similarly, including the need to classify, think in terms of binary opposites, and impose order.

HERMENEUTICS AND OTHER VENTURES INTO BELIEF, MEANING, AND BEHAVIOR

Poststructuralists focused on the symbolic representations of myth and ritual through interpretative approaches within a contextual framework of social interaction. According to Clifford Geertz, religion is a system of symbols. "Sacred symbols function to synthesize a people's ethos—the tone, character, and quality of their life, its moral and aesthetic style and mood—and the worldview—the picture they have of the way things in sheer actuality are, their most comprehensive idea of order."[16] Critics recognize this venture into hermeneutics by Geertz and others as an interpretation of an interpretation because the information collected is the researcher interpreting the view of the narrator's own interpretation.

Recent studies of religion no longer search for origins and definitions but acquire a more humanistic and cognitive approach to understand the meanings associated with religious practices (e.g., prayer). One of the common characterizations of religious behavior is related to older adults with a general assumption that people become more religious as they age. In my research in gerontology, I found that growing older does not mean that an individual is more religious. Although that is a question researchers often attempt to answer, it is the wrong question. The questions that need answers are those that provide meaning to how one's beliefs are revealed in dealing with everyday life. Based on a collection of life stories of older African American women, those who considered themselves to be religious voiced their beliefs in a higher power as a major coping strategy in times of stress or need. Instilled with the belief that God answers prayers, they explained that when prayers went unanswered, it was "God's will." Religious belief systems have a built-in explanation that allows individuals to accept outcomes or unresolved problems that prayers did not erase. In this case, the women did not openly challenge their beliefs, but by seeming to accept the circumstances their faith remained intact. It is widely accepted that religion enhances the spiritual and perhaps physical well-being. Conversely, a dependency on prayer as a coping mechanism may repress individual initiative in problem-solving.[17] This does not mean religion is tied to needs but that individual beliefs often guide behavior. Religion as a coping strategy may be a "real and observable mechanism for dealing with day-to-day transactions; or it may represent an ideal that in effect exists within the mind of the individual."[18]

SPACE AND PLACE IN THE PRODUCTION OF SACRED SITES

Going beyond faith and religious practices, the concept of space and place in architecture, philosophy, anthropology, geography, and tourism may provide another perspective on what is sacred. Space as used here is a demarcated area as part of the landscape that can be mapped, photographed, and unearthed to reveal the contents of habitation in the past or a specific sector within a larger area. Landscape is important as a way of defining both the natural environment as well as socially constructed places.[19] Tuan explains, "In experience, the meaning of space often merges with that of place. 'Space' is more abstract than 'place.' What begins as undifferentiated space becomes place as we get to know it better and endow it with value."[20] Place in common usage denotes a locale special to an individual or group entrenched with special humanistic qualities engaging the senses as when Dorothy in the *Wizard of Oz* says: "There's no place like home." This attachment to place encompasses more than the relationship between people and their surroundings. The meaning of place is recognized through individual feelings of identity and belonging. Anthropologists are concerned with "how experience is embedded in place and how space holds memories that implicate people and events."[21] Sacred space is inclusive of group values and cultural bonds that call attention to both natural and socially constructed environments.

Roger Stump, a geographer, explains that "within the context of religion, the definition of sacred space serves specifically to connect the meanings of a system's worldview and ethos to recognizable spatial constructions."[22] He identifies themes that concern both geographers and anthropologists and are essential to an understanding of the relationship between space and religion. These include: "the spatial dynamics of religious distribution; the contextuality of religious belief and practices; religious territoriality in secular space; and the meaning and uses of sacred space."[23] These are briefly addressed in the following sections through the notion of the sacralization of space, contextualizing religious practice in relation to the larger society, and religious territoriality and the contestation of space.

THE SACRALIZATION OF SPACE

Whether as a part of nature, a plant, an animal, human-made object, or artistic creation, the concept of sacralization provides a cultural paradigm for seeing how belief is transmitted in a communal way through pilgrimages, performance, art, and ritual.[24] The natural environment such as mountain tops and forest trails may be deemed sacred sites simply as part of nature or because of myths and legends surrounding real or imagined events that occurred there. According to Angrosino, the natural environment—mountains, rivers, and deserts—have always been related to religious beliefs and practices. It is easy to believe that volcanic mountains possess superhuman natural powers and rivers bring the water for drinking that is necessary for life but just as easily bring disaster through flooding. "Three of the world's great religions—Judaism, Christianity, and Islam—all arose out of a desert environment."[25]

The sacred site may replicate pilgrimages taken by a group's ancestors to pay homage to their past. Sacred items believed to have special powers are acquired or created and used for healing or to appease the gods and protect the bearer against present dangers. Two examples are taken from David Maybury-Lewis's (1992) PBS TV series and companion book *Millennium: Tribal Wisdom and the Modern World* to convey the way belief and ritual are practiced to bring order to the universe and restore balance and harmony.

The Huichol Indians of Central Mexico assemble for a yearly pilgrimage to Wirikuta, as their ancestors had done in the past. They spend nights in prayer, dancing, chanting, and fasting, and in the daylight they search for peyote—the hallucinogenic food of the gods. When eaten, this adds to their feelings of ecstasy complete with color visions that to them result from the spiritual experience. They make offerings to the gods and offer prayers to balance the world.[26] MacLean (2001) interviewed a shaman in Mexico who explained that the color visions are a form of communication from the gods and spirits, and the sacred colors provide guidance.

In the second example, Billy Yellow, a Navaho medicine man in Monument Valley, Utah, creates a sand painting to cure his sick grandson. The "hogan"—or earth-covered Navaho dwelling—becomes a sacred place for the performance of a healing ritual. Once the colorful sand painting is finished, the boy sits on it as Billy Yellow chants to bring about balance and harmony. Once the chanting stops, the boy is healed and the sand painting, having done its work, is destroyed.[27] In both examples, the space of the natural environment and the colored sand on the floor of the hogan has become sacred for a time as a place of healing and renewal.

In reading Dean MacCannell's article on sightseeing as related to tourist attractions in modern society, I immediately saw a connection based on his model of sacralization to the designation and handling of sacred objects and locations. He refers to this as "sight sacralization" in reference to sightseeing as a modern ritual and the distinguishing characteristics that make places significant. In fact, Graburn explains his ritual theory of tourism as "a stream of alternating contrasts" in which he compares the alteration between the sacred/nonordinary and the profane/workaday/at home experiences.[28] MacCannell identifies five stages of sacralization. The first is "when a site is marked off from similar objects as being worthy of preservation" (e.g., the Great Pyramids of Giza or an object that has been named as having historical or other social values). The second entails "framing and elevation." This is most likely seen by putting it on display (e.g., a figurine placed on a pedestal, a cross hung above the pulpit, a religious painting). Third is a form of "enshrinement" (e.g., setting an object apart by encasement such as the copy of the Gutenberg Bible at the Library of Congress). Fourth, the "mechanical reproduction" of the object is found at tourist sites as well as religious centers and bookstores (e.g., postcards, books, prints, photographs, and souvenirs). The final stage is one of "social reproduction when groups, cities, and regions begin to name themselves after famous attractions" (e.g., The Holy Land).[29]

The concept of the sacralization of space or objects is useful in thinking about the way people make sacred something that is ordinary. The circumstances directly or indirectly responsible for the creation of a site lend credence to an awareness of the sacredness of place and the power it retains to evoke a response or satisfy a need. All over the world, examples reveal the power of place in the creation of what becomes a temporary or permanent sacred space and one that is either public or private. People create altars or shrines in their homes or in public places to express symbolic meaning, self-expression, or a space for contemplation and affirmation.[30] Sacred space need not be a building but can just as well be a makeshift memorial leaving flowers and tokens of remembrance at the actual site where someone died. We see this along the roadside of a fatal automobile accident, on the sidewalk in front of a home, embassy, or palace, and at the Apple offices after the death of founder Steve Jobs in 2011.

Prominent sites become sacred as people respond to national tragedies such as the bombing of the Alfred P. Murrah Federal Building in Oklahoma City and the attacks on September 11, 2001, at the World Trade Center in New York, the Pentagon, and the loss of life as Flight 93 crashed to the ground in Shanksville, Pennsylvania. Ten years later, on September 11, 2011, a waterfall cascades over the sides of the footprint of the two towers as part of the memorial park constructed on the site.

The Vietnam Veterans Memorial grounds located in Constitution Gardens on the National Mall in Washington, D.C., is considered by some veterans as a sacred place. The wall with over 58,000 names etched into the black granite panels, the Three Soldiers Monument, and the Vietnam Veterans Women's Memorial are places of reverence and commemoration.[31] These and other historical places, memorials, and grave sites become, paradoxically, both a spectacle as a tourist attraction and a place of mourning and memorialization.[32]

GLOBALIZATION, TRANSNATIONAL MIGRATION, AND RELIGIOUS TERRITORIALITY

The production of sacred space does not occur in isolation and can only be understood within the context of place and time—past and present. We live in an age of rapid globalization as economic, political, and cultural influences spread throughout the world. An understanding of these dynamics is essential to making the right decisions in the production of sacred space. The impact of globalization, transnational migration, and religious territoriality produces changing conditions that can create challenges for architects and all service providers in a multicultural environment. What emerges today is the interplay of local, regional, national, and transnational populations with the transference of people, objects, and culture across what may be considered ever-changing boundaries. Push-pull factors are operative as people relocate through labor migration, escape from political or religious persecution, or simply follow a dream. Those who leave their homeland often leave other family members behind, forcing them to share not only their resources but also their emotional ties with the land and culture they knew. This may include a different way of practicing their religion or forgoing an important aspect of who they are. The attempt to resolve this in the new land creates a challenge worth considering as new space must be carved out to fulfill old obligations to a belief system that may be at risk. Questions worth considering are: What no longer fits into the view people hold of their religion? What is essential to maintaining their identity and sense of place? In what way does the politics of space intervene in what is possible?

While sacred sites may be thought of as all inclusive, the idea of religious territoriality often leads people in power to exercise exclusivity based on race, ethnicity, gender, age, or ideology. Religious territoriality and the contestation of space is an ongoing problem found at home and abroad, often without consideration of the spiritual meaning and cultural value of a site, the significance of sacred objects, or the views of indigenous populations. Federal claims have been filed by American Indian groups over the taking of sacred land for public use. Conflict arises over the issue of control when property is involved.[33] The Native American Graves Protection and Repatriation Act of 1990 (NAGPRA)[34] addresses this issue of contestation over what is sacred with an effort of returning items or human remains—now in museums—to the descendants. This is not a simple process and meets with controversy on both sides.

Religious territoriality crosses borders of ideology as well as land at times erupting in violence. Eller writes of religion and violence in *Cruel Creeds, Virtuous Violence,* creating a broad, cross-cultural approach using examples from Christianity, Judaism, and Islam, as well as Eastern religions and tribal religions. He explains, "These manifestations include sacrifice, self-destructive behavior, persecution, ethnoreligious conflict, war, and homicide and abuse."[35] With the media coverage of church burnings, car bombings, and internal and external warfare, we are made aware of the contestation of territory and ideology on a daily basis wherever it occurs. The long unrest between Palestine and Israel is a prime example of the contestation over sacred space. In this case, both believe in the sacredness of the land; however, they see this in different ways. Whether classified as local or regional protest or the potential of domestic or foreign terrorism, the structural violence may be related to religious ideology, inequality, or the disparity of power. It seems to be a continuing state of affairs with no easy solution.

OLD AND NEW MOVEMENTS: EXAMPLES OF REVITALIZATION

Throughout history, religious movements have emerged to provide answers to uncertainty, renew faith, or create new religions. Cultural pluralism stimulates religious creativity and contributes to a blending of old and new as well as "the esoteric and the popular, scientific, and religious discourses, ideas, and practices from various parts of the world."[36] For example, Albert B. Cleage (1972) led the movement in Black Christian Nationalism by establishing the Shrine of the Black Madonna in Detroit, Michigan, during the period of unrest following the riots of 1967. The eighteen-foot mural of the Black Madonna hangs above the altar to provide an overpowering experience for visitors to the Shrine, exemplifying a transcendental moment through the power of color and form that Kandinsky (1977) would call the language and color of spiritual art. Cleage also established the Shrine of the Black Madonna in Atlanta with a painting of the Black Madonna and child painted by Carl Owen.

Alternative religions continue to emerge with charismatic leaders, and extremes of beliefs and practices have been labeled as "cults" (e.g., the Branch Davidians of Waco, James Jones and the People's Temple, and others). But "one person's cult is another's religion."[37] What they all have in common is the search for something new and meaningful. For a variety of reasons, there is a need to adopt a change that seems to satisfy deeper needs not addressed by the status quo. Anthony Wallace would call this a revitalization movement and a way to "reorganize culture in such as manner that a better way of life is brought into being to take the place of the old."[38] Those who believe will follow. The contestation of territory, ethnoreligious conflict, antireligious movements, violence, and warfare will undoubtedly result in careful decision-making. Conversely, nonviolence and peace movements may offer an opportunity for a different dialogue. Either will result in a challenging exercise in creativity.

TRANSCENDING ARCHITECTURE IN THE PRODUCTION OF SACRED SPACE

As architects are being asked to transcend the boundaries of their profession in the production of sacred space, the anthropological perspective may be useful as part of the total design process. Concepts of worldview, values, memory, and power are all relevant to the sacralization of space and the production of special places. Michel Foucault introduces a different perspective in his commentary on the relationship between space and power in regard to religious architecture. "Space is fundamental in any form of communal life; space is fundamental in any exercise of power." On invitation by architects to do a study of space, he explained his term for space "heterotopias," referred to as "those singular spaces to be found in some given social spaces whose functions are different or even opposite of others."[39] Foucault articulates his limited views of architecture, noting that in addition to the obvious design considerations, architecture is "not only considered as an element in space, but is especially thought of as a plunge into a field of social relations in which it brings about some specific effect."[40] The following reminders simply provide a starting point for effecting change:

- Religion is universal and all people possess a belief system.
- Myths, symbols, and rituals may guide beliefs and activities and take the believer to a higher plane of spirituality and emotion transcending the ordinary daily experiences.
- By identifying religious practices as culture specific, we risk engaging in stereotyping and making judgments about what is meaningful and sacred based on our own ethnocentric values and biases.
- Sacred spaces are created by people with collective as well as individual differences on what is sacred.

Finally, in recalling Otto's concept of the numinous, anthropologists can make a contribution, not in terms of the origins of religion or the ontological argument but in relation to the meanings of what is sacred. This humanistic and cross-cultural perspective on the role of the sacred in people's lives and meanings intrinsic in age-old myths, rituals, and the politics and contestation of space are essential to the idea of transcending architecture or going beyond the normal practices in an ever-changing world. As sacred space is re-created, the meaning may change with the emergence of a new set of players and a new ethos. Indeed, it may be necessary to transcend architecture to embrace the concept of "the other" with a new view of greater possibilities and a deeper understanding of the numinous.

12 ARCHITECTURAL CATALYSTS TO CONTEMPLATION

On the website introducing the interdisciplinary symposium for which this chapter was originally written—a wide-ranging conference titled with the double (maybe triple) entendre "Transcending Architecture: Aesthetics & Ethics of the Numinous," Julio Bermudez presents the following daringly exuberant claim: "Architecture is called to do a lot more than to guarantee the public health, safety and welfare of building users.... At its highest, architecture has the ability to turn geometric proportions into shivers, stone into tears, rituals into revelation, light into grace, space into contemplation, and time into divine presence."[1] I, for one, am persuaded by these lofty contentions concerning ways that built forms can play a crucial role in, as Bermudez writes, "moving us from the ordinary to the extraordinary, from the profane to the sacred." But if we aim now for a somewhat

finer point on these bold assertions, how, more precisely, can we describe the relationship between the physical forms of architecture and religious experience?

In this chapter, I will propose three quite different answers to that question—and all that I have to say is predicated on the tensions between these three significantly different ways of conceiving of the relations between built forms and religious experience. In fact, if you are unpersuaded that these are three distinct alternatives, then you are not likely to find any of my comments persuasive. The first, which I designated as the "*theatric mode*," considers the prospect of architectural forms that provide something like the stage-setting or backdrop for theatrical ritual activities, ceremonial occasions that presumably rouse (or arouse) participants and onlookers to have some sort of transformative experience. The second reply, tendered under the heading of the "sanctuary mode," will direct attention to architectural forms that simply provide boundaries between the wider, presumably more prosaic, environment and some special "sacred space" within which worshippers are afforded an experiential engagement with "the divine." And the third way of conceiving the relationship between architecture and religious experience, which I will term the "contemplation mode," involves built forms that serve as props for reflection and devotion, that is, built architectural configurations that devotees engage in direct and purposeful ways as objects of sustained, often meditative, attention.

Readers of my *Hermeneutics of Sacred Architecture* may recognize these as three of the eleven general sorts of so-called "ritual-architectural priorities" that I enumerate in that work.[2] In any case, of these three possibilities, it is the third—the one that deals with architecture and contemplation—that vexes me most in the present context; but discussion of the first two can prepare the way for my comments on the third.

THE COMPARATIVE HISTORY OF RELIGIONS AS A RESOURCE FOR MAKING ARCHITECTURE

Attending a symposium populated largely by architectural theorists and, yes, real architects, I feel myself very much a historian, or, more properly, a historian of religions who emerges from that hermeneutical school of thought that most readers probably know via the work of one of my teachers, Mircea Eliade. Operating from that disciplinary frame of reference, then, I should forewarn you that I am much more comfortable talking about what architecture, in various contexts, *has*

done in the past than about what architecture *could* or *should be doing* in the future. Neither ethical nor aesthetic judgments about good or bad architecture, nor prescriptive recommendations about how we can improve our built environment, are, as a rule, part of my scholarly game.

Moreover, while I share Eliade's generous bent toward all faith traditions, and thus am similarly uninclined to make rulings about good versus bad religion, you will note at several points my willingness to acknowledge that "religion," broadly conceived, can be an insidious and destructive as well as healthy and improving force in people's lives. In fact, where Eliade is routinely associated with a "hermeneutics of retrieval" wherein one celebrates the diversity of ingenious ways that people exercise their religious inclinations, and thus he is often criticized for inordinate generosity, this chapter is, in large part, an exercise in the more skeptical "hermeneutics of suspicion" wherein one brings to the fore discrepancies and distortions in the ways that previous scholars have interpreted architectures of old.[3] It is, in short, a contribution to—and an interrogation of—the history of ideas about supposedly sacred architecture.

Additionally, in the spirit of self-disclosure, I should note my childhood aspirations to becoming an architect—that is, a person who actually designs and builds something—got me only so far as an undergraduate degree in environmental design before I left (or maybe *descended* from) the world of "making" to that more humble universe wherein historians, critics, and theorists subsist via their second-order reflections on the world-shaping efforts of architects. This symposium has reaffirmed my self-deprecating surmise that architects are real athletes whose creative performances can engender standing ovations or, on occasion, similarly exuberant boos and brickbats; but historians are only commentators, wannabes, and "wished-they-weres" whose observations are, as a rule, easily ignored by all but their other academic cohorts.

On the one hand, then, my disappointed self-assessment that I lacked the "right stuff" to be an architect has left me with a very lofty—perhaps excessively charitable—assessment of those who do actually design and build things. To be sure, I hold many architects in awe and thus wonder why and how a mere historian of religions made it into this edited collection. But, on the other hand, I also persist with the opinion—or maybe hope—that historians of religions can indeed make a constructive contribution to the world-shaping efforts of working designers, and that hopeful confidence accounts in large part for my great pleasure at being included in a conversation where I feel like something of a black sheep. It is, in other words, my very strong opinion, for one, that we contemporary Westerners, professional designers included, tend to persist with quite impoverished appreciations of all that architecture can do in facilitating a richly rewarding religious life. But, for two, I am also convinced that a widely cross-cultural survey of the myriad of ways that architecture supports, frames, expresses, and enables "religious experience," again broadly conceived, can provide a very practical resource for working architects, that is to say, a valuable means of mitigating otherwise too-modest evaluations of all that built forms can do to enhance religious sensibilities.

In this respect, I am reminded of a little anecdote wherein an art instructor submits her students to a two-part drawing assignment. First, she asks them to remain at their desks, *imagine* a tree, and then draw it. Then the instructor requires the pupils to go outside, find a specific tree and draw that. The contrast between the two sets of sketches is drastic and telling. The exercise in imagination leads to uniformity, an abundance of those proverbial lollipop trees, more simple and symmetrical than any that one can find in nature. The second exercise—wherein the students conduct themselves more like empirically grounded historians of religions who train their attentions on specific cases—leads to vastly more diversified, intricately eccentric, and thus far more interesting depictions of "real trees." The dual point of the anecdote is, in other words, that our personal imaginations, invariably confined by our personal experiences and sociocultural horizons, remain very limited—but also that those limitations can be greatly alleviated, sometimes even exploded, by more wide-searching observations of what really is out there in the world.

With this appreciation of the richness of historical specificities in mind, I re-echo the comparative morphology of Mircea Eliade insofar as I draw ideas and inspiration from a host of deliberately far-spaced cross-cultural contexts; at the same time, I have, however, taken a special interest in the pre-Columbian architectures of Mesoamerica—that is, the built forms that persist as ruins at such sites as Teotihuacán, Chichén Itzá, Palenque, Tikal, and Monte Albán, all of which qualified in their primes as pre-Columbian cities. And thus, while raising some very general issues and engaging some widely disparate examples, I want to reflect especially on the supposed connections between built forms and religious experience in those ancient urban contexts.

More specifically, to the extent that this chapter ventures a somewhat original thesis, I will be arguing that students of Mesoamerican architecture—most notably, archaeologists and art historians—have had little trouble imaging that these ancient architectural configurations, when they were up and running as pre-Columbian cities, facilitated religious experiences in the first two ways that I enumerated at the outset. That is to say, lots of scholars and commentators have hypothesized (or often just assumed) that these huge stone structures were designed in order to, and seemingly succeeded in working as, either (a) the stage-setting for large-scaled and highly theatrical ritual proceedings or (b) boundary markers that delimited, or marked off, a privileged "sacred place" wherein one could partake of some sort of special engagement with "the divine." These first two possibilities have been well worked, indeed probably overworked; and I will suggest reasons why that has been the case. The third possibility, however—namely, that these stone formations were intended and utilized as, what I'll term, props to contemplation—is a possibility that has received, I think, too little serious consideration, at least among mainstream scholars. The impetus for this manuscript was, in other words, a troubled observation concerning the extreme unevenness with which the three modes have been respectively applied to pre-Columbian Mesoamerican architecture, especially the overrepresentation of the theatric mode and the severe underrepresentation of the contemplation mode.

I will explore that disconcertingly wide discrepancy by following the same three-step format for each of the three ways of conceiving the relation between built forms

and religious experience, though allowing greater time and attention for the third. In other words, for each possibility, I will first quickly characterize the alternative in very general terms; second, I will provide a couple of instructively salient exemplars of that heuristic option; and third I will inventory in a succinct fashion ways in which that alternative has (or has not) been deployed as an explanation of the logic of pre-Columbian Mesoamerican architecture. The final conclusions—which direct attention to the very large disparities between the respective ways in which professional scholars and "New Age" enthusiasts engage the ancient ruins—return to the possibility that consideration of these specific cases may (or may not) provide insights and inspirations for practicing architects, including those who are unencumbered by any special interest in Mesoamerica.

ARCHITECTURE AS THEATER: SETTING THE STAGE FOR RITUAL PERFORMANCE

The distinctions between these three alternatives—(a) architecture as stage-setting, (b) architecture as sanctuary, and (c) architecture as props for devotion—are heuristic and by no means absolute. Assuredly, in actual practice, these are, not infrequently, mutually supportive design strategies. Nevertheless, I can present them as three discrete alternatives or three "modes of ritual-architectural presentation," and thereby appreciate the very wide spectrum of different relations between built forms and religious experience, via consideration of two sorts of distinctions: *inclusivist* versus *exclusivist* experiences of architecture, and *direct* versus *indirect* experiences of architecture (see chart on p. 174).

This first so-termed "theatric" option,

	Indirect apprehensions of architectural forms: *Architecture as an ambience for ritual activity*	Direct apprehensions of architectural forms: *Architecture as an object of devotion*
Inclusive: Performative / spectator-oriented ritual events—*in which the priority is encouraging wide participation*	**Theater mode**	**Contemplation mode**
Exclusive: Cloistered, esoteric ritual events—*in which the priority is the protection of purity, sanctity*	**Sanctuary mode**	**Contemplation mode**

wherein built forms provide the backdrop for ritual performance, involves ritual-architectural configurations that are designed to be *inclusive* insofar as the incentive is more often to cajole spectators into involvement than to restrict access to the proceedings. In other words, by contrast to the second "sanctuary" alternative, wherein built forms are *exclusivist* insofar as they restrict access to some sacred place, theatric configurations are expressly inviting, enticing, welcoming, even seductive. The ceremonial proceedings that they support are, by and large, non-elitist and encouraging of widespread participation; these ritual events are more often collectivistic than individualized. Indeed, involvement in these events is, in many instances, mandatory and coerced rather than voluntary and self-initiated.

Moreover, with respect to the second tension, such theatric architectural arrangements enhance the experience of those ceremonial proceedings in an *indirect* fashion insofar as they involve the layout of the stages, backdrops, ambiences, and atmospheres that

enable and support those performative activities. That is to say, by contrast to the *direct* engagements that we will encounter in the third "contemplative" alternative, in this first option, the built forms themselves are not, for the most part, objects of the direct circumspections of ritual participants. In these cases, it would be more accurate to say that people experience *the ritual performances* that the architecture facilitates rather than experiencing the architecture per se. In these cases, the built forms are "working on" ceremonial patrons in *indirect* ways of which those persons are largely unaware.

Furthermore—and this helps to explain the deep ambivalence with which many assess this alternative—it is this theatrical option that draws us most fully into a swirl of subtly interrelated themes concerning not only ritual performance and persuasion but, more specifically, architecture's and ritual's relationships to emotion, sentiment, and sensory stimulation. In many instances, expressions of this mode involve the elaborations of pageantry, procession, and spectacle.

Here we are, generally speaking, trafficking in the *affective* dimension of the experience of sacred architecture, the evocation of awe, wonderment, and sentiment. Often loud and spine-tingling in their affect, theatrically presented architectural events, as a heuristic type, are those that work, in very concerted ways, to make an impression, to influence, touch, impress, sway, and persuade the assembled audiences and participants. In these events, where pomp and panache tend to prevail, feeling supersedes critical thinking.

Consequently, and perhaps not unfairly, of the three options, it is theatrical configurations that draw by far the most frequent accusations of both superficiality and manipulation. Often, this means of engaging an audience is assessed as a pandering to emotion, a kind of ceremonial sentimentality rather facilitation of a "real encounter" with the divine; instead of illuminating onlookers, they are simply aroused, maybe "juiced up" and titillated—and thus the charges of superficiality. Likewise, because this inclusivistic version of ritual-architectural choreography is designed to grab the attention of even reticent onlookers—in an important sense, to take control of their emotions and thereby rearrange their sentiments and convictions— there is, not surprisingly, a notoriously close relationship between highly dramatic ceremonialism and religiopolitical propagandizing. It is the theater mode that shows best architecture's potential for suasion, coercion, and ideological realignment, even against considerable resistance.

Thus, instead of deepening insights and awareness, these ritual-architectural experiences often do precisely the opposite insofar as disparities of socioeconomic power are obfuscated and reinforced; often, instead of enlightening, these events indoctrinate—and thus the charges of manipulation. Among ample relevant cases, the infamously exuberant public rallies of the Third Reich, assuredly "religious" rituals in some sense, provide quintessential exemplars of this mode of evoking attitude-altering experiences. That is to say, this theatrical mode may facilitate the sort of lofty, life-enhancing experiences that many discussions of architecture and "spirituality" are likely to celebrate, but they are likewise prone—much more prone than the other two options—to facilitate those sorts of "religious experiences" that are easily derided as disturbingly propagandistic, politically manipulative, mystifying, even conspiratorial. Here, then, the too-simple presumption that ostensibly sacred architecture prompts only high-minded and magnanimous "spiritual experiences" is quickly dispelled. Architecturally abetted ceremonialism is, to be sure, a resource that can be put to either altruistic or pernicious purposes.

SPECIFIC EXAMPLES: CHRISTIAN DEBATES OVER THE SUITABILITY OF THEATRICAL RITUAL

The highly emotive stagecrafting of Baroque architecture and statuary arguably provides the quintessential Western exemplar of this heuristic option. Nonetheless, for present purposes, a quick appeal to the interminable debate among Christians as to the suitability (or lack thereof) of such theatrical modes should help us appreciate the very mixed— in fact, invariably polarized—assessment that theatrical modes of ritual-architectural choreography spawn. On the one hand, Christians in numerous contexts have embraced highly theatric liturgical celebrations as assuredly the most expeditious means of making the faith both appealing and accessible, especially to the unlettered; and, on the other hand, there are Christian critics of a more iconoclastic bent who, with equal vigor and certainty, reject entirely the prospect that the essential truths of Christianity can be served via the elaboration of art, architecture, and ritual, least of all via the choreography of emotion- and sensory-driven ceremonialism.

Historical case in point: the competition and interaction between circular and longitudinal European church plans, and particularly the controversy and eventual rejection of Italian architect Donato Bramante's sixteenth-century design for the round rebuilding of Saint Peter's in Rome, illustrate very well a complex play of ritual-architectural priorities and the eventual victory of theatric—in this case, liturgical—considerations. In his account of that controversy, Rudolf Wittkower argues that the shift from the basilican cross form to centralized church plans was the architectural expression of a fundamentally changed conception of the godhead that separated the Middle Ages from the Renaissance: the medieval Christ, the "Man of Sorrows," suffered on the cross for humanity and the Latin cross plan was the symbolic expression of his crucifixion; by contrast, the Renaissance Christ was the essence of perfection and harmony, the "Pantocrator," whose truth and omnipotence were best captured in a mathematical architecture of centers, circles, and spheres.[4] Moreover, Wittkower notes that Christian martyria were likewise traditionally circular in plan.

Thus, whether Bramante conceived of Saint Peter's as an enormous martyrium for the Father of the Church,[5] or perhaps as an architectural symbol of God's perfection,[6] his original idea called for a centrally planned building. In either case, the circular plan was severely criticized as inadequate to the needs of ecclesiastical ceremony: It had no adequate sacristy, few chapels for the worship of individual saints, and, worst of all, no nave, a feature essential to house a large congregation and to provide a suitable setting for opulent liturgical processions.[7] That is to say, Bramante's plan could accommodate neither the lavish ritual proceedings nor, accordingly, the popular experiential sensations that large audiences could derive from their participation in those elaborate ceremonies. Accordingly, after several attempts at compromise, round symmetry was jettisoned in favor of the Latin cross plan—the most propitious stage to grand processionary ritual—that exists at Saint Peter's today.

The resistance to centrally planned churches, in other words, stemmed largely from the liturgical, and to that extent affective, potency that the basilican plan had demonstrated during the Romanesque period. The longitudinal shape, originally borrowed from the form of the pagan Roman basilica, had endured hundreds of years of transformation and refinement to bring it into accord with the demands of Christian ceremonialism, an evolution that perhaps culminated in the third abbey church of Cluny (1088–1130).[8] Even better than Saint Peter's, in fact, the similarly shaped Cluny church well demonstrates the ascendency of theatric, liturgical priorities insofar as, here, gigantic scale, munificent lavishness, and sublime symbolism collaborate in a longitudinal basilica that was designed, above all, to provide the backdrop for grandiose procession and ceremony. Of the single-minded agenda at Cluny, Wolfgang Braunfels, for instance, writes: "Building was to one end only: the life of the monks was almost exclusively devoted to the celebration of liturgy, to such long drawn-out services that by comparison meditation and study were virtually, and bodily labor wholly, neglected."[9] In the eyes of its patrons and priests, the opulent theatrics of Cluny, honed and refined over several generations, were unprecedentedly successful in evoking the desired flood of emotions; it was a masterful design solution to abet Christian liturgy and thus stimulate a distinct and, in their view, wholly legitimate sort of religious experience. Yet, from other, still-Christian perspectives, the very same agenda was condemned as completely misguided and inappropriate. Among the most articulate critics, Saint Bernard of Clairvaux, for example, espoused a radically different arrangement of ritual-architectural priorities and was, therefore, adamant that the ostentation of Cluny was an obstacle to proper Christian spirituality rather than an enhancement. According to Bernard, "the soaring heights and extravagant lengths and unnecessary widths of the churches, … their expensive decorations and their novel images, … catch the attention of those who go to pray, and dry up their devotion."[10]

Saint Bernard was prepared, it would then seem, to acknowledge that Cluny's ceremonialism was highly effective in evoking an experience of sorts—but it was, in his view, one that was actually distracting from, rather than in conformity with, the proper ideals of Christianity. He did not doubt that Cluny's shimmy and splendor incited intense experiences; but it was, in his view, the wrong type of experience. In Bernard's protestations, then—and even more in his own Cistercian monastic building program (a featured example relative to the forthcoming sanctuary mode)—we are apprised of a wide and very

enduring strain of Christian architecture that strives in a most deliberate fashion to absent itself from the theatrical mode (at least as I have defined it). Embracing plainness over grandeur, intellectualism over sensuality, the design tradition epitomized by Bernard's Cistercians and their Trappist inheritors—not unlike the great majority of Protestant architectures in this respect—does *not* aspire to foster an emotional sense of wonderment.

Nonetheless, albeit in a somewhat backhanded way, Bernard's condemnation of Cluny's ritual-architectural agenda constitutes a very strong affirmation of architecture's proficiency in educing powerful human experiences and emotions; but it is likewise a stern warning that architecture is even more proficient in evoking sensations that draw one away from Christianity than into the fold. According to Bernard—and, in the broad strokes, a host of later Protestant thinkers—architecture can, when configured in the very different ways that I will address with respect to the second alternative (i.e., "the sanctuary mode"), make fabulous contributions to the advancement of Christian spiritualities; but theatrical configurations—precisely because of their effectiveness in summoning intense sensations and passions—are invariably subject to skepticism and liable to be derided as among the most egregious obstacles to Christian advancement.

In any case, I turn now to the abundant, albeit ambivalent, ways in which this notion of architecture as theater has been applied to pre-Columbian Mesoamerican architecture, a context that provides yet another arena in which to debate the mixed merits of this mode of ritual-architectural choreography.

PRE-COLUMBIAN ARCHITECTURE AS THEATER: HEAPS OF CONGRATULATORY CONDEMNATION

Irrespective of the usually pejorative valences that accompany the assessment of architecture as "highly theatrical"—or, actually, precisely because of those negative connotations—this has been, assuredly, the most common way in which both lay and academic commentators have made sense of the enormous outlay of labor that ancient Mesoamericans invested in their architectural elaborations. From the Spanish Conquest forward, when confronted by the ruined remains of magnificent processional ways and "pageant-spaces" of ancient Mexico, even those reporters who were usually content with formal descriptions have been swept into imaginative (re)creations of the supposed histrionics of pre-Columbian ritual-architectural performances.[11] In the musings of seventeenth-century Spanish Franciscan historian López de Cogolludo, for instance, the long-abandoned and overgrown pyramids of Yucatan conjured simultaneously fascinating and repulsive images of the "horribly exciting" spectacle of Maya human sacrifice, which he guessed transpired atop those tall structures.[12] And for a Spanish bishop of the Roman Catholic Archdiocese of Yucatán, Diego de Landa, whose own grizzly orchestrations of sixteenth-century inquisitional ritual-architectural events demonstrated a "superb theatrical sense,"[13] those same ruins similarly evoked an imagined scene of the "great show and company of people," which, in his view, must have accompanied the steamy dramaturgy of Maya public ceremony.[14]

So, too, in the nineteenth century, British explorer Frederick Catherwood's imagination filled the still ruins of the Yucatec Maya with "great exhibitions of pomp and splendor," while his American traveling partner, John Lloyd Stephens, likewise envisaged "the theater of great events and imposing religious ceremonies" that must have characterized pre-Columbian Yucatan.[15] In the heart of the southern Maya zone, the obviously amphitheatric arrangement of the main court of Copán, bounded on three sides by artificial ramparts and low platforms, and on the fourth by a three-hundred-foot-wide stairway, inspired equally graphic imaginings of ritual spectacle and panache: Guatemalan historian and poet Francisco de Fuentes (c. 1700) pictured "the great circus of Copán";[16] American art historian Herbert Spinden considered that "the plaza [of Copán] is surrounded by a stepped wall as if it were a sort of theater";[17] and art historian Pal Kelemen, going directly for a parallel to the theatrical Baroque churches of Bernini, described the Copán plaza as "an ideal arena … Baroque it is—in feeling, in its complication of design and ebullience of detail, in the dramatic dynamics of its whole conception, in the untrammeled freedom of its execution … a ceremony witnessed here must have been immensely awe-inspiring."[18]

By the same token, the long vacant and dilapidated but still sumptuous mountaintop Great Plaza of Monte Albán inspired William Henry Holmes (1895), a typically impassive American archaeologist, to muse that "civilization has rarely conceived anything in the way of amphitheatric display more extensive and imposing than this,"[19] an assessment re-echoed a hundred years later when art historian George Kubler was moved to an uncharacteristic flourish on "the stirring fusion of stone and ritual … the sumptuous life of religious pageantry" that must have transpired on the platforms

FIGURE 12-1. THE GREAT PLAZA AT THE ZAPOTEC SITE OF MONTE ALBÁN, OAXACA, A MESOAMERICAN SITE IN THE "THEATRIC MODE." SCHOLARS HAVE OFTEN CONCLUDED THAT THE BUILT FORMS PROVIDED THE STAGE-SETTING FOR DRAMATIC CEREMONIAL OCCASIONS THAT PRESUMABLY AROUSED MANY PARTICIPANTS AND ONLOOKERS TO TRANSFORMATIVE EXPERIENCES.

and stairways of Monte Albán, "the most grandiose of all American temple centers."[20] And likewise in the Aztec case, even William Prescott (1843), among the first to bring what he termed the "horrid wonders" of Aztec ritual to North American readers, despite his inclination to characterize the "barbarian" Mexica as superstitious heathens rather than astute politicians, nevertheless imagined the gory showmanship of human sacrifice at the Templo Mayor was intended more for the large audience than for the actual participants, let alone for the deities of Mesoamerica. In Prescott's Victorian prose: "From the

FIGURE 12-2. THE GREAT PLAZA OF CHICHÉN ITZÁ CAN
COMFORTABLY ACCOMMODATE THE MORE THAN THIRTY
THOUSAND VISITORS WHO ATTEND THE DESCENT OF
THE "SERPENT OF LIGHT" ALONG THE BALUSTRADE OF
THE MAIN CASTILLO PYRAMID EACH SPRING EQUINOX.
SUCH ARCHITECTURAL SPACES WERE SITES OF THE CER-
EMONIAL EVENTS CHARACTERISTIC OF THE THEATRIC
MODE.

construction of [the Aztecs'] temples, all religions services were public. The long processions ascending their massive sides, as they rose higher and higher toward the summit, and the dismal rites of the sacrifice which were performed there, were all visible from the remotest corners of the capital, impressing on the spectator's mind a superstitious veneration for the mysteries of his religion, and for the dread ministers by whom they were interpreted."[21]

The romantic excesses of Prescott notwithstanding, state-of-the-art excavation and interpretation of the Aztecs' Templo Mayor have done little to dispel his vision either of the lushness of the ceremonial theatrics or of the inclusivistically public character of the proceedings. Ethnohistorian Johanna Broda, for instance, explains how each successive Aztec ruler enlarged the Templo Mayor, not in its entirety but particularly in a fashion that produced an increasingly spectacular frontal view;[22] it was appearances that mattered most. Moreover, Broda recounts how, in the wake of each remodeling, selected lords of allies and enemies alike were then invited—or, more properly, forced—to witness extravagant inaugurations that began with displays of the architectural embellishments and tributes of luxury goods from the conquered provinces and then climaxed in massive human sacrifices of captives from resisting populations.[23] Likewise, historian of religions David Carrasco has also emphasized that the Aztecs' Templo Mayor ceremonials were, among other things, spectacular "dramas of intimidation" wherein motion, color, sound, and gesture were all choreographed with a very specific audience in mind: "The ritual extravaganza was carried out with maximum theatrical tension, paraphernalia

and terror in order to amaze and intimidate the visiting dignitaries who returned to their kingdoms trembling with fear and convinced that co-operation and not rebellion was the best response to Aztec imperialism."[24]

In sum, then, with respect to this first option, there is a surfeit of commentators— and, believe me, I could assemble many more—for whom the notion of highly emotive, lavishly orchestrated public ceremony provides the most obvious way of (re)conceptualizing the design logic that led to these huge pre-Columbian urban complexes. That is to say, rather than overlooking the prospect of architecture as theater, that notion provides the default hypothesis for what was happening when these ruins were in full operation as living cities. But there is also a deep ambivalence in those assessments. On the one hand, ancient Mesoamericans are praised and congratulated for their triumphs in ritual-architectural showmanship. In that technical respect, pre-Columbian architects win enthusiastic commendations for demonstrating a skill at ritual-architectural choreography that rivals, or perhaps even exceeds, that of Cluny or Bernini.

On the other hand, however, those approbations are invariably laced with even stronger negative evaluations insofar as the Aztecs' and Mayas' proficient preoccupation with glitzy and gory ritual is utilized as among the surest signs of their barbarity. Not unlike Saint Bernard's judgment that the refinement of Cluny's ceremonial dramaturgy actually signaled superficiality and misplaced priorities, assessments of ancient Mesoamericans as ritual showmen of the highest order is a version of praise that actually eventuates in a condescending dismissal of their culture and religion. Imagining these great urban complexes as, first and foremost, "theaters of intimidation," wherein shock-and-awe ritual strategies—most notably, dramatically staged human sacrifices—prevailed, allows one to dismiss the ancient Indian rulers as self-serving totalitarians and the native masses as superstitious, easily manipulated pawns to their leaders' ritual-architectural propaganda. In short, the pervasive focus on the theatrical quality of Mesoamerican architecture leads to (or arises from) deeply ambivalent assessments that their design initiatives are spectacular but not sophisticated, provocative but not profound, stirring but not subtle.

In any case, I will have more to say concerning the forces that underlie this frequency with which pre-Columbian architecture has been interpreted as an expression of primarily theatrical incentives; but let me first turn toward the second way of conceiving the relationship between built forms and religious experience—namely, architecture as sanctuary.

ARCHITECTURE AS SANCTUARY: DELIMITING CONTROLLED AND SACRED SPACES

A second, much less ambiguous way of conceiving of the relationship between built forms and religious experience—a very widely recognized option that I address under the rubric of "architecture as sanctuary"—depends upon the demarcation of a "threshold,"[25] that is, a boundary, limit, frontier, or picket between, in Eliadean terms, two "modes of being"—between "a profane outside" and "a sacred inside."[26] In the emblematic case of a walled city or compound, for instance, Eliade contends that outside one may have the not-altogether-rewarding sensation of the ordinary and mundane, of

chaos, confusion, and danger; but to be inside opens the possibility of experiencing the security, "reality," and "being" that come only via accessibility to "the Sacred."[27]

As privileged places that open the way to privileged experiences, sanctuary shelters and enclosures have the appearance, however illusory, of perfection, if only within tightly circumscribed boundaries. Historian of religion Jonathan Smith, for example, directs attention to what is distinctive about this second alternative when he argues that a crucial feature of a sanctuary space is not some qualitatively different ontological status but rather that it has been "marked off" and then carefully groomed with such deliberation and meticulous order that nothing random or insignificant is allowed to remain. And, as Smith explains, that exclusion of disorder and distraction has a salient experiential effect: "When one enters a temple, one enters marked-off space (the usual example, the Greek *temenos*, derived from *temno*, 'to cut') in which, at least in principle, nothing is accidental; everything, at least potentially, demands attention. The temple serves as a focusing lens, establishing the possibility of significance by directing attention, by requiring the perception of difference. Within the temple, the ordinary (which to any outside eye or ear remains wholly ordinary) becomes significant, becomes 'sacred,' simply by being there."[28]

This option, then, which engenders none of the ambivalence associated with the theatrically staged ritual-architectural events, may seem, at first, to be essentially synonymous with many generic conceptions of "sacred space." Again, however, the distinctions between (a) inclusivist versus exclusivist and (b) direct versus indirect experiences of architecture can be useful in appreciating sanctuary as an option different from either the so-termed theatric or contemplative modes. Unlike the embracing, *inclusivist* pageant spaces and public spectacles typically associated with the theatric mode, the delimitation of a sanctuary space is invariably characterized by a measure of *exclusion* and restricted access. Instead of persuading even reticent onlookers into involvement, often by appeals to emotion, sanctuary configurations are designed to guard the integrity of the occasion by limiting involvement to some select socioreligious contingency. Sanctuary spaces fence in and fence out, thus blocking access, insulating, and protecting the sanctity, or maybe insidious secrecy, of the ceremonial (or perhaps not-so-ceremonious) proceedings.

Nonetheless, the architecture in theatrical configurations works on ritual participants in largely *indirect* ways that are effective irrespective of worshippers' self-conscious awareness of the built forms. In sanctuary configurations, people are really experiencing the space delimited by the architecture rather than the constructed features themselves. Unlike contemplation modes, to which I will turn next—that is, circumstances wherein worshippers engage the physical forms of architecture in *direct* and purposeful ways— sanctuary spaces facilitate religious experience *indirectly*, by creating an environment of special possibility. As a heuristic possibility, the so-termed sanctuary mode, like the theatric mode in this respect, is *not* concerned with the presentation and apprehension of actual objects of devotion but instead with the construction of a ritual ambience, a background or setting that can then serve to facilitate any number of very different sorts of subsequent ceremonial and/or meditative

proceedings. Even immediately after an event within such a controlled space, however, again not unlike many theatric arrangements, worshippers may have considerable difficulty in describing in any detail the physical aspects of the environment. Sanctuary configurations, which frequently do little more than demarcate between a prosaic outside and a sacred inside, often succeed by their inconspicuousness.

SPECIFIC EXAMPLES: JEWISH SYNAGOGUES, ROMAN ARCHITECTURE, AND CISTERCIAN MONASTERIES

Though this alternative is straightforward enough not to require great elaboration, three brief cases exemplify architectural programs that explicitly eschew more ambitious roles in favor of the modest function of differentiating a sacred inside from profane outside. In the first case, Jews, consonant with their celebrated iconoclasm, are, however (in)appropriately, sometimes awarded credit as "the first to voluntarily assemble to erect a structure for prayer and study, *and not to house a visible God*."[29] Though claims both to chronologic priority and drastic discontinuity with past practice are overstated, according to this argument, the architecture and institution of the synagogue (from the Greek word meaning "assembly" or "assembling together"), which arose largely in response to the destruction of the Jerusalem Temple, was, in spirit and use, the very opposite of the ancient Near Eastern temple or, for that matter, of the tabernacle and the Jewish temple of earlier times.[30] Instead of symbolic "Houses of God" designed to signal the glory of the Almighty or cultic centers designed to facilitate ritual sacrifices, synagogues were originally conceived simply as meetinghouses for prayer—that is, sanctuary spaces—the efficacy of which depended neither on any specific physical form nor location. Entirely different from Cluny's evocation of highly emotive "religious experiences" via splendiferous ceremonialism, synagogues were designed to cultivate the sort of intellectualized "religious experiences" that one achieves via communal study and prayer.

The early synagogue constituted, then, ironically, a special place in which Jews experimented with the possibility that one's devotional obligations to God could be fulfilled in *any* place, not only in the now-desecrated Jerusalem Temple. Since these structures had more the character of schools than shrines, here the architecture was called upon to do considerably less; the design agenda was more modest. Instead of marking the site of some hierophanic manifestation of God or even the place of some fateful event in Jewish sacred history, synagogues were located wherever there was a community of Jews, providing, in a sense, a kind of "portable fatherland."[31] Moreover, unlike most exhortative, inclusivistic, theatrically arranged ritual contexts, there was little attempt to beckon or even allow the involvement of outsiders. Likewise, the notion that worshippers would meditate directly upon the actual architectural features (as in the contemplative mode, to which I turn next) was repugnant to iconoclastic Jews. And furthermore, unlike most propitiatory exercises in buildings wherein one expects some sort of "cosmic compensation" for undertaking the labor and expense of erecting religious structures, both the synagogue's visual appearance and mode of construction (or often simply the expropriation of an existing construction) were largely inconsequential so long as the congregation was, in the end, afforded a safe interior space in which to study the Torah, pray, and foster a sense of community in Diaspora.

A second, similarly strong demonstration of the historical ascendancy of the sanctuary mode—and thus of a building agenda of containment, control, and exclusion—though stimulated by quite different sociocultural forces, comes in Vincent Scully's account of the transition from Hellenistic to a radically divergent tradition of Roman building.[32] In Scully's view, the Classic Greek temple was outstanding both for its reciprocal relationship with nature, its "outward-looking design" as he terms it, and for its sculptural representation of the abstract attributes of specific deities, say, Hera, Demeter, Artemis, or Aphrodite. While wide-open in a certain respect, Classic temples provided virtually no sheltering space and thus served less as "ritual contexts" per se into which officiates and worshippers entered than as sculpture-like objects of meditation and reflection, in Scully's phrase "articulated sculptural bodies," which were viewed and appreciated from outside. In that respect, then, the experience of Classic Greek temples instantiates the sort of direct engagement of built forms characteristic of the contemplative mode.

The incentives and uses of Roman building were, however, Scully argues, profoundly different in virtually all important respects. Instead of an intimate integration of architecture and nature wherein apprehensions of the built forms were inseparable from those of the features of the landscape, Roman builders, generally speaking, aimed for complete disconnectedness from the landscape—that is, for the creation of highly restrictive sanctuary spaces. "Roman theaters, like those at

Orange in southern France and Aspendos in Asia Minor," Scully explains, "were intended, like most Roman buildings, to provide an enclosed experience totally shut away from the outside world."[33] In a military empire like that of Rome, then, the objectives of security and dominion ascended to priority even in the realm of explicitly religious architecture so that, unlike the Classic Greek temple's sculptural analogy to the attributes of a deity, the Roman temple was rigidly symmetrical, logical, self-sufficient, and bastioned.[34] Again venturing to accomplish somewhat less (religiously speaking) with the actual built forms, the fabric of the Roman structure was no longer itself holy; it, like the Jewish synagogue, simply enclosed space—and thereby provided an ambience for the cultivation of a more thoughtful than emotive version of religious experience.

Third, while all monasteries are pertinent to this discussion, the building agendum of Saint Bernard of Clairvaux and his Cistercians provides the consummate exemplar of what I am terming the sanctuary mode. Bernard is especially instructive, first, because of his explicit, fully informed, and vehement rejection of the similarly Catholic logic that had eventuated in the opulent decoration, sculpture, stained glass, and towers of Cluny; he rejected, in other words, the appropriateness of decidedly theatric modes of ritual-architectural presentation. Even more famously well documented and equally adamant (though somewhat qualified) is Bernard's patent dismissal of the anagogical Gothic machinations of his contemporary, Abbot Suger, whom I will discuss momentarily in connection with contemplation modes.[35] Not only was Bernard certain that Christian ritual-architectural agenda should

not be working to further the socioeconomic interests of the state, nor was he favorably disposed to the notion, which Suger among many promulgated, that a Christian church building could serve in some tangible sense as "the house of God."[36]

Alternatively, Bernard, in formulating the design of Cistercian communities, imagined that a church building ought to be first and foremost an oratorium, the place of the soul's communion with God, a kind of sanctuary within a sanctuary insofar as he believed also that the entire monastery complex ought to be a pristine, autonomous refuge wherein all energies were enlisted in perfect conformity to the Rule of Saint Benedict.[37] Life in the Cistercian cloister was to be an image and foretaste of paradise, an ideal that Bernard termed "*paradisus claustralis.*"[38] The monastic ideal espoused then and now required a lifestyle of compromiseless devotion to God: "Everything in our life tends to protect us from the turmoil of the world and of our passions, to guarantee us solitude of the spirit, the heart and the will, in order that our monasteries may be sanctuaries of silence filled with the fragrance of prayer."[39]

To achieve that ideal, then, unlike the overtly politicized ritual-architectural agenda of Abbot Suger, Bernard (who was by no means oblivious to the wider, worldlier ramifications of his plan of action) opted for a monochromatic architecture of simplicity and geometrical clarity. Instead of stimulating the senses, he aspired to austere architectural configurations that would quiet them; instead of winning converts, his more exclusivist approach aimed to facilitate the ideals of poverty, retreat from the world, and a renewed spirit of Benedictine regulation. It is ironic, then, but perhaps not too surprising, that Bernard's economical plan for Clairvaux won sufficient acclaim that it was repeated in some 742 Cistercian monasteries, virtually all of which were located at similarly remote rural sites—and while visitors to these monasteries may well feel a kind of stirring of emotion, in principle, the built forms are not doing anything more than delimiting a space in which dedicated and disciplined Christians can undertake their fully clearheaded engagements with the divine.

PRE-COLUMBIAN ARCHITECTURE AS SANCTUARY: WIDESPREAD NONCONTROVERSIAL ACKNOWLEDGMENTS

As an explanation for the logic of numerous features of pre-Columbian Mesoamerican ritual-architecture design, the sanctuary mode has been invoked with only somewhat less regularity than the theatric option—though I should note, with none of the ambivalence that is associated with ritual-architectural dramaturgy. To the contrary, this is a heuristic possibility that anthropologists and religionists working in nearly every cultural context have recognized, and there has been no reason to suspect that ancient Mesoamericans would stand as an exception to the apparently universal urgency for clearly partitioning the exceptional from the prosaic in every architectural medium and scale. It is, quite plainly, what people do. In fact, while there may be vigorous disagreement as to whether the devotional activities that Toltecs, Aztecs, and Mayas undertake within their sanctuary spaces are best characterized as astute, vulgar, or simply specious, there is virtual unanimity that the meticulous delimiting of specific zones in which to conduct those ritual exercises is entirely healthy and normal. Accordingly, a very brief sampling of the abundant observations relative to the sanctuary option should be adequate to signal the widely acknowledged diversity and ingenuity with which pre-Columbian designers pursued this mode of ritual-architectural presentation.

Perhaps the most elemental strategy for acknowledging specially sacred places amidst the wider environment is the expropriation of some sort of natural sanctuary, most obviously, a cave, or "a womb of the earth" as they are so often conceived; such places are alluring already by virtue of seemingly inherent cosmological or mythological significance. The spectacular system of underground passageways at Balankanche near Chichén Itzá is but one of countless examples wherein ancient Mesoamericans co-opted natural caves as ritual-architectural "sanctuaries" with the confidence that such caverns are intrinsically potent places wherein the efficacy of their ritual propitiations would be greatly intensified.[40] Likewise, very common are those circumstances in which the sanctity and potent rebirth symbolism of entering and exiting a cave is architecturally (re)created quite apart from any natural cavern. The abundant cave-like "earth monster" temples of the Rio Bec-Chenes area with their face-like facades and tooth-lined doorways, a luridly elegant effect that Paul Gendrop describes as "mythical surrealism," provide one large set of exemplars;[41] and art historian Richard Townsend comments, for instance, on the sense in which the Mt. Tlaloc temple enclosure in the mountains outside the Aztec capital was "a diagrammatic womb of the earth, containing the source of water and regenerative forces," an artificial sanctuary configured to resemble a natural one.[42]

Though the incentive to build cave-like structures eventuated in many very elaborate constructions, other Mesoamerican sanctuary configurations are of the most unextravagant and transient sort. Bishop Diego de Landa, for instance, provides the quaint example of four sixteenth-century Maya priests holding a rope to tether off a temporary sacred context for the performance of the *emku* or Yucatecan coming-of-age ceremony;[43] and Karen Bassie-Sweet contributes the parallel southern Maya case of a "tying dance" at Copán wherein a cord was apparently stretched around four inner columns, presumably in order to form "a quadrilateral space just as the deities tied off the quadrilateral world."[44] That is to say, from a Maya view, even the gods are inclined to exercise this version of spatial planning.

Other Mesoamerican expressions of this mode involve only slightly more elaborate and lasting structures that serve as preparatory refuges, that is, transitional spaces to which ritual celebrants retreat for a matter of hours, days, or even months, either to cultivate a sense of renewal or, in other cases, to purify themselves in advance of their participation in the main ritual event. Bishop Bartolomé de las Casas, for instance, reported that the highland Mayas in Guatemala were "accustomed to separate from their wives and take up residence in special men's houses near the temples for 60, 80, or even 100 days before some great festival"; and, in the same vein, Landa observed that before major ceremonies in Yucatan, "all had to sleep, not in their homes, but in houses which for the time of the penance were near the temples."[45]

Along with these temporary and transitional sanctuary spaces, there is, of course, a plethora of larger and more substantial

FIGURE 12-3. MESOAMERICAN ARCHITECTURE, WHILE LARGELY DEVOID OF LARGE INTERIOR SPACES, DOES FEATURE COUNTLESS WINDOWLESS AND NARROW STRUCTURES SUCH AS THIS MAYA BUILDING IN THE INITIAL SERIES GROUP AT CHICHÉN ITZÁ, CHARACTERISTIC OF THE "SANCTUARY MODE." IN THIS SACRED SPACE, WORSHIPERS COULD ENGAGE WITH "THE DIVINE."

FIGURE 12-4. CONFIGURATIONS LIKE THE SUNKEN PATIO AT MONTE ALBÁN INSTANTIATE THE MUTUALLY SUPPORTIVE DESIGN STRATEGIES OF THE SANCTUARY MODE AND THE THEATRIC MODE. ALL WHO ASSEMBLE WITHIN THE RECESSED PLAZA ARE URGED TO TRAIN THEIR ATTENTIONS ON RITUAL PERFORMANCES THAT OCCUR ON THE CENTRAL PLATFORM.

expressions of the need to control and restrict access. Archaeologists working at nearly every site comment on walls and gateways that, while ostensibly serving military purposes, invariably functioned also—not infrequently, *only*—to differentiate in very clear ways between profane and sacred spaces. Monte Albán, for instance, is just one of numerous ancient cities wherein an extensive system of walls apparently served both as very practical fortifications and as symbolic dividers between the rigorously controlled urban space and the wider, wilder surroundings. Additionally, to cite an even more ingenious ritual-architectural means of differentiating that which is normal (or profane) from that which is special (or sacred), the pre-Hispanic designers at work in the lush tropical forests of southern Mesoamerica relied on blocky monumental forms accentuated by rigid straight lines and bright colors, which, as Broda explains, "created an artificial order in contraposition to nature; [such design tactics] imposed a new structure, a 'human order' upon the 'natural order.'"[46]

Finally, while carving out refuges and controlled spaces may appear at first a means of *dis*engaging from social conventions and hierarchies, scholars are likewise quick to note even more Mesoamerican instances in which sanctuary configurations work to reinforce and perpetuate the status quo. In the simple two-room plan of the pre-Hispanic Zapotec *yohepèe*, for example, literally the "house of *pè*" (i.e., of wind, breath, or spirit), the outer room that one encounters first at the top of the stairway entrance was open to anyone who wished to make an offering; the actual sacrifices, however, were performed on an altar called the *pecogo* or *pe-quie* (the stone of *pè*) in a second, "more sacred" room to which no lay-

person was ever admitted, but that the priests rarely left.[47] At the scale of whole settlements, Landa describes the concentric arrangement of sixteenth-century Yucatecan Maya villages, like Mayapan for instance, wherein there was an unmistakable correlation between levels of social prestige and access to the sacred center: "The houses of the lords and priests [were at the center of the city, near to the temples], and then those of the most important people.... [Then] came the houses of the richest and those who were held in highest estimation nearest to them, and at the outskirts of town were the houses of the lower class."[48]

Robert Carmack likewise describes a pre-Columbian sociospatial circumstance in the Quiché Maya capital of Utatlán in Guatemala wherein residents' social identities were defined in a fully public way by the structures that they could or could not enter: "Buildings occupied by the lineages became as important symbolically as the lineages themselves—hence the name *nim ja* ('big house') as the general term for lineage."[49] In short, controlled access to architectural spaces and access to social influence were mirror reflections of one another.

To summarize then, in ancient Mesoamerica, just as in virtually all traditional contexts, the utilization of architecture simply as a means of containment and controlled access has been undertaken with diversity, ingenuity, and great frequency—and those efforts have been widely acknowledged. By contrast to theatric modes, sanctuary configurations are *exclusionist* (not inclusionist) insofar as they fence out "profane" distractions, unsuitable people included, and thereby "mark off" an ambience of possibility in which devotees are allowed, so long as they do their worshipful part, an engagement with the exceptional and "sacred"; but, by contrast to the so-termed contemplation mode (to which my attention now turns), the built forms in these cases contribute to religious experiences only *indirectly*. In sanctuary configurations, the physical elements are called upon to do little more than cordon off a zone of purity and perfect order, in short, to distinguish an inside from the outside. Thus, instead of either congratulations or condemnations, the Mesoamerican demarcation of sanctuary spaces has been assessed, by and large, as neither deficient nor outstanding; it is simply par for the course, if you will. Probably because such sanctuary configurations afford art and architecture the sort of modest and indirect role in facilitating religious worship that even Protestant skeptics of ritual can accept; pre-Columbian exercises of this mode evoke no accusations of superficiality, superstition, or heathenism. This is, by far, the least controversial of the three options.

At any rate, consider now another more vigorously contested alternative in which the demands and expectations of architecture's role in the cultivation of religious experience are both more direct and far more grandiose.

ARCHITECTURE AND CONTEMPLATION: PROVIDING DIRECT CATALYSTS TO SPIRITUAL ASCENT

In Puebla, a state in central Mexico famously abundant with spectacularly tiled, carved, and stuccoed colonial churches, two modestly sized but stupendously decorated exemplars stand out: Santa María Tonantzintla and Santuario San Francisco Acatepec.[50] Both reflect the paired efforts of Spanish architects and indigenous craftsmen. As though the winners in some tournament to create

the most crowdedly ornamental facades and surfaces, the interior of each of these small nineteenth-century churches features literally hundreds of small cherubic faces scattered through a riot of gold-leafed Churrigueresque decoration in which Catholic motifs are integrated with indigenous ones. Upon entering either structure, the earliest in a chain of sensations is an experience of affectivity as visitors are stunned or surprised by its decorative, histrionic hyperbole. Sitting in the back near the door, one hears an audible gasp from nearly everyone who enters, particularly if this is their first time.

The initial sensation of these Mexican churches, which can be overwhelming, is, then, of that emotive sort characteristic of the experience of the theater mode. But then, very likely (at least in my experience), this very same fantastic array of angelic visages sustains continued interest as the patron's attention fastens on one, or maybe a series, of the exuberant elements in the decoration as a kind of mandala-like object of meditation. The beholder's mode of architectural apprehension, the nature of one's relationship to the built forms, can shift, in other words, perhaps in the matter of a few moments, from that of the theatrical sort to that which is characteristic of what I now consider under the rubric of the "contemplation mode."

Consequently, where, in the cases considered thus far, built forms contribute to the experience of ritual *in*directly, either by crafting constructional elements into a stage for the performance and witness of ritual enactments (as in the theater mode) or by providing an environment of distractionless purity (as in the sanctuary mode), my present concern is with a sort of ritual-architectural presentation in which the link between building elements and worshippers is *direct*, purposeful, immediate, and unmitigated. These are ritual-architectural events that depend on the explicit engagement with, or sustained meditative attention on, the actual physical forms of the architecture itself. The so-termed contemplation mode, in other words, concerns architecture that serves variously as an object of concentration, a prop or focus for devotion, an aid to spiritual exercise or ascent, a support or a guide—in short, a *direct* catalyst to religioritual experience. With respect to this alternative, we encounter frequently claims that the architectural elements are not just helpful but instead are absolutely crucial in instigating the subsequent religious experience.

Regarding that tension between inclusive versus exclusive modes, the term contemplation, which I am using here in a quite specific if somewhat idiosyncratic way, connotes a whole complex of introspective, perhaps esoteric meditative practices; and indeed, many expressions of the contemplation alternative are, like the sanctuary mode, *exclusivistic* insofar as they restrict access to a minority of largely self-selected, sophisticated, and deep-thinking religious experts. But as the example of the Puebla churches and others that I will cite momentarily demonstrate, even more often the cache of the contemplation mode, like the *inclusivistic* theater mode, is its ability to reach unschooled and less than fully enthusiastic audiences. Thus, where the contemplation mode may find its most glamorous instantiation in highly self-reflective, rarified, and esoteric art-assisted introspections of monks and mystics, this mode of ritual-architectural presentation can pertain likewise in unremarkably mundane, pedantic, and popular devotions—say, direct and purposeful interactions with paintings,

posters, banners, stained glass, statues, stelae, and totem poles, as well as with geometrically decorated floors, domes, and towers. In short, while, by heuristic definition, every expression of contemplation mode depends upon a concentrated, sustained, and productive engagement with the physical features of architecture, this may involve either *exclusive* or *inclusive* audiences.

Likewise, as in the case of the theatric mode, there is, in principle, no reason why "contemplative" engagements with art and architecture could not be put to malicious as well as beneficent and mind-expanding purposes; and recall that Saint Bernard, for instance, speaks for a very large (and otherwise diversified) iconoclastic camp when he argues that art-reliant programs of religious proselytism like that of Abbot Suger's Gothic cathedral (to be discussed momentarily) involve trade-offs that make them ultimately deterrents rather than aids to healthy spiritual development. The contemplative mode, like the theatric, has harsh critics as well as staunch supporters. Yet, *un*like the theatric mode, scholarly treatments of this less discussed possibility, as a general rule, display much less of the ambivalence and far fewer charges of superficiality and political manipulativeness than do discussions of highly theatrical ritual-architectural histrionics. To the contrary, scholars who train their attentions on this sort of deliberative, "contemplative" engagement with art and architecture tend generally—and generously (maybe overgenerously)—to associate it with personal spiritual enhancement rather than socioeconomic manipulation.

Anthropologist Jacques Maquet, for instance, describes the "contemplative encounter" between art object and beholder as less methodical, intense, and "radical" than meditation per se, but nonetheless "a special mode of consciousness," an "insight-oriented process" that is irreducible either to cognition or to affectivity, which participates in the character of meditation insofar as it entails a "disinterested engrossment."[51] Philosopher of aesthetics Harold Osborne argues similarly that purposeful encounters with art and architecture invariably entail a "weakening of the ego," "nonattachment," or a "reduction of self-interest."[52] These contentions that, to an important degree, "selflessness makes contemplation possible and thus is reinforced by contemplation,"[53] likewise accord with Hans-Georg Gadamer's notion that the "productivity" of such deliberative encounters with art and architecture is largely contingent on a measure of self-abandonment and acceptance of vulnerability as one enters "the closed world" of the work, accepts the wager that the situation offers, and thus commits to abiding by rules that may be less than pleasant.[54] And art historian David Freedberg puts a similarly affirmative, apolitical spin on what he terms "image-assisted meditation" when he writes that "the aim of this kind of meditation is to grasp what is absent, whether historical or spiritual. It is predicated on the view that since our minds are labile, meditation profitably begins in concentration. By concentrating on physical images [or perhaps on an architectural form], the natural inclination of the mind to wander is kept in check, and we ascend with increasing intensity to the spiritual and emotional essence of that which is represented in material form before our eyes—our external eyes and not the eyes of our mind."[55]

In short, albeit an imperfect generalization, scholars who devote serious attention to the so-termed contemplation mode (irrespective of whether or not they use that precise term) have tended to assess these sorts of engagements with built forms, whether deservingly or not, as signs of spiritual sincerity, sophistication, and even selflessness—a positive affirmation that, I'll opine in the following discussion, accounts in large part for the very oddly skewed application of this alternative to pre-Columbian Mesoamerican architecture. But before turning to that context, consider first a couple of famously pertinent cross-cultural examples.

SPECIFIC EXAMPLES: GOTHIC CATHEDRALS AND BUDDHIST MANDALA ARCHITECTURE

In a longer chapter, I could provide, for instance, Egyptian and Hindu examples of this same sort of expansive expectation for a very direct role of architectural forms in the enhancement of religious experience.[56] Even among Muslims, especially but not strictly within Sufi traditions, one finds architecture conceived as a means of "structuring" that facilitates contemplative ascents from "the Manifest" (*Zahir*) to "the Hidden" (*Batin*).[57] But for present purposes, two very prominent, deliberately far-spaced, examples should suffice to reveal this as a distinct heuristic alternative.

The first is Abbot Suger's much-discussed deployment of Dionysius the Pseudo-Areopagite's metaphysical theory of anagogical illumination to the realm of Gothic architecture. As noted, Christians debate at great length among themselves the appropriate role (or lack thereof) of art and architecture in religious devotion. If Saint Bernard represents an especially articulate spokesman for only highly restricted and indirect reliance on architecture, his French contemporary, Abbot Suger, provides an even more fascinating counterargument via his total confidence that images and works of art can indeed facilitate a "transport from the material to the immaterial," an assertion that finds its most spectacular architectural climax in his conception of the Gothic cathedral.

Abbot Suger's innovative design for the abbey church at St. Denis near Paris, often termed "the first Gothic cathedral," provides the preeminent example particularly because he produced a manuscript that thoroughly documents what he hoped to achieve with his massive twelfth-century building program. Among the most fortuitous documents in architectural history, Suger's treatise makes explicit both his intention to adapt fully the Pseudo-Areopagite's anagogical theory to the realm of architecture, and, moreover, his obvious self-satisfaction in having succeeded.[58] Invoking beautifully expansive language, Suger explains how contemplation of the architectural elements of St. Denis, in this case the precious stones and altar ornaments, lifted him (and, presumably, anyone else who visits there) out of his quotidian boundedness, up to a "strange region" of ethereal bliss, which lies somewhere between heaven and earth. Few statements capture better what is at issue in this presentational mode than Suger's poetical account of his own personally transformative apprehension of St. Denis:

When—out of my delight in the beauty of the house of God—the loveliness of the many-colored stones has called me away from external cares, and worthy meditation has induced me to reflect, transferring that which is material to that which is immaterial, on the diversity of the sacred virtues: then it seems to me that I see myself dwelling, as it were, in some strange region of the universe which neither exists entirely in the slime of the earth nor entirely in the purity of Heaven; and that by the grace of God, I can be transported from this inferior to that higher world in an anagogical manner.[59]

Suger, then, like the designers of Borobudur's massive gilded surfaces and flamboyant narrative reliefs that I will discuss next,[60] contrived at St. Denis, in every way possible, to construct an atmosphere of sumptuousness and ostentation. The dramatic effect is unmistakable, and there is most assuredly an appeal to the senses. Yet the (anticipated) experience of the Gothic, again like that of Borobudur, is *not* primarily of the affective, theatric sort; nor is it simply a sensation of quietude like that enabled by the hermetic architectural spaces of the sanctuary mode. Alternatively, at St. Denis, the relation between the human and the architectural forms is (intended by the designers to be) more direct. The artistic forms are "effective symbols"[61] insofar as they are specifically responsible for stimulating or triggering a transformative experience—an experience that Suger considered not simply as psychological but, moreover, religious.

Thus, to the extent that Suger prevailed in his grand plan—success and failure would have to be assessed on a case-by-case basis—meditating directly on the shiny surfaces of Saint Denis's liturgical objects and "altar furnishings,"[62] or even more famously on the light that filters through the Gothic stained glass, induces a trance-like state, a mesmerizing sensation described by Erwin Panofsky as "spiritual illumination."[63] The constructed elements of the cathedral were intended as, in Joan Gadol's terms, "referential symbols";[64] in Otto von Simson's phrasing, "objects of mystical contemplation … gateways leading the mind to ineffable truths;"[65] or in Suger's own words, "anagogical windows [that] urge us onward from the material to the immaterial."[66] Art and architecture are, in this case, not only helpful guides to transcendence; they are indispensable. In fact, for Suger, the *only* route to God is through material things.

A second example, the similarly famed Buddhist monument of Borobudur in Java, depends upon the "architecturalization" of the logic of the mandala. Mandalas, in perhaps their most simple form, are two-dimensional diagrams that represent, at once, maps of the entire universe and of human consciousness itself. Accordingly, the famous mandala paintings that hang in Tibetan monasteries, beyond a merely decorative or even pedagogical function, serve very pragmatically as aids to devotion, or as objects of contemplation. By concentrating on these two-dimensional, microcosmic paintings, Buddhist monks, in a sense, "enter" that world that is represented there, and thus are allowed to "travel" through the larger macrocosm, and thus, in an important sense, to make the cathartic ascent of the mythical Mount Meru, which corresponds both to the center of the world and to the center one's being.[67] In Guiseppe Tucci's Jungian language, these mandalas serve as "the concretization of a psychological state," that is, as "psycho-cosmogrammata that lead the neophyte by revealing to him the secret play of the forces that operate in the universe and in us, on the way to reintegration of consciousness."[68] In Romi Khosla's terms, "The initiated *arhat* seeking to realize the mandala is compelled to concentrate upon it and enter within it so as to eventually merge completely with the central deity within."[69]

Moreover, in addition to these flat, cos-mogrammatic wall hangings, the mandala concept is likewise expressed in a more explicitly architectural fashion in the layout of the entire Tibetan monastery. Thus, besides contemplating the two-dimensional mandala diagrams, moving through the monastery itself becomes a figurative sort of journey around the universe, or, perhaps, more psychologically speaking, around one's consciousness. As Kholsa explains, "The Tibetan temple within the compound of the monastery is also a mandala. Just as the disciple mentally enters the spiritual realm of the diagram through concentrated meditation, he too, by physically entering the temple, arrives within a spiritual realm."[70]

This architecturalization of the mandala concept finds arguably its grandest expressions in the cosmogrammatic monuments of Angkor Vat in Cambodia and Borobudur in Java. Praised as no less than "the most complex and sophisticated conception of deity in the whole history of religious iconography,"[71] the huge pyramidal structure of Borobudur is a monumental vehicle for devotion, the physical ascent of which provides what Tucci would term a "means of psychic integration." In other words, where "reading" a Tibetan painted mandala diagram—a devotional activity presumably undertaken in a stationary seated posture—requires concentrating on the painting's pattern and effecting a kind of "liberation through sight" that is typically reserved for initiated *arhats* (or monks),[72] the analogous, though perhaps more flexibly egalitarian, sort of spiritual transformation that Borobudur facilitates requires that pilgrims literally walk along the circuitous paths of the ninth-century shrine. This devotional exercise stretches the label "contemplation" insofar as the ambulatory experience of the monument is bodily as well as simply cerebral, and multisensory as well simply visual.

The transformative, carefully choreographed journey proceeds in several stages. At the base of Borobudur, according to Hiram Woodward's interpretive reconstruction, the pilgrim is confronted with nearly two miles of didactic reliefs of the elementary laws of cause and effect, a kind of cautionary primer on the ubiquity of karma. From there, the pilgrim enters a "monster gate" and begins to climb through a series of four corridor-like galleries that encircle the monument, creating spaces open to the sky but otherwise closed off to the outside world. These galleries are lined with life-sized images of the Buddha and with a succession of relief panels based upon the life and enlightenment of Gautama, and on the *Gandavyuha-sutra*, there is a Mahayana text telling the story of the edification of a pilgrim named Sudhana, with whom visitors presumably identify.[73] Emerging from this confining space and passing through a second monster doorway, the pilgrim is finally granted an open view of the great crowning *stupa*, encircled by seventy-two smaller *stupas*, each containing an image of the Buddha and, perhaps, symbolizing seventy-two elements or *dharmas* of existence.

Woodward, insisting that the meaning of Borobudur be interpreted against "an international Buddhist context," finds an important analogy between the two main levels of the huge Javanese monument and the two complimentary mandalas of Japanese Shingon Buddhism.[74] He believes, in other words, that Borobudur actually consists of a pair of superimposed mandalas: the dim lower galleries correspond to the "womb mandala," the real world or the trial, while that the upper open terraces and apical *stupas*

correspond to the "diamond mandala," the ideal world as known by the Bodhisattvas, the reward for lessons learned in the dark galleries.[75] Thus, according to Woodward, ascending the monument entails a preparatory sort of education, a daunting experience of confinement, and then, finally, at the top, a crowning sense of freedom and exhilaration. Upon emerging into the open air at the summit of the monument, Woodward imagines that "even the visitor who has understood little from the reliefs in the galleries should be deeply stirred."[76]

Though the specific analogy to Shingon Buddhism will not persuade everyone, Woodward's interpretation of the pilgrim's experience of Borobudur does illustrate very clearly the profoundly transformative potential of this sort of monument.[77] Not unlike the "anagogical illumination" that is accomplished via an engagement with Gothic architecture, pilgrims are "transported" to previously inaccessible awarenesses. Furthermore, Woodward's discussion helps to foreground the specific mechanism of growth and change that is more generally characteristic of contemplation modes of ritual-architectural presentation and apprehension: beyond simply creating a dramatic ambient background (as in the case of theater or sanctuary modes), the reliefs and built forms of Borobudur—like the images in the two-dimensional mandala diagrams—are engaged directly and deliberatively. The art and architectural elements are, in this case, absolutely indispensable to the pilgrim's spiritual ascent; the transfiguration of the pilgrim, when the work of the monument succeeds, is not one that could have happened otherwise.

PRE-COLUMBIAN ARCHITECTURE AND CONTEMPLATION: COMPETING BIASES AND OVERLOOKED POSSIBILITIES

Consideration of this heuristic possibility as an explanation of the logic of pre-Columbian Mesoamerican architecture has been tellingly sparse and even more tellingly uneven. A scour of the relevant literature for intimations of the contemplation mode turns up infrequent exceptions such as the great German Americanist Eduard Seler who, in the beginning of the twentieth century, interpreted portions of the *Codex Borgia*, a set of Mixtec pictographs and hieroglyphics, after the fashion of a mandala;[78] and influential British Mayanist Eric Thompson, on occasion, described the intentionally circuitous routes and manipulations of open and closed spaces in Maya planning as a design strategy that recalls the pilgrim's choreographed path at Borobudur.[79] Neither suggestion, however, received an enthusiastic reception. In the 1970s a handful of scholars—Laurette Séjourné, Irene Nicholson, and Frank Waters—employed Jungian perspectives to interpret Mesoamerican decorative motifs, particularly Quetzalcoatl and the quincunx pattern at Teotihuacan, as mandala-like symbols that functioned as props for psychic unity and reinterpretation.[80] But their work has been largely (maybe unfairly) consigned to the fringe of pre-Columbian art history.

At present, if still generally ignored by well-established scholars, the view that the renowned pre-Columbian monuments were products of something like an overlooked strain of ancient "Mexican mysticism," and thus designed as catalysts of direct and purposive contemplation, does find very loud advocacy among those popular writers, that is, aficionados of Mesoamerican culture who deliberately position themselves outside of mainstream academia. These authors win audiences—often very wide audiences!—in large part by presenting reinterpretations of the ruins that they claim have been either missed or, for more sinister reasons, deliberately suppressed by "establishment scholarship."[81] In this intrepid and controversial literature, one encounters frequent admonitions that the pre-Hispanic structures continue to stand as repositories of profound ancient wisdoms and, therefore, highly efficacious "props for devotion," if only audiences have the informed receptivity to capitalize on those architecturally embedded insights. From this free-swinging perspective, neither Abbot Suger nor the designers of Borobudur were one iota more insightful or ambitious than the architects of Teotihuacán and Chichén Itzá.

The still-growing throngs of spiritually inclined visitors who nowadays flood into Mexico's archaeological ruins each spring equinox—these days, every major archaeological tourist site attracts tens of thousands of visitors on that day—testify, on the one hand, to the very wide appeal of these venturesome ideas. That is to say, popular audiences are entirely game to embrace the prospect that these monuments constitute Gothic-like vehicles to transcendence, and thus enduring, still-evocative exercises of the contemplation mode. Yet, on the other hand, professional Mesoamericanists, instead of imagining that this veritable explosion of devotional enthusiasm each spring might actually provide a helpful clue as to the original pre-Columbian usages of these ancient monuments, feel compelled to deride the New Age enthusiasts as ridiculously misinformed and completely at

FIGURE 12-5. MESOAMERICAN SITES PRESENT MANY
HIGHLY ELABORATE FAÇADES SUCH AS THE CHAAC-
MASKS ADORNING THE CODZ-POP PALACE AT THE
PUUC MAYA SITE OF KABAH, YUCATÁN. THESE TYPES
OF ARCHITECTURAL MANIFESTATIONS WOULD HAVE
ENABLED WORSHIPPERS TO ENGAGE IN DIRECT,
SUSTAINED, AND PURPOSEFUL "CONTEMPLATION."

odds with the sensibilities of the monuments'
original builders. To be sure, the chasm
between popular and professional interpretations of the ruins is vast, with no sign of
narrowing in the foreseeable future.

In sum, then, while conjecture that
ancient Mesoamerican architecture was primarily animated by theatric concerns is abundant in the extreme, and while interpretive
proposals concerning the sanctuary mode are

as prevalent here as they are in other Western and Asian contexts, the prospect that
pre-Columbian architecture presented props
for purposeful contemplation and reflection
is subject to a striking difference of opinions.
On the popular "fringe" of Mesoamericanist
studies, the possibility enjoys very strong,
seemingly growing support; but within the
more professionalized scholarly mainstream,
advocates for the likelihood that these

structures were designed to serve as guides or catalysts to otherwise inaccessible spiritual ascents are almost wholly absent.

How can we explain this stark discrepancy in views? What accounts for the great swell of popular enthusiasm? And how do we explain the lacuna of scholarly support? Is this the historical fact of the matter? Were ancient Mesoamerican architects truly uninterested in advancing the sorts of "anagogical" ritual-architectural programs that we observe at St. Denis and Borobudur? Is this design option—which scholars are so quick to discern in European, Asian, Middle Eastern, and Egyptian contexts[82]—actually irrelevant to indigenous American architecture? Or could there be other forces that account for the weird skew with respect to this interpretive possibility?

Exercising a suitably skeptical "hermeneutic of suspicion," one has to conclude that the deficiency lies in the history of the scholarship rather than the architectural history of Mesoamerica per se. More specifically, as I move now toward a more general conclusion, I isolate two relevant biases that grow from that academic study of religion's exceptionally tangled roots in modernity: Protestantism and colonialism. Together, these two biases concerning ritual, contemplation, and art-assisted devotion, I would wager, have precluded a full and fair treatment of all of the ways that pre-Columbian built forms stimulated religious experiences. These two usually unspoken prejudices, intriguingly enough, account for a pair of nearly antithetical attitudes with respect to what I am terming contemplative modes of ritual-architectural design. One reflects the lingering legacy of iconoclasm insofar as it dismisses as superficial all versions of art-assisted worship,

the contemplation mode included; but the second bias actually romanticizes mysticism, and thus issues in an overgenerous, uncritical commendation of the contemplation mode.

In any event, following brief comments on these two competing distortions, I will provide some closing thoughts that return again to this very marked discrepancy between scholarly versus lay assessments of the architectural remains of ancient Mesoamerica.

The Dismissal of Art-Assisted Contemplation: Lingering Legacies of Iconoclasm

There is no denying that the scholarly practices of "comparative religion" have deep and tangled roots that, for better or worse, can be traced to the processes of colonialism, to the Enlightenment, and, more specifically, to certain versions of liberal Protestantism. It is perhaps not too surprising, then, that one pervasive and enduring bias within the academic study of religion reflects that strain in Abrahamic religion, to which I have already alluded, that is never fully persuaded that the merits of art-assisted religiosity outweigh the potentially idolatrous dangers. Though Protestant spokesmen against art-assisted devotion are abundant, the polemical opinions of medieval Catholic Saint Bernard are again useful in focusing on the still-relevant issues. While emphatically dedicated to meditation and contemplation in a general sense, we have noted that Bernard launches diatribes against the luxuriant dramatics of Cluny's ritual-architectural program (i.e., against theatric modes) that apply likewise to the Suger's notion that one's Christian aspirations might require the use of artistic or architectural props for devotion (i.e., the contemplation mode).[83] Bernard, in other words, collapses the distinction between the *indirect* reliance on architecture characteristic of the theatric mode and the *direct* reliance on art and architecture characteristic of the contemplation mode—and then rejects both.

Nevertheless, even Bernard, iconoclast that he is, provides a highly qualified, if condescending, endorsement of contemplative presentational modes by acknowledging their usefulness—but only among the spiritually immature. He says, for instance, that "bishops have a duty toward both the wise and foolish. They have to make use of material ornamentation to rouse devotion in a carnal people, incapable of spiritual things"; but he then quickly explains that, as monks, "we no longer belong to such people," and, thus, art is necessarily more distracting than inspiring for the contemplative practice of the serious Cistercians.[84] That is to say, according to Bernard, artistic and architectural elaborations are crutches that might support the naïve and sophomoric, but able-minded grown-ups with more mature religious outlooks should have the good sense to toss them aside.

Modern scholars of religion also like to imagine themselves as "no longer belonging to such people"; and thus they, too, like Bernard, have been wont to lump what I have termed "contemplative approaches" together with theatric ones, and then to dismiss both with the same broad brush as superstitious and unreflectively gullible—that is, the virtual opposite of individuated, self-critical meditative introspection. From that perspective, which is much accentuated by the tacitly Protestant leanings of religious studies and anthropology, art-assisted contemplation of the sorts I just discussed *is* "ritualistic"; art-assisted contemplation is a kind of lingering legacy of (or similarly puerile parallel

to) medieval, magico-mechanistic delusions concerning the supposed inherent efficacy of sacramental actions and objects.

From this view, then, the orchestration of art-assisted devotion is not a viable religious alternative but rather a sign of immaturity and the "foolishness" of those who are "incapable of spiritual things." Early students of Mexico's native culture and religion, such as E. B. Tylor, author of *Primitive Culture* (1871), for instance, were willing to imagine the existence of an evolutionary stage in which native peoples believed in "fetishism," an outlook that, to the extent that it involves accessing supernatural power via direct engagements with material objects (stones, rattles, carvings, or, by extension, whole buildings), participates in the logic of the contemplation mode. But, for Tylor, native peoples' adherence to the notion that strategic interactions with material things, architecture included, could actually provide access to "the immaterial" was a sort of childlike error that signaled their standing on a fairly low rung of the unilinear evolutionary ladder.

In the century and a half since Tylor, Mesoamericanists, still more like Bernard than Suger, have remained largely unpersuaded by the proposition that there are indeed nuanced and sophisticated ways wherein art and architecture can engender "spiritual ascents"; and thus, the heuristic option of diagnosing some other culture—especially some indigenous culture—as involved in the utilization of art and architecture as a healthy and mature means of fostering religious insights and awarenesses essentially disappears. Thus, while, as noted, this way of interpreting the logic of pre-Columbian architecture is no less than the dominant explanation among "New

FIGURE 12-6. WHILE EVERY VISITOR TO THE ZAPOTEC-
MIXTEC SITE OF MITLA SINCE THE EIGHTEENTH CENTURY
HAS COMMENTED ON THE AMPLE AND DIVERSE GEO-
METRIC DESIGNS THAT COVER MANY OF THE BUILDING
FAÇADES, ALMOST NO ONE HAS SERIOUSLY ENTERTAINED
THE PLAUSIBLE POSSIBILITY THAT THOSE INTRICATE
DECORATIONS SERVED AS PROPS FOR DEVOTION IN THE
SENSE THAT THEY WERE OBJECTS OF SUSTAINED "CON-
TEMPLATIVE" ATTENTION.

Age" audiences, mainstream scholars remain even now very hesitant—I'll argue, much too hesitant—to hypothesize that ancient Mesoamericans could have been engaging their monuments in the "contemplative" ways that we have described relative to Gothic cathedrals and Borobudur.

In short, while the next prejudice to which I now turn tends to elevate the contemplative mode too high, this first bias—the lingering legacy of iconoclasm—leads scholars to dismiss that heuristic prospect much too soon.

The Romanticization of Art-Assisted Contemplation: Privileging Mysticism

The second bias, which is also endemic in academic religious studies (and even more conspicuous in *popular* religious studies), curiously enough, pulls in nearly the opposite direction and, therefore, mitigates and sometimes overrides the first prejudice. Perhaps counterintuitively, the very same rationalist and Protestant propensities that tend to denigrate theatric modes of ritual-architectural presentation as superficial and meretricious work in precisely the opposite direction with respect to appraisals of contemplation and meditation. That is to say, contemplative and especially "mystical" practices (however vaguely and broadly defined), whether observed in Western or Eastern contexts—because they are presumed to constitute the most highly intellectualized, nuanced, explicitly cognitive, and cerebral strains of those traditions (particularly in contrast to the seemingly basely emotive and bodily character of theatric ritual practices)—have routinely garnered very generous academic reviews. Though often in implicit rather than explicit ways, scholars of religion have invariably judged contemplation and meditation

to be the most "hard thinking," maybe the most responsibly self-controlled of devotional approaches, and thus the most sophisticated and deserving of respect. Moreover, the (only sometimes correct) perception of such activities as nonthreateningly apolitical and "specifically religious" also enhances this aura of sincerity and discipline; contemplation and mysticism are, in this view, if impractical, at least benignly harmless. Contemplative and mystical practices are presumed to be the abstrusely metaphysical cogitations of spiritual experts, "worshipful" or "prayerful" activities that barely qualify as "ritual"—again just opposite of theatrically choreographed ceremonial events.

There has been and remains, then, on the one hand, ironically, a kind of Western romanticization, sometimes exoticism, of the mentalist introspection associated with contemplation, particularly, but not only, in the case of Asian religions.[85] Yoga, Zen, Vedanta, and other versions of mindfulness meditation—these are ranked as both the healthiest and most unthreatening of religious practices. Commentators who are deeply skeptical of Christian institutions can nonetheless be enthusiastically affirming of "contemplatives" from Meister Eckhart, Teresa of Avila, and St. John of the Cross to Thomas Merton; many who are wary of mainstream Islam are quite at ease with Sufism and Rumi's mystical poetry; and lots who are generally indifferent to mainline forms of Judaism nevertheless embrace the esoteric and "mystical" ideas of Kabbalah. That is to say, oddly enough, from a liberal Protestant frame, that mysticism especially—because it seems to correspond most closely to the counterinstitutionalized, personalistic, and otherworldly "essence" of "spirituality"—has enjoyed a special privilege in the comparative history of religions, which has only lately begun to be exposed and challenged.[86] In these meditative-mystical practices, according to the presumptions of many academic (and popular) assessments, the superficial differences of cultural-specificity are erased and the transhistorical crux of religion laid bare. Mystical contemplation, so these generous assessments go, involves essential insights that are transcultural and eternal, and thus shareable across the boundaries of time and space.

Therefore, from one solidly established scholarly sight-line, contemplation of all sorts, including where art and architecture are involved, is granted a kind of noncritical, overgenerous commendation. By contrast to the iconoclastic strain that collapses the distinction between theatric and contemplative modes, this mysticism-privileging perspective actually polarizes those two heuristic options: theatrical ritual, especially when highly politicized, is seen as religion at its worst; but cerebral contemplation (including that which relies on art and architectural supports) is, from the same vantage, religion at its best. Where theatrical ritual is condemned as self-serving and manipulative, art-assisted contemplation is, as we've seen, praised for its supposed dependence upon and reinforcement of a "reduction of self-interest."[87] From this perspective, then, to assess pre-Columbian architecture as an expression of the contemplation mode—something that happens frequently in "anti-establishment" venues but very *in*frequently in the mainstream academic literature—involves granting ancient Mesoamericans an exceptionally high compliment.

CLOSING COMMENTS: MESO-AMERICAN RUINS AS RESOURCES FOR SEEKERS, SCHOLARS, AND/OR ARCHITECTS

In the wake of this chapter's sustained "hermeneutic of suspicion," we can, I hope, begin to appreciate that appraisals of ancient Mesoamerican architecture, even those of the most rigorously academic sorts, have been, in larger part than we might expect, occasions to exercise a whole host of modern Western ambivalences about art, ritual, and mysticism as well as enduring colonialist ambivalences about indigenous peoples. Though most seem quite benign, interpretations of these ruins are, in no case, simply objective and empirical retrievals of a pre-Columbian past. To the contrary, these long-abandoned ceremonial centers—not least because they are accompanied by almost no contemporaneous alphabetical texts—offer fabulously provocative vehicles for imaginative rumination on these (and many other) vexing issues, and distressingly little in the way of resistance. By contrast to much more richly documented European and Asian contexts, the extreme elusiveness of the "facts" about ancient Mesoamerican religion and design have, for better or worse, allowed these ruins to stand as richly provocative and highly flexible resources. The range of interpretations they evoke allows these old buildings to act as palimpsests, Rorschach-like canvases, as it were, onto which Western audiences can project all sorts of complaints and aspirations that may have very little to do with the historical realities of this region.

The spectrum of responses and interpretations that these multivalent monuments elicit—the range the creative and interested "revalorative" uses to which the old buildings are put—is exceptionally variegated and indeed ever-widening.[88] Nevertheless, consideration of the highly disparate views of three sorts of audiences—"seekers," scholars, and architects—can provide one final means of addressing the very different statuses of the three modes of ritual-architectural presentation with which I began.

SEEKERS: RUINS AS RESOURCES FOR "SPIRITUAL" INSIGHTS AND ENHANCEMENTS

First, by the imperfect term "seekers" I refer to those persons who visit and engage Mesoamerica's ruins not simply with academic or recreational incentives but with expectations of some sort of "spiritual" enhancement. It is, of course, dangerous and sloppy to generalize as to the attitudes and expectations of the tens of thousands who attend the present-day spring equinox ceremonies at Chichén Itzá, Teotihuacan, and other sites. For many of them, a tour of the ruins is simply a vacation side trip with casual investments akin to thumbing through the *National Geographic Magazine*.[89] Others, however, are impassioned in the extreme and deeply invested in the "popular literature" on ancient Mesoamerica by authors such as José Argüelles, "the man who first introduced the date December 21, 2012, to public consciousness,"[90] and Hunbatz Men, the increasingly high-profile and controversial Maya "daykeeper," a self-proclaimed "New Age" workshop leader and author of *Secrets of Maya Science/Religion* (1990) and *The 8 Calendars of the Maya: The Pleiadian Cycle and the Key to Destiny* (2009).

In these widely read works—which I suspect, at present, substantially outsell more rigorously academic books on the same area—one finds not simply different interpretations of Maya history but a wholesale antimodernist, antirationalist (or maybe transrationalist) critique of mainstream scholarship, which is to say, an explicit rejection of the very premises of "the academic establishment," which, in the view of Argüelles and Men, is largely blind to the esoteric messages that reside in monuments like Chichén Itzá's Castillo. These authors are, in the main, critics of positivism, doubters of the entire Enlightenment project, as well as harsh critics of the current consumerist and materialist preoccupations of Western society; and because they imagine that ancient Mesoamericans represent instructive antidotes on both those fronts, their assessments of pre-Columbian peoples are, instead of ambivalent, fully congratulatory, even eulogizing. These authors aspire not only to study the creations of Mexico's ancient architects but to be replenished by them.

With respect, then, to the first of those two competing biases within religious studies, this popular constituency largely exempts itself from of "the lingering legacy of iconoclasm" insofar as its adherents are, as a rule, completely at ease with the prospect of art-assisted religious devotion. One could say that they find Abbot Suger's anagogical approach to design far more persuasive than Saint Bernard's protestations. However, with respect to the second bias—that is, the tendency to privilege "mysticism" as the surest sign of religious truth and sophistication—so-termed New Age audiences are quintessentially implicated. That is to say, this group does all that it can to downplay the political dimensions of pre-Columbian ritual-architectural design; among enthusiasts of Argüelles and Men, one hears frequent and emphatic rejections of the re-creations of the viciously autocratic, human-sacrificing Classic Maya that one encounters, for instance, in Mel Gibson's 2006 film, *Apocalypto*.[91] Accordingly, on the one hand, these authors almost never make the case that ancient Mesoamerican configurations were designed as the stage-setting for the sorts of highly dramatic, often propagandistic ritual performances that are characteristic of the theatric mode.

On the other hand, however, this popular literature takes every opportunity to accentuate and celebrate the supposed extent to which ancient Mesoamerican priests and architects were no less than mystical savants whose fabulous intellectual and calendrical insights remain available to those astute enough to read them out of the symbolism of their still-standing architecture. Consequently, their (re)constructions of the purported logic of pre-Columbian architectural design invariably and overwhelming presume something like what I term "the contemplation mode." In their view, the notion that the long-abandoned pyramids worked—and can continue to work!—as "direct catalysts to spiritual ascent" is a perfectly accurate description of the still-relevant genius of pre-Columbian architecture. For them, Suger's confidence that Gothic architectural forms can indeed "transport one from the material to the immaterial" is fully transferable into the Mesoamerican context.

SCHOLARS: RUINS AS RESOURCES FOR HISTORICAL AND (SUPPOSEDLY) ACADEMIC INSIGHTS

Second, mainstream scholars, by contrast, though often contentious among themselves, are nearly unanimous in taking issue with virtually every aspect of the New Age stance. In academic critiques, the ideas and practices

of equinox aficionados are decried variously as innocently naïve, insidiously harmful, or simply ridiculous. For scholars versed in the five-hundred-year history of Western ideas about indigenous American culture, the present generation of antiestablishment thinkers may be garnering an unprecedentedly wide following—and one might look to a host of technological and economical factors that enable the unprecedentedly huge book sales and the gigantic crowds at equinox ceremonies—but the current "spiritual" enthusiasm for the ruins is actually just the latest expression of a very long-running tendency to romanticize pre-Columbian peoples. A long view could find precedents in the discourses of "noble savages," which begin with Columbus's arrival in the New World; or, in a tighter timeframe, one could contextualize these current movements in relation to the raft of eccentric and historically preposterous nineteenth- and twentieth-century theories about the Mayas and Toltecs described in Robert Wauchope's *Lost Tribes and Sunken Continents: Myth and Method in the Study of American Indians* (1962) and a host of more recent works on the Eurocentric imaginings of indigenous peoples.

From these critical perspectives, the huge equinox crowds simply represent the newest version of a very old "primitivism" wherein poorly informed, if perhaps well-intentioned, "spiritual travelers" are willing to deploy highly distorted, inordinately romantic depictions of ancient Americans as a means for launching their own critiques against the excesses of modern Western culture and consumerism. Moreover, while most of these "seekers" explicitly differentiate themselves from the churchgoing mainstream, and thus would reject this assertion, scholarly critics would maintain that these seemingly countercultural equinox enthusiasts are also instantiating a characteristically Protestant, highly individuated, and experience-driven conception of "religion" (which they would rather term "spirituality"); that is to say, New Age practitioners are also unwitting emissaries of the very modernist attitudes toward religion that they claim to reject and disdain. In short, for well-trained historians of religions and ideas, both the protestations and the enthusiasms of these pilgrims to the ruins are eminently predictable.

Consequently, academics may concede that adherents to the ideas of Argüelles, Men, and other venturesome writers deserve scholarly attention—but as a "new religious movement" rather than as reliable interpreters of past traditions.[92] Scholars insist, in other words, that the ideas and exercises in "ritualization" undertaken by these contemporary spiritual sojourners bear virtually no significant continuity with the pre-Columbian mindsets and practices that they claim to be recovering. Instead, most Mesoamericanists—lots of who are deeply offended by what they regard as the wholesale distortion of the historical record—are adamant that we can learn absolutely nothing from these imaginative thinkers and practitioners about the pre-Hispanic past (or, for that matter, the present or future), a thoroughgoing dismissal that is often leveled with ridicule and sarcasm. Thus, while New Age enthusiasts accuse scholars of being "uptight" and imprisoned by their commitments to rational positivism, academics return the insult by assessing them as flaky and gullible, insufficiently critical either of their own motives or of the historical data. Expect no meeting of the minds between these two camps.

Be that as it may, I hope to have shown that scholarly as well as popular ideas about pre-Columbian architectural design invariably reflect unspoken, often unnoticed, biases and prejudices that have very little do with "what really happened in ancient Mesoamerica." More specifically, revisiting the literature with a skeptical-minded hermeneutic of suspicion, as I have tried to do throughout this chapter, has led me to the following set of hypotheses regarding the troubling discrepancies with which academic commentators appeal to the three alternative modes of ritual-architectural presentation.

First, *with respect to theatric modes*, while present-day aficionados intent on accentuating the "religiomystical" (not political) priorities of the ancient Maya deliberately reject this alternative, we nonetheless observe that this has been and remains, far and away, the most prevalent means of interpreting the logic of pre-Columbian architecture. The accounts of sixteenth-century conquistadors and colonial-era Spanish priests routinely accentuated the Indians' garish, emotion-evoking, and politically manipulative ritual-architectural showmanship, an assessment that provided a dexterous means of simultaneously congratulating and condemning the accomplishments of native architects. Moreover, the theatric mode has endured as the default explanation of pre-Columbian design, so it would seem, in part, because it is an accurate assessment, but even more because it is a kind of backhanded compliment that provides the quintessential expression of what colonial historian Lewis Hanke (and countless others) have identified as an insidiously pervasive Eurocentric ambivalence about Indians, that is, a conflicted admiration and disgust for the native peoples of New World[93]—and it is, therefore, worrisome that contemporary scholars continue to appeal with such regularity to this interpretive alternative.

Second, *with respect to sanctuary modes*, a skeptical view reveals that the fairly common acknowledgments—among both scholars and popular writers—that ancient Mesoamerican architects were indeed very skillful and ingenious in delimiting privileged "sacred spaces" within the wider natural and urban environment provides a more modest way of working through conflicted feelings toward Indians. Conceding that they were artful and highly proficient in cordoning off specific zones in which to conduct their ritual exercises is a largely neutral assessment insofar as it allows students of this region, on the one hand, to affirm the able accomplishments of pre-Columbian designers, and, nonetheless, on the other hand, to abstain on the moral (im)propriety of the activities that were undertaken in those spaces. This is, as noted, the least controversial of the three options.

Third and last, *with respect the contemplation mode*, we discover that serious scholars, unlike their more popular counterparts, have been distressingly (perhaps even increasingly) unwilling to appeal to this explanation. Despite the wide acknowledgment of contemplative modes in the so-called "great world religions" (from which I, too, have drawn my primary examples), academic interpreters of sacred architectures outside those major faiths—that is, among so-called "archaic," traditional, or tribal contexts—very seldom appeal to this sort of explanation. Here, then, Christocentric and modernist biases are laced with colonialist ones insofar as Euro-American researchers have had particular difficultly in imaging that "indigenous" peoples (long

labeled "primitive" peoples), ancient Mesoamericans included, might have the inclination and/or wherewithal to undertake the sort of deep, abstract thinking required of contemplative modes of ritual-architectural design and apprehension. Native peoples' ritualized interactions with art objects and constructions have been routinely diagnosed as "fetishism," a condescending diagnosis that assigns to them a naïve, childlike version of contemplative modes; but, especially since the 1980s, rigorous scholars, unlike popular commentators, have been increasingly reticent to attribute the sort of "mysticism" to ancient Mesoamerican architects that would likewise attribute to them more nuanced and sophisticated exercises of the contemplation mode.[94]

Oddly enough, then, at least where serious consideration of the contemplation mode is concerned, the often reckless ruminations of "New Agers" on Mesoamerica's ruins might actually constitute a healthy corrective to mainstream scholarship. That is to say, while professionalized Mesoamericanists are vehement—and I'd say right—their scholarly practices and critical standards are drastically different from those of their more popular counterparts, on this particular point, "establishment academics" would, I think, do well to borrow a page or two from the interpretive catalogue of those free thinkers. More specifically, while a large majority of the claims that one finds in the antiestablishment literature are, shall we say, intriguingly unpersuasive, I am persuaded that the so-termed contemplation mode was, after all, a highly relevant priority in the design of many pre-Columbian buildings—a prospect that is, therefore, deserving of much more serious scholarly attention than it has received. Why, after all, when European, Asian, and Egyptian designers have all made such effective use of contemplative modes of ritual-architectural presentation, should ancient Mesoamerican architects stand as an exception?[95]

ARCHITECTS: RUINS AS RESOURCES FOR DESIGN INSIGHTS AND INSPIRATIONS

Finally, then, I end by quickly revisiting the question of the ways in which these monuments, and my skeptical reflections on the myriad interpretive controversies that swirl around these old pyramids and palaces, might (or might not) be of interest and use to architects and designers. In that spirit, I circle back to the hopeful proposition with which I tried to justify my presence in this book—namely, that observations emerging from the comparative history of religions can serve, among other purposes, as resources for practicing architects, that is, as tools and means of "deprovincialization" that broaden horizons with respect to all that architecture can do in facilitating and supporting religious experiences. And, in that respect, I remind you of my opening anecdote about the paired tree-drawing assignments, whereby I tried to suggest that, to quote myself, "the efforts of imagination are invariably improved by consideration of specific empirical examples," in this case consideration of the specific cities of ancient Mesoamerica.

But whether or not these dilapidated old buildings, and the interminably debate that they continue to evoke, might really provide some practical insights and inspirations for working designers is not a query that a mere historian of religions can answer. Instead, I leave it to you—the world-shaping architects whom I hold in such high esteem—to answer that for yourselves.

13 TRANSCENDING AESTHETICS

The title of this chapter, "Transcending Aesthetics," seeks to respond to the title of the symposium that ushered in the present volume, "Transcending Architecture: Aesthetics and Ethics of the Numinous." I find this title interestingly ambiguous: transcending suggests going beyond. But is "architecture" in the title to be understood as subject or object? Who or what here is doing the transcending, architecture or human observers? Is it we who must transcend architecture, which in this sense would have to be gone beyond or left behind, if we are to open ourselves to the numinous? Or is it perhaps architecture that in some sense must transcend itself? I shall return to these questions.

The following remarks develop some considerations advanced in a subsequently published lecture, "Untimely Meditations on the Need for Sacred Architecture," given as part of the conference "Constructing the Ineffable: Contemporary Sacred Architecture," organized by Karla Cavarra Britton in 2007.[1] That lecture began and concluded with the claim that the sacred needs architecture if it is not to wither and that similarly architecture needs the sacred. This twofold claim invites a twofold challenge: today architecture would seem to thrive without the sacred; and does the sacred still require architecture? That the two should not be tied quite so closely together may seem to be suggested by the title given to the symposium that originated this book: "Transcending Architecture: Aesthetics and Ethics of the Numinous."

The shape of our modern age seems to render both claims: that the sacred needs architecture and that architecture needs the sacred, hopelessly backward looking. But in the face of what may seem evident, I want to reassert the claim that the sacred needs architecture if it is not to wither and that similarly architecture needs the sacred, and now add that if that twofold need is to be met, our thinking about architecture needs to take its leave from aesthetics, that aesthetics as it has evolved is an obstacle to an adequate understanding of architecture. Hence the title I have given this chapter: Transcending Aesthetics.

As suggested, I chose the title to engage and call into question the title given to the symposium in which I was invited to participate: "Transcending Architecture: Aesthetics and Ethics of the Numinous." In the invitation I was sent, a brief explanation suggested what the title intended—that sacred architecture should transcend itself as a material thing: "At its highest, architecture has the ability to turn geometric proportions into shivers, light into grace, space into contemplation, and time into divine presence. A transcending architecture disappears in the very act of delivering us into the awesome and timeless space of the holy." This seems to assert that, at its highest, sacred architecture is somewhat like a bridge that transports us into an inner spiritual realm that allows us to enter an inner subjective space. As we cross that bridge, everything material, and with it architecture, is transcended as the solitary subject discovers within him- or herself "the awesome and timeless space of the holy" or the "numinous." Architecture is understood here as occasioning an experience of the numinous. So understood, it would seem, the numinous does not really reside in the architecture but in the subject.

But to do justice to the sacred, we must look not just to the subject but to things, places, and texts in which the divine is experi-

enced as present; we must look to the mystery of incarnation. With this the relationship of the sacred to the aesthetic and, more especially, to the beautiful and the sublime becomes problematic: sacred objects need not be, indeed often are not, aesthetically distinguished.[2] As will become clearer, there is indeed tension between aesthetic experience as it has come to be understood ever since the eighteenth century and encounters with the sacred, and that means also with sacred architecture. Constitutive of the sacred, I would like to claim, is the inseparable unity of spirit and matter. And spirit here may not be sought within the observing subject but in a reality that transcends whatever human artifice can form and create. The sacred breaks into the horizontality of the mundane and establishes a vertical that unites heaven and earth. The divine logos descends into the visible. Meaning is incarnated in matter. Matter becomes the bearer of divinity. That gives objects we experience as sacred their special aura.

But what sense can we still make today of such incarnation except as a projection of a spiritual significance into things that do not really belong to them? Have objects that once were experienced as sacred not lost the aura of the sacred for us moderns? In this chapter, I can do no more than approach this question by taking a closer look at the phenomenon of aura.

Today, invocations of aura are likely to bring to mind Walter Benjamin's famous claim that in this age of technical reproduction, works of art have to lose whatever aura they once possessed.[3] That recalls Hegel's claim that today art and architecture, in their highest sense, belong to a never-to-be-recovered past. And like Hegel, who proclaims the death of art in this highest sense even as he invites us to affirm that death is a necessary consequence of humanity's coming of age, Benjamin proclaims the loss of the aura works of art once possessed, even as he invites us to affirm that loss as a necessary byproduct of the progress of technology, progress that he took to be essential to the progress of humanity: and does technology, promising to render us the masters and possessors not just of nature without but of our own nature, not also promise true autonomy and happiness to all? This, to be sure, presupposes, as Benjamin reminds us, that a society is "mature enough to incorporate technology as its organ"[4] instead of allowing technology to become an instrument used by those in power to reduce nature and human beings to material to be used and dealt with as one sees fit. We have had to learn that such maturity cannot be assumed.

As his work in its entirety shows, Benjamin, too, found it difficult to let go of what in "The Work of Art in the Age of Mechanical Reproduction" he seems so ready to relegate to a never-to-be-recovered past. In that essay, this is hinted at by an example he offers, where it is significant that it is taken not from art but from nature: "If, while resting on a summer afternoon, you follow with your eyes a mountain range on the horizon or a branch which casts its shadow over you, you experience the aura of those mountains, of that branch."[5] The experience is familiar: the musical outline of a distant mountain range, observed on some warm, lazy summer afternoon, hints at some elusive magical other that will not yield its magic to the camera: the camera may well give me an image that will preserve a trace of this magical moment, but it will not allow me to hear in the same

way the beckoning call of those distant mountains, as if up there I would find home. The material object seen is experienced here as a figure of utopia. That figural significance gives the perceived its special resonance and depth. Something similar can be said about many works of sacred art or architecture.

Is it this figural significance of the perceived that the word "aura" is meant to capture here? The Greek "aura" meant "breath" or "breeze," the Latin "aura" a gentle wind or current of air; "aura" thus came to name the subtle emanation of some substance, for example the special odor of a rose. In this sense, an artificial rose can be said to lack the aura of the original. In all these cases, "aura" names a perhaps elusive but definitely physical phenomenon that can in principle be measured. Aura here has a material basis. That basis became more elusive, was spiritualized, when aura came to be understood in the nineteenth century as a "subtle emanation around living beings." In that sense, one might speak of the special aura issuing from a charismatic person or from someone we love. And is there not a similarity between the aura of the beloved and the aura of a work of sacred architecture? Does such a work not hint at a happiness that cannot be captured in words? The camera fails to adequately preserve that aura. It only helps us to recall it.

What Benjamin has in mind here would not appear to be a material phenomenon: this at least is suggested by his definition of aura "as the unique phenomenon of a distance, however close it may be."[6] The chosen examples shift our attention away from smell and touch, senses that are more immediately involved with matter, to the more spiritual eye. Sight, to be sure, presupposes distance: whatever is seen is seen at a distance and in principle that distance can be measured. Benjamin's invocation of a "unique phenomenon of a distance, however close it may be," forces us to link the phenomenon of aura as he understands it here not to a physical but to a psychical distance, where this psychical distance also has a temporal dimension as Benjamin points out in his elaboration of this thought in "On Some Motifs in Baudelaire" (1939): "To perceive the aura of an object we look at is to invest it with the ability to look at us in return." He adds to this explanation: "This endowment is a wellspring of poetry. Wherever a human being, an animal, or an inanimate object thus endowed by the poet lifts up its eyes, it draws him into the distance. The gaze of nature thus awakened dreams and pulls the poet after its dreams."[7] Looking at some sacred object, we are similarly drawn to something nameless and far removed from the cares and concerns that bind us to the here and now.

Psychical distance, along with its bracketing of the everyday and its temporality, has been discussed as a defining characteristic of the aesthetic experience ever since Kant. That phenomenon was given authoritative expression by Edward Bullough in his "'Psychical Distance' as a Factor in Art and as an Aesthetic Principle." Bullough gives the example of the way we experience the world in a fog, where everything seen seems strangely distant, even when close, everything heard strangely close, even when distant. The fog lets us become oblivious to our everyday cares and see things "'objectively,' as it has often been called, by permitting only such reactions on our part that emphasize the 'objective' features of the experience and by interpreting even our 'subjective' affections not as modes of our being but rather as char-

acteristics of the phenomenon." The thing is strangely transfigured, "seemingly possessed by human affections." So transfigured the phenomenon acquires a flavor of "concentrated poignancy and delight," as if illuminated by "the passing ray of a brighter light."[8] The quasireligious significance of aesthetic experience so understood is underscored by Jacques Maritain, when he says that beauty, following the medievals, possesses "the flavor of the terrestrial paradise, because it restores, for a moment, the peace and simultaneous delight of the intellect and the senses."[9] For that very reason, beauty can also pose a threat to the sacred, for the very analogy between terrestrial paradise and the beautiful object can cause the latter to substitute for the former, to usurp the place of the sacred.

The promise of such a utopian home also seems inseparable from Benjamin's experience of the aura possessed by his distant mountain range: it, too, seems to possess a spiritual significance. That something of the sort is indeed constitutive of aesthetic experience and is hinted at by Bullough when he suggests that when transfigured into an aesthetic object a thing found in nature acquires a quasihuman presence: the aesthetic experience of natural objects involves a humanizing identification with them: spirit without now seems to answer spirit within. And is such a process of identification not also, as Hegel suggested, at work in all artistic creation? Is this not at the heart of the story of Pygmalion? Benjamin, too, understands aura in terms of such an identification, which lets the natural appear as more than just natural.

But is this not only an appearance, an illusion, something read into nature by the human observer? As Benjamin's friend Theodor Adorno put it, "Aesthetic appearance means always: nature as the appearance of the supernatural." But as he also reminds us: "Art is not transcendence, but an artifact, something human, and ultimately: nature."[10] So understood, the phenomenon of aura veils the perceived with an illusion of transcendence. But does not reality demand that our eyes open to all that threatens to destroy dreams of happiness, open to hunger and disease, to injustice and exploitation. And was that not true especially in 1935 when Benjamin wrote his essay, at a time when such long familiar scourges were being raised to an up to then unknown, higher level by the terror being rained on millions by leaders hungry for power and deaf to outmoded appeals to human dignity, very much attuned to the new means of domination and destruction made available by the progress of technology?

If, as his loving description of the distant mountain range and many similar passages show, Benjamin knew all too well the seductive call of the aura that seems to issue from works of art, nature, and persons, he also had good reason to be suspicious of the spiritual, quasireligious significance "aura" so readily suggests. Had not Marx called religion "the opium of the people": "at the same time, an expression of real suffering and a *protest* against real suffering. Religion is the sigh of the oppressed creature, the sentiment of a heartless world, and the soul of soulless conditions."[11] And since human suffering and oppression remain, even as that death of God proclaimed by Nietzsche would seem to deny those truly of this modern age the consolation religion once was able to provide, cannot the artwork and its aura offer at least some compensation for what had been lost by offering a substitute, if only illusory, transcendence? But, especially in 1935, the

state of the world made such an escape into the aesthetic seem irresponsible to Benjamin. What was needed, he insisted, was not the consolation offered by beautiful illusion that willingly turns its back on ugly reality but active intervention that will change the world for the better. Precisely because he was unwilling to accept the distance that on the aesthetic approach must separate beautiful illusion from reality, Benjamin, in this respect quite representative of his generation, had to resist the aesthetic approach to art, which the phenomenon of aura so readily invited.

I have suggested that "aura" invites interpretation as just another variant of the experience of the aesthetic object: has the aesthetic experience not been described in terms of a distance that preserves the integrity and autonomy of the aesthetic object, a distance that lets the observer become fascinated and absorbed by the aesthetic object's unique presencing? Notwithstanding the death of God, such absorption in the beautiful promised a secular redemption.[12] The celebration of aura would thus seem to belong with the cult of beauty that is so much a part of the aesthetic approach to art. Benjamin is a modernist in his resistance to that cult: "To pry an object from its shell, to destroy its aura, is the mark of a perception whose 'sense of the universal equality of things' has increased to such a degree that it extracts it even from a unique object by means of reproduction."[13]

The last quote expands on and at the same time demands reconsideration of aura as an aesthetic phenomenon. Key here is Benjamin's emphasis on the unique materiality of the auratic object, which is said to be challenged by the proletarian's "Marxist communal egalitarian sense." Benjamin here links aura to originality, where "the presence of the original" is said to be "the prerequisite of the concept of authenticity." "Chemical analyses of the patina of a bronze can help to establish this, as does the proof that a given manuscript of the Middle Ages stems from an archive of the fifteenth century. The whole sphere of authenticity is outside technical—and, of course, not only technical reproducibility."[14]

The way Benjamin links aura to a particular piece of matter invites further consideration. So understood, aura is destroyed by reproduction, where thinking of such essentially reproducible artworks as woodcuts and engravings—to which Benjamin himself calls the reader's attention in his essay—we may well wonder whether the concern for authenticity does not lose sight of the art character of art and distances Benjamin's understanding of aura from aura as understood by the aesthetic approach. For a defining characteristic of the aesthetic approach to art, captured by the rhetoric of "beautiful illusion" (*schöner Schein*), would seem to be precisely the dissociation of the aura of the aesthetic object from its materiality, from what Heidegger calls its "thingliness." Benjamin's critique of aura is also a critique of Heidegger's emphasis on the thingliness of the work of art.

And must we not grant Heidegger at least this much: whatever else works of art may be, they are also things. But is it really so obvious that the artwork must be a thing? In the case of a sculpture or a work of architecture, it may seem natural to identify the thing, the material object, with the work of art. But when I see some painting in a reproduction, am I not also encountering the unique work of art, perceiving its special aura, if in a more or less deficient mode, depending on the quality of the reproduction? Just how

important is the unique materiality or what Heidegger calls the "thingly quality" of the work of art? Have artists like Duchamp and Warhol not taught us what should have been evident all along: that this thingly quality is not essential to the work of art? And is this not what Benjamin himself insists on when he opposes to what he takes to be the backward-looking auratic understanding of art to the forward-looking political understanding that he associates with Marxism, where he also recognized the importance of Dada in destroying the matter-bound aura of the art work? Marcel Duchamp thus declared that he "wanted to get away from the physical aspect of painting," that he "was interested in making painting serve [his] purposes, and in getting away from the physicality of painting."[15] The politicization of art advocated by Benjamin is not so different, although he had no doubt very different purposes in mind than the self-absorbed Duchamp.

Much recent concept art could be cited in support of what Benjamin has to say about the shift from an auratic art to a political art. To be sure, there will always be some material thing that mediates the aesthetic experience, but that experience will transcend the mediating thing and render it quite unimportant, no more than an occasion to engage the thoughtful observer.

And should something similar not be said of sacred architecture? What case can be made for the importance of some unique piece of matter? Kant already had called the importance of the thingly character of the work of art into question: for him, the aesthetic object is in an important sense not a thing at all. And is he not supported in an obvious way by such arts as music or poetry? When we speak of Beethoven's Fifth

Symphony, are we speaking of a thing? If so, how is "thing" understood here? Can it be weighed or located in time and space? That can be said of some particular score and every performance takes place in space and time—but we also would not want to identify with the Fifth Symphony, which will continue to be when these are long gone.

Certainly, paintings and sculptures are things, and for those of us who lack a sufficiently strong imagination, aesthetic experience depends on objects that present themselves to our senses. But does a pure aesthetic experience not surpass the material object and leave it behind? The material thing, it would seem, is here like a gate that grants access to the beautiful forms that are the object of a purely aesthetic and that means for Kant a spiritual understanding. A distinction between material thing and aesthetic object is demanded by Kant's understanding of the disinterested character of aesthetic experience. Given such an aesthetic understanding of art, the technical reproducibility of works of art should pose no threat to their art character or aesthetic aura. It only threatens those who would fetishize the thing in the work of art.

Heidegger could be cited as an example. He, too, takes for granted that a work of art is more than just a mere thing. It does indeed seem obvious that an artwork is a thing that has been made: made to be appreciated as an aesthetic object. Artwork = (material) thing + (spiritual) aesthetic component. Applied to architecture, this becomes: works of architecture = functional shed + aesthetic addendum. And isn't it the addition of this aesthetic component that makes something a work of art or architecture? Heidegger, however, claims that such an understanding obscures the nature of great art such as a Greek temple or a medieval cathedral, which stands in a different and more intimate relationship to things. Benjamin might say Heidegger refuses to let go of a more archaic auratic understanding of the artwork that remains focused on its thingly character. And Heidegger would have to grant this, aware that his emphasis on the unique materiality of a work of art cannot be reconciled with the modern understanding of the artwork as an aesthetic object, an understanding that subordinates the artwork's materiality to the beautiful illusion it creates. Heidegger's emphasis on the thingly character of the work of art claims that something essential is lost in this aesthetic transformation of the aura that once belonged to works of art. And Benjamin would seem to agree, even if such agreement does not mean that he thinks it is either possible or desirable to return to art its lost aura.

Benjamin recognizes that his matter-based concept of aura casts light not so much on the aesthetic approach to art as on an older understanding that placed art at the service of ritual: "We know that the earliest art works originated in the service of a ritual—first the magical, then the religious kind."[16] And that older understanding, even if not in keeping with the spirit of the times, retains its hold on us. Benjamin thus finds it "significant that the existence of the work of art with reference to its aura is never entirely separated from its ritual function."[17] Ritual is constitutive of aura and by extension of the sacred.

Heidegger would have agreed; although more optimistic—or, should we say, more nostalgic?—than Benjamin, he seeks to preserve that archaic origin: he looks to it to distinguish what great art once was and perhaps still can be from the aesthetic art that is demanded by this age of the world picture. That distinction is said to show itself in the very different ways in which works of art are "set up":

When a work is brought into a collection or placed in an exhibition we also say that it is "set up." But this setting up differs essentially from setting up in the sense of erecting a building, raising a statue, presenting a tragedy at a holy festival. Such setting up is erecting in the sense of dedication and praise. Here "setting up" no longer means a bare placing. To dedicate means to consecrate, in the sense that in setting up the work the holy is opened up as holy and the god is invoked into the openness of his presence. Praise belongs to the dedication as honor to the dignity and splendor of the god.[18]

But the modern world picture has no room for either gods or the holy: the world of temple and statue has perished. Although both may still have a place in our modern world as valued aesthetic objects, as such they have lost their basis in religious ritual. To be sure, we can grant Benjamin that "this ritualistic basis, however remote, is still recognizable as secularized ritual even in the most profane forms of the cult of beauty."[19] This poses the question of how to understand this modern cult of beauty: as a secularized pursuit of grace, where the artist assumes the role of the priest, or as a nostalgic attempt to hold on to something that in fact has disappeared from our modern world—in other words, as an example of bad faith? More resolutely modern than any celebration of the artwork's special aura would seem to be Kant's understanding of beauty as an object of an entirely disinterested satisfaction. It entails the reproducibility of what from an aesthetic point of view is essential in the work of art: its beautiful form. As Benjamin observes, "The

extent to which the cult value of the painting is secularized the ideas of its fundamental uniqueness lose distinctness. In the imagination of the beholder the uniqueness of the phenomena that hold sway in the cult image is more and more displaced by the empirical uniqueness of the creator or of the creative achievement."[20] This uniqueness transcends the material work of art, transcends the thing on which Heidegger placed so much weight. What matters about art, in this view, belongs to spirit rather than matter, belongs to the human spirit.

Just this, however, is challenged by Heidegger when he takes one task of art to be the presentation of the earth. At issue is his conviction that an acceptance and preservation of the incommensurability of our understanding and reality is a condition of finding meaning in life, that meaning cannot finally be invented by us but must be discovered. All meaning is a gift. In this sense, I also want to claim, responding to clues I find not just in Heidegger's work but also in Kant's *Critique of Judgment*, that an auratic appreciation of reality is needed to ground ethics and politics and that we need art and architecture to re-present and thus recall for us the aura of nature, especially our own nature. The beautiful here blurs with the sacred.

But I have been moving too fast. Let me slow down and return to the claim that our understanding and nature are incommensurable. It is sufficient to contemplate any natural object, say a rock, a tree, or some ears of wheat, to know about the inadequacy of all our attempts to really get hold of its reality, sufficient to let us recognize that reality will finally always transcend and elude our grasp. As Heidegger puts it,

A stone presses downward and manifests its heaviness. But while this heaviness exerts an opposing pressure upon us it denies us any penetration into it. If we attempt such a penetration by breaking open the rock, it still does not display in its fragments anything inward that has been disclosed. The stone has instantly withdrawn again into the same dull pressure and bulk of its fragments. If we try to lay hold of the stone's heaviness in another way, by placing the stone on a balance, we merely bring the heaviness into the form of a calculated weight. This perhaps very precise determination of the stone remains a number, but the weight's burden has escaped us. Color shines and wants only to shine. When we analyze it in rational terms by measuring its wavelength, it is gone. Earth thus shatters every attempt to penetrate into it. It causes every merely calculating importunity upon it to turn into a destruction.[21]

We can, of course, try to lift some stone, feel its weight. Feeling its weight, we may say it's heavy. To give a more exact answer, we may state its weight in kilograms. But such statements, no matter how detailed and accurate, lose the weight that I experience with my whole straining body that lets me experience also myself as an essentially embodied self. Challenging any understanding of reality that makes our ability to describe clearly and distinctly its focus, I want to maintain that we experience that something is real only as long as we remain aware that we are unable to fully understand whatever is before us. Reality transcends our understanding and language. Inseparable from our awareness of the reality of things is an awareness of what I want to call "material transcendence." With that expression, I point in the same general direction as Heidegger does with his "earth" or Kant with his "thing-in-itself," which is present to us only as appearance. What

invites such talk is the fact that, even if inevitably mediated by our language or concepts and as such appearance, what thus appears is experienced as not created by our understanding, but as given. Inseparable from our experience of things is a sense of this gift, an awareness that our understanding is bound to our bodies and finite, and that means also that the reach of our concepts and words is limited. Everything real is infinitely complex and can never be fully translated into words. The rift between thing and word cannot be closed, and it is this rift that gives everything we experience as real its distinctive aura.

Benjamin would have objected to what he might have called a fetishizing of matter incompatible with the positivist spirit of modern materialism. And thus he links the aura of the authentic work of art not so much to the unique, material thing it is as to the way it is "imbedded in the fabric of tradition."[22] History and memory are given greater importance than nature. Reproduction is said to tear the artwork out of its historical context and thus destroy its aura. This claim invites a broader application: in the age of mechanical reproduction, must not nature, too, and finally even human nature lose that special aura that distinguishes the original from its simulacrum? And if so, what are the implications of the loss of aura for ethics?

Benjamin's loving description of the true collector—he knew what he was talking about, having been just such a collector himself—offers a pointer to just how much is at stake in the refusal to let go of the artwork's aura: human happiness. We may well ask: but what does it matter that I own this particular material object, this surviving exemplar of some rare edition, rather than some readily available and perhaps much more informative critical edition of the same text? Why should I care about the book's provenance, its previous owners?

Benjamin's portrait of the collector underscores the way aura grants to things an almost human presence.[23] The acquisition of a book, for example, is described by him in a way that suggests a marriage. The aura some book or work of art possesses for the true collector is not unlike the aura that any person possesses whom we encounter and cherish as such. He invests what he collects with his own humanity, experiences it as if it were a person. That helps to explain its aura and his bliss.

It is indeed the person in the work of art, Benjamin suggests, that provides a last refuge to what remains of the cult value once possessed by works of art:

In photography, exhibition value begins to displace cult value all along the line. But cult value does not give way without resistance. It retires into an ultimate retrenchment: the human countenance. It is no accident that the portrait was the focal point of early photography. The cult of remembrance of loved ones, absent or dead, offers a last refuge for the cult value of the picture. For the last time the aura emanates from the early photographs in the fleeting expression of a human face. This is what constitutes their melancholy, incomparable beauty.[24]

And is there not a sense in which it is the human countenance of a painting, even an abstract painting, say by Jackson Pollock, that, while offering us no more than traces, nevertheless is experienced as a kind of self-portrait that here, too, offers what once was the cult value of painting a last refuge? We get a hint here that the cult value of certain objects is tied to the way they place us in an ongoing human context. That can also be said of works of architecture. The loss of

aura means spiritual homelessness. The age of mechanical reproduction threatens the triumph of nihilism.

As his discussion of the collector suggests, the paradigm behind all experiences of aura is for Benjamin the experience of another person: "Looking at someone carries the implicit expectation that our look will be returned by the object of our gaze. Where this expectation is met (which, in the case of thought processes, can apply equally to the look of the mind and to a glance—pure and simple), there is an experience of the aura to the fullest extent."[25] There is to be sure a profound difference between experiencing the gaze of the other and experiencing the aura of a writer or a composer in one of his or her creations. When I experience the other person, the experience of his or her distinctive aura is the experience of an incarnation of spirit and matter so complete that there is no distance between the two. The mystery of aura is the mystery of such incarnation, which is fully realized when two lovers look into each other's eyes: "The person we look at, or who feels he is being looked at, looks at us in return."[26] But something of the sort is present in every experience of aura: to experience the aura of something, say a work of architecture, is to experience it as if it were another person, capable of speech. Benjamin no doubt would have us underscore the "as if": "Experience of the aura thus rests on the transportation of a response common in human relationships to the relationship between the inanimate or natural object and man."[27] In this interpretation, it is the human subject who invests an essentially mute nature with something like spirit of soul. But must we who are truly of this modern world not recognize that such an investment is at bottom a self-deception?

Today, a child may still experience rocks and animals as animate, endowed with the power of speech; and fairy tales preserve traces of an older magical experience of the aura of all things. But the reason that it is a presupposition of our science and technology has to render nature mute and meaningless. Such a reason cannot make sense of the phenomenon of aura except as a projection of meaning into matter that as such lacks meaning.

But are human beings not part of nature? Descartes promised a science that would render human beings the masters and possessors of nature. Today, the spirit of such mastery presides over our world: artifice threatens to embrace the environment so completely that at moments it seems to all but vanish in the embrace, pushed to the peripheries of our postmodern culture, where in wilderness preserves we may still meet with vestiges of what once was "the desert of the real itself."[28] The last is an expression I borrowed from Baudrillard. Baudrillard conjures up a world in which image is no longer "the reflection of a profound reality," no longer "masks and denatures a profound reality," no longer even "masks the absence of a profound reality" but instead "has no relation to any reality whatsoever" and "is its own pure simulacrum."[29] Let me accept Baudrillard's dismal prophecy as at least an illuminating caricature of our world where the boundary that separates real from virtual architecture seems to get increasingly blurred. What then makes this caricature so disturbing? How are we to understand our nostalgia for a natural environment uncontaminated by simulacra, for beauty not born of artifice? Just what is wrong with artifice? Why not compensate ourselves for the ugliness of an environment shaped by our own understanding of what constitutes an acceptable standard of living, including demands for cheap energy, for a high degree of physical and spiritual mobility, with images that let us dream of a very different world, a world that increasingly seems to belong to a past that cannot be recovered? Why not enjoy such images without having to surrender comforts that have come to seem almost an inalienable right? And what is wrong with artificial environments that mimic beautiful nature but without the ants, scorpions, centipedes, and jellyfish that can make Caribbean beaches quite unpleasant? Are such artificial environments not anticipations of that paradise regained on the basis of technology of which already Francis Bacon and Descartes, these founding heroes of modernity, were dreaming?

Why then do such environments frighten us—at least some of us? Do such artificial environments not have their own beauty? Why should anticipations of some future world that would no longer have an outside at all, that really would be what Baudrillard takes our world already to be, a world of simulacra, why should such figures disturb us?

Because, I want to suggest, in such a world we would find ourselves increasingly disembodied and alone. In such a world, our own being, along with the being of persons and things, would lose its weight, would become unbearably light. Our sense of reality, inseparably tied to a sense of our own reality, demands that we remain open to that rift within us between spirit and body, where openness to the body is also openness to what eludes all our attempts to master and possess reality. Full self-affirmation demands an affirmation of what Heidegger called the earth.

The awareness that what we have before us is not really rock but only simulates one threatens to reduce what presents itself to our eyes to a mere spectacle. Mock rock loses the aura of the real. But such loss inevitably diminishes our sense of our own reality. And the same is true of an environment of simulacra. To the derealization of things corresponds the derealization of the subject. Openness to the reality of the real, whose vestiges, according to Baudrillard, persist in the increasingly artificial environment we have created, lets the self return to itself. Is it not this that lets us long for wilderness?

In the *Critique of Judgment*, Kant wonders how it would affect us to learn that what we thought was the call of a nightingale was in fact produced by a boy an innkeeper had hired some beautiful summer evening to heighten the enjoyment of his guests. The assumption here is that what is heard remains indistinguishable from the song of the true nightingale. From a purely aesthetic point of view, it would seem that there should be no reason to rank one above the other. We might even prefer the simulacrum, which demonstrates the skill of the performer. Nevertheless, Kant suggests, once we learn of the deception, what we hear loses its aura; we hear the same melody but without the former interest and pleasure, which shows that more is involved in our appreciation of beautiful nature than just the appreciation of beautiful forms. What matters to Kant is that these forms are experienced by us as products of nature, as not born of artifice. Something in nature here appears to respond to our intellect and its demands, and Kant here does not hesitate to invoke the medieval understanding of nature as a text: the beauties of nature present themselves to us as ciphers addressed to us.[30] Spirit without speaks to our own spirit. In beautiful nature, we feel at home. The experience of the beauty of the environment promises a genuine homecoming.

But has Benjamin not taught us to recognize the self-deception that supports such an experience? What sense can we still make of talk of spirit dwelling in nature? A religious person might have an answer. But has the progress of science not replaced the book of nature with an understanding of nature as the totality of essentially mute facts, to be used by us as we see fit and are able? More questions are raised by Kant's claim that "an immediate interest in the beauty of nature … is always the mark of a good soul," that the appreciation of the beauty of nature is "akin to the moral feeling."[31] How are we to understand such kinship?

What links the two is that both involve something like a recognition of an incarnation of spirit in matter. To be sure, as Kant emphasizes, science can know nothing of such an incarnation. And yet such incarnation is a presupposition of any ethics. Morality presupposes that we experience others as persons deserving respect. But this is to say that we must be able to experience the other person as more than just a material object among objects, say as a very complicated robot governed by a computer so complicated that it successfully simulates human intelligence. The other must present him- or herself to me as spirit incarnated in this particular matter. I must experience that person's special aura. Were I to learn that what I took to be a person was just some mechanical reproduction, I would no longer experience the aura that alone lets me recognize the other as a person, like myself. I would lose what lets me know that I am not alone.

But even if we grant that the recognition of persons presupposes an experience of aura that is more than just a registration of mute facts, that here we experience incarnations of spirit in matter, what justifies Kant's claim that recognition of beauty in nature, too, presupposes an openness to meaning of which we are not the authors. Kant might answer that even though science cannot know anything resembling an incarnation of spirit in matter, its pursuit of truth nonetheless presupposes experiences of the intelligibility, or as he would put it, of the purposiveness of nature. Kant's theory of knowledge thus has its foundation in his understanding of aesthetic experience or of beauty. And this claim can be generalized: the very self-assertion that leads human beings to oppose themselves to nature as its masters and possessors presupposes not just sensation but a perception of significant patterns or family resemblances, as Schopenhauer and, following him, Wittgenstein were to put it. All concept formation presupposes perceptions of meaning in matter, of meaning that cannot be manufactured but must be received as a gift. Kant takes such perception to be an experience of beauty, understood as purposiveness without a purpose. There is thus an intimate link between my ability to appreciate the beauty of the natural environment and my ability to experience the other as a person. Both are perceptions of spirit incarnated in matter, answering to our own spirit. Both give us the understanding that we are not lost in the world but at home in it.

At this point, you may be wondering whether in embracing this central argument of Kant's *Critique of Judgment* I have not forgotten the beginning of this chapter. Does the medieval understanding of nature as a book in which God speaks to us not lie so thoroughly behind us that Kant's invocation of it should be understood as no more

than just a rhetorical embellishment, not to be taken too seriously? And what modern aesthetician would follow Kant in placing the beauty of nature so decisively above the beauty of art? Did Hegel not have good reason to exclude the beauty of nature from his *Aesthetics*? Hegel justifies this exclusion by insisting that "the beauty of art is the beauty that is born—born again, that is—of the mind; and by as much as the mind and its products are higher than nature and its appearances, by so much the beauty of art is higher than the beauty of Nature."[32]

Nature is thought by Hegel, in characteristically modern fashion, first of all as mute material to be understood, appropriated, and used by us as we see fit. A crystal can be called beautiful, but the beauty of its geometric faces is really the product of our own spirit, which recognizes in their geometry something of itself. With greater justice a work of architecture can be called beautiful, or just a ploughed field. In both cases, human beings have labored to impose an order on matter. Nature has been subjected to the human spirit. Considered just in itself, Hegel insists, nature cannot really be considered beautiful. Kant had a very different understanding of beauty: he leaves no doubt that for him the ground of all artificial beauty finally is the beauty of a nature that transcends our understanding.

Hegel knows, of course, that human beings are also animals and as such part of nature. But human beings are animals that by virtue of their reason raise themselves above nature, become conscious of it, experience it, including their own nature, as not simply given but as material to be understood, shaped, and bent to their will instructed by their reason. Their spirit places human beings in opposition to nature, demands mastery over it. In something as simple as a child throwing stones into the water and enjoying the rings formed, Hegel finds evidence of this drive. Already in such childish play, human beings seek to appropriate the natural given by transforming it in their own image, and this means first of all in the image of their own spirit. History is understood by Hegel as the progress of such appropriation. Art, like religion, is part of the effort to make the natural and sensible our own, to rob it of its character of being a mute, alien other by investing it with the aura of the human, and thus to help transform the earth into a dwelling place fit for human beings, into something that deserves to be called "home." The goal of art also is such humanization of the sensible, where humanization here means spiritualization. So understood, art prefigures technology, which allows for a far more effective mastery of nature and for that very reason eventually overtakes art and leaves it behind.

Here we have a key to Hegel's thesis of the death of art in its highest sense, which, if accepted, entails also the death of sacred architecture. And just as decisively as Hegel would have us place the beauty of art above the beauty of nature, he would have us place the beauty of artificial environments above the beauty of natural environments. Kant's nightingale argues for a very different understanding of nature.

Regardless of details, in its essentials Hegel's determination is difficult to get around. *If* we grant him the importance he grants spirit and freedom, do we not grant him the substance of his case? If human freedom demands that the individual liberate him- or herself from the accidents of what happens

to be the case, then our real home should not be sought by looking toward the aura of some mountain range or branch, to some particular place and its *genius loci*. Must our real home not be a spiritual home to which nothing sensible can finally do justice? Consider in this connection the recurrent insistence on the inessential nature of what is considered the accident of location, birth, gender, and race. Is the attempt to discover one's home in a particular place not born of a nostalgia that we should not allow to rule our lives and build us our homes? Hegel's philosophy is born out of the confidence that human beings, bound only by the authority of their own reason, today find themselves on the threshold of true autonomy. Our aggressive appropriation and transformation of the environment appears from this perspective as but an aspect of humanity's coming of age. Are there not many today who feel already more at home in cyberspace than in any natural environment? The death of sacred architecture is a corollary.

Let me return once more to Kant's two nightingales. Kant, as I pointed out, assumes that the song of the artificial nightingale cannot be distinguished from that of its natural counterpart: the relevant aesthetic object would seem to be the same in the two cases. And yet the song of the real nightingale, he insists, has an aura that its simulacrum does not possess. The loss of that aura lets us become bored with the latter, lets us dismiss it as no more than rather superficial entertainment. Something analogous can be said about real flowers and their simulacra, and of buildings that we experience as clones of other buildings.

But just what is it that gives the real nightingale or the real flower its special aura?

How are we to understand this sense that what we are experiencing is not something artificial, that it is not a product of our own spirit that here seems to speak to us, but spirit incarnated in nature? Whatever it is, it must be a bit like feeling the heaviness of the stone. It weighs on us, touches us. It is essentially the same sense that gives a special aura to each individual: we are touched. The other's plight weighs on us; the other's joy lifts us, too. Suppose a person we thought we loved turned out to be a mechanical puppet: our love would disintegrate.

Kant's example of the two nightingales teaches us that beauty alone is not enough. Representations or reproductions of beautiful nature need not preserve the aura of the original. That is the lesson of Kant's nightingale: the beauty of nature, including human nature, lets us feel at home in the world as artificial beauty is unable to do. The beauty of art must remain grounded in the beauty of nature. We need art to open windows in the house objectifying reason has built, windows to nature, including our own nature.

But how does this apply to sacred architecture? It also must be grounded in and answer to an experience of the world as a gift that speaks to us of our place. That is to say, we need to reappropriate the wisdom buried in the traditional understanding of architecture as repetition and image of the cosmos. This to be sure presupposes that we can still experience in some sense our world as a cosmos, that is to say as rather like a house, a house of which we are not the authors.

PART III   RESPONSE FROM ARCHITECTURAL PRACTICE

MICHAEL J. CROSBIE

14 CALLING FORTH THE NUMINOUS IN ARCHITECTURE

One of the primary roles of sacred architecture is to facilitate an encounter with the "holy," divine, or metaphysical. Given the centrality of this issue to any discussion of sacred space and architecture, it is essential to consider the concept of the "numinous" as advanced by Rudolf Otto, the German religious scholar and thinker, in his book *Das Heilige*, published in 1917 (its first English translation, *The Idea of the Holy: An Inquiry into the Non-Rational Factor and the Idea of the Divine and Its Relation to the Rational*, was published in 1923).

Otto devised the term "numinous" to describe the power or presence of the holy, but without its moral factor. The numinous is the common denominator for all religious experience, in every culture around the world. He wrote, "There is no religion in which it does not live as the real innermost core, and without it no religion would be worthy of the name."[1]

Otto coined the word "numinous" from the Late Latin word *numen*, which means "an influence perceptible by the mind but not by the senses."[2] Sociologists use the word numen to refer to the belief in the magical powers of an object, such as a talisman, stone, or other object invested with the spirit of potential.[3] The term "numinous" is related to, but not derived from, the Greek word *noumenon*, which describes the knowing of an object or event (if it can be known at all) not by seeing, touching, smelling, tasting, or hearing it. Not through the senses at all, but simply in the mind, a knowing of something without evidence of an everyday variety, through sensory experience.[4] It is knowledge received not through direct sensory experience but perhaps only through openness, stillness, by invitation of one's self.

The numinous can be discussed, debated, hinted at, and speculated about, but Otto tells us that it cannot be defined. The numinous is a mental state that is "irreducible to any other."[5] The numinous is not inside us, but outside. It is sensed inside of us, but it resides apart from us. The numinous, Otto writes, is "felt as objective, and outside the self."[6] How do we arrive at the numinous? How can we possibly understand it? Otto tells us that we must be led; we must be guided through our own consideration and discussion of it, through one's own mind, until the numinous inside each one of us "begins to stir." It cannot be taught, it can only be awakened.[7]

How do we make the numinous, as a state of mind, "ring out," as Otto describes it?[8] He suggests that we seek it out, with "sympathy and imaginative intuition,"[9] wherever it is found, and one place where the numinous consciousness is directed, he tells us, is in "the atmosphere that clings to old religious monuments and buildings, to temples and churches."[10] That element, as Otto calls it, is the "*mysterium tremendum*."[11]

How do we become possessed of this state? Otto describes the feeling of it as a gentle tide sweeping over us, imparting "a tranquil mood of deepest worship"[12] to still the turbulence of the mind's worldly distractions. As it submerges us, it may be "thrillingly vibrant and resonate,"[13] until it washes back out to the great sea of numinousness, as it were, leaving one's soul high and dry in its "profane" state of everyday existence. At other times, this feeling might erupt from "the depths of the soul"[14] without warning, transporting us to

ecstasy. Or, Otto consoles us, it may become "the hushed, trembling, and speechless humility"[15] we experience in the presence of … the presence of what? In the presence of the mystery of mysteries—inexpressible, and yet at the very core of the holy.

In this presence, we tremble. We tremble not in fear, Otto explains—we tremble in awe. Otto considers examples of fear in scripture—the fear of God (in Exodus it is the dread sent forth by Yahweh)—but fear of this type lacks the dimension of awe. It is less something that we sense, comprehend, and then "fear" in response. The sense of awe that Otto describes is one in which we completely fail to comprehend what we are witnessing. It is other-worldly; perhaps we sense it as impossible. We have no reference point for it; we cannot measure it with our personal experience or our shared human experience. But this feeling, Otto posits, "forms the starting-point"[16] for religion in human history and a new realm of experience in human beings. And in the recognition of this overpowering, "aweful majesty,"[17] we are reduced to trembling in the realization of our own powerlessness, nothingness, the alienation of our "selfhood," or the fact that we are just "dust and ashes," as Otto describes it so aptly, which, he writes, "forms the numinous raw material for the feeling of religious humility."[18]

Otto argues that the term *mysterium tremendum* should not be understood as one state that implies the other. You can have mystery without tremor, and you can have awe without mystery. Otto means the word mysterious in its religious sense: "the 'wholly other,' that which is quite beyond the sphere of the usual, the intelligible, and the familiar."[19] For Otto, mystery is a component of the numinous that "fills the blank mind with wonder and astonishment."[20] And, he adds, fascination. For the experience of the "aweful majesty" of the numinous is accompanied by an allure, a potent charm. One feels dread but also attraction to it, an impulse to turn toward it, Otto writes, "to make it somehow his own."[21]

Where is art and architecture in the creation of the numinous? What is its role in helping us to "ring it out," as Otto describes the evidence of this feeling, the numinous? In *The Idea of the Holy*, Otto considers the role of art and architecture in calling forth the numinous. Otto claims that art and architecture cannot be numinous, but they can represent the numinous in the sublime, especially architecture. Architecture, in its lasting materials, in its scale, in its decoration, has, for Otto, a "magical" presence, which can suggest the numinous.[22]

In the West, Otto sees no greater numinous form of architecture than Gothic architecture and art.[23] It is sublime, and the most sublime of all—of course it is in Otto's native Germany—is the tower of the Cathedral in Ulm, as portrayed in Wilhelm Worringer's book *Formprobleme der Gotik*. From his description of the cathedral, it appears Otto is carried away with the sublimity of the cathedral's tower, because he contradicts himself by actually pronouncing Ulm Cathedral as "numinous," as distinct from merely "magical."[24] He notes that the difference between the two can nowhere be better felt than in the picture of the tower in Worringer's book. This is quite a statement, given that Otto's experience of the tower's "numinousness" is suggested by only a picture, not the actual building. No doubt Otto had visited the cathedral, and the photo in Worringer's book

FIGURE 14-1. THE WEST FAÇADE OF ULM MINSTER (ALSO KNOWN AS THE ULM CATHEDRAL) IN ULM, GERMANY, WHICH FOR RUDOLF OTTO WAS "NUMINOUS."

FIGURE 14-2. THE INTERIOR OF ANTONI GAUDI'S SAGRA-
DA FAMILIA IN BARCELONA.

sparked a memory of the numinous that the theologian must have felt in its presence.

While the sublime and the magical in architecture can represent the numinous in architecture, Otto believes that there are three more direct methods of suggesting the numinous: darkness, silence, and emptiness. The darkness is not absolute: Its presence is made all the more mysterious and overwhelming when contrasted with some last flicker of light, such as a candle just before it sputters out. Otto writes, "The semi-darkness that glimmers in vaulted halls … strangely quickened and stirred by the mysterious play of half-lights, has always spoken eloquently to the soul, and the builders of temples, mosques, and churches have made full use of it."[25]

Of silence, Otto argues that it is our spontaneous reaction to the presence of the numinous. And of emptiness, Otto speaks of it as "the sublime in the horizontal."[26] Nowhere is this more forcefully achieved for Otto than in Chinese architecture, in its placing buildings in space, with unfolding courtyards and vistas—capturing nothingness, as it were.

Can architecture create the numinous? Can architecture call it forth or "ring it out," as Otto writes? It seems that for this theologian, architecture can, at best, only symbolize the numinous; it can suggest its presence beyond architecture, transcending stone and metal, wood and glass, paint and clay. Architecture can make a place for the numinous to manifest. It can host that magical, sublime combination of darkness tinged with light, of silence so loud that you can hear the heart beat, and of spatial expanses that imply the void each of us must prepare for the numinous.

Julio Bermudez has done extensive work in

FIGURE 14-3. THE SUNDIAL AT THE TOP OF THE BRICK LANE MOSQUE REMINDS PASSERSBY THAT "WE ARE BUT SHADOWS."

this area, collecting accounts of people in the throes of the numinous experience.[27] One of the most poignant is from a visitor to Antoni Gaudi's Sagrada Familia in Barcelona, who recounts every element of the numinous that Otto identifies:

I was immediately overcome by the sheer scale of the structure I had entered. Despite the clutter of scaffolding, I felt somehow lifted into the space. As I entered further I was amazed by the intensity. And I turned and saw a wall of stained glass full of life and color abstracted in form. It became a part of me. Despite its religious context, I felt as though I understood it … and that somehow … it

… understood me. I don't know how to describe the "it" part, but I certainly was unable to ignore the penetrating bond that was created. I sat down where I was able and did what I could to hold back the tears, pretending to blow my nose as the rest of the visitors passed by me. I eventually went back and took a picture of the place, but it serves only as a reminder. The image conjures the fringe of the feelings that were generated, but can't quite simulate the overpowering nature of the event.[28]

Architecture most often celebrates the numinous, recognizes the holy, through exalted decoration, triumphant and precious materials, and achievements of human craft quite extraordinary. Less often celebrated, but just as essential to making us ready for the numinous, is the recognition of our dependence, our own insignificance, our transitory existence, our ultimate powerlessness, our speechless humility, our status as "dust and ashes," as Otto describes it. For this, one compelling example is offered. On Brick Lane, in the City of London, there stands a building constructed in 1743. It was first built as a place of worship for the French Huguenots, and in 1819 it became a Methodist chapel. By 1897 it had passed to a Jewish congregation and became the Spitalfields Great Synagogue. Seventy-nine years later, the Jamme Masjid acquired the building, and it is now the Brick Lane Mosque, one of the largest mosques in the city. This one building has been home to all three Abrahamic faiths.[29]

In the tympanum of its brick gabled façade is a sundial, inscribed with the building's date of construction and the words *Umbra Sumus*, inspired by the poet Horace. Every day, for all those years, the sundial has reminded those who look up at it, going there to worship or simply passing by: "We are but shadows."

15 ELEMENTAL SIMPLICITY

A few days ago, I heard a lecture by Juhanni Pallasmaa at the Finnish Embassy concerning the architecture of silence. Today, life is driven by speed, rush, and chaos, neglecting our need to pause and experience calm and serenity. We long for stillness and silence in our culture and in our life. In light of his observations and my own belief in the role of art and nature in creating silence, I thought it would be appropriate to begin with an art piece by Walter de Maria, *The Lightning Field* (1977). This artwork is in the desert of New Mexico. It is a site that is one mile by one kilometer, and it is filled with four hundred stainless steel rods. They all reach the same height but are shorter or longer depending on the rolling terrain. The average height of these poles is twenty feet. To see the art, people are taken by car to a small cabin and left there for twenty-four hours (a long time to stare at one piece of art), but as the hours pass they become aware of the changes occurring in tiny incremental steps. They realize the vast land around the lightning field, the sky, and the way the rods change when the light changes. You don't simply gaze at De Maria's work—the work of art is making you aware of the desert, the sky, and the transformations produced by light. The rods become pink and orange and red at dawn and sunset, and at noon and night they completely disappear. You become aware of eternity, infinity, and stillness. There is a quiet, calm light—a sense of strange familiarity, serenity, and elemental simplicity.

Art makes us see the world differently and enhances our awareness. Mark Rothko's *Orange and Yellow* (1956) embodies this. After seeing his paintings at the National Gallery, you see the sky differently. Consider now Cy

FIGURE 15-1. WALTER DE MARIA, *THE LIGHTNING FIELD*, 1977. QUEMADO, NEW MEXICO.

FIGURE 15-2. MARK ROTHKO, *ORANGE AND YELLOW*, 1956.

Twombly's *Untitled* (1970). This painting is four meters tall. When confronted with it, you wonder how to start. Where do things begin and end? It seems to have been created out of a mindless gesture; simple words written over and over again, but to the eye they become amazing wild clouds with remarkable depth. Yet another example is a sculpture by Nooni Reatig that I have in my office. It is made of folded, galvanized steel plates, and its name is *All Real All Steel*. It has the virtue that it constantly changes throughout the day. Its power stems from its amazing combination of geometric and organic forms, how the sharp and hard materials feel soft like a fabric, and how light magically changes the metal into something soothing as opposed to harsh. The presence of the natural in these works brings familiarity and, consequently, comfort to the viewer.

I would like to discuss two works that deal with gravity. The first is *Delineator* by Richard Serra (1974–1975). It consists of two plates, one on the floor and one on the ceiling. When I look at this, or experience it, there is only the feeling of intimidation or terror caused by the prospect of walking between these two plates. The second example is also by Serra and, I think, his best work: *Equal (Corner Prop Piece)*. It is one of his first efforts (1969–1970) and is composed of two pieces of lead: a plate and a tube. The silent power of this piece delicately operates like a ballerina, but it makes you aware that the balance can tilt at any moment. It is like life. Things look balanced, but you really do not know what may happen next.

By exposure to nature and art, we can strive to create architecture that brings about spiritual comfort. The work of two inspiring architects illustrates this: Luis Barragán and Louis Kahn.

Being in Luis Barragán's house in Mexico City is a spiritual experience. The simplicity, the modesty. Nothing is extra. No clutter, but a very powerful experience. For example, his living room brings the outside to the inside in the simplest, most minimal way. In the afternoon, he would go out and sit in this outer room, sit under the sky, just surrounded by white walls and the sky. Here, the architecture encourages us to become aware of the outside, and once we are aware of the sky and earth, we become aware again of the walls surrounding us and the tranquility to be found in the house's simplicity.

Kahn's Salk Institute in La Jolla, California, is another spiritual experience. The open space framed by the buildings, the sky, and the ocean shows how architecture can make us see nature differently.

FIGURE 15-3. NOONI REATIG, *ALL REAL ALL STEEL #2*, 2003. GALVANIZED STEEL.

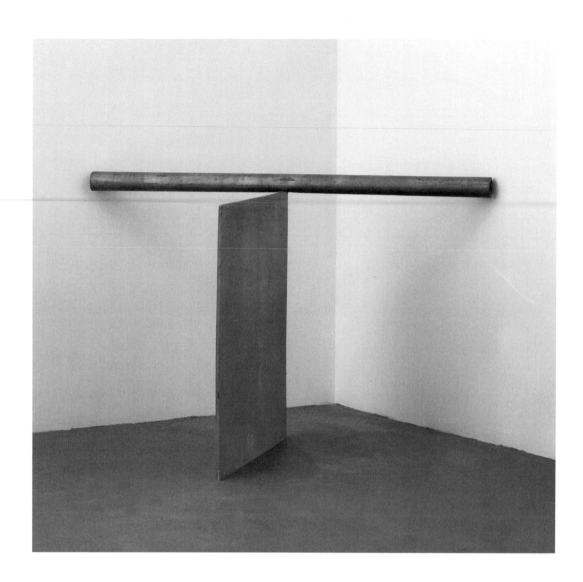

FIGURE 15-4. RICHARD SERRA, *EQUAL (CORNER PROP PIECE)*, 1969–1970.

I will conclude these short reflections with a brief reference to my work. First, I would like to discuss the Metropolitan Community Church that I was commissioned to design in 1989 and was completed in 1993. The question was how to conceive a spiritual building for a group of people who are discriminated against. Other churches were rejecting them. Their neighborhood did not want them around. The building site was in a dangerous neighborhood, and they hardly had any money. So it had to be a simple building with simple materials. The plan is very elemental: a rectangular sanctuary wrapped by an L-shaped wing holding programmatic services. Opening the building and welcoming the neighborhood encourages the client's acceptance within the community. Even with simple ordinary materials: steel, concrete masonry, and glass, the building changes

FIGURE 15-5. MAIN COURTYARD OF THE SALK INSTITUTE
BY LOUIS KAHN. LA JOLLA, CALIFORNIA.

FIGURE 15-6. METROPOLITAN COMMUNITY CHURCH BY
SUZANE REATIG ARCHITECTURE, 1993.

constantly as the light changes. At dusk, it becomes completely gold. The openness, light,
and the reflective glass generate a feeling of
eternity and serenity.

I am showing very briefly some residential
work we do. Most of our work is for nonprofit, with modest budgets. We always provide
a cross-ventilation and a few exposures to
each apartment unit which usually requires
having a court. By blurring the line between
inside and outside, we encourage nature and
our own self and private space to interact and
blend. This simplicity, openness, and oneness

with the elements inherently bring us serenity
and tranquility. Light changing during the
day makes us conscious of our surroundings,
the time, and the seasons. Architecture as
art makes us see the world differently and
enhances our awareness of nature and reality.

I want to end with a quote by James
Turrell. He said, "The best magic of all is the
magic that is real. I am interested in working
straight with that power."[1]

DUNCAN G. STROIK

16 TRANSCENDENCE, WHERE HAST THOU GONE?

When I think of the numinous (i.e., the experience of the Holy) and architecture, I am reminded of the work of Anders Sövik, who called his work the architecture of the "non-church."[1] Like many people who devote their lives to religious architecture, Anders Sövik is not well known in the profession. I think this is what Karla Britton is partially talking about in her chapter in this volume. Sövik may not be held in high regard today, but—at least in the 1960s and 1970s—he was a very important architectural voice who influenced the design of many parish churches. Anders Sövik had a successful practice and referred to the "numinous" quite often, quoting Rudolf Otto. This is how I learned about the concept of the numinous, from the dissertation by Mark Torgerson written at Notre Dame many years ago.[2]

While there are many elements of sacred architecture shared across religions, we can also say that there are distinctive qualities characterizing different faiths or religious traditions. It is these distinctive aspects that make the architecture of those traditions unique or special and give them identity. My own study of sacred architecture over the past two decades has led me to the conclusion that transcendence is one of the three essential dimensions crucial to sacred architecture, alongside procession and beauty.

That being said, I am particularly interested in determining the elements that make architecture transcendent. And I would like to ask, are there particular gifts that the Christian tradition has brought us? As we know, the Christian faith grows up within the milieu of Roman-Pagan religion and culture. During that time, Pagan temples were extroverted, with the sacrifice happening on

the outside, on substantial marble altars. And that was very typical of most religions in that age. The extroverted nature of these temples meant that only very few people could go inside: priests, the nobility, maybe the divine Caesar. They were not really places for the common person to enter. The revolutionary thing that Christianity did was to build large buildings that people could worship within. In other words, it proposed an introverted type of sacred architecture. The early basilicas were very large spaces that allowed thousands of faithful to attend the ritual gathering, with tall ceilings that allowed light to come from above and a heavenly illumination along with directionality, both vertical and horizontal. And then there was a focus on a place of mystery formed by an apse with a half dome, the raised sanctuary probably shrouded with a colonnade (a predecessor to the *iconostastis)*, and an altar that was also veiled. In short, early Christian architecture offered some remarkable new elements to the history of architecture, which I would call an interior of transcendence.

But why should a church or other kind of temple express transcendence? There are any number of reasons, yet I would emphasize that the goal of transcendence is to express the "other," the beyond, the eternal. As Father Seasoltz mentions in his chapter in this book, architecture seeks to give a taste of eternity, a taste of the Divine. In fact, sacred architecture in some way is meant to symbolize or embody the Godhead.

Related, and using a different metaphor, we can think of a Christian sanctuary as a gateway to heaven. And here one remembers Jacob's Ladder and how Jacob says that such a gate is none other than the house of God,[3] an expression that to this day continues to be

FIGURE 16-1. SANTA MARIA IN TRASTEVERE. ROME, ITALY.

used as a way to refer to the church building: a gateway through which we depart the material world and enter into the sacred realm to go beyond, into the "other."

Fundamental to the experience of transcendence is height. However, it is not sufficient to have a tall building to gain an experience of transcendence. Vertical proportions are also needed. For instance, compare the Houston Astrodome, dubbed the eighth wonder of the world in 1965, at 200 feet tall with St. Peter's basilica in Rome, with a nave only 150 feet tall. The Astrodome is much grander, much more vast, and maybe even more impressive to many adherents of the sports religion. But I would argue that while the stadium is huge and shocking, it is not transcendent. So, what are the things that differentiate St. Peter's and make it transcendent? The vertical proportions, the way light enters, fine materials, and the particular architectural syntax all combine to express transcendence. There is not one single reason but many that come together to create a sense of transcendence. And most of these principles can be seen in the broad expanse of religious architecture, but they are particularly evident in the Christian tradition.

In the modern age, some of these architectural elements calling forth the sacred have continued to be used, especially the idea of height and verticality. Yet the other aspects endemic to transcendence which we see exhibited at St. Peter's basilica have disappeared.

If one defines transcendence using these principles, some might suggest that the architects of the great modernist churches were not really interested in transcendence. In fact, if you read Karla Britton's chapter, you will see that most of the great modern churches were designed by agnostics. So what does an architect do if he wants to design a powerful modern church but is not an agnostic?

And, maybe more importantly, what should the average person do? There are these great monuments, these great cathedrals that they can visit. But what about the average church they go to, whether it is once a week or only on Easter and Christmas? What does it do for them? People in the pew will naturally compare their church built in the last fifty years to a church built at an earlier time. It may come as a surprise to architects that many pew-sitters do not believe that the average Catholic church built during the past half century exhibits any transcendence, much less an intimation of heaven. Or, as Pope John Paul II exclaimed upon visiting a church from the 1960s in Rome, "There is little sense of the sacred in these modern churches."[4]

Some might say an intimation of heaven is a rather tall order. Yet not so long ago it was common for architects to be able to create a sense of transcendence that could be appreciated by the average person. And, in fact, this sense of transcendence continues to be appreciated. That is one of the challenging things about architecture. While it is considered architectural dogma that one should create an architecture of our time that meets modern needs, the reality is that most buildings go beyond our time. And churches, especially, need to be thought of in that way.

Going back to our principles of Christian sacred architecture, I would argue that height/verticality is one of the first things to address in an architecture of transcendence. Yet we encounter great trouble when trying to design and build tall structures. Why? Because we are building in small towns or even in suburban locations with restrictive

FIGURE 16-2. NOTRE DAME DU HAUT. RONCHAMP, FRANCE.

building codes. The standard height limit in this country for buildings is thirty-five feet. So, for a one-story building that happens to be sixty or seventy-five feet tall, one must convince the neighbors and the city to give a variance.

What are some of the other things that are important? The temple upon the hill, the building itself that appears like it is a hill or a place to go up to. I had the opportunity to design a pilgrimage church in Wisconsin

that sits on the side of the hill. You cannot drive up to it and are forced to make a short pilgrimage.

The tower is another important consideration in building sacred Christian architecture. We all agree that towers are not only a place for bells, but they point heavenward. There are many ways to design towers. For instance, I love the Ulm Cathedral and its numinous Gothic tower. The other typology relevant to us here is the dome. The church

FIGURE 16-3. OUR LADY OF THE MOST HOLY TRINITY,
THOMAS AQUINAS COLLEGE. SANTA PAULA, CALIFOR-
NIA, 2009.

FIGURE 16-4. OUR LADY OF GUADALUPE SHRINE.
LACROSSE, WISCONSIN, 2009.

building with its tower and its dome rises up like a mountain or a little city on a hill.

When you enter a church, it is as if you are entering through a gateway from the profane toward the sacred. On the way, you many enter into a narthex, a place of transition somewhere between the outside world and the holy place of the interior. It is in this place of transition that historically the baptistery was located since this sacrament is thought of as a dying to the world and a new life in God. The nave, whether in a parish church or a cathedral, should have a sense of verticality. The ceiling, the vaulting, the decoration, and the ribbing are all ways to give a sense of transcendence. Along with verticality, a temple also needs a sense of the infinite, accomplished often by colonnades, side chapels, and aisles, which leads the visitor into these other spaces and even toward those occupants of the infinite, the angels, and the saints.

In the Christian tradition, inspired by the Incarnation, the icon or image is crucial. Through painting and sculpture, glass and mosaic, we re-present the figures that have gone on before us. In fact, in a sacramental architecture that speaks to people, icons are crucial to helping us participate in the heavenly realm, which these "holy others" are participating in already.

The transept, while not necessary, is a wonderful way to create a layer of complexity and a modulation of our approach to the holy of holies. The dome can reflect the heavens due to its spherical shape and vertical proportions. At the Shrine of Our Lady of Guadalupe, it was painted with the constellations, as they would have been seen on December 12, 1531, the day of the Virgin's appearance to the peasant Juan Diego.

Light is crucial, not just for illumination but also as an expression of beauty. And a talented lighting designer has an important role to play, not only in working with natural sources (e.g., stained glass) but also with electric lighting, which allow us to illuminate the temple at all times of day and night.

Another essential element in the creation of transcendence in a church is the sacred location and design of the altar, possibly using a *baldacchino* or some other device to set it apart. Just as Mary Magdalene anointed the body of Christ, so the altar of sacrifice is anointed with oil when it is dedicated. And that which is consecrated and not consumed is left in the smallest *tempietto* of all, in a tabernacle, for prayer and adoration outside of the liturgy.

If it is true that famous modern architects are not particularly interested in transcendence, then it may not be surprising that this quality is not present in most contemporary religious structures. In its stead we find other characteristics, such as impressive size, sculptural lighting, or structural complexity. For many talented agnostic architects, the goal may be an architecture of absence rather than transcendence.[5] This is because the concept of transcendence in architecture implies belief in an invisible reality that is not materially quantifiable.

17 ARCHITECTURAL QUESTS INTO THE NUMINOUS

A search of the numinous travels well beyond the great historical examples of sacred architecture. Indeed sacred architecture has never failed to be one of the best expediters for such a quest. We all readily understand design driven by spiritual metaphor when it comes to religious architecture. For millennia, from the animists like the Hopi, to the Egyptians, the Greeks, and Romans, to the great world religions of Judaism, Christianity, Islam, Hinduism, and Buddhism, all have relied on succinct mythical metaphors to shape their edifices of worship and their heritage. These spiritual lyrics are at the heart of their messages, and their architecture has always sung their stories. It is why we continue today to design synagogues that collect the minions, cathedrals that mass us together to celebrate the light above, mosques that simply lift us into triangular clouds to surrender to God's greatness, and stupas to churn us in the milk of the sea of consciousness and Samsara. The Greek gods are still lyrics for our everyday classical want-to-be architecture.

How this human poetic can carry on into the modern world in its own democratic idiom is a new and daunting horizon, especially in light of the numinous loss to materialistic modernism. Attempting to design modern architecture, even the so-called mundane and profane buildings, to come alive with renewed numinosity requires an open examination of our vast cultural landscape with direct involvement through a freshly informed modernity. We need a new way to explore our emerging architecture inspired by the ancients, a way to live in buildings that evoke enduring primordial wisdom. This resonance of human spirit is, of course, diversely demonstrated in regional vernacular architecture that is historical. At the same time, the numinous is beginning to find its way into modern architecture through cultural imprints that are inherently driven in mankind's mythological heritage. I call this resurrection of man's numinosity in today's new architecture "the Mythic Modern," an intoxicating new horizon in contemporary design vocabulary.

In 1970, as a graduate student at the University of New Mexico, I and a half-dozen other students went on a ten-day camping trip with a mentor, Harvard professor and author J. B. Jackson, to Chaco Canyon, the site of remote pre-Columbian ruins built a thousand years ago by the Pueblo peoples. As the dawn light rose over the mighty cliff edges, my heart took flight. Numinous yellow clouds shimmered and purple cacti flowered as rosy rock striations rippled into view. In the distance, the Rinconada Kiva tipped the first rays of the sun, spilling across the dappled chamisa brush. From the clouds, it seemed as if a hundred Kachina dancers were snaking their way steadily downward into the *sipapu*, the birthing navel of the earth. As the sun pitched onward to its zenith, the great semicircle of stacked stones passively melted the night snows back into the clouds. As always, I wondered how such a marvelous structure had been designed. How was such a massive shape directed: was it simply the obvious survival instinct of facing the south sun for warmth, or was it perhaps better understood as a building design blessed with a sacred shape directed by watchful tribal shamans?

For decades the answer to this symbiosis for me has been always embedded in a simple, joyful paradox of design: "both" seems to be the best answer. Nature and man

distinctly different, yet intrinsically interwoven, creating our great architecture in a seamless paradox, entwining the physical and the metaphysical. For me, the numinous in architectural form is just such a mix; it is the metaphysical memory that exudes in particular forms derived in our shared subconscious as well as our shared cosmic conscience. I share the Eliadean belief that a noncorporeal body, the sacred, is embedded in all things, and while at times it may not be seen by blinded eyes, or by being of a diluted quality, there is a numinous essence embedded in the stories told, evoked, and/or remembered in these things. If one has any doubts about this notion, one only need visit a profoundly profane space like the back alley of a bar or a sterilized modern mall to feel the lack of numinosity. The ensuing emptiness becomes self-evident.

The crisscrossed layers and crusts of cultures globally with landscapes graced by mankind's built legacies are a source of never-ceasing joy to me. Yet alarmingly, while the accelerated speed of modern industrialism has brought us a phenomenal reprieve from the drudgery of rural slavery, our landscapes and, even more importantly, the poetics of our cultural heritage are confronting a looming loss. The flow of cultural homogenization is creeping rapidly across the built world. The speed of today's industrial growth is blanketing a tsunami of artistic loss. Never has this been more apparent than in our soulless architectural landscape. Auto-driven sprawl, ubiquitous malls, and the excess of one-liner high-rises have plundered our historical spirit from the built environment. There isn't a country I know of today—from Peru to Nepal, India, Ireland, Finland, and, especially, the United States—that isn't struggling with a loss of authenticity. The critical poetics of regional architecture is quietly being lost under the mud of homogenization. Our historical architectural response to climate and to the human imagination is increasingly waning under our massive fossil fuel indulgences.

Even more disconcerting in our accelerating globalization is the portending shape of the future, a future where homogenized buildings augmented by nostalgically watered-down exterior decorating will shape our very human character into one monochromatic, bland whisper. Our built environments do shape our character just as much as we do. This new character, or lack thereof, sadly may be as empty as the structures we are building. Already we are filling that feeling of emptiness with an even more vacuous virtual, electronic reality that not only alienates us but, more dreadfully, numbs us to our environment and our fellow humans. Our common stories, myths, and authentic fiber will continue to fade away if they are not retold and revived in our modern works.

There is another design path worth the venture, a way to rekindle our souls in a modern idiom. I have sought metaphysical guidance from a number of mentors: Mircea Eliade, Plato, Carl Jung, and the magnificent modern guru Joseph Campbell. I immersed my own architectural works in the very nature of mankind's ethos, sacred metaphors, and cultural order to find the essential traits of the psyche that we all share, those that guide our lives in our common dreams, our embedded myths. I wanted to find our deepest metaphors—besides nature itself—to guide modern architecture both in form and material. I have essentially called for increasing the very nature of programming

architecture to go beyond the key elements of function, budget, and site. The social behavior added to this list as cultural function is adequate. I'm calling for the mythical story in each piece of building to be told in form and styling as an overriding design determinant. I say mythical largely to specifically point out that individual modernist conceits are not satisfactory, the common dreams and the deepest lyrics of the numinous must be evoked. To this end, I have built numerous projects with this in mind and equally importantly, I have formed a crucible of design investigations and testable interventions to gauge such ideas.

What better way to seek fresh answers for a new language for modern architecture than to enlist the best and brightest young minds, innovative architectural students, as my fellow explorers? Pragmatically, together with an array of cultural masters, we have uncovered a plethora of human legends and metaphors for almost eighteen years. We have sought out key lyrics of the soul that evoke the heartfelt landscapes of each culture we encountered. In turn, we shaped *their* stories into descriptive sculptures, and then, with furious revisions, we forged them into a single design. We further tested our mettle in the most extraordinary landscapes of the world under trying conditions as we built each of these projects in an astonishing nine days. Designing inspired pieces is hard enough work, but considering that the students had little if any construction experience, building these projects in such short order is a feat within itself. These expeditions started as a class titled "The Spirit of Place-Spirit of Design" taught at the Catholic University of America in concert with Explorer in Residence Wade Davis at the National Geographic Society. Each year, a cultural and spiritual lyric was examined, a numinously embedded design evolved, and then on site and within a remote culture we built that project at the edge of the world as we know it.

Among many examples, we explored the meaning of Incan spatial constructs through the Mayu star gazing of the dark voids above the Andes that indeed formed the building of Machu Picchu; or the shaping of Thin Places in western Ireland that reveals portals into the Celtic soul; or exploring and building forms that transport the modern Finn into the shamanistic time warp of the Kalevala mythology; or evoke in a temple the very reincarnations of the Magar ancestors of pre-Hindu Nepal. The real litmus test over the years has been the outpouring of testimonials from the residents of local cultures who visit them: each has attested to hearing their own echoes in the shapes and textures of the constructs. In a way, all we have done is simply to raise a mirror in a distant land and then ask the inhabitants to gaze into it. Our goal was to have their selves seen as they are seen, to see their deepest values through us in a new design. As the world dramatically shifts, these designs are an attempt to retain the mythical numinosity of the diverse cultures of the world while also ushering in a new and destined modernism that each culture hungrily is entering.

Sixteen such architectural expeditions into the spirit of place have evolved an initial road map for pursuing a new design language, *The Mythic Modern*.[1] These investigations and built interventions have elicited a singular Socratic question: are there enduring cultural values that can be reinvigorated into the emerging modern architectural landscape? We have opened a new direction for our next

FIGURE 17-1. THE KALEVALAKEHTO, HELSINKI, FINLAND. BUILT AUGUST 2010 (DC AIA AWARD WINNER 2011).

FIGURE 17-2. THE KALEVALAKEHTO, HELSINKI, FINLAND.
DEDICATION CEREMONY, 2010.

century, one in which we will improve the authenticity and meaningfulness of modern architecture with a revived humanism and spiritual numinosity. Our goal and success have been the creation of a modern architecture embedded again and again with humanity's deepest dreams, its richest stories, and the wisdom of its enduring myths. The numinous is embedded in these forms as is the human character. The eighteen expeditions that have unfolded span over four continents and nearly two decades. In the Spirit of Place

installations, we have reawakened the stories of the numinous within modern architecture that tells the tales of our souls. So, too, in my commercial, institutional, and residential architecture this same thirst for the numinous is bearing fruit.

These expeditions of built projects are a voyage to distant lands and diverse cultures with daring and immensely talented young architects. As analytics, the resulting installations are a groundbreaking educational pedagogy—one that I believe will eclipse

FIGURE 17-3. MEMORIAL TO JAMES HOBAN, ARCHITECT OF THE WHITE HOUSE. DESART/CALLAN, IRELAND. BUILT AUGUST 2008 (DC AIA AWARD WINNER 2010).

the equally imperative "green" movement. Each expedition came at great expense and hard work by students and patrons alike. The greatest rewards are no doubt seeing the students working with their newfound friends for life while building cultural legacies. The students became true travelers, never to be idle passive tourists again. The humanistic rewards are beyond measure. Joyfully in the purist Socratic spirit, the expeditions sought out to address our modern world's most difficult challenge: the revival of the numinous in the everyday. We hope that this effort will reopen the door of wonder for designers and celebrate humanity's creative spirit for the twenty-first century's modern architectural renaissance. For certain, the installations speak to the complexity of the numinous as a way to see its essence. Indeed, these projects speak louder than writing, as they are testimonies to architects that such words can become form and indeed inform us all that the numinous continues to find its way into our built environments. These projects

FIGURE 17-4. THE MAGAR MEMORIAL TO THE ANCESTORS. NAMJE-THUMKI, NEPAL. BUILT JUNE 2011 (DC AIA AWARD WINNER 2011).

are a clarion call for a new language of the numinous in architecture, one that has just reawakened in a modern idiom. In search of the numinous in the new architectural form is a quest for the mythic modern.

> Swirling air and legs alight and the lands are
> formed
> the Eggs open spilling out the mystery of
> Creation
> launching windswept Vessels transporting the
> sage song-weaver Vainamoinen
> always to be rekindled
> recreated in Sampo's fiery light washed upon
> the shores
> in a whirling quiet of creativity.[2]

The lyrics, with English words mirrored in Gaelic, progress from initial invocations of struggle and adversity (rendered in opaque glass), through strength gained to expressions of triumph and accomplishment.

> The sea of souls churns while dancing around
> mortal woes ...
> tipping time's ancestral future ...
> here is there, and there again ...
> embracing the unspoken
> knowing ...[3]

Where the "Sadhu watches the trees eating rocks singing odes to the metamorphosis of the soul."[4]

FIGURE 17-5. TRAVIS PRICE RESIDENCE. WASHINGTON, D.C., HISTORIC PARK AREA. BUILT IN 2003 (DC AIA AWARD 2006).

18 REACHING FOR THE NUMINOUS

The main title of this book, *Transcending Architecture*, could be read as a double entendre. As a modifier, the word "transcending" describes architecture as a means for delivering human beings to an experience of what is a numinous episode. However, as a verb, the word "transcending" also suggests to me a movement *beyond* our conventional expectations of how architecture functions as a pathway from the profane to the sacred.

On one hand, it is difficult to disagree that architecture has a role in shaping cultures, attitudes, and value systems. It does. Some edifices can transport even the most cynical person to heights never imagined. On the other hand, one must ask if there are realities, still emerging, not fully understood, that are altering the role architecture plays in the hunt for a holy experience. My perspective will be focused on religious architecture in the United States, more specifically architecture for worship.

In the texts of the Torah and the Koran there is the story of Jacob, son of Isaac and Rebecca. While seeking a spouse in a foreign land, he dreams of a ladder set upon the earth but reaching to the heavens. He imagines angels going up and down the ladder. Seeing God by his side, Jacob proclaims, "This is none other than the house of God ... the gate of heaven."[1] Although there are different interpretations of this biblical story, it complements the diverse philosophies and theologies that later would also claim that God is mysterious but accessible not only by faith and good work but also because of a wild imagination.

Dualities often shape our imaginations. We use contrasting words to organize and categorize ideologies and realities: words like left and right, heaven and hell, rich and poor, good and bad. The word "mystery" is often used when something real cannot be explained. Other words such as ineffable, transcendent, liminal, and numinous offer possibilities for rising above the situation. These words give promise and hope. However, they are not strategies for successful living or discipleship. These words imply that what we call divine is outside ourselves, unknown and removed from what and where we are. We then have to figure out how to attain it or get there by climbing Jacob's Ladder.

However, what if the holy other is more present than we ever imagined? Annie Dillard wrote, "Beauty and grace are constantly performing whether we will it or sense them; all we can do is be present when they happen.[2] Countless human experiences are testimonies that the holy other is frequently met face to face in real time without the aid of a stepladder, a religious building, an artistic venue, or the quiet beauty of a desert.

Human relationships and our attention to each other and the environment are found in our homes, places of worship, neighborhoods, favelas, battlefields, and flooded towns. Here the experience of the numinous is cradled in times of joy and hardship. The arts, architecture, language, music—all works of human hands—serve as narratives expressing and affirming our lived experiences. Sometimes they endorse nothing more than the status quo, bolstering what is already familiar and comfortable. Sometimes they offer new insights, boldly helping us see things in new ways, taking us to new places. What the arts and architecture know best is the human spirit. They can play back to us our stories. Architect James Ingo Freed called the Holocaust Memorial a "resonator." They can also shake our foundations.

For many who are searching for a holy experience, the time-honored principles employed to create stimulating architectural forms symbolized by Jacob's Ladder may still be effective. A linear, vertical orientation, expansive volume, profuse light, the harmonious organization of organic materials, all in proper scale and with delightful proportions can serve, in Jungian terms, as outward expressions of innermost longings. Joseph Campbell reminded us that buildings can reveal in a temporal way what is mysteriously illusive.

However, these architectonic expressions are not constrained by time, location, or a specific building typology. An appreciative study of architectural and religious history provides emotional if not empirical evidence that the experience of the numinous, especially in places of worship, knows no boundaries and may be discovered in the simplest ritual chamber, great cathedrals, and temples as well as in contemporary mosques and churches.

Jacob's Ladder then, is just one of many archetypal examples of a link between us and what is thought to be mysteriously beyond us. Mountains, rivers, and deserts serve the same purpose. The Ladder also suggests that there is a hieratic order in creation that, regretfully in my mind, separates the creatures from the creator. For example, churches in western Christianity that disconnect, by design and distance, clergy from the laity, the holy of holies from the nave, are good examples of such dissociation. These churches disregard, in a Christian context, the significance of the incarnate God and the belief that Jesus changed forever the notion that God is an intangible deity. They ignore the Pauline understanding of the people of God as living stones—the dwelling places of the holy one. Such compartmentalized churches spurn the early Christian writers who eschewed temples and altars and understood the people to be the body of Christ.

Given the unique (and huge) challenges of our time along with the limitations of a hierarchical interpretation of Jacob's Ladder, we should ask for ways to transcend the conventional rules defining how built forms take us to a numinous or liminal experience. Indeed, can theologians, architects, and artists help others to perceive, recognize, and respect other humans, 8.7 million species, and innumerable but not inexhaustible natural resources? Can clients, architects, and artists work to create spaces and objects of beauty that reveal and celebrate the cosmic enterprise that is not out there somewhere but one that embraces us here?

The use of the thematic word "transcending" as a verb can stimulate a movement beyond the conventional understanding of the role of religious architecture in convening sacred experiences. In describing the daily human dance in Grand Central Terminal in New York City, the writer Alastair Macaulay asks, "Are the people at Grand Central different?" He was writing about the impact of the terminal on human behavior, comparing it with that of the stale and dull Pennsylvania Station across town. In the article, he recalls a story his mother told him. Her employer had a maid from Milan to whom she once said politely, "I understand the cathedral in Milan is very beautiful." The maid replied, "Oh, but Madame! You should see the railway station!"[3]

This brings me then to the question of the teleology or end purpose of a built form, especially one that is defined as a convener of numinous experiences—forms that we casually call sacred spaces. Is the purpose of such structures fulfilled just with their completion? It is the goal of these buildings to satisfy the architect or client alone? Or, rather, is the intention of this architecture to transcend what is tangible, something even larger but not always apparent, something not confined by categories or dualistic thinking? Could the purpose of architecture be to shape our imaginations about the deep dimensions of the creative process we are part of and then transform us and the way we live?

Buildings, especially in urban settings, that are sustainable in design, ecologically sensitive, and easy to navigate are places where the human spirit can be lifted up. Places of worship that also house soup kitchens, food pantries, and child care centers are expressions of how human beings can elevate themselves, climb that ladder, in the face of dire circumstances. Imagine such buildings with windows that look out to a city street or to nature. Such glazing would ground the congregation or individual in the immanent expression of God's presence. Imagine if during worship the assembly sat in concentric circles rather than long rows facing one direction? A centralized arrangement of seats would help people focus on their collegial embodiment of the holy other and their common ritual performance designed to praise and thank the creator.

If the architect can also incorporate the components mentioned earlier—light, volume, materials, scale, and proportion—and still manage to render the space delightful, functional, sustainable, and accessible to all, then architecture can be a servant to humanity rather than an icon to be revered by us.

When religious architecture is dull and

unimaginative, when it fails to stir the mind, the body, and the human spirit, it is easy to see why people are flocking to concert halls and museums. The maid from Milan seemed to be saying that other venues can also provide a spiritual stimulus. What is going on in these places that evoke a sense of something beyond or bigger than a world view? Is it a bold, fresh architectural style alone or is it more about the story that is being told? Could it be that we humans want to be refreshed and inspired now, to live peacefully with dignity in our own time, that we do not want to wait for paradise to show up somewhere beyond reality? Do we want to find it here and now?

Further, if religious *behavior* can provide us with any clues about the teleology or purposefulness of building types that are *expected* to provide stepping stones to a liminal or numinous experience, what is the shift in religious behavior in this country and elsewhere telling us? The extensive research conducted by the Pew Forum on Religion and Public Life,[4] among other studies, provides glaring statistics. Twenty-eight percent of Americans have left their childhood religion. Forty-four percent have switched to another religion. Sixteen percent practice no faith, a number that has doubled since 1990. Latest studies on the millennial generation point out that the age group of eighteen- to thirty-nine-year-olds claims to be spiritual but not religious.

Studies are showing that while mainstream religions are concerned about dwindling congregations, independent, nondenominational churches are growing. These communities are known for hospitality, lively music, charismatic preachers, advanced technology in proclaiming God's Word, and outreach programs in their communities. They are *not* known for building places of worship that replicate the architectural, artistic, and symbolic conventions usually employed by more traditional religious groups. There is no Jacob's Ladder in these places other than the spiritual experience of being connected with others in the same search for peace, stillness, and holiness.

If architecture is not essential in the search for what is spiritual or sacred in the lives of these large numbers of people, these emerging Christian and Jewish groups, what can be said about the power of religious architecture and art in triggering a connection with the supernatural or numinous one?

As the place of mainline religion goes through a time of transformation, could it be that the role of architecture as a stimulant of what is good, true, and beautiful is indeed also changing? Are other places, not necessarily categorically defined or recognized as sacred, being used to convey the experience of what is liminal and numinous in life?

The story of Jacob's Ladder is an excerpt from a biblical passage filled with intrigue, war, multiple marriages, dueling brothers, and the emergence of imperialistic nations. In the end, the story does give birth to new ways of living. Perhaps the lesson is that the search for the gentle touch of a loving, unpredictable creator is found no where else than in the untidiness, the imperfection, and the instability of human nature.

19 EXPLORING TRANSCENDENCE

One only needs to peruse the table of contents to know that this volume is a rich panorama on the theme of transcendence. Gathered here are insights from architects, theologians, anthropologists, social workers, historians, and many other voices. There are commentaries on religious ceremonies, art, buildings, urban design, culture, and ethics. There is a discussion of individual perspectives and an analysis of transcendence as it is experienced by communities of believers. The content is intentionally diverse, stretching our minds and challenging us to take in new horizons. But such breadth also comes with risk. It is an intellectual journey that can leave us bewildered with a confusing grab bag of fragments rather than a sense of the whole.

Stepping into this dilemma with what I hope is a constructive approach, I come as a pilgrim to the vast arena of transcendence and ponder notions that suggest common ground, that bring pieces into more coherent focus. In the end, my aspirations are twofold: to indicate where we are and where we may need to go. Of course, if you layer on these musings your own understanding of what we have achieved and the frontiers yet to be explored, all the better.

So what pathways do we take? The first is the experience of transcendence as *dialogue*. A second is the question of transcendence and *scale*. Third, we probe transcendence as *sensual*. Finally, in a skeptical world, I am convinced we must reassert the very possibility—as well as the value—of transcendence.

TRANSCENDENCE AS DIALOGUE

One notion of transcendence is that it exists beyond—beyond our humanness and beyond physical reality. In this scenario, there are gateways or bridges—a sacred space, a ritual, a work of art, nature, or meditation—that unveil, allow us to move closer, or even enter this "other world." Transcendence is discovered but not shaped by mere mortals. The attraction of this threshold profile is its elegant simplicity. We need only find the pathway and key and we are in. Moreover, a spectrum of religious traditions professes to share these otherwise hidden means with us and, with faith and guidance, the door is opened. Intriguingly—and for me, more persuasively—several contributors to our symposium suggest an alternative definition of transcendence. It is not beyond us but within us, a connection with our souls. Here the experience of transcendence is found in a nuanced dialogue with the very realities of our world rather than crossing a threshold to something extraterrestrial. In our cluttered existence, there are innumerable distractions and this deeper dialogue must be "designed" with effort and commitment. Architecture, art, and nature can, and do indeed, help frame and give focus to the discussion, but in the end what we find is that transcendence only exists if it is enriched by the human touch. It is a vision that confirms and ennobles our humanity, and I find that compelling.

In his chapter about the intersection of the numinous and domestic architecture, Thomas Barrie offers a litany of sacred spaces where the image of a house has inspired the design—the Greek temple, the Shinto Naiku Shrine of Ise Jingu, the Early Christian house church, the Navaho hogan, and, of course, Laugier's oft-cited "primitive hut." It is a distinguished pedigree that links the elemental and the cosmos, that ties the basics of living now with a world that is beyond the present. The analysis is intellectually

impressive but, for me, most intriguing is how Barrie extrapolates his insights into a small house he designed for two artists and their two children in the rugged terrain of the Berkshires in Western Massachusetts. A ten-foot-high concrete block wall is aligned to geographic north and transforms the site into a giant sundial. The studio—clad in rough-sawn cedar—rests on top of the wall with a galvanized roof that mediates between earth and sky. A modest gateway aligns with a lake to the east and a mountain to the west, inviting a process from earth to sky, from outside to inside, from public to private. The home is modulated by time. Materials weather, some rooms are oriented to the mornings while others come alive in the evenings. And in the end, Barrie has a vision of the house as an enigmatic ruin on the landscape. It is easy to understand this artists' dwelling as a transcendent experience. What is important to note is that transcendence here—and I believe always—is discovered in a dialogue. It is not a formula or a fait accompli but emerges as the interaction between an environment and those in that environment—in this case, in axes and procession, in savoring the diversity of the natural environment, in enjoying the uniqueness of each interior space as it is animated with vistas and light, in the sensuous and symbolic use of materials.

Mark Wedig articulates another example of this transcendent dialogue in his description of Steven Holl's Chapel of St. Ignatius on the campus of Seattle University. Wedig sees this special place as a refuge from the hyperkinetic realities of contemporary life and describes it as "bottles of light tightened by the compression of space." The chapel is all about experiences. Interior views are as if "one were within a box camera" with a carefully positioned lens. Movement is dramatized by shifting displays of light that highlight the contrasts of interior/exterior, religious/secular, and action/meditation. Its framed and interwoven forms juxtapose "light, color, shadow, window view, opacity, and surface … to effect a symphony of subjective responses" to the point where, while St. Ignatius was conceived and is used primarily as a Roman Catholic environment, it is now home for Buddhist, Muslim, and various Christian groups. In one venue, the transcendent dialogue touches those from many traditions.

Taking things further in what I am convinced is an important amplification, some writers in this volume expand the dialogue as it relates to transcendence to include an ethical mandate. This suggests a conversation that, in one direction, leads to self-discovery, then can move outward as a call for action. We uncover the spiritual essence inside ourselves and feel compelled to share the implications of that reality with others. This contrasts with conventional thinking where action is guided by external commands—if we believe we do as we are told. In the dialogue that reveals transcendence, the truth we discover inspires action. Two chapters demonstrate this dynamic.

A social worker, Michael Sheridan contends that equality and justice must go beyond the idea of a safety net to providing opportunity. Architecturally, this means creating spiritual spaces—environments that stimulate our senses and imagination, that encourage interaction and break down social barriers, that respect and do not degrade the world we are given. She dubs this a "justice-seeking, spirit-growing architecture" and illustrates how this strategy would affect housing, public spaces, and community centers. It is a powerful direction. Although her thinking is initiated by seeking to serve the neglected segments of society, the tenets she spells out inevitably inspire a spirituality for all of humanity.

Landscape architect and artist Rebecca Krinke and planner and urban designer Maged Senbel take the conversation and moral imperative related to transcendence to an even more expansive level. Krinke highlights several extraordinary places where the intersection of people, nature, and spirituality become an exchange connecting the soul, the earth's landscapes, and the divine. For Krinke, these epiphanies demand a response, one she sees exemplified in Wangari Maathai's Green Belt Movement initiated in Kenya. Now a worldwide phenomenon, the act of tree-planting is reinterpreted as a lesson in values: love for the environment, gratitude and respect for the Earth's resources, self-empowerment and self-betterment, and promoting a spirit of service and volunteerism. Paralleling this emphasis on environmental concerns, the transcendent dialogue is also an ethical dialogue for Senbel. He advocates "reverential urbanism" where architecture and city-building fulfill "spiritual, social and ecological needs." The goal is a less consumptive society, one that resonates with the modes of nature and leaves a better world for future generations. Here cities engage inhabitants in conversations that "symbolize and support compassion, humility, and fairness." And interestingly, the icon for these communities is not a building or skyline but the garden, "a physical reminder of the preciousness of life and the cosmic cycles of life, death, and rebirth."

TRANSCENDENCE AND SCALE: PERSONAL OR COMMUNAL EXPERIENCE

Related to the issue of dialogue is an assessment of transcendence as personal or communal. As individuals, spiritual epiphanies can be moving and memorable. Each of us can, no doubt, recall (and even look forward to) such moments. Personally, for instance, each time I enter the Pantheon in Rome, I am drawn into a conversation—about the order of the universe, about my place in that universe, and, as I move back through the portico into the bustle of the day-to-day reality, about the principles that guide my actions and relationships. It is stunning and transformative. It is memorable and enduring. And not unexpectedly, many can recount their own versions of this rendezvous, some quite poetically.

In his commentary, Juhani Pallasmaa distinguishes between "designated" and the more remarkable "ideated" experiences of sacredness. The former is predetermined by and for the community and is associated with religious places and events. The latter is discovered in subjective encounters with architecture, art, and nature. These personal connections with the sacred are powerful and clearly Pallasmaa's main interest. Their essence is found in light and silence. Referring to works by Louis Kahn, Steven Holl, Rembrandt, Caravaggio, Constantin Brancusi, James Turrell, and others, Pallasmaa poetically describes the significance of light: "Natural light connects us with cosmic dimensions and brings life into architecture"; in art, chiaroscuro gives light "an experiential materiality, plasticity, and heighted presence"; and "the delicacy of reflected color suggests a spiritualized existence." With regard to silence, he notes: "Great architecture is petrified stillness, silence turned into matter"; when struck by a profound piece of art, "the work silences us and we find ourselves listening to our own existence"; and in silence, "we are, perhaps, rediscovering the virtue and expressive power of tranquility." For Pallasmaa, ideated sacredness is that elevating moment that changes how we see ourselves and the world.

Karsten Harries looks at the sacred from a similarly personal point of view. He is interested in mediating among the nature, the material, and the sacred. To connect these, he invokes the concept of "aura," which "veils the perceived with an illusion of transcendence." This "auratic distance" takes the individual beyond the here and now so that an object—perhaps a work of art or an impressive building—is experienced "as if it were another person, capable of speech." It is a critical link for Harries who then sees this dynamic as a gateway to natural beauty and the vast majesty of our world. Applying this to the realm of sacred architecture, his counsel to each of us is a blend of optimism and caution: "We need to reappropriate the wisdom buried in the traditional understanding of architecture as repetition and image of the cosmos. This, to be sure, presupposes that we can still experience in some sense our world as a cosmos, that is to say as rather like a house, a house of which we are not the authors."

The language is moving, but there is a subtle tension in the shadow of these narratives. Certainly, we are touched by the sacred as individuals, sometimes quite powerfully. But if it ends there, transcendence becomes idiosyncratic and solipsistic when it should connect as well as inspire humanity. Pallasmaa and Harries emphasize the intimate, but that is not enough. Just as the dialogue related to the sacred ranges from conversations about details to discussions concerning the environment and urbanism, so the meeting with the sacred must span the scales of the personal and the communal.

In this context, Lindsay Jones's chapter is an essential counterpoint. Pondering the pre-Columbian architecture of Mesoamerica, he proposes that these temple complexes with their orthogonal layout, dramatic stairs, mix of open spaces, terraces, interior pavilions, and intricate decoration can be interpreted in three very distinct ways. Most common is to see them as theater where procession and ritual mesmerized (and perhaps terrorized) citizens and visitors alike. As sanctuaries, walls and the delineation of exclusive domains became another way to explain the meaning and use of these religious spaces. Finally, Jones's own scholarly contribution is to classify these monuments "as catalysts of direct and purposive contemplation." He highlights mandala-like decorative motifs and the throngs that make a pilgrimage to these sites for the spring equinox. For me, the message of this critique is not to discern which view is correct but rather to note that—across all three interpretations—the sacred is regarded as a community experience. Further, Jones elaborates that theater, sanctuary, and contemplation are modes of engaging the faithful in all major religions.

Anthropologist Sue Ann Taylor articulates additional dimensions of communal sacredness. It reinforces key values and behaviors. It endows certain sites and places as special and unique. It provides a way to connect past and present. And it can unite all these with ritual as process for moving from the ordinary to the extraordinary.

Of course, the understanding and interpretation of these elements can vary widely based on the cultural and historical traditions from which they emerge, and also with the passing of time. Kevin Seasoltz illuminates this evolutionary aspect in his history of community and sacred space in the Roman Catholic Church. While acknowledging the timeless primacy of people (Jesus' incarnation and presence in our world and his call to personal transformation) over place in the Christian faith, he carefully explains how the built reality of this message shifted significantly from one historical era to another. He calls out the sense of gathering and interiority in Early Christian basilicas; the notions of enclosure, verticality, and hierarchy manifest in the Romanesque period; the blending of heavenly light and the order of the cosmos in Gothic cathedrals; and the idea of theater that drove design and ritual in seventeenth-century Baroque churches.

Putting many viewpoints together, we end up with a deeper understanding of the sacred experience. Pallasmaa and Harries write about it as a compelling personal encounter. Jones, Taylor, and Seasoltz explore how it is also communal. In the end, there is no choice to be made. The two visions complement and inform each other, demonstrating the breadth and richness of this arena.

TRANSCENDENCE AS SENSUAL

The discussion of dialogue, of individual and community, and of ritual all surround another theme that must be part of our overview—the sensual. The experience of transcendence and the sacred is made manifest through the senses. The visual dimension is easily understood. Light, form, space, vistas are mentioned by most of the authors in this volume. Juhani Pallasmaa speaks poetically of the "miracles of light:" light reshaped by fog, smoke, or snow or shadowed by rounded surfaces; light as floating panels in a James Turrell sculpture or as an elusive point of brightness in blackness. Susanne Reatig comments on the pure volumes of Luis Barragán's home in Mexico City and the plaza of the Salk Institute in La Jolla, California, framed by the buildings, the sky, and the sea.

Touch is also implied. Rebecca Krinke describes her Table for Contemplation and Action as a plane of wood with a copper box on top of which is a handmade glass vessel. Thomas Barrie painstakingly selects the materials in his house for two artists—a concrete block wall, a studio of western red cedar, a galvanized steel roof. Lindsay Jones makes note of the mystical patterns carved into the walls of pre-Columbian temples. And the beautiful projects by Travis Price and his students are all the more stunning because of their meticulously chosen materials and fabrication—the textures of wood and stone, the seams of copper cladding, the reflections that radiate from glass surfaces.

Sound is barely alluded to. Kevin Seasoltz talks about the three different rhythms that need to be orchestrated in liturgical space: "a visual rhythm (what we see), an aural rhythm (what we hear), and a kinetic or motor rhythm (how we move about or act)." But he does not really elaborate on the topic. Pallasmaa calls out the power of silence in his analysis: "A powerful architectural experience eliminates noise.... In an impressive space, we hear only our own heartbeat." But while that may be true for the individual, an auditory experience other than silence is often integral to the communal sense of the sacred: the call to prayer; the hymn at key points in a

service; a sung reading; a musical interlude by organ, brass, bells, or orchestra; a chant that rallies believers; a repeated tone as the background to meditation. Like physical space and light, what we hear can unite a group and become the threshold to transcendence.

Smell can also convey the sacred. It is a powerful trigger, igniting memories, marking the boundaries of a place, announcing the seasons, and setting the stage for prayer and rituals. Certain locales have a unique scent—from landscapes to specific rooms. On other occasions, scents are associated with specific times of year and events—in the Christian West, the pines at Christmas or the candles at Easter. In other instances—the use of incense comes to mind—the smell can be symbolic (prayers ascending heavenward) and establish the ambiance for a liturgy, service, or moment of contemplation.

Of course, there is also taste. Perhaps not a major feature of transcendence, but still possible. The sharing of a ritual meal, a communion service, and other similar activities can even make taste part of the sacred experience.

THE RELEVANCE OF TRANSCENDENCE IN A SKEPTICAL WORLD

So where does these musings leave us? I think above all, they indicate the robustness and multidimensional nature of transcendence and the sacred. We need the many and diverse chapters in this volume because transcendence and the sacred can appropriately be viewed from so many perspectives. They are dynamic, a lively conversation—experiences that continuously change and expand our view of the world. They can be a dialogue of such import that they become a call to action, a mandate for those of us engaged in the discussion to not only see the world different-ly but to change the world. They touch us as individuals at the same time that they bring us together as a community. They confirm our uniqueness and value but also our mutual dependence. Finally, they reach into our souls through all the senses, deeply memorable en-counters that heighten how we see ourselves *and* how we one with our brothers and sisters and the world around us.

I am convinced these criteria can be used to interpret and discover meaning in any of the chapters in this book. But in a secu-lar world, in a world skeptical that there is anything beyond the here and now, we are compelled to ask if there is any relevance to exploring transcendence and the sacred. Fortunately, as I see it, our response must be unequivocally YES! Before celebrating triumph, however, know that I arrive at this conclusion with one important caveat. If the goal of such an investigation is to reveal the God or gods that have framed—and maybe even continue to shape—the cosmos and our human existence, then our studies will prove, at best, inconclusive and, at worst, frustrating and disappointing. We will find ourselves in the inevitable stalemate between believers and nonbelievers.

The reason is that transcendence and the sacred do not lead us to a God or gods, but to ourselves. What we see in crossing the ineffa-ble threshold of transcendence and marking the sacred is a new and better view of our-selves. The dialogue makes us aware of others and the extraordinary universe in which we live. The tension between the individual and the community confirms an astounding unity—that from past through present and into the future, all generations are connected. And the senses become pathways into the

rich mysteries of these realities. To say we live in a secular and skeptical world is only an ex-cuse to avoid the challenging journeys toward transcendence and the sacred present. But to those willing to move into these realms—in-cluding the thought-provoking contributors to *Transcending Architecture*—the rewards are tremendous: the revelation of an enno-bling vision of who we are as human beings and how we touch and understand our little earth and the great cosmos in which it exists.

ENDNOTES, BIBLIOGRAPHY, CONTRIBUTORS, INDEX

NOTES

1. INTRODUCTION

1. Le Corbusier, *New World of Space* (New York: Reynal & Hitchcock, 1948); Rudolf Otto, *The Idea of the Holy* (New York: Oxford University Press, 1970); Robert Twombly, ed., *Louis Kahn: Essential Texts* (New York: W. W. Norton & Company, 2003).

2. Juhani Pallasmaa, *Encounters, Architectural Essays* (Helsinki, Finland: Rakennustieto Publishing, 2008). See also John Dewey's definition of an aesthetic experience as when an experience becomes itself an experience in *Art as Experience* (New York: Wideview/Perigee Book, 1934).

3. I am here referring to philosophies in which beauty is conceived as a central component of human life and understood as a disinterested and emotionally arousing experience that is immediately accessible through sense-perception, and with the ability to deliver profound insights and pleasures (e.g., Plato, Aristotle, Kant, Schopenhauer, Stolnitz). Modern and postmodern philosophies, in contrast, see beauty as "aesthetics," an area of secondary importance among other more regarded forces and interests (e.g., epistemology, science, language, ethics) wherein "aesthetic appreciation" depends on mental effort and not sensual

and emotional faculties because it is the content or meaning of a work (not its appearance) that matters (e.g., Danto, Foucault, Nehamas, Wittgenstein).

4. Karsten Harries, *The Ethical Function of Architecture* (Cambridge, Mass.: The MIT Press, 1997); Alberto Perez-Gomez, *Built Upon Love* (Cambridge, Mass.: The MIT Press, 2006)

5. Michael Benedikt, *God Is the Good We Do: Theology of Theopraxy* (New York: Bottino Books, 2007).

6. Michael Benedikt, *God, Creativity, and Evolution: The Argument from Design(ers)* (Austin, Tex.: Centerline books, 2008); Karla Britton, *Constructing the Ineffable* (New Haven, Conn.: Yale School of Architecture, 2011); Renata Hejduk and Jim Williamson, *The Religious Imagination in Modern and Contemporary Architecture: A Reader* (New York: Routledge, 2011), see their introduction chapter; Julio Bermudez, "The Extraordinary in Architecture," *2A—Architecture and Art Magazine*, Autumn Quarter, no. 12 (2009): 46–49; Moyra Doorly, *No Place for God: The Denial of Transcendence in Modern Church Architecture* (San Francisco: Ignatius Press, 2007); Michael Crosbie, "The 'S' Word" (editor's page), *Faith & Form* 45, no. 1 (2012):

4, available online: http://www.faithandform.com/editorial/archive/45-1.php (accessed March 24, 2012).

7. Over the past five years or more, new groups have assembled (e.g., the Forum for Architecture, Culture and Spirituality), old ones are growing (e.g., IFRAA, Faith & Form), the number of conferences (e.g., Constructing the Ineffable at Yale University in 2007; the ACS Forum consecutive annual symposia since 2009; the "Spirituality of Place" meeting at the Savannah College of Art and Design in 2011) and publications on the topic (see the number of books cited in this introduction) have increased, and new and old graduate programs are paying more attention to these matters (e.g., Sacred Space and Cultural Studies at the Catholic University of America School of Architecture and Planning, Sacred Architecture at Texas A&M College of Architecture).

8. In book V, chapter II of his *The Hunchback of Notre Dame*, Victor Hugo describes the central historical role of architecture in civilization: "[F]rom the very beginning of things down to the fifteenth century of the Christian era inclusive, architecture is the great book of the human race, man's chief means of expressing the various stages of his development, whether physical or mental." Hugo then argues that the advent of the printed book is to bring down such a situation, something that he summarizes in his famous forecast, "This will kill that. The book will kill the edifice." Victor Marie Hugo, *Notre Dame De Paris*, vol. XII (New York: P.F. Collier & Son, 1917), reprint, Bartleby.com, 2000, http://www.bartleby.com/312/0502.html (accessed March 22, 2012).

9. In fact, and no longer surprising, the book is being transcended by the digital networks. The recent announcement (March 2012) by *Encyclopedia Britannica* that it has stopped its print edition after 244 years (2010 was its last) to concentrate on its Internet presence is the latest sign that we are witnessing the death of the physical book, if not for good, at least in the format that we have come to know since the start of Gutenberg's revolution of the 1450s.

10. Following, more or less, Victor Hugo's thesis, other arguments propose that architecture ceased to be the best representation of the human worldview after the scientific and technological revolution started by the European Enlightenment transcended the Euclidean-Aristotelian paradigm (what many claim to be common sense experience) sometime in the early to mid-nineteenth century. The arrival of non-Euclidean geometry and other complex mathematics, evolutionary theory, fields theory, and electromagnetism, and later nuclear physics, psychoanalysis, relativity, and so forth, made it increasingly difficult to physically embody/represent the discovered properties, phenomena, order, and processes of reality through architecture. See, among those making this argument, Marcos Novak, "Transmitting Architecture," in *Architects in Cyberspace* (*AD Profile #18*), 1996, 42–47.

11. See Michael Benedikt, *Cyberspace, First Steps* (Cambridge, Mass.: The MIT Press, 1992); Marcos Novak, "Transmitting Architecture"; Marcos Novak, "TransTerraFirma: After Territory," *Sites 26* (1995): 34–53.

12. Kevin Seasoltz, *Sense of the Sacred: Theological Foundations of Christian Architecture and Art* (New York: Continuum, 2005). See also his chapter in this book.

13. Lindsay Jones. See his chapter in this book.

14. This may be particularly clear in Protestant churches which, although often highly respected and crafted buildings, bring little if any attention to themselves in order to become background facilitators of the foreground religious liturgy and ritual.

15. Lindsay Jones, *The Hermeneutics of Sacred Architecture* (Cambridge, Mass.: Harvard University Press, 2000).

16. See Jonathan Shear, *Explaining Consciousness: The Hard Problem* (Cambridge, Mass.: The MIT Press, 1999); David J. Chambers, *The Character of Consciousness* (New York: Oxford University Press, 2010).

17. For testimonies describing an aesthetic transcendence of architecture, see Le Corbusier, "The Parthenon," in his *Journey to the East*, ed. and trans. Ivan Zaknic in collaboration with Nicole Pertuiset (Cambridge, Mass.: The MIT Press, 1987); Steven Holl, "Archetypal Experiences of Architecture," in *A+U: Questions of Perception* (1994), 121–35; "Frank O. Gehry," in *Studio Talk: Interview with 15 Architects*, ed. Yoshio Futagawa (Tokyo: A.D.A. EDITA, 2002), 6–57; "Bernard Tchumi," in *Studio Talk: Interview with 15 Architects*, ed. Yoshio Futagawa (Tokyo: A.D.A. EDITA, 2002); 512–41; Antoine Predock, "Antoine Predock on the Alhambra," in *Architects on Architects*, ed. Susan Gray (New York: McGraw-Hill, 2002), 146–53; Tadao Ando, "Tadao Ando on Le Corbusier," in *Architects on Architects*, ed. Susan Gray (New York: McGraw-Hill, 2002), 11–17.

18. I conducted two large surveys on "Extraordinary Architectural Experiences" between April 2007 and April 2008. The polls, one in English and the other in Spanish, gathered nearly 2,900 responses, the largest number of such testimonies ever collected. The statistical and interpretive analyses of the results have been published in a variety of venues, including

Julio Bermudez, "Mapping the Phenomenological Territory of Profound Architectural Atmospheres: Results of a Large Survey," in *Electronic Proceedings of the International Symposium "Creating an Atmosphere"* (2008), http://www.cresson.archi.fr/PUBLI/pubCOLLOQUE/AMB8-1Bermudez.pdf (accessed March 15, 2012); Julio Bermudez, "Amazing Grace: New Research into 'Extraordinary Architectural Experiences' Reveals the Central Role of Sacred Places," *Faith & Form* 42, no. 2 (2009): 8–13; Julio Bermudez, "Profound Experiences of Architecture: The Role of 'Distancing' in the Ineffable," *2A—Architecture and Art Magazine*, Spring Quarter, no. 17 (2011): 20–25; Julio Bermudez, "Empirical Aesthetics: The Body and Emotion in Extraordinary Architectural Experiences," in *Proceedings of the 2011 Architectural Research Centers Consortium: "Considering Research,"* ed. P. Plowright and B. Gamper (Detroit: Lawrence Tech University), 369–80; Julio Bermudez and Brandon Ro, "Extraordinary Architectural Experiences: Comparative Study

of Three Paradigmatic Cases of Sacred Space," in *Proceedings of the 2nd International Congress on Ambiances*, ed. J. P. Thibaud and D Siret (Montreal, Canada, 2012), 689–94, http://halshs.archives-ouvertes.fr/docs/00/74/55/45/PDF/ambiances2012_bermudez_ro.pdf (accessed April 23, 2013).

19. Among these books are: Britton, *Constructing the Ineffable*; Rebecca Krinke, *Contemporary Landscapes of Contemplation* (New York: Routledge, 2005); Thomas Barrie, *The Sacred In-Between: The Mediating Roles of Architecture* (New York: Routledge, 2010) and *Spiritual Path, Sacred Place: Myth, Ritual, and Meaning in Architecture* (Boston: Shambhala, 1996); Pallasmaa, *Encounters*; Jones, *Hermeneutics of Sacred Architecture*; Harries, *Ethical Function of Architecture*; Perez-Gomez, *Built Upon Love*; Hejduk and Williamson, *Religious Imagination*; and Benedikt, *God Is the Good We Do*.

20. Henry Thoreau, *Walden* (Boston: Houghton, Mifflin, 1894).

2. LIGHT, SILENCE, AND SPIRITUALITY IN ARCHITECTURE AND ART

1. "Architecture is not only about domesticating space, it is also a deep defence against the terror of time. The language of beauty is essentially the language of timeless reality." Karsten Harries, "Building and the Terror of Time," *Perspecta: The Yale Architecture Journal*, issue 19 (1982).

2. Maurice Merleau-Ponty, as quoted in Iain McGillchrist, *The Master and His Emissary: The Divided Brain and the Making of the Western World* (New Haven, Conn.: Yale University Press, 2009), 409.

3. Jean-Paul Sartre, *What Is Literature?* (Gloucester, Mass.: Peter Smith, 1978), 272.

4. Ibid., 3.

5. Jean-Paul Sartre, "What Is Literature?" *Basic Writings*, ed. Stephen Priest (London: Routledge, 2001), 264.

6. Ibid., 271.

7. Louis I. Kahn, as quoted in John Lobell, *Between Silence and Light: Spirit in the Architecture of Louis I. Kahn* (Boston: Shambala, 1985), 20.

8. Kahn, as quoted in Lobell, *Between Silence and Light*, 22.

9. Paul Valéry, "Euphalinos, or the Architect," *Dialogues* (New York: Pantheon Books, 1956), 107.

10. Martin Jay, as quoted in David Michael Levin, "Introduction," *Modernity and the Hegemony of Vision*, ed. David Michael Levin (Berkeley: University of California Press, 1993), 14.

11. Constantin Brancusi, as quoted in Eric Shanes, *Constantin Brancusi* (New York: Abbeville Press, 1989), 57.

12. Gaston Bachelard, *The Flame of a Candle* (Dallas: The Dallas Institute Publications, 1988).

13. Louis I. Kahn, paraphrasing Wallace Stevens in "Harmony between Man and Architecture," in *Louis I. Kahn Writings, Lectures, Interviews*, ed. Alessandra Latour (New York: Rizzoli International Publications, 1991), 343.

14. As quoted in Arthur Zajonc, *Catching the Light: The Entwined History of Light and Mind* (Oxford: Oxford University Press, 1995), 326.

15. James Turrell, *The Thingness of Light*, ed. Scott Poole (Blacksburg, Va.: Architecture Editions, 2000), 1, 2.

16. Ibid.

17. Max Picard, *The World of Silence* (1948) (Washington: Gateway Editions, 1988), 145.

18. Erich Fromm, *Pako Vapaudesta* [Escape from Freedom] (Helsinki: Kirjayhtymä, 1976).

19. Picard, *The World of Silence*, 212.

20. Edward O. Wilson, *Biophilia: The Human Bond with Other Species* (Cambridge, Mass.: Harvard University Press, 1984), 1.

21. Picard, *The World of Silence*, 145.

22. Rainer Maria Rilke, *Letters to a Young Poet* (New York: Random House, 1986), 106.

23. Ibid., 54.

24. Picard, *The World of Silence*, 231.

25. Ibid., 168.

26. Ibid., 162.

27. Wallace K. Harrison invited his friend Alvar Aalto to participate in the preliminary planning of Lincoln Center. Cöran Shildt, *Alvar Aalto A Life's Work—Architecture, Design and Art* (Helsinki: Otava Publishing Company Ltd., 1994), 103.

28. Luis Barragán, acceptance speech for the 1980 Pritzker Architecture Prize.

29. Arthur Zajonc, *Catching the Light: The En-twining History of Light and Mind* (Oxford: Oxford University Press, 1995), 5.

30. Picard, *The World of Silence*, 161.

31. Ibid., 139.

32. Guy Debord, *The Society of the Spectacle* (New York: Zone Books, 1994).

33. Donald B. Kuspit in *Modernin ulottuvuuksia* [Dimensions of the Modern], ed. Jaakko Lintinen, trans. Juhani Pallasmaa (Helsinki: Taide, 1989).

34. Bo Carpelan, *Homecoming*, trans. David Mc-Duff (Manchester: Carcanet, 1993), 111.

3. THE DOMESTIC AND THE NUMINOUS IN SACRED ARCHITECTURE

1. For a full discussion, see R. D. Dripps, *The First House: Myth, Paradigm, and the Task of Architecture* (Cambridge, Mass.: The MIT Press, 1997), 3–18.

2. E. Baldwin Smith, *Egyptian Architecture as Cultural Expression* (New York: D. Appleton-Century Company, 1938), 11.

3. Ibid, 29.

4. Thomas Barrie, *The Sacred In-between: The Mediating Roles of Architecture* (New York: Routledge, 2010), 4–5.

5. Religion has generally served similar roles. The Latin *religare* means "to bind together," suggesting its principal role of connecting and completing. Religious beliefs and practices from around the world, in all their variety, share a goal of connecting the individual to broader communal, cultural, and theological contexts. They can be understood as intrinsic to the archetypal human endeavor of establishing a "place" in the world.

6. E. Baldwin Smith, *The Dome: A Study in the History of Ideas* (Princeton, N.J.: Princeton University Press, 1950), 6.

7. Norman Crowe, *Nature and the Idea of a Man-made World: An Investigation into the Evolutionary Roots of Form and Order in the Built Environment* (Cambridge, Mass.: The MIT Press, 1995), 42–46.

8. Lindsay Jones, *The Hermeneutics of Sacred Architecture, Experience, Interpretation, Comparison, Vol. 2* (Cambridge, Mass.: Harvard University Press, 2000), 100.

9. Luke 6:46-49.

10. 1 Kings 6:1–8:13.

11. Joseph Rykwert outlines an extensive history of reconstructions of this first house for god and suggests the lasting influence it has garnered. See Rykwert, *On Adam's House in Paradise* (New York: The Museum of Modern Art, 1972), chapter 5. See also 1 Kings 6:1-38 and Ezekiel 40 and 41.

12. Otto von Simson, *The Gothic Cathedral* (Princeton, N.J.: Princeton University Press, 1956), 93–94.

13. George Michell, *The Hindu Temple: An Introduction to Its Meaning and Forms* (Chicago: The University of Chicago Press, 1977), 61.

14. Ibid., 73.

15. Ibid., 71.

16. Spiro Kostof refers to Saqqara as the "first interpretation of the brick, timber, and plant forms of Egyptian architecture in the hard medium of Tura limestone." Spiro Kostof, *A History of Architecture, Settings and Rituals* (New York: Oxford University Press, 1985; 2nd ed., 1995), 71.

17. Smith, *Egyptian Architecture as Cultural Expression*, 67

18. Rykwert, *On Adam's House in Paradise*, 166.

19. Peter Nabokov and Robert Easton, *Native American Architecture* (Oxford: Oxford University Press, 1989), 38.

20. Ibid., 82–91.

21. Ibid., 76–86.

22. Ibid., 85.

23. Christopher Carr and D. Troy Case, eds., *Gathering Hopewell: Society, Ritual, and Ritual Interaction* (New York: Springer, 2006), 468.

24. Ibid., 468–73.

25. William F. Romain, *Mysteries of the Hopewell: Astronomers, Geometers, and Magicians of the Eastern Woodlands* (Akron, Ohio: The University of Akron Press, 2000), 158.

26. Ibid., 157–60.

27. In some examples, frescos depict detailed erotic scenes, a particular type of postmortem paradise.

28. See Rykwert, *On Adam's House in Paradise*, 183, 190.

29. Wayfarers and travelers were under Jupiter's protection.

30. In Buddhism, this is described as "relative" and "ultimate" reality.

31. Donald Keene, *Anthology of Japanese Literature: From the Earliest Era to the Mid-Nineteenth Century* (New York: Grove Press, 1955), 206–7.

32. Thomas Barrie, *Spiritual Path, Sacred Place: Myth, Ritual and Meaning in Architecture* (Boston: Shambhala Publications, 1996), 180–212.

33. But, of course, the significance of the *hojo*, like most religiously motivated architecture, is not so simple. Koto-in was built by an important member of the military aristocracy who retired there (presumably) to spend his days studying and practicing Zen. But it is likely he, like others, retained power and influence and so, like much of the domestic architecture of its time, communicated symbols of prestige. The house in this case, as we can observe in others, derives its authority from a range of sources.

34. Henry David Thoreau, *Walden* (Roslyn, N.Y.: Walter J. Black, Inc., 1942), 114.

35. Barrie, *The Sacred In-between*, 64–79.

36. I began my work by spending a day and a night at the site, watching the sun set behind the mountain to the west; sleeping on its hard ground surrounded by the smells of its fields and pine trees; listening to the sounds of wind, water, and animals; awakening to see the sun rising over the lake.

37. Norman Crowe, *Nature and the Idea of a Man-Made World* (Cambridge, Mass.: The MIT Press, 1995), 30.

38. Mohsen Mostafavi and David Leatherbarrow, *On Weathering, The Life of Buildings in Time* (Cambridge, Mass.: The MIT Press, 1993), 42.

39. Thomas Moore, *The Re-Enchantment of Everyday Life* (New York: HarperCollins Publishers, 1996), 42.

40. Alberto Perez-Gomez, *Built upon Love: Architectural Longing after Ethics and Aesthetics* (Cambridge, Mass.: The MIT Press, 2006), 129.

41. Thoreau, *Walden*, 135–36.

42. Gaston Bachelard, *The Poetics of Space* (Boston: Beacon Press, 1969), 5.

4. NATURE, HEALING, AND THE NUMINOUS

1. Linda Zagzebski and Timothy D. Miller, *Readings in Philosophy of Religion: Ancient to Contemporary* (New York: Wiley-Blackwell, 2009), 119.

2. Josephine Klein, *Jacob's Ladder: Essays on Experiences of the Ineffable in the Context of Contemporary Psychotherapy* (New York: Karnac Books/Other Press, 2003), 2.

3. Christopher Thacker, *The History of Gardens* (Berkeley: University of California Press, 1979), 2.

4. See Richard Louv, *The Nature Principle: Human Restoration and the End of Nature Deficit Disorder* (Chapel Hill, N.C.: Algonquin Books, 2011), for a good overview of this research.

5. N. Gerlach Spriggs, R. E. Kaufman, and S. B. Warner Jr., *Restorative Gardens: The Healing Landscape* (New Haven, Conn.: Yale University Press, 1998), 9–10.

6. See Rachel Kaplan and Stephen Kaplan, *The Experience of Nature: A Psychological Perspective* (Cambridge: Cambridge University Press, 1989).

7. See http://www.greenexercise.org/Research_Findings.html (accessed on April 14, 2013).

8. See http://www.iriswellbeing.com/negative_ions.html (accessed on April 14, 2013).

9. See http://www.hphpcentral.com/article/forest-bathing (accessed on April 14, 2013).

10. Christopher Witcombe, *Sacred Places*. http://witcombe.sbc.edu/sacredplaces/ise.html (accessed on April 14, 2013).

11. Heinrich Hermann, "On the Transcendent in Landscapes of Contemplation," in *Contemporary Landscapes of Contemplation*, ed. Rebecca Krinke (London: Routledge, 2005), 60.

12. "Map of Memory, an Interview: Michael Singer with Rebecca Krinke," in *Contemporary Landscapes of Contemplation*, ed. Rebecca Krinke (London: Routledge, 2005), 75.

13. Ibid., 83.

14. United States Environmental Protection Agency, "The Inside Story: A Guide to Indoor Air Quality," 1. http://www.epa.gov/iaq/pubs/insidestory.html (accessed on April 14, 2013).

15. For results of controlled clinical research on the health benefits of expressive writing, see James W. Pennebaker, *Opening Up: The Healing Power of Expressing Emotions* (New York: Guilford Press, 1997).

16. Wangari Maathai, *Replenishing the Earth: Spiritual Values for Healing Ourselves and the World* (New York: Doubleday, 2010), 14–16.

17. American Community Gardening Association. *http://communitygarden.org/learn/* (accessed on April 14, 2013).

18. Thomas Brendler and Henry Carey, "Commu-

nity Forestry, Defined," from *What Is Community Forestry and Why Does It Matter?* National Community Forestry Center, August 2000, 5. *http://www.yellowwood.org/what.pdf* (accessed on April 14, 2013).

19. Anne C. Bellow, Katherine Brown, and Jac Smit, *Health Benefits of Urban Agriculture*, 7. *http://www.foodsecurity.org/UAHealthArticle.pdf* (accessed on April 14, 2013).

20. Robert Pogue Harrison, *Forests: The Shadow of Civilization* (Chicago: The University of Chicago Press, 1992), 247.

21. Gilles A. Tiberghein, *Land Art* (Princeton, N.J.: Princeton University Press, 1995), 59.

22. Robert Pogue Harrison, *Gardens: An Essay on the Human Condition* (Chicago: The University of Chicago Press, 2008), 47.

23. Ibid., x.

5. FROM BIOREGIONAL TO REVERENTIAL URBANISM

1. William Rees, "The Ecological Crisis and Self-Delusion: Implications for the Building Sector," *Building Research and Information* 37, no. 3 (2009): 300–311; "Human Nature, Eco-Footprints and Environmental Injustice," *Local Environment*, 13, no. 8 (2008): 685–701; and Mathis Wackernagel and William Rees, *Our Ecological Footprint* (Gabriola Island, BC: New Society Publishers, 1996).

2. Maged Senbel, Timothy McDaniels, and Hadi Dowlatabadi, "The Ecological Footprint: A Non-Monetary Metric of Human Consumption Applied to North America," *Global Environmental Change* 13, no. 2 (2003): 83–100.

3. Rees, "The Ecological Crisis and Self-Delusion: Implications for the Building Sector," 300.

4. See special issue of *Building Research and Information*, 2012.

5. Arne Naess, "The Shallow and the Deep, Long-Range Ecology Movement: A Summary," *Inquiry* 16, no. 1 (1973): 95–100; *Ecology, Community, and Lifestyle: Outline of an Ecosophy*, trans. and ed. David Rothenberg (Cambridge: Cambridge University Press, 1990).

6. Mike Carr, *Bioregionalism and Civil Society: Democratic Challenges to Corporate Globalism* (Vancouver: UBC Press, 2005).

7. Robert Venturi, Denise Scott Brown, and Steven Izenour, *Learning from Las Vegas: The Forgotten Symbolism of Architectural Form* (Cambridge, Mass.: The MIT Press, 1977).

8. Christopher Alexander, Sara Ishikawa, and Murray Silverstein, *A Pattern Language: Towns, Buildings, Construction* (New York: Oxford University Press, 1977).

9. Robert McLeman, "Impacts of Population Change on Vulnerability and the Capacity to Adapt to Climate Change and Variability: A Typology Based on Lessons from a Hard Country," *Population and Environment* 31, no. 5 (2010): 286–316.

10. Tom Spector, "Codes of Ethics and Coercion," in *Architecture and Its Ethical Dilemmas*, ed. Nicholas Ray, 101–12 (New York: Taylor and Francis, 2005).

11. Netta Weinstein, Andrew K. Przybylski, and Richard M Ryan, "Can Nature Make Us More Caring? Effects of Immersion in Nature on Intrinsic Aspirations and Generosity?" *Personality and Social Psychology Bulletin* 35, no. 10 (2009): 1315–29; Andrea Faber Taylor and France E. Kuo, "Is Contact with Nature Important for Healthy Child Development? State of Evidence," in *Children and Their Environments: Learning, Using and Designing Spaces*, ed. Christopher Spencer and Mark Blades, 124–40 (Cambridge: Cambridge University Press, 2006); Richard Louv, *Last Child in the Woods: Saving Our Children from Nature Deficit Disorder* (Chapel Hill, N.C.: Algonquin Press, 2005).

12. Barbara Goodwin and Keith Taylor, *The Politics of Utopia: A Study in Theory and Practice* (Bern: Peter Lang AG, 2009).

13. Rees, "The Ecological Crisis and Self-Delusion: Implications for the Building Sector."

14. Yves Charles Zarka, "The Meaning of Utopia," *The New York Times*, *Opinionator*, August 28, 2011. http://opinionator.blogs.nytimes.com/2011/08/28/the-meaning-of-utopia/ (accessed on April 15, 2013).

15. Graham Harman, *Prince of Networks: Bruno Latour and Metaphysics* (Melbourne, Australia: re.press, 2009).

16. Goodwin and Taylor, *The Politics of Utopia*, 274.

17. Bron Taylor, "Earth and Nature-Based Spirituality (Part II): From Earth First! and Bioregionalism to Scientific Paganism and the New Age," *Religion* 31, no. 3 (2001): 225–45.

18. Marianne Barracund, "The Garden as a Reflection of Paradise," in *Islamic Art and Architecture*, ed. Markus Hattstein and Peter Delius, 490–94 (Potsdam, Germany: H. F. Ullmann, 2004).

19. Attilio Petruccioli, "Nature in Islamic Urbanism," in *Islam and Ecology*, ed. Richard C. Foltz, Frederick M. Denny, and Azizan Baharuddin,

499–510 (Cambridge, Mass.: Harvard University Press, 2003).

20. Maged Senbel, "Ecology and Spirituality in Cities: Towards a Spirit Enriching Urban Environment," *2A: Architecture and Art* 12 (2009): 68–70; Leonie Sandercock and Maged Senbel, "Spirituality, Urban Life and Urban Professions," in *Postsecular Cities: Space, Theory and Practice*, ed. Justin Beamont

and Christopher Baker, 87–103 (London: Continuum, 2011).

21. Annette Kim and Phil Thompson, "God's Plan: A Podcast on Faith and City Planning," *Polis: A Collaborative Blog about Cities*. 2012. http://www.thepolisblog.org/2012/01/gods-plan-podcast-on-faith-and-city.html (accessed on January 10, 2012).

6. THE RISK OF THE INEFFABLE

1. Karl Gruber, *Bilder zur Entwicklungsgeschichte einer deutschen Stadt* (Munich: F. Bruckmann, 1914).

2. Rudolf Wittkower, *Architectural Principles in the Age of Humanism* (London: Warburg Institute, 1949).

3. Erwin Panofsky, *Gothic Architecture and Scholasticism* (New York: Meridian Books, 1957).

4. Augustus Welby Pugin, *Contrasts: Or, a Parallel between the Noble Edifices of the Middle Ages, and Corresponding Buildings of the Present Day, Shewing the Present Decay of Taste* (London: Charles Dolman, 1841).

5. Sigfried Giedion, *The Eternal Present* (New York: Bollingen Foundation, 1962).

6. Vincent Scully, *The Earth, the Temple, and the Gods: Greek Sacred Architecture* (New Haven, Conn.: Yale University Press, 1962).

7. Joseph Rykwert, *The Idea of a Town* (Princeton, N.J.: Princeton University Press, 1976).

8. Jürgen Habermas, "The Resurgence of Religion: A Challenge to the Secular Self-Interpretation of Modernity," *Castle Lectures*, Yale University, October 2008.

9. Rafael Moneo, "Architecture as a Vehicle for Religious Experience: The Los Angeles Cathedral," in *Constructing the Ineffable: Contemporary Sacred Architecture*, ed. Karla Britton (New Haven, Conn.: Yale School of Architecture, 2011), 159.

10. www.nytimes.com/2010/08/20/nyregion/20muslims.html?pagewanted=all&_r=0 (accessed May 15, 2013).

11. http://www.nytimes.com/2009/11/30/world/europe/30swiss.html (accessed May 15, 2013).

12. Britton, *Constructing the Ineffable*.

13. Le Corbusier, "L'Espace indicible," in *L'Architecture d'Aujourd'hui*, January 1946, numero hors serie "Art," 9–10. English translation, "Ineffable Space," published in Le Corbusier, *New World of Space* (New York: 1948), 7–9.

14. Le Corbusier, "Ineffable Space," in *Architecture*

Culture 1943–1968, ed. Joan Ockman (New York: 1993), 66.

15. Ibid.

16. Mies van der Rohe, "Wir stehen in der Wende der Zeit," *Innendekoration* 39 (1928): 262, quoted in Fritz Neumeyer, *The Artless Word: Mies van der Rohe on the Building Art* (Cambridge, Mass.: The MIT Press, 1991), xii.

17. Ibid.

18. Rudolf Schwarz, *Vom Bau der Kirche* (Heidelberg: Schneider, 1938). English trans., *The Church Incarnate* (Chicago: H. Regnery Co., 1958).

19. Mohammed Arkoun, "Spirituality and Architecture," in *Architecture Beyond Architecture: Creativity and Social Transformations in Islamic Cultures*, ed. Cynthia Davidson and Ismail Serageldin (London: Academy Editions, 1995).

20. Comparing El-Wakil's work with Le Corbusier's and Louis Kahn's deep sense of the sacred, for example, Vincent Scully has noted that whereas for the two modernist architects the sacred is based in the darkness of the cavern and in savage sacrifice, El-Wakil's work in contrast "embodies a more gentle primitivism, something bright and clear." Vincent Scully, "The Earth, the Temple, and Today," in Britton, *Constructing the Ineffable*, 44.

21. Luis Barragán, "1980 Laureate Acceptance Speech," Pritzker Architecture Prize, www.pritzker.com/laureates/1980.

22. Gianni Vattimo, *Etica dell'interpretazione* (Turin: Rosenberg & Sellier, 1989), 23, quoted in Marta Frascati-Lochhead, *Kenosis and Feminist Theology* (Albany: SUNY Press, 1998), 82.

23. Martin Heidegger, "Building Dwelling Thinking," in *Poetry, Language, Thought* (New York: HarperCollins, 1971).

24. Gianni Vattimo, *Belief* (Stanford, Calif.: Stanford University Press, 1999), English trans. of *Credere di Credere* (Milan: Garzanti Libri, 1996).

1. Rudolf Otto, *The Idea of the Holy* (New York: Oxford University Press, 1970). For a good and short introduction to Otto's definition of the numinous, the reader needs to go no further than Michael Crosbie's chapter in this book.

2. While Otto would not approve the term "sublime" to refer to a spiritual or religious experience of the numinous, he does argue that the sublime is a profound aesthetic event conducive to the numinous. He calls it a "schema" for the Holy but not the Holy itself. The sublime connects and conjoins the numinous but does not make us evolve into the numinous. Ibid., 41–43.

3. Alberto Campo Baeza, *Principia Architectonica* (Madrid: Mairea Libros, 2012); Steven Holl, "Archetypal Experiences of Architecture," in *A+U: Questions of Perception* (1994); Juhani Pallasmaa, *Encounters: Architectural Essays* (Helsinki, Finland: Rakennustieto Oy, 2008) and his chapter in this book; Claudio Silvestrin, *Claudio Silvestrin* (Basel, Switzerland: Birkhäuser, 1999).

4. Lindsay Jones, *The Hermeneutics of Sacred Architecture: Experience, Interpretation, Comparison*, 2 vols. (Cambridge, Mass.: Harvard University Press, 2000), 1:97, 102.

5. Alberto Pérez-Gómez, *Built Upon Love: Architectural Longing after Ethics and Aesthetics* (Cambridge, Mass.: The MIT Press, 2006), 109.

6. My three-year-long search (part of an in-progress book investigating extraordinary architectural experiences) resorted to all types of sources, assistance, and advice to locate first-person accounts in the published record of architecture. The result has been a handful of trustable testimonies that could be said to present some transcendent or numinous state. Among them are the extraordinary experiences of Bruno Taut at Katsura in Kyoto (Bruno Taut, *Houses and People of Japan* [Tokyo: The Sanseido Co., 1937]); Frank Gehry at the Chartres Cathedral ("Frank O. Gehry," in *Studio Talk: Interview with 15 Architects*, ed. Yoshio Futagawa [Tokyo: A.D.A. EDITA, 2002]); Bernard Tschumi while visiting the city of Chicago ("Bernard Tschumi," in *Studio Talk: Interview with 15 Architects*, ed. Yoshio Futagawa [Tokyo: A.D.A. EDITA, 2002]); Antoine Predock at the Alhambra (Antoine Predock, "Antoine Predock on the Alhambra," in *Architects on Architects*, ed. Susan Gray [New York: McGraw-Hill, 2002]); Tadao Ando at Ronchamp (Tadao Ando, "Tadao Ando on Le Corbusier," in *Architects on Architects*, ed. Susan Gray [New York: McGraw-Hill, 2002]);

Steven Holl at the Pantheon (Steven Holl, "Archetypal Experiences of Architecture," *A+U: Questions of Perception* [1994]); Juhani Pallasmaa at Karnak (Juhani Pallasmaa, "The Aura of the Sacred," in *The Religious Imagination in Modern and Contemporary Architecture: A Reader*, ed. Renata Hejduk and Jim Williamson [New York: Routledge, 2011], see esp. 237); and Alberto Campo Baeza at the Pantheon (Alberto Campo Baeza, *Principia Architectonica* [Madrid: Mairea Libros, 2012], 85–92). I did find a few literary pieces (e.g., Henry James's "The Last of the Valerii") that definitely and beautifully narrate the architectural extraordinary, but these stories are fictional and therefore cannot be used for a fact-based phenomenological inquiry.

7. Arguments and evidence explaining the biases of our discipline against the qualitative, phenomenological, and axiological may be found in several books. For example, Alberto Pérez-Gómez, *Architecture and the Crisis of Modern Science* (Cambridge, Mass.: The MIT Press, 1985); Karsten Harries, *The Ethical Function of Architecture* (Cambridge, Mass.: The MIT Press, 1997), "The Ethical Significance of Environmental Beauty," in *Architecture, Ethics, and the Personhood of Place*, ed. Gregory Caicco (Lebanon, NH: University Press of New England, 2007), and his chapter in this book; Luis Barragán, "1980 Laureate Acceptance Speech," Pritzker Architecture Prize, accessed May 15, 2013. http://www.pritzkerprize.com/1980/ceremony_speech1. And the always-contemporary Gaston Bachelard, *The Poetics of Space* (Boston: Beacon Press, 1964).

8. Pérez-Gómez explains the lack of institutional interest (or censorship) in addressing transcending experiential states thus: "This is the state that irritates theologians and technocrats—understood by Socrates as an authentic glimpse of truth, despite its dangers. Although this state may threaten historical rationality and even deontological human action, the unknowing it reveals to our experiences is crucial for the construction of any truth: the seductive power of the poetic images is the foundation of signification" (*Built Upon Love*, 84).

9. This event is depicted in the chapter titled "The Parthenon," in Le Corbusier, *Journey to the East*, ed. and trans. Ivan Zaknic (Cambridge, Mass.: The MIT Press, 1987). The original French text, *Le Voyage d'Orient*, was published in 1966.

10. Mostly descriptive accounts of Le Corbusier's experience of the Parthenon/Acropolis are offered in M. Christine Boyer, *Le Corbusier, Homme De Lettres*

(New York: Princeton Architectural Press, 2011); Nicholas Fox Weber, *Le Corbusier, a Life* (New York: Alfred A. Knopf, 2008); H. Allen Brooks, *Le Corbusier's Formative Years* (Chicago: University of Chicago Press, 1996); Stanislaus von Moos and Arthur Rüegg, *Le Corbusier before Le Corbusier* (New Haven, Conn.: Yale University Press, 2002); Geoffrey H. Baker, *Le Corbusier—The Creative Search* (New York: Van Nostrand Reinhold, 1996). Of all these authors, Weber and Baker provide the best accounts (i.e., detailed descriptions) of the event, even though they avoid getting too involved in the phenomenology of the episode.

11. Von Moos and Rüegg, *Le Corbusier before Le Corbusier*; Baker, *Le Corbusier—The Creative Search*, esp. 174–87. In addition, refer to Anthony Vidler, "Framing Infinity: Le Corbusier, Ayn Rand, and the Idea of 'Ineffable Space'," in *Warped Space: Art, Architecture and Modern Culture* (Cambridge, Mass.: The MIT Press, 1999).

12. I will list a good number of scholars who support this claim in the next section. However, it is worth noting that a small minority disagree. For example, H. Allen Brooks argues that the Carthusian monastery in the Ema Valley near Florence "was perhaps the most important experience he [Le Corbusier] ever had" (31). This is why, Brooks says, he chose to go through it one more time at the end of his "journey to the East" and would use some of what he learned there for other projects later on. See H. Allen Brooks, "Le Corbusier's Formative Years at La Chaux-De-Fonds," in *Le Corbusier: The Garland Essays*, ed. H. Allen Brooks (New York: Garland Publishing, 1987).

13. Karla Britton provides some rationale behind the prejudice against the sacred or spiritual in contemporary architecture in her chapter in this book and also in her work *Constructing the Ineffable: Contemporary Sacred Architecture* (New Haven, Conn.: Yale School of Architecture, 2011). Additionally, see Renata Hejduk and Jim Williamson, "Introduction: The Apocryphal Project of Modern and Contemporary Architecture," in *The Religious Imagination in Modern and Contemporary Architecture: A Reader*, ed. Renata Hejduk and Jim Williamson (New York: Routledge, 2011). Michael Benedikt offers more proof of this bias in the introduction to his book *God, Creativity and Evolution: The Argument from Design(ers)* (Austin, Tex.: Center for American Architecture and Design, 2008).

14. Refer to Arthur C. Danto, *The Abuse of Beauty* (Peru, Ill.: Carus Publishing, 2006); Alexander Nehamas, *Only a Promise of Happiness* (Princeton, N.J.:

Princeton University Press, 2007); Roger Scruton, *Beauty: A Very Short Introduction* (New York: Oxford University Press, 2011); Hans-Georg Gadamer, *The Relevance of the Beautiful and Other Essays*, trans. Nicholas Walker (New York: Cambridge University Press, 1986).

15. At the start of his book on Le Corbusier, Kenneth Frampton asks why he should conduct yet another study of the famous architect when there is so much already available and concludes that it is precisely such wealth of knowledge of his life that provides scholars with a perfect context to explore or validate a great variety of architectural ideas and questions. Kenneth Frampton, *Le Corbusier* (New York: Thames & Hudson, 2001). As to how big the body of scholarship on Le Corbusier is, scholar Nicholas Weber says: "There are nearly four hundred monographs devoted to Le Corbusier's work, among them detailed accounts of his early years and some excellent books on specific aspects of his career." Nicholas Fox Weber, *Le Corbusier, a Life* (New York: Alfred A. Knopf, 2008), xvii.

16. Paul V. Turner, *The Education of Le Corbusier* (New York: Garland Publishing, 1977); H. Allen Brooks, "Foreword" in H. Allen Brooks, ed., *Le Corbusier: The Garland Essays* (New York: Garland Publishing,1987), vii–x; Jean-Louis Cohen, ed., *Le Corbusier, Le Grand* (New York: Phaidon Press, 2008). See also Le Corbusier *Creation Is a Patient Search*, trans. James Palmes (New York: Frederick Praeger, 1960).

17. Le Corbusier's decision to publish his *Journey to the East* weeks before dying is discussed by Turner, *The Education of Le Corbusier*; H. Allen Brooks, *Le Corbusier's Formative Years* (Chicago: University of Chicago Press, 1996); Cohen, ed., *Le Corbusier, Le Grand*. For those wondering why Le Corbusier waited fifty-four years to get such important testament published, Ivan Zaknic discusses two unsuccessful attempts at publishing the trip journal as a full manuscript: one in 1912 that failed for no known reasons and the other in 1914 that was stopped by the outbreak of war. He adds that there seems to have been a third try at the end of WWI (Ivan Zaknic, "Editor's Preface," in Le Corbusier, *Journey to the East*, viii–xiv). According to Boyer, extracts of "The Parthenon" were published in a 1925 article titled "Sur l'Acropole," in *Almanac D'Architecture Moderne* (M. Christine Boyer, *Le Corbusier, Homme De Lettres* [New York: Princeton Architectural Press, 2011]). However, and although Le Corbusier often pointed at his early trip to the East in talks, books, and works, the actual full account was never published until after his death. What propelled

Le Corbusier to finally go ahead and publish it is still best explained in the preface to the 1966 first printing of the book: to inspire young people into undertaking a trip of this kind. Several facts support this interpretation. First, Le Corbusier affirmed the importance of such journey in his first and still most popular book *Vers une Architecture* ("Toward a New Architecture" in English) and throughout his life, something that the publication of his trip notes would support. Second, by leaving the text basically untouched Le Corbusier demonstrates his desire to preserve the raw, passionate, and at times naïve writing of the experiences which, as Jose M. Torres Nadal says in his prologue to the Spanish version of *Le Voyage d'Orient*, is one of the most beautiful texts he ever wrote and likely to resonate with young people. This would have been an important consideration in Le Corbusier's committed pedagogic agenda. Le Corbusier, *El Viaje De Oriente*, 2nd ed. (Valencia, Spain: Artes Graficas Soler S.A., 1993).

18. Le Corbusier, quoted in von Moos and Rüegg, *Le Corbusier before Le Corbusier*, 93.

19. Zaknic, "Editor's Preface," in Le Corbusier, *Journey to the East*, xiv.

20. Le Corbusier, *Toward a New Architecture*, trans. John Goodman, 2nd ed. (Los Angeles: Getty Research Institute, 2007), 239.

21. Le Corbusier, *New World of Space* (New York: Reynal & Hitchcock, 1948), 66. Notice that in this talk, Le Corbusier mistakenly says twenty-three instead of the actual twenty-two years of the time passed since his first visit to the Acropolis. He made the same mistake in the quote covered in note 18.

22. For example, see Simon Richards, *Le Corbusier and the Concept of Self* (New Haven, Conn.: Yale University Press, 2003), 11; Baker, *Le Corbusier—The Creative Search*, 187; Cohen, ed., *Le Corbusier, Le Grand*, 19; Brooks, "Le Corbusier's Formative Years at La Chaux-De-Fonds," 34; von Moos and Rüegg, *Le Corbusier before Le Corbusier*, 183; Turner, *The Education of Le Corbusier*, 98; Le Corbusier, *Journey to the East*, viii; Frampton, *Le Corbusier*, 13; Vidler, "Framing Infinity: Le Corbusier, Ayn Rand, and the Idea of 'Ineffable Space'"; *El Viaje De Oriente*; Spyros Papapetros, "Le Corbusier and Freud on the Acropolis: Notes on a Parallel Itinerary," in *Architects' Journeys: Building, Traveling, Thinking*, ed. Craig Buckley and Pollyanna Rhee (New York: GSAPP Books, 2011).

23. For example, Stanislaus von Moos, "Chapter 1: Voyages en Zigzag," in Weber, *Le Corbusier, a Life*; von Moos and Rüegg, *Le Corbusier before Le Corbusier*; Richard A. Etlin, "The Parthenon in the Modern Era,"

in *The Parthenon: From Antiquity to the Present*, ed. Jenifer Neils (New York: Cambridge University Press, 2005).

24. William J. Curtis, *Le Corbusier: Ideas and Forms* (New York: Rizzoli, 1986), 43.

25. von Moos and Rüegg, *Le Corbusier before Le Corbusier*, esp. 182–85; Vidler, "Framing Infinity: Le Corbusier, Ayn Rand, and the Idea of 'Ineffable Space'"; Turner, *The Education of Le Corbusier*; Baker, *Le Corbusier—The Creative Search*; Etlin, "The Parthenon in the Modern Era"; Le Corbusier, *Journey to the East*.

26. An English translation of Renan's *Prière sur l'Acropole* is available online at http://www.archive.org/stream/recollectionsofmoorenauoft#page/60/mode/1up. This is a scan of Ernest Renan, *Recollection of My Youth* (London: Chapman and Hall Limited, 1897). His "Prayer on the Acropolis" is on 49–61. This same translation is also available online at http://www.lexilogos.com/document/renan/acropolis.htm (accessed May 15, 2013).

27. See Stanislaus von Moos, *Le Corbusier: Elements of a Synthesis* (Cambridge, Mass.: The MIT Press, 1980), 14. Brooks, "Le Corbusier's Formative Years at La Chaux-De-Fonds."

28. Baker, *Le Corbusier—The Creative Search*; Weber, *Le Corbusier, a Life*; Francesco Passanti, "Architecture: Proportion, Classicism and Other Issues," in *Le Corbusier before Le Corbusier*, ed. Stanislaus von Moos and Arthur Rüegg (New Haven, Conn.: Yale University Press, 2002); Le Corbusier, *Journey to the East*. Brooks provides us with an example of the doubts raised by Jeanneret's three-year delay in writing the testimony. He points out that "The Parthenon" is the best chapter of *Journey to the East* because it probably took advantage of the criticism his early notes had received, recommendations of his adviser William Ritter, lots of leisure time, and more reading of books and articles. This train of thought pushes scholar Brooks to pronounce "how much his ideas about Greece had changed during these three years, we don't know." Brooks, *Le Corbusier's Formative Years*, 281.

29. For example, in one representative passage, Brooks says: "Yet Jeanneret, as Francophile and Germanophobe, was in no way prepared to give credit where credit was due. Therefore, for the sake of posterity, he subsequently invented the more romantic image of undergoing a sudden conversion to classicism at the foot of the Acropolis, thereby avoiding mention of the arduous and often painful evolution that ultimately made him receptive to what he saw in Greece." Ibid., 210.

30. According to Turner and others, the experience of the Parthenon thoroughly convinced Jeanneret of the aesthetics and values of Southern-Mediterranean cultures (classic, monastic, spiritual) over the Northern European ethos (i.e., practical, rational, material), something advanced in books of Cingria-Vaneyre and Ruskin that Jeanneret had read by the time he visited the Parthenon. Turner, *The Education of Le Corbusier*.

31. Julio Bermudez and Brandon Ro, "Memory, Social Interaction and Communicability in Extraordinary Experiences of Architecture," in *Proceedings of the 2013 Architectural Research Centers Consortium*, ed. C. Jarrett, K.-H. Kim, and N. Senske (University of North Carolina–Charlotte: ARCC, 2013), http://arccweb.org/conferences/proceedings/ARCC2013_UNCC%20Conference%20Proceedings.pdf (accessed May 15, 2013). Julio Bermudez, "Empirical Aesthetics: The Body and Emotion in Extraordinary Architectural Experiences," in *Proceedings of the 2011 Architectural Research Centers Consortium*, ed. Philip Plowright and Bryce Gamper (Lawrence Tech University, Detroit, Mich.: ARCC, 2011), http://arccweb.org/conferences/proceedings/ARCC2011_Lawrence%20Tech%20Conference%20Proceedings.pdf (accessed May 15, 2013).

32. Le Corbusier, *Journey to the East*, 235. Ivan Zaknic, the translator of the English edition of *Le Voyage d'Orient*, explains that "resin wine in the East is an ancestor of absinthe," which is the medicine that was used to combat cholera at the time. Ibid., 235.

33. Weber, *Le Corbusier, a Life*, 91, 97.

34. Ibid., 55. He says that Jeanneret's sexual abstinence had to do with his religious upbringing.

35. Pérez-Gómez, *Built Upon Love*; Alberto Pérez-Gómez, *Polyphilo or the Dark Forest Revisited: An Erotic Epiphany of Architecture* (Cambridge, Mass.: The MIT Press, 1994).

36. Otto, *The Idea of the Holy*, 46–47.

37. There are two "interludes" in my study of Jeanneret's experience. While not essential to the general interpretation of the text, they do provide important contextual background that will clarify and add nuance to the situation being considered. I leave it up to the reader to engage or bypass this extra layer of information.

38. See Lynne Withey, *Grand Tours and Cook's Tours: A History of Leisure Travel, 1750–1915* (New York: William Morrow & Co, 1997). By the early twentieth century, the "Grand Tour" tradition had been transformed but the cultural custom still remained (as it does at least as an ideal to this day).

39. For example, Baker (1996) argues that Jeanneret's main reason for the trip was the Acropolis-Parthenon as demonstrated by a letter to his mentor William Ritter written on March 1, 1911, where he says that "the prime intention of his journey was to visit Athens." Baker, *Le Corbusier—The Creative Search*, 138. In return, Ritter encourages and advises him. For more on this, see section "Interlude One." I only found one scholar who disagrees on this matter: von Moos maintains that "the goal, and in many respects the raison d'etre, of their 'reverse Grand Tour' was of course not the Acropolis but Istanbul where they spent seven weeks." "Cat. No. 11 Athens," in von Moos and Rüegg, *Le Corbusier before Le Corbusier*, 182–85.

40. Le Corbusier, *Journey to the East*, 216.

41. Turner, *The Education of Le Corbusier*; Baker, *Le Corbusier—The Creative Search*; H. Allen Brooks, "Foreword," in Brooks, ed. *Le Corbusier: The Garland Essays*, vii–x; Frampton, *Le Corbusier*.

42. Turner, *The Education of Le Corbusier*; von Moos, *Le Corbusier: Elements of a Synthesis*; Frampton, *Le Corbusier*; H. Allen Brooks, "Foreword," in Brooks, ed. *Le Corbusier: The Garland Essays*; Alan Colquhoun, "The Significance of Le Corbusier," in *Le Corbusier: The Garland Essays*, ed. H. Allen Brooks (New York: Garland Publishing, 1987).

43. Turner, *The Education of Le Corbusier*, 12.

44. Ibid; von Moos, *Le Corbusier: Elements of a Synthesis*, 11; Frampton, *Le Corbusier*.

45. Jeanneret's family followed Catharism, a persecuted Christian sect that challenged much of the established dogmas of the Catholic Church and other Christian traditions. See Adolf Max Vogt, *Le Corbusier: The Noble Savage*, trans. Radka Donnell (Cambridge, Mass.: The MIT Press, 1998); Frampton, *Le Corbusier*; Weber, *Le Corbusier, a Life*. For more on the impact of religion and spirituality in young Le Corbusier, see Le Corbusier and Pierre Jeanneret, *Oeuvre Complète 1910–1929* (Switzerland: Les Editions d'Architecture, 1964).

46. Turner, *The Education of Le Corbusier*; Frampton, *Le Corbusier*; Weber, *Le Corbusier, a Life*; von Moos and Rüegg, *Le Corbusier before Le Corbusier*; Cohen, ed. *Le Corbusier, Le Grand*; Curtis, *Le Corbusier: Ideas and Forms*.

47. "German Vice," Turner speculates, also relates to pragmatism, functionalism, "lack of gracefulness and calm order," "fine organization but little art," and "harsh and brutal" buildings. Turner, *The Education of Le Corbusier*.

48. Ibid; Baker, *Le Corbusier—The Creative Search*.

49. Le Corbusier, *Journey to the East*. The two cita-

tions in the previous paragraph are from pages 195 and 214, whereas the stand alone quote is from page 214.

50. Le Corbusier refers to the month of September in Le Corbusier *Voyage D'orient: Carnets*, trans. Mayra Munson and Mege Shore (Milano: Mondadori Electa spa, 2002), 123. The exact date, September 12, is provided by Brooks (Brooks, *Le Corbusier's Formative Years*, 280) and confirmed by von Moos and Rüegg (von Moos and Rüegg, *Le Corbusier before Le Corbusier*, 182).

51. Le Corbusier, *Journey to the East*, 216.

52. Ibid. Scholar von Moos advances that Jeanneret waited until late afternoon to climb up to the Acropolis in order to *"keep up with the literary tradition of the Hellenic traveler."* "Cat. No. 11 Athens," in von Moos and Rüegg, *Le Corbusier before Le Corbusier*, 183. Papapetros says Jeanneret's intention was to be at the Acropolis during sunset. Spyros Papapetros, "Le Corbusier and Freud on the Acropolis: Notes on a Parallel Itinerary," in *Architects' Journeys: Building, Traveling, Thinking*, ed. Craig Buckley and Pollyanna Rhee (New York: GSAPP Books, 2011), 145.

53. Le Corbusier, *Journey to the East*, 217.

54. Sigmund Freud, "A Disturbance of Memory on the Acropolis," in *The Standard Edition of the Complete Psychological Works of Sigmund Freud*, ed. James Strachey, Anna Freud, and Angela Richards (London: Hogarth Press, 1966).

55. Vidler, "Framing Infinity: Le Corbusier, Ayn Rand, and the Idea of 'Ineffable Space'," 57.

56. Le Corbusier, *Journey to the East*, 232, 234.

57. This interpretation matches the anxiety I myself experienced while walking up to the Acropolis for the first time. There is no question that my stress came from feeling not prepared enough to encounter the extraordinary, in not being pure or open or free enough to meet the architectural perfection "up there" (and not due to some Freudian psychological disturbance). I was scared that nothing would happen, that I would miss my chance at the numinous. If I was very apprehensive at forty-six, so must have been young Jeanneret at half my age!

58. For example, see Papapetros, "Le Corbusier and Freud on the Acropolis: Notes on a Parallel Itinerary"; Daniel Naegele, "Object, Image, Aura: Le Corbusier and the Architecture of Photography," *Harvard Design Magazine* (Fall 1998).

59. Le Corbusier, *Journey to the East*, 217, 220; emphasis added.

60. Ibid., 220; emphasis added.

61. Jeanneret is operating under a condition termed "distancing" by philosophical aesthetics. He is far from home in a different culture, country, language, and so forth. It is worth noticing that all the reported extraordinary experiences of architects (see note 6) happen away from their motherland, tongue, and more. For more on this, see Julio Bermudez, "Profound Experiences of Architecture: The Role of 'Distancing' in the Ineffable," *2A—Architecture and Art Magazine* Spring Quarter, no. 17 (2011). The fact that Jeanneret is alone, silent, in a more or less empty (i.e., nonsocially distracting or constraining) environment adds even more power to conditions suitable for an exceptional phenomenology.

62. Arriving at a nondual state may be seen as "regression" or "progression" depending on one's vanishing point, beliefs, or arguments. For example, from some perspectives it does look like a "reversion" to an animalist, "dionysian," preconscious state (a return to an oceanic, pre-ego, infantile developmental stage). From other perspectives (and I would here include most spiritual traditions), it is an evolution to an "enlightened" or "blessed" state that could be very embodied but represents a "growth" in consciousness or sensibility that transcends intellectual or self-centered operations. When we consider "peak" experiences, another possibility of understanding becomes available (by itself or in conjunction with "regressive" or "progressive" interpretations).

63. Ibid., 236.

64. Jeanneret wrote "The Parthenon" toward the middle of 1914, as WWI was brewing, if it had not already started. Additionally, the harsh and violent term "annihilation" may also have to do with a twenty-three-year-old male ego being completely bruised by the sheer power of the moment that forced him to confront the always uncomfortable (especially for a young person) sense of existential fragility.

65. In his testimony, Jeanneret himself tells us that he arrived in Athens at 11 a.m. He then says he spent all afternoon drinking coffee and reading his mail after having an early lunch and securing hotel accommodations, which puts us at 3–4 p.m. He then states that he walked around "waiting for the sun to go down" (let us say one hour, getting us to 4–5 p.m.). Early September sun in Athens sets at around 7 p.m., about the time the Acropolis closes for visitors, as we gather from the narrative. If we now consider some thirty-minutes walking time from old downtown Athens to the Acropolis (at a brisk pace), we get about 1.5 to 2.5 hours left at the top.

66. Architect Claudio Silvestrin beautifully summarizes this type of nondual aesthetic experi-

ence thus: "When one actually sees the solidity of a mountain or the vastness of the sea, when one comes upon it suddenly, there it is in its monolithic presence. Everything, including one's own ego, has been pushed aside, except the majesty of that mountain or that sea. Such a sight absorbs you completely—it is beauty itself. If you are fortunate enough, think of a building that absorbs you with the same intensity—that building I call architecture: the others are nothing but edifices." Claudio Silvestrin, *Ad* (*Architectural Design*): *Aspects of Minimal Architecture II* (Waltham, Mass.: Academy Press, 1999), 9.

67. William James, *Varieties of Religious Experiences* (New York: Touchstone, 2004). Consistent with seeking nondual consciousness to access the Holy, Trappist monk Thomas Keating explains that the ultimate goal of Catholic contemplative prayer is reaching the place "… in which *the knower, the knowing and that which is known are all one*. Awareness only remains. This is what *divine union* is… Union on the spiritual level is the infusion of love and knowledge together, and, while it is going on, it is *non-reflective*." Thomas Keating, *Open Mind, Open Heart* (New York: Continuum, 2009), 69; emphasis added. See also Thomas Merton's chapter, "Transcendent Experience," in *Zen and the Birds of Appetite* (New York: A New Direction Book, 1968). Zen Buddhist masters usually refer to the "death of the self" as a most difficult, necessary, yet frightful step to attain enlightenment. Contemporary philosopher Ken Wilber discusses at length the nondual state of consciousness that characterizes the most profound spiritual experiences, offering many references, in Ken Wilber, *Integral Spirituality* (Boston: Shambala, 2006), *Integral Psychology* (Boston: Shambala, 2000).

68. Otto, *The Idea of the Holy*, 21. Otto emphasizes that only the removal of the "personal I" will deliver the greatest "plenitude of being" wherein the self realizes "I am naught, Thou art all."

69. Le Corbusier, *Journey to the East*, 217.

70. Papapetros, "Le Corbusier and Freud on the Acropolis: Notes on a Parallel Itinerary," 155. "Heroic self-fulfillment" has at least a word-resemblance to what in Zen is called "self-fulfilling Samadhi," that is, a difficult-to-attain state of consciousness. Self-fulfilling Samadhi is sustained for its own sake (without purpose), without striving, and without a witness.

71. Richard Etlin argues that Le Corbusier's response to the Parthenon was not due to the beauty of the building but to something much more vast and powerful, closer to experiencing Mont Blanc (i.e.,

nature)—thus deploying a romantic and pleasing interpretation of the sublime. He says, "Unlike beauty, which is man's 'domain,' sublimity transports the observer to a place and to a condition 'beyond and above us.'" However, it is of no use to this essay to discriminate between this or that type of beauty (depending on this or that philosophical position). Instead, we are interested in the capability of some external phenomena to quicken us into a numinous state. Richard A. Etlin, "Le Corbusier, Choisy, and French Hellenism: The Search for a New Architecture," *The Art Bulletin* 69, no. 2 (June 1987): 270.

72. Confronted with our limited sense of self against something "other" so vast and beyond our comprehension, we may feel threatened with extinction and recoil in horror and disgust (negative) or rejoice and be eager to join in the loving embrace (positive). In one case, the letting go of ego's control and separateness would be perceived as terrifying and maddening (awful sublime) whereas in the other circumstance as liberation, pleasure, and ultimate intimacy (ecstatic sublime). Put differently, the former response refuses nonduality while the latter welcomes it. Otto's discussion on the "majestic" quality of the numinous further clarifies this matter. Faced with the overwhelming might of the transcendent, we are frightened for what it feels as sure annihilation. However, Otto says if we manage to "transmute" that "plenitude of power" into a "plenitude of being," awfulness turns into bliss. Otto, *The Idea of the Holy*, 21. In the end, actual sublime experiences are likely to fall within a continuum between rejection and embrace, thus giving rise to a rich variety of psychological, physical, and/or spiritual outcomes.

73. Mihaly Csikszentmihalyi, *Flow: The Psychology of Optimal Experience* (New York: Harper & Row, 1990). Regarding "positive psychology," refer to M. E. P. Seligman and M. Csikszentmihalyi, "Positive Psychology: An Introduction," *American Psychologist* 55, no. 1 (2000); Martin E. P. Seligman, *Authentic Happiness: Using the New Positive Psychology to Realize Your Potential for Lasting Fulfillment* (New York: Atria Books, 2003); S. R. Snyder, Shane J. Lopez, and Jennifer Teramoto Pedrotti, *Positive Psychology: The Scientific and Practical Explorations of Human Strengths* (Thousand Oaks, Calif.: Sage, 2011). For other good information on this topic, see the International Positive Psychology Association, http://www.ippanetwork.org/ (accessed June 1, 2013).

74. In one passage, Heidegger says, "Standing there, the building [i.e., the temple] rests on the rocky ground. This resting of the work draws up out of the

rock the mystery of the rock's clumsy yet spontaneous support. Standing there, the building holds its ground against the storm ranging above it and so first makes the storm itself manifest in its violence. The lust and gleam of the stone, though itself apparently glowing only by the grace of the sun, yet first brings to light the light of the day, the breath of the sky, the darkness of the night. The temple's firm towering makes visible the invisible space of air." Martin Heidegger, *Poetry, Language, Thought*, trans. Albert Hofstadter (New York: Harper & Row, 1971), 42.

75. John Dewey, *Art as Experience* (New York: Wideview/Perigee Book, 1934); James Elkins, *Pictures and Tears* (New York: Routledge, 2001); Mark Johnson, *The Meaning of the Body* (Chicago: University of Chicago Press, 2007). I discuss nondual states in the context of architectural experiences in two articles: Julio Bermudez, "Non-Ordinary Architectural Phenomenologies: Non Dualist Experiences and Husserl's Reduction," *Environmental & Architectural Phenomenology (EAP)* 21, no. 2 (2010) and "The Extraordinary in Architecture," *2A—Architecture and Art Magazine* Autumn Quarter, no. 12 (2009). Although influenced by a limiting Freudian view of nonduality as infantile (as renowned psychoanalyst Carl Jung later showed), John Abell presents an interesting conversation on this topic in "On 'That Oceanic Feeling': Architectural Formlessness, Otherness and Being Everything," *Quarterly Architectural Essays Journal* 3, no. 1 (Fall 2007).

76. Le Corbusier, *Journey to the East*, 226.

77. Ibid., 209, 212.

78. Ibid., 212.

79. Ibid., 230.

80. Many spiritual traditions discuss the relationships and/or parallels between states of consciousness, states of mind, and states of reality. For example, see the Vajrayana-Vedanta schools, Theosophy, and Gurdjieff's Fourth Way. For a thorough discussion on lucid dreaming and subtle states of consciousness, see Wilber, *Integral Spirituality*.

81. Otto, *The Idea of the Holy*, 37.

82. Ibid., 236; emphasis added.

83. Philosopher Mark Taylor's insightful discussion of the "absential" dimension of the Holy provides more clarity and nuance to Jeanneret's situation. See Mark Taylor, "The Nonabsent Absence of the Holy," in *Tears* (Albany: State University of New York Press, 1990). We can find more understanding in Mother Teresa's confession that the most unbearable thing in her entire life was the nearly fifty-year-long absence of God after having experienced His graceful presence. See David

Van Biema, "Mother Teresa's Crisis of Faith," *Time Magazine* August 23, 2007.

84. Weber, *Le Corbusier, a Life*, 95.

85. Vidler, "Framing Infinity: Le Corbusier, Ayn Rand, and the Idea of 'Ineffable Space,'" see esp. 55.

86. Baker, *Le Corbusier—The Creative Search*, 187. This statement could be turned on its head if we accept that Jeanneret reached a nondual state. In such case, the battle between the building and Jeanneret ended up with the "annihilation" of the latter which is exactly what permitted his experiential breakthrough.

87. Le Corbusier, *Journey to the East*, 238.

88. Otto, *The Idea of the Holy*, 33–34.

89. Here is yet another reason why casting Jeanneret's breakthrough at the Parthenon as awful and negative is twisted and incorrect. Unless one is psychologically disturbed, nobody uses dreadfulness to motivate oneself and advance one's career or life for fifty-four years!

90. Le Corbusier, *Journey to the East*, 228.

91. Jeanneret quoted in Ivan Zaknic, *The Final Testament of Père Corbu: A Translation and Interpretation of Mise Au Point by Ivan Zaknic* (New Haven, Conn.: Yale University Press, 1997), 9. It is important to note that by the time Jeanneret had arrived in Athens, he had stopped writing travel notes (but not sketching). As noted earlier, he would write his account of Athos and Athens two-plus years after finishing his journey to the East.

92. Le Corbusier makes patently clear the importance of phenomenology while affirming his extraordinary moment at the Parthenon. In the following quote, and referring to himself in third-person, he comments, "The columns of the North façade and the architrave of the Parthenon were still lying on the ground. Touching them with his fingers, caressing, he grasps the proportions of the design. Amazement: reality has nothing in common with books of instructions. Here everything was a shout of inspiration, a dance in the sunlight … and a final and supreme warning: do not believe until you have seen and measured … and touched with your own fingers." *Creation Is a Patient Search*, 21. Scholar Baker claims that the architect placed great importance in seeing works for himself as the direct way to discovery. Baker, *Le Corbusier—The Creative Search*, 138. Le Corbusier extended his lack of faith in formal and indirect learning to schooling in general, which explains his autodidactic education. He would say, "I acquired a positive terror for the teaching of the architectural schools, and of all planning recipes, infallible a priori methods, etc.; for even at this uncertain period I had

appreciated the necessity of having resources to one's own judgment. I used my savings to travel, keeping well away from schools of architecture and earning my living by practical work. I began to open my eyes." Jeanneret, *Oeuvre Complète 1910–1929*, 13.

93. Le Corbusier does acknowledge that his term "ineffable space" was one built upon years of observation, that is, evolution. He says it very clearly: "I am the inventor of the phrase 'ineffable space,' which is a reality that I discovered as I went on." Le Corbusier, quoted in André Wogensky, *Le Corbusier's Hands*, trans. Martina Millá Bernad (Cambridge, Mass.: The MIT Press, 2006), 81.

94. See "Interlude One."

95. Le Corbusier, *New World of Space*, 8. The quotations in the previous paragraph are also from the same source and page. The power of ineffable space to "efface the walls and drive away all contingent presences" quite closely resembles Jeanneret's first encounter with the Parthenon when only the most essential aspects of the experience appear in consciousness (the temple, earth, and the sky). For more on "ineffable space," see Britton, *Constructing the Ineffable: Contemporary Sacred Architecture*, as well as her chapter in this book.

96. Wassily Kandinsky, during his last push toward total abstraction, initially recoils against the disappearance of objecthood, possibly pointing at some Burkean sublimity. He says, "A terrifying abyss of all kinds of questions, a wealth of responsibilities stretched before me. And most important of all: what is to replace the missing object?" Kenneth C. Lindsay and Peter Vergo, eds., *Kandinsky: Complete Writings on Art* (New York:

Da Capo Press, 1994), 370. Kandinsky's experience is not unlike the one that Kazimir Malevich himself had as he also approached ultimate abstraction when painting his black square on a white background in 1913. In the Suprematist Manifesto, and referring to such moment, he states, "Even I was gripped by a kind of timidity bordering on fear when it came to leaving 'the world of will and idea,' in which I had lived and worked and the reality in which I had believed."

97. Naegele, "Object, Image, Aura: Le Corbusier and the Architecture of Photography," 41.

98. Several books have come out (re)claiming the spiritual dimension of Le Corbusier. For example, Frampton, *Le Corbusier*; von Moos, *Le Corbusier: Elements of a Synthesis*; Simon Richards, *Le Corbusier and the Concept of Self* (New Haven, Conn.: Yale University Press, 2003); J. K. Birksted, *Le Corbusier and the Occult* (Cambridge, Mass.: The MIT Press, 2009). These scholars show how the spiritual interest of Le Corbusier surfaces in the figurative imagery in many of his post-1930s buildings and drawings, the long, twisting, and provocative "Poem of the Right Angle" written over many years (1947–1953), his alchemical connotations along with a number mysticism, as well as his interest in Carl Jung. These expressions of a so-called modern Le Corbusier should not surprise us. Richards tells us that "mysticism and occultism have been acknowledged as central to much of modernist art and literature. In fact, the general picture that emerges is that it would be unusual for an artist not to have some connection with them." Richards, *Le Corbusier and the Concept of Self*, 125.

99. Frampton, *Le Corbusier*, 13.

8. THE CHRISTIAN CHURCH BUILDING

1. See Mircea Eliade, *Images and Symbols: Studies in Religious Symbolism* (Princeton, N.J.: Princeton University Press, 1991).

2. Alexander Schmemann, *The World as Sacrament* (London: Longman, Darton & Todd, 1965), 16.

3. John Habgood, "The Sacramentality of the Natural World," in *The Sense of the Sacramental: Movement and Measure in Art and Music, Place and Time*, ed. David Brown and Ann Loades (London: SPCK, 1995), 27–28.

4. Joel P. Brereton, "Sacred Space," in *The Encyclopedia of Religion*, ed. Mircea Eliade (New York: Macmillan, 1995), 9:526–35. See also Mircea Eliade, *The Sacred and the Profane: The Nature of Religion* (New York: Harper & Row, 1959), 20–67 and *Patterns*

in Comparative Religion (New York: Sheed & Ward, 1958), 367–87.

5. See Robert L. Cohn, *The Shape of Sacred Space: Four Biblical Studies* (Chico: Scholars Press, 1981).

6. Karl Rahner, *The Church and the Sacraments* (London: Burns & Oates, 1963), 76–117; Lambert J. Leijssen, *With the Silent Glimmer of God's Spirit: A Postmodern Look at the Sacraments* (New York: Paulist Press, 2006), 1–8.

7. Judith Kubicki, *The Presence of Christ in the Gathered Assembly* (New York: Continuum, 2006), 33–59; Gordon W. Lathrop and Timothy J. Wengert, *Christian Assembly: Marks of the Church in a Pluralistic Age* (Minneapolis: Fortress Press, 2004).

8. See Eliade, *Images and Symbols*.

9. Diana Eck, "Sacred Mountains," in *Encyclopedia of Religion*, ed. Eliade, 9:130–34; see also Cohn, "Mountains in the Biblical Cosmos," in *Shape of Sacred Space*, 25–41.

10. See Exod. 28; 29; Lev. 8-10.

11. Yves Congar, *The Mystery of the Temple* (London: Burns & Oates, 1962), 3–9; Jean Daniélou, *Le Signe du temple ou de la présence de Dieu* (Paris: Gallimard, 1942); H.-M. Féret, "Le temple du Dieu vivant," in *Prêtre et Apôtre* (Paris: Bonne Presse, 1947), 103–5; 135–37, 166–69, 181–84.

12. See Jer. 31, 33, 34; Ezek. 36:25-26.

13. Leslie J. Hoppe, *The Synagogue and Churches of Ancient Palestine* (Collegeville: Liturgical Press, 1994); Robert Wilken, *The Land Called Holy: Palestine in Church History and Thought* (New Haven, Conn.: Yale University Press, 1992); Steven Fine, *This Holy Place: On the Sanctity of the Synagogue during the Greco-Roman Period* (Notre Dame: University of Notre Dame Press, 1997).

14. See Rafael Aguirre, "Early Christian House Churches," *Theological Digest* 12 (Summer 1985): 151–55; L. M. White, *Social Origins of Christian Architecture*, vol. 1, *Building God's House in the Roman World: Architectural Adaptation among Pagans, Jews, and Christians* (Valley Forge: Trinity Press International, 1990), 110.

15. Paul Post, "Dura Europos Revisited: Rediscovering Sacred Space," *Worship* 86 (May 2012): 254–70. See also *Dura-Europos: Crossroads of Antiquity* (Boston: McMillan Museum of Art, 2011).

16. Roger Stalley, *Early Medieval Architecture* (New York: Oxford University Press, 1999), 17–22. See also Marcel Mezger, *History of the Liturgy: The Major Stages* (Collegeville: Liturgical Press, 1997), 64–112.

17. François Louvel, "Le mystère de nos églises," *La Maison-Dieu* 63 (1960): 5–23.

18. Stalley, *Early Medieval Architecture*, 17–22.

19. Christian Norberg-Schulz, *Meaning in Western Architecture* (New York: Praeger Publishers, 1975), 119. See also Richard Krautheimer, *Early Christian and Byzantine Architecture* (New Haven, Conn.: Yale University Press, 1992), 21, 41; Paul Corby Finney, *The Invisible God: The Earliest Christians on Art* (New York: Oxford University Press, 1994).

20. See George Zarnecki, *Romanesque* (New York: Universe Books, 1971), 14–54; Stalley, *Early Medieval Architecture*, 37–57; Rolf Toman, ed., *Romanesque Architecture, Sculpture, Painting* (Cologne: Könemann, 1970), 32–255.

21. Norberg-Schulz, *Meaning in Western Architecture*, 150.

22. See Kenneth J. Conant, *Carolingian and Romanesque Architecture* (Baltimore: Penguin Books, 1959), 1–2. Ernst Short, *A History of Religious Architecture*, 3rd rev. ed. (New York: W. A. Norton), 145.

23. J. A. Jungmann, "The Defensive Battle against Teutonic Arianism and Its Immediate Reaction," in *Pastoral Liturgy* (New York: Herder and Herder, 1962), 23–32.

24. Cheslyn Jones et al., *The Study of the Liturgy*, rev. ed. (London: SPCK, 1992), 535–37. See also F. Bond, *Screens and Galleries* (Oxford: Oxford University Press, 1908).

25. See Edwin Mullins, *Cluny: In Search of God's Lost Empire* (New York: Blue Bridge, 2006).

26. See Terryl N. Kinder, *Cistercian Europe: Architecture of Contemplation* (Grand Rapids, Mich.: Eerdmans, 2002) and *Architecture of Silence: Cistercian Abbeys of France* (New York: Harry N. Abrams, 2002); *Studies in Cistercian Art and Architecture*, 4 vols., ed. Meredith Parsons Lillich (Kalamazoo, Mich.: Cistercian Publications, 1980, 1984, 1987, 1993).

27. See Conrad Rudolph, *The "Things of Greater Importance": Bernard of Clairvaux's Apologia and the Medieval Attitude toward Art* (Philadelphia: University of Pennsylvania Press, 1990), 287–93.

28. Norberg-Schulz, *Meaning in Western Architecture*, 185.

29. Ibid., 185–87. See also *The Art of Gothic: Architecture, Sculpture, Painting*, ed. Rolf Thoman (Cologne: Könemann, 1999).

30. See Karl H. Dannefeldt, ed., *The Renaissance: Basic Interpretations* (Lexington: Heath, 1974); John W. O'Malley, Thomas M. Izbicki, and Gerald Christianson, eds., *Humanity and Divinity in Renaissance and Reformation* (New York: Brill, 1993); Anthony Levi, *Renaissance and Reformation* (New Haven, Conn.: Yale University Press, 2002); Peter Burke, *The Italian Renaissance: Culture and Society in Italy* (Princeton, N.J.: Princeton University Press, 1986).

31. Louis Bouyer, *Liturgical Piety* (Notre Dame: University of Notre Dame Press, 1954), 5–6.

32. Norberg-Schulz, *Meaning in Western Architecture*, 252.

33. See Brian Tierney, *Foundations of the Conciliar Theory* (Cambridge: Cambridge University Press, 1955).

34. See M. H. Carré, *Realists and Nominalists* (Oxford: Oxford University Press, 1946).

35. See Craig Kallendorf, ed., *Humanist Educational Treatises* (Cambridge, Mass.: The Tatti Renaissance Library, 2002).

36. See James White, *Protestant Worship: Traditions in Transition* (Louisville: Westminster John

Knox, 1989), 122–29 and *Catholic Worship: Trent to Today* (Collegeville: Liturgical Press, 2003), 1–23.

37. See Donald K. McKim, ed., *The Cambridge Companion to Martin Luther* (New York: Cambridge University Press, 2003).

38. Bruce Gordon, *The Swiss Reformation* (New York: Manchester University Press, 2002).

39. See T. H. L. Parker, *Calvin: An Introduction to his Thought* (New York: Continuum, 2002).

40. See Margaret Miles, *Images as Insight: Visual Understanding in Western Christianity and Secular Culture* (Boston: Beacon Press, 1985), 101, 113–20; A. L. Mayer, "Renaissance, Humanism und Liturgie," *Jahrbuch für Liturgiewissenschaft* 14 (1934): 123–70.

41. Bouyer, *Liturgical Piety*, 6.

42. Frank C. Senn, *Christian Liturgy: Catholic and Evangelical* (Minneapolis: Fortress Press, 1997), 538–39.

43. See J. Ernest Rattenbury, "Methodist Spirituality," in *Protestant Spiritual Traditions*, ed. Frank C. Senn (New York: Paulist Press, 1986), 217–73.

44. R. Kevin Seasoltz, "Liturgical Movement," *The Encyclopedia of Christianity*, ed. Erwin Fahlbusch et al., 5 vols. (Grand Rapids, Mich.: Eerdmans Publishing Company, 2003), 3: 314–19.

45. Guerric DeBona, James Wallace, and Robert Waznak, *Lift Up Your Hearts* (New York: Paulist Press, 2004), 251–52.

46. These reflections on the baptistry and other furnishings of the interior of a church reflect the excellent commentary on furnishings in the document issued by the U.S. Bishops' Committee on the Liturgy, *Environment and Art in Catholic Worship* (Washington, D.C.: National Conference of Catholic Bishops, 1978), 34–51. See also Irish Episcopal Commission for Liturgy, *The Place of Worship* (Dublin: Veritas, 1994); Canadian Conference of Catholic Bishops, *Our Place of Worship* (Ottawa: Publications Service Canadian Conference of Catholic Bishops, 1999), 23–41.

47. R. Kevin Seasoltz, *God's Gift Giving: In Christ and through the Spirit* (New York: Continuum, 2007), 71–77.

48. "Dedication of an Altar," *The Rites of the Catholic Church as Revised by the Second Vatican Ecumenical Council*, vol. 2 (New York: Pueblo Publishing Company, 1980), 250–73.

49. See Philip Jenkins, *The Coming of Global Christianity*, 3rd ed. (New York: Oxford University Press, 2011); Richard R. Gaillardetz, *Ecclesiology for a Global Church: A People Called and Sent* (Maryknoll: Orbis Books, 2008).

50. See Eileen D. Crowley, *Liturgical Art for a Media Culture* (Collegeville: Liturgical Press, 2007).

51. See Richard S. Vosko, "Liturgical Technology, Social Media, and the Green Church," *Liturgical Ministry* 20 (Spring 2011): 87–92; Gloria L. Schaab, "Environment, Ecology, and Creation Theology: Visions and Revisions in the Christian Tradition," *Liturgical Ministry* 20 (Spring 2011): 57–67.

52. Quoted in "U.S.A. National Symposium on Environment and Art," *Notitiae* 160 (November 1979): 659.

53. Armand Veilleux, "Monasticism and Culture-Encounter," *Tjuringa* (May 1975): 48.

9. ECCLESIAL ARCHITECTURE AND IMAGE IN A POSTMODERN AGE

1. Albert Borgmann, *Crossing the Postmodern Divide* (Chicago: University of Chicago Press, 1992), 96.

2. The emerging work of these theologians can be first anthologized in *The Postmodern God: A Theological Reader*, ed. Graham Ward (Oxford: Blackwell Publishing, 1997).

3. Graham Ward, "Introduction, or, a Guide to Theological Thinking in Cyberspace," in *The Postmodern God: A Theological Reader*, ed. Graham Ward (Oxford: Blackwell Publishing, 1997), xlii.

4. Rosemary Haughton, *Images for Change: The Transformation of Society* (New York: Paulist Press, 1997), 45–56.

5. Borgmann, *Crossing the Postmodern Divide*, 110–47.

6. Ibid., 145–47.

7. Jean-Yves Lacoste, *Expérience et Absolu: Questions disputes sur la humanité de l'homme* (Paris: Presses Universitaires de France, 1994).

8. Ibid., 34–48.

9. Steven Holl, *The Chapel of St. Ignatius* (Princeton, N.J.: Princeton Architectural Press, 1999), and *Architecture Spoken* (New York: Rizzoli International Publications, 2007).

10. David Lasker, "International and Regional— Tales of Two Architects," *Canadian Interiors* 36, no. 3 (1999): 6–7.

11. Jean-Yves Lacoste, "Presence and Parousia," in *The Blackwell Companion to Postmodern Theology*, ed. Graham Ward (Oxford: Blackwell Publishing, 2006), 395.

12. Holl, *Architecture Spoken*, 45.

13. For the purposes of this chapter, the author has collected anecdotes about the various religious uses of the Chapel of St. Ignatius.

14. Catherine Pickstock, "Justice and Prudence: Principles of Order in the Platonic City," *The Blackwell Companion to Postmodern Theology*, ed. Graham Ward (Oxford: Blackwell Publishing, 2006), 173.

15. Borgmann, *Crossing the Postmodern Divide*, 113–14.

16. Ibid., 116.

17. For a synopsis of those reforms, see Mark E. Wedig, "Edifice and Image: Reform of the Roman Catholic Worship Environment," *New Theology Review* 15, no. 3 (August 2002): 5–15.

18. Mark E. Wedig, "No Neutral Zones: Hermeneutics and the Interpretation of Liturgical Space," *Liturgical Ministry* 14 (Winter 2005): 1–7.

19. Second Vatican Ecumenical Council, *Constitution on the Liturgy: In Decrees of the Ecumenical Councils, Vol. II Trent to Vatican II;* English ed. Norman P. Tanner, SJ (Washington, D.C.: Sheed and Ward and Georgetown University Press, 1990), 122–30.

20. Sacred Congregation for Divine Worship, *General Instruction of the Roman Missal*, translated by ICEL, Liturgy Documents Series 2 (Washington, D.C.: United States Conference of Catholic Bishops, 2003), 288–318.

21. Ward, "Introduction, or, a Guide to Theological Thinking in Cyberspace," xlii.

10. SPIRITUALITY, SOCIAL JUSTICE, AND THE BUILT ENVIRONMENT

1. Frank M. Loewenberg, *Religion and Social Work Practice in Contemporary American Society* (New York: Columbia University Press, 1988); Philip R. Popple and Leslie Leighninger, *Social Work, Social Welfare, and American Society* (Boston: Allyn & Bacon, 2005).

2. Roberta W. Imre, "The Nature of Knowledge in Social Work," *Social Work* 29, no. 1 (1984): 41–45; Max Siporin, "Contribution of Religious Values to Social Work and the Law," *Social Thought* 12, no. 4 (1986): 35–50.

3. Robin Russel, "Spirituality and Religion in Graduate Social Work Education," *Social Thought* 18, no. 2 (1998): 17.

4. Edward R. Canda and Leola D. Furman, *Spiritual Diversity in Social Work Practice: The Heart of Helping*, 2nd ed. (New York: Oxford University Press, 2010).

5. Council on Social Work Education, *Educational Policy and Accreditation Standards* (Washington, D.C.: Council on Social Work Education, 2008).

6. Canda and Furman, *Spiritual Diversity in Social Work Practice*, 113.

7. Canda and Furman, *Spiritual Diversity in Social Work Practice*; Michael J. Sheridan, "The Spiritual Person," in *Dimensions of Human Behavior: Person and Environment*, ed. Elizabeth D. Hutchison, 163–208 (Thousand Oaks, Calif.: Sage, 2011).

8. Canda and Furman, *Spiritual Diversity in Social Work Practice*, 75; emphasis added.

9. Ibid., 76; emphasis added.

10. Ibid., 87.

11. Ibid., 88.

12. Ibid., 89.

13. Ibid.

14. Council on Social Work Education, *Educational Policy and Accreditation Standards*; National Association of Social Workers, *Code of Ethics* (Washington, D.C.: NASW, 2008); Jerome C. Wakefield, "Psychotherapy, Distributive Justice, and Social Work Part I: Distributive Justice as a Conceptual Framework for Social Work," *Social Service Review* 62, no. 2 (1988): 187–210.

15. Charles Frederick Weller, "Needy Families in their Homes," in *Proceedings of the National Conference of Charities and Corrections*, ed. Isabel C. Barrows (Boston: George H. Ellis Company, 1902) , 272.

16. Margaret Gibelman, "The Search for Identity: Defining Social Work—Past, Present, Future," *Social Work* 44, no. 4 (1999): 298–310.

17. John Stuart Mill, *Utilitarianism* (London: Parker, Son, and Bourn, West Strand, 1863), 9.

18. John Rawls, *A Theory of Justice* (Cambridge, Mass.: Harvard University, 1971); *A Theory of Justice*, rev. ed. (Cambridge, Mass.: The Belknap Press of Harvard University Press, 1999); *Justice as Fairness: A Restatement* (Cambridge, Mass.: The Belknap Press of Harvard University Press, 2001).

19. Rawls, *A Theory of Justice*, 100–1.

20. Ibid., 277.

21. Ibid., 276.

22. National Association of Social Workers, *Code of Ethics*, preamble; emphasis added.

23. Josephine Figueira-McDonough, "Policy Practice: The Neglected Side of Social Work Intervention," *Social Work* 38, no. 2 (1993): 179–87; Michael Reisch, "Defining Social Justice in a Socially Unjust World," *Families in Society: The Journal of Contemporary Human Services* 83, no. 4 (2002): 343–54; Carol R. Swenson, "Clinical Social Work's Contribution to a Social Justice Perspective," *Social Work* 43, no. 6

(1998): 527–37; Wakefield, "Psychotherapy, Distributive Justice, and Social Work Part I."

24. Wakefield, "Psychotherapy, Distributive Justice, and Social Work Part I," 200.

25. Loretta Pyles and Mahasweta M. Banerjee, "Work Experiences of Women Survivors: Insights from the Capabilities Approach," *Affilia* 25, no. 1 (2010): 43–55; Loretta Pyles, "The Capabilities Approach and Violence against Women: Implications for Social Development," *International Social Work* 51, no. 1 (2008): 25–36; Patricia M. Morris, "The Capabilities Perspective: A Framework for Social Justice. Families in Society," *A Journal for Contemporary Human Services* 83, no. 4 (2002): 365–73.

26. Mahasweta M. Banerjee and Edward R. Canda, "Comparing Rawlsian Justice and the Capabilities Approach to Justice from a Spiritually Sensitive Social Work Perspective," *Journal of Religion & Spirituality in Social Work: Social Thought* 31, nos. 1–2 (2012): 9–31.

27. Amartya K. Sen, *The Idea of Justice* (Cambridge, Mass.: The Belknap Press of Harvard University Press, 2009), 18.

28. Amartya K. Sen, *Commodities and Capabilities* (Amsterdam: Elsevier Science Publisher, 1985), 15; emphasis added.

29. Amartya K. Sen, *Inequality Reexamined* (New York: Russell Sage Foundation, 1992), 40.

30. Sen, *Commodities and Capabilities*, 16.

31. Martha C. Nussbaum, *Creating Capabilities: The Human Development Approach* (Cambridge, Mass.: The Belknap Press of Harvard University Press, 2011), 20.

32. Ibid., 210.

33. Ibid., 30.

34. Nussbaum, *Creating Capabilities: The Human Development Approach*, 36.

35. Martha C. Nussbaum, "Women and Equality: The Capabilities Approach," *International Labor Review* 138, no. 3 (1999): 234.

36. School of Architecture and Planning, the Catholic University of America, *Transcending Architecture: Aesthetics and Ethics of the Numinous* [Brochure] (Washington, D.C.: The Catholic University of America Press, 2011), 1.

37. Nussbaum, *Creating Capabilities: The Human Development Approach*, 33.

38. Emily Anthes, "Building Around the Mind," *Scientific American Mind* 20, no. 4 (2009): 52–59; John Zeisel, *Inquiry by Design: Environment/Behavior/Neuroscience in Architecture, Interiors, Landscape, and Planning*, rev. ed. (New York: Norton, 2006).

39. Nussbaum, *Creating Capabilities: The Human Development Approach*, 33–34.

40. Pieter Desmet, *Designing Emotions* (Delft: Delft University Press, 2002); Esther M. Sternberg, *Healing Spaces: The Science of Place and Well-Being* (Cambridge, Mass.: The Belknap Press of Harvard University Press, 2009); and Esther M. Sternberg and Matthew A. Wilson, "Neuroscience and Architecture: Seeking Common Ground," *Cell* 127 (2006): 239–42.

41. Nussbaum, *Creating Capabilities: The Human Development Approach*, 34.

42. Dwayne Huebner, "Education and Spirituality," *Journal of Curriculum Theorizing* 11, no. 2 (1995): 13–34.

43. Nussbaum, *Creating Capabilities: The Human Development Approach*, 34.

44. Ibid.

45. Ronald Mace, *Universal Design: Housing for the Lifespan of All People* (Rockville, M.d.: US Department of Housing and Urban Development, 1988); Molly F. Story, James L. Mueller, and Ronald L. Mace, *The Universal Design File: Design for People of All Ages and Disabilities*, rev. ed. (Raleigh: The Center for Universal Design, North Carolina State University, 1998).

46. Nussbaum, *Creating Capabilities: The Human Development Approach*, 34.

47. Stephen Kellert and Edward Wilson, eds., *The Biophilia Hypothesis* (Washington, D.C.: Island Press, 1993); Edward O. Wilson, *Biophilia: The Human Bond with Other Species* (Cambridge, Mass.: Harvard University Press, 1984); "Biophilia and the Conservation Ethic," in *Evolutionary Perspectives on Environmental Problems*, ed. Dustin J. Penn and Iver Mysterud (New Brunswick, N.J.: Transaction Publishers, 2007), 249–57.

48. David Cumes, "Nature as Medicine: The Healing Power of the Wilderness," *Alternative Therapies* 4 (1998): 79–86; Robert M. Hamma, *Earth's Echo: Sacred Encounters with Nature* (Notre Dame: Sorin Books, 2002); Stephen Kaplan, "The Restorative Benefits of Nature: Toward an Integrative Framework," *Journal of Environmental Psychology* 15 (1995): 169–82.

49. Yannick Joye, "Architectural Lessons from Environmental Psychology: The Case of Biophilic Architecture," *Review of General Psychology* 11, no. 4 (2007): 305–28.

50. Nussbaum, *Creating Capabilities: The Human Development Approach*, 34.

51. Linnea M. Anderson, "'The Playground of Today Is the Republic of Tomorrow': Social Reform and Organized Recreation in the USA, 1890–1930s."

2007. http://www.infed.org/playwork/organized_rec-reation_and_playwork_1890-1930s.htm (accessed March 8, 2013).

52. Mark Francis and Ray Lorenzo, "Seven Realms of Children's Participation," *Journal of Environmental Psychology* 22 (2002): 157–69.

53. Andrea Oppenheimer Dean and Timothy Hursley, *Rural Studio: Samuel Mockbee and an Architecture of Decency* (New York: Princeton Architectural Press, 2002).

54. Ibid., 5.

55. Ibid., 17.

56. Ibid.

57. Dean and Hursley, *Rural Studio*.

58. Ibid., 98.

59. Vernon Mays, "The New Rural Studio." *Architect*, November 2, 2007. http://www.architectmaga-zine.com/educational-projects/the-new-rural-studio.aspx (accessed March 8, 2013).

60. "Hunts Point Riverside Park," http://www.majoracartergroup.com/services/case-histories/hunts-point-riverside-park/ (accessed March 8, 2013).

61. Brunner Foundation, "2009 Rudy Brunner Award: Silver Medal Winner Hunts Point River-side Park." 2009. http://brunerfoundation.org/rba/pdfs/2009/Hunts%20Point.FINAL.pdf (accessed March 8, 2013).

62. Ibid., 70.

63. Ibid.

64. Clifford Pearson, "Inner-City Arts: Phase III," *Architectural Record*, February, 2009. http://archrecord.construction.com/projects/portfolio/ar-chives/0902innercity-1.asp (accessed March 8, 2013).

65. Ibid.

66. Ibid.

67. Christopher Hawthorne, "Coming Clean in the Inner City: A Downtown Arts Center Signals Constancy and Community," *Los Angeles Times*, December 15, 2008. http://www.latimes.com/enter-tainment/arts/la-et-inner-city-arts15-2008dec15-story.html (accessed March 8, 2013).

68. See http://www.onbeing.org/program/architec-ture-decency/feature/rural-studio/1584 (accessed May 20, 2014).

11. RITUAL, BELIEF, AND MEANING IN THE PRODUCTION OF SACRED SPACE

1. The term "primitive" is repeated here because it was in common usage at the writing of the original documents. Today, the term is derogatory and no longer used.

2. Dorothy Lee, "Religious Perspectives in Anthro-pology," in *Magic, Witchcraft, and Religion: A Reader in the Anthropology of Religion*, 8th ed., ed. Pamela A. Moro and James E. Myers (New York: McGraw-Hill, 2010 [1952]), 20–27.

3. Jack David Eller, *Cruel Creeds, Virtuous Violence: Religious Violence across Culture and History* (Amherst, N.Y.: Prometheus Books, 2010), 45.

4. Emile Durkheim, *The Elementary Forms of the Religious Life*, trans. Joseph Ward Swain (New York: The Free Press, 1965[1912]), 62.

5. George P. Murdock, "The Comparative Study of Cultures." Revised version, "World Ethnographic Sample," *American Anthropologist* 59 (August, 1957): 664–87; Guy E. Swanson, *The Birth of the Gods: Origin of Primitive Beliefs* (Ann Arbor: The University of Michigan Press, 1964), 232.

6. Nancy Bonvillain, *Cultural Anthropology*, 2nd ed. (Boston: Prentice Hall, 2010), 354.

7. Conrad Phillip Kottak, *Cultural Anthropology: Appreciating Cultural Diversity*, 14th ed. (New York: McGraw Hill, 2011).

8. Bonvillain, *Cultural Anthropology*, 370–72.

9. See, for example, David Hicks, *Ritual and Belief: Readings in the Anthropology of Religion*, 3rd ed. (Lan-ham, Md.: AltaMira Press, 2010); William A. Lessa and Evon Z. Vogt, *Reader in Comparative Religion: An Anthropological Approach*, 3rd ed. (New York: Harper & Row, 1975 [1958]); Pamela A. Moro and James E. Myers, *Magic, Witchcraft, and Religion: A Reader in the Anthropology of Religion*, 8th ed. (New York: McGraw Hill, 2010); Richard Warms, James Garber, and R. Jon McGee, eds., *Sacred Realms: Readings in the Anthropology of Religion*, 2nd ed. (London: Oxford University Press, 2008).

10. Kim Knott, "Spatial Theory and the Study of Religion," *Religion Compass* 2, no. 6 (2008): 1104.

11. Robert Mugerauer, "Eliade: Restoring the Possibilities of Place," in *Interpretations on Behalf of Place: Environmental Displacements and Alternative Responses*, 52–64 (Albany: State University of New York Press, 1994), 56.

12. Robert A. Segel, *Myth: A Very Short Introduc-tion* (Oxford: Oxford University Press, 2004), 56.

13. Thomas Barrie, *Spiritual Path, Sacred Place: Myth, Ritual, and Meaning in Architecture* (Boston: Shambhala, 1996), 4.

14. Anthony F. C. Wallace, *Religion: An Anthropo-*

logical View (New York: Random House, 1966), 102.

15. Claude Lévi-Strauss, Myth and Meaning: Cracking the Code of Culture (New York: Schocken Books, 1995 [1978]), 11–12.

16. Clifford Geertz, The Interpretation of Cultures (New York: Basic Books, 1973), 89–90.

17. Sue Ann Taylor, "Religion as a Coping Mechanism for Older Black Women," Quarterly Contact 5, no. 4 (1982): 2–3.

18. Sue Ann Taylor, "Mental Health and Successful Coping among Aged Black Women," in Minority Aging: Sociological and Social Psychological Issues, ed. Ron C. Manuel (Westport, Conn.: Greenwood Press, 1982), 100.

19. See, for example, Eric Hirsch, "Introduction," in The Anthropology of Landscape: Perspectives on Place and Space, ed. E. Hirsch and M. O'Hanlon (Oxford: Clarendon Press, 1995), 1–30.

20. Yi-Fu Tuan, Space and Place: The Perspective of Experience (Minneapolis: University of Minnesota Press, 1977), 6.

21. Setha M. Low and Denise Lawrence-Zúñiga, eds., The Anthropology of Space and Place: Locating Culture (Malden, Mass.: Blackwell Publishing, 2005), 185.

22. Roger W. Stump, The Geography of Religion: Faith, Place, and Space (Lanham, Md.: Rowman & Littlefield Publishers, 2008), 301.

23. Ibid., 18–19.

24. See, for example, Robert Farris Thompson, Flash of the Spirit: African & Afro-American Art & Philosophy (New York: Vintage Books, 1984).

25. Michael V. Angrosino, The Culture of the Sacred: Exploring the Anthropology of Religion (Longrove, Ill.: Waveland Press, 2004), 177.

26. David Maybury-Lewis, Millennium: Tribal Wisdom and the Modern World (New York: Viking, 1992).

27. Ibid.

28. Nelson H. H. Graburn, "Secular Ritual: A General Theory of Tourism," in Tourists and Tourism: A Reader, ed. Sharon Bohn Gmelch (Long Grove, Ill.: Waveland Press, 2004), 23–34.

29. Dean MacCannell, "Sightseeing and Social Structure: The Moral Integration of Modernity," in Tourists and Tourism: A Reader, ed. Sharon Bohn Gmelch (Long Grove, Ill.: Waveland Press, 2004), 55–70.

30. Jean McMann, Altars and Icons: Sacred Spaces in Everyday Life (San Francisco: Chronicle Books, 1998).

31. Sue Ann Taylor, "At or Near: An Analysis of Proximity," in Vietnam Veterans Memorial Center: Site Selection Study, ed. James Cummings, appendix F (Washington, D.C.: Vietnam Veterans Memorial Fund, 2005), 1–15; "Public Commemoration and Private Remembrance," Anthropology News (September 2011). http://www.anthropology-news.org/index.php/toc/an-table-of-contents-september-2011-526/ (accessed March 27, 2012).

32. Marita Sturken, Tourist of History: Memory, Kitsch, and Consumerism from Oklahoma City to Ground Zero (Durham: Duke University Press, 2007).

33. Marcia Yablon, "Property Rights and Sacred Sites: Federal Regulatory Responses to American Indian Religious Claims on Public Land," Yale Law Journal 113 (2004): 1623–62; Richard O. Clemmer, "'The Legal Effect of the Judgment': Indian Land Claims, Ecological Anthropology, Social Impact Assessment and the Public Domain," Human Organization 63, no. 3 (2004): 334–45; Frank D. Occhipinti, "American Indian Sacred Sites and the National Historic Preservation Act: The Enola Hill Case," Journal of Northwest Anthropology 36, no. 1 (2002): 3–50.

34. "The NAGPRA provides a process for museums and federal agencies to return certain cultural items— human remains, funerary objects, sacred objects, or objects of cultural patrimony—to lineal descendants and culturally affiliated Indian tribes and Native Hawaiian organizations." http://www.nps.gov/nagpra/FAQ/INDEX.HTM (accessed March 27, 2012).

35. Eller, Cruel Creeds, Virtuous Violence, 9.

36. Galina Lindquist and Don Handelman, eds., Religion, Politics & Globalization: Anthropological Approaches (New York: Berghahn Books, 2011), 42.

37. Chris Mikul, The Cult Files: True Stories from the Extreme Edges of Religious Beliefs (New York: Metro Books, 2010), 7.

38. Anthony F. C. Wallace, Religion: An Anthropological View (New York: Random House, 1966), 164. See also Anthony F. C. Wallace, "Revitalization Movements," American Anthropologists 58, no. 2 (1956): 264–81.

39. Michel Foucault, "Space, Knowledge, and Power," in The Foucault Reader, ed. Paul Rabinow (New York: Pantheon Books, 1984), 252.

40. Ibid., 253.

1. Julio Bermudez, "Transcending Architecture: Aesthetics and Ethics of the Numinous," School of Architecture and Planning, The Catholic University of America, http://www.sacred-space.net/symposium/ (accessed May 20, 2013).

2. Lindsay Jones, *The Hermeneutics of Sacred Architecture: Experience, Interpretation, Comparison*, vol. 2, *Hermeneutical Calisthenics: A Morphology of Ritual-Architectural Priorities* (Cambridge, Mass.: Harvard University Press, 2000). On the one hand, this chapter, in route to making my argument about overused and overlooked approaches to pre-Columbian Mesoamerican architecture, borrows liberally from that work, especially chapters 21, 24, and 22, which treat, respectively, architecture as theater, architecture as sanctuary, and architecture and contemplation. On the other hand, I appeal to themes from that book as a basis with which to explore an idea about which I have not written before—namely, the neglect of the contemplation mode as a viable explanation of the logic of pre-Columbian Mesoamerican architecture.

3. Regarding the contrast (and complementariness) between a skeptical "hermeneutic of suspicion" and a more generous "hermeneutic of retrieval (or restoration)," see, for instance, Giles Gunn, *The Culture of Criticism and the Criticism of Culture* (New York: Oxford University Press, 1987), 194; or Jones, *Hermeneutics of Sacred Architecture*, I:16–20.

4. Rudolf Wittkower, *Architectural Principles in the Age of Humanism* (New York: W. W. Norton and Co., 1971), 20–30.

5. Peter Murray, *The Architecture of the Italian Renaissance* (New York: Schocken Books, 1963), 118, 125, for instance, discusses circular Christian martyria and argues that this was Bramante's intention for Saint Peter's.

6. In contrast to Murray, Wittkower, *Architectural Principles in the Age of Humanism*, 24–26, argues that Bramante intended Saint Peter's to be a symbol of God's perfection.

7. A number of authors discuss the history and controversy of the sixteenth-century rebuilding of Saint Peter's. Besides Wittkower, *Architectural Principles in the Age of Humanism*, pt. 1; and Murray, *The Architecture of the Italian Renaissance*, 124–25; see the editor's introduction to Anthony Blunt, ed., *Baroque and Rococo Architecture and Decoration* (New York: Harper & Row, 1978), 25–26.

8. Bruno Zevi, *Architecture as Space: How to Look at Architecture*, trans. Milton Gendel, ed. Joseph A. Barry, rev. ed. (New York: Horizon Press, 1974), 78–85, for instance, explains that the most significant Christian modification of the Roman basilica involved shifting the principal entrance from the long side of the building to the short (or front) side, accentuating the longitudinal axis of the church and forcing one's attention along a processionary path that culminates at the altar. J. G. Davies, *Temples, Churches and Mosques: A Guide to the Appreciation of Religious Architecture* (Oxford: Basil Blackwell, 1982), 95–96, among many, also comments on the dramatic effect of the "basilica as path." See also Whitney S. Stoddard, *Art and Architecture in Medieval France* (New York: Harper and Row, 1972), 53.

9. Wolfgang Braunfels, *Monasteries of Western Europe: The Architecture of the Orders* (Princeton, N.J.: Princeton University Press, 1972), 51.

10. Saint Bernard, quoted in Louis J. Lekai, *The Cistercians: Ideals and Reality* (Kent, Ohio: Kent State University Press, 1977), 263.

11. I borrow the apt term "pageant-spaces" from George Kubler, "The Design of Space in Maya Architecture," in *Miscellanea Paul Rivet, octogenario dicata* (Mexico: Universidad Nacional Autónoma de México, 1958), 528.

12. López Cogolludo, *Historia de Yucatán*; quoted by John L. Stephens, *Incidents of Travel in Yucatan* (1846; New York: Dover Publications), I:192–93.

13. Inga Clendinnen, *Ambivalent Conquests: Maya and Spaniard in Yucatan, 1517–1570* (Cambridge: Cambridge University Press, 1987), 114–17, for instance, comments on Bishop Landa's "superb theatrical sense" in orchestrating both building and ritual productions, specifically elaborately staged inquisitional *autos de fe*, which served at once to intimidate the Indians and to allow his friars "to become habituated to the exercise of violent physical domination while distancing their actions from the zone of the personal and the personally culpable" (115).

14. Diego de Landa, *Relación de las Cosas de Yucatán*, trans. and ed. Alfred M. Tozzer (Cambridge, Mass.: Harvard University Press, 1941), 119.

15. Frederick Catherwood, *The Views of Ancient Monuments of Central America, Chiapas and Yucatan* (London: Owen Jones, 1844); reprinted in Victor Wolfgang von Hagen, *Frederick Catherwood, Archt.* (New York: Oxford University Press, 1950), 126–29, seems to have simply extrapolated William Prescott's notion of Aztec ritual (which I will address later this chapter) into the Maya context. John L. Stephens,

Incidents of Travel in Central America, Chiapas and Yucatan (New York: Dover Publications, 1969), I:143, seems to have used Cogolludo as his main inspiration for Maya ritual; also see Stevens, *Incidents of Travel in Yucatan*, I:192–93.

16. Francisco de Fuentes, writing of Guatemala in about 1700; cited by Stephens, *Incidents of Travel in Central America, Chiapas and Yucatan*, I:131.

17. Herbert J. Spinden, *A Study of Maya Art: Its Subject Matter and Historical Development* (New York: Dover Publications, 1975), 96. Similarly, George Kubler, *The Art and Architecture of Ancient America*, 3rd ed. (New York: Penguin Books, 1984), 217, agrees that "a primary platform [of Copan], rightly called the acropolis … provides a theatrical setting for the ball court."

18. Pal Kelemen, *Medieval American Art* (New York: Macmillan, 1943), I:57–61.

19. William Henry Holmes, *Archaeological Studies Among the Ancient Cities of Mexico* (Chicago: Field Columbian Museum, 1895–1897), 221.

20. Kubler, *Art and Architecture of Ancient America*, 163.

21. William H. Prescott, *The Conquest of Mexico* (1843), 45; quoted in Catherwood, *The Views of Ancient Monuments of Central America, Chiapas and Yucatan* (1844); reprinted in von Hagen, *Frederick Catherwood, Archt.*, 126.

22. Johanna Broda, "Templo Mayor as Ritual Space," in *The Great Temple of Tenochtitlán: Center and Periphery in the Aztec World*, ed. Johanna Broda, David Carrasco, and Eduardo Matos Moctezuma (Berkeley: University of California Press, 1987), 40–41.

23. Ibid.

24. David Carrasco, "Templo Mayor: The Aztec Vision of Place," *Religion* 2 (1981): 275–97; or David Carrasco, *Quetzalcoatl and the Irony of Empire: Myths and Prophesies in the Aztec Tradition* (Chicago: University of Chicago Press, 1982), 186.

25. Though Eliade (among others) very often writes of "thresholds" in this respect, the wide currency of that term, as exemplified in the opening quote to this chapter, is more appropriately traced to Arnold van Gennep's *Rites of Passage* (1909). Note, though, that van Gennep adheres to an explicitly Durkheimian notion of "sacred" versus "profane," which thus aligns his perspective of "sacred space" more closely with that of Jonathan Smith than of Eliade.

26. See, for instance, Mircea Eliade, *The Sacred and the Profane: The Nature of Religion*, trans. Willard R.

Trask (New York: Harcourt Brace Jovanovich, 1959), 25–26, 49.

27. J. G. Davies, "Architecture," in *Encyclopedia of Religion*, 2nd ed., ed. Lindsay Jones (Detroit: Macmillan Reference, 2005), I:462–63, for instance, formulates the problem in a fashion very similar to that of Eliade: "The sacred place, defined by the religious building or precinct, is first of all a means of ensuring the isolation and so the preservation of both the sacred and the profane. The wall that keeps the one out also serves to keep the other in; it is the demarcation line (*demeans, tempus, templum*) between the two worlds. But within the sacred enclosure, the profane world is transcended and hence the existence of the holy place makes it possible for humans to pass from one world to another."

28. Jonathan Z. Smith, *To Take Place: Toward Theory in Ritual* (Chicago: University of Chicago Press, 1987), 104.

29. Anita Abramovitz, *People and Spaces: A View of History through Architecture* (New York: Viking Press, 1979), 76, borrows this line from Paul Thiry, Richard M. Bennett, and Henry L. Kamphoefner, *Churches and Temples* (New York: Reinhold Publishing Corp., 1953); emphasis added.

30. Abramovitz, *People and Spaces*, 76. Jeanette Mirsky, *Houses of God* (Chicago: University of Chicago Press, 1965), 105, for instance, among others, repeats a very similar argument about the origins of the Jewish synagogue.

31. See ibid., 105.

32. See Vincent Scully, *The Earth, the Temple and the Gods: Greek Sacred Architecture* (New Haven, Conn.: Yale University Press, 1962), chapter 10.

33. Scully, *The Earth, the Temple, and the Gods*, 194.

34. Ibid., 211–12. Note also that Gottfried Richter, *Art and Human Consciousness*, trans. Burley Channer and Margaret Frohlich (Spring Valley, N.Y.: Anthroposophic Press, Inc, 1985), 75–77, contrasts the "outward orientation" of the Greek temple, not with its Roman counterpart but with the "strong inward orientation" of the Egyptian temple, which likewise instantiates, among other things, a exercise of the sanctuary mode.

35. The distinction between the respective building agendas of Saint Bernard and Abbot Suger is a central issue in Panofsky's introduction to Abbot Suger's treatise, *On the Abbey Church of Saint Denis and Its Art Treasures*, ed. and trans. Erwin Panofsky (Princeton, N.J.: Princeton University Press, 1979). That interesting contrast could be further illumined, I think, by

the use of Victor Turner's categories "iconophilia" (or image lovers) versus "iconoclast" (or image breakers); see particularly Victor Turner and Edith Turner, *Image and Pilgrimage in Christian Culture* (New York: Columbia University Press, 1978), 234–36, 253. Also relevant in that respect is the discussion of two alternative types of Christian theological aesthetics—namely naturalism or "abundant means" versus asceticism or "scanty means"—provided by Gerardus van der Leeuw, *Sacred and Profane Beauty: The Holy in Art*, trans. David E. Green (New York: Holt, Rinehart and Winston, 1963), 177–89, 303–27.

36. Bernard and the Cistercians were not, however, totally unsympathetic to art (as they are often portrayed). On the aesthetic sensibilities of Cistercians, see, for instance, David Freedberg, *The Power of Images: Studies in the History and Theory of Response* (Chicago: University of Chicago Press, 1989), 301–3.

37. See, for instance, Braunfels, *Monasteries of Western Europe*, chapter 5.

38. Otto Von Simson, *The Gothic Cathedral: Origins of the Medieval Concept of Order* (Princeton, N.J.: Princeton University Press, 1956), 44.

39. *Le Directoire Spirituel des Cisterciens Reformes* (Bricquebec, 1910), quoted in Thomas Merton, *The Waters of Siloe* (New York: Meriner Books, 1979), xxvii.

40. On this cave near Chichén Itzá, see, for instance, E. Wyllys Andrews, IV, *Balankanche: Throne of the Tiger Priest*, Publication 32 (New Orleans: Middle American Research Institute, 1970). For a more general and more extensive treatment of caves in Mesoamerica, see Doris Heyden, "An Interpretation of the Cave Underneath the Pyramid of the Sun in Teotihuacan, Mexico," *American Antiquity* 40 (April 1975): 131–47, and "Caves, Gods and Myths: World-View and Planning in Teotihuacan," in *Mesoamerican Sites and World-Views*, ed. Benson, 1–35; and Karen Bassie-Sweet, *At the Edge of the World: Caves and Late Classic Maya World View* (Norman: University of Oklahoma Press, 1996).

41. Paul Gendrop, "Dragon-Mouth Entrances: Zoomorphic Portals in the Architecture of Central Yucatan," in *Third Palenque Round Table, 1978, part 2*, ed. Merle Greene Robertson (Austin: University of Texas Press, 1980), 138–50, describes the stylistic variation and geographical distribution of dragon-mouth entrances. On the same temples, also see, for instance, H. E. D. Pollock, "Architecture of the Maya Lowlands," in *Handbook of Middle American Indians* (Austin: University of Texas Press, 1965), II:427–28; or Kubler, "The Design of Space in Maya Architecture," 515.

42. Richard F. Townsend, "The Mt. Tlaloc Project," in *To Change Place: Aztec Ceremonial Landscapes*, ed. Davíd Carrasco (Niwot, Colo.: University Press of Colorado, 1991), 29.

43. See Landa, *Relación de las Cosas de Yucatán*, 103–4, 153.

44. Bassie-Sweet, *At the Edge of the World,* 26.

45. J. Eric S. Thompson, *Maya History and Religion* (Norman: University of Oklahoma Press, 1970), 172–75, describes preparation for Mayan ceremonies, citing not only Las Casas and Landa but a number of strong ethnographic references; and Alfred M. Tozzer, *Chichén Itzá and its Cenote of Sacrifice: A Comparative Study of Contemporaneous Maya and Toltec* (Cambridge, Mass.: Harvard University, 1956), 76, provides more sources on the same issue. Also relevant here is the remote Guatemalan *raxaja*, or "green house," so named because this temporary hut was kept ever new and pure with fresh leaves that were continually replaced as they dried out, where a Quiché Maya priest would do penance for up to a year, bleeding himself and offering gifts to the deities; Las Casas's description of this Guatemalan refuge is summarized in Robert M. Carmack, *The Quiché Maya of Utatlán: The Evolution of a Highland Guatemala Kingdom* (Norman: University of Oklahoma Press, 1981), 198. Alfredo López Austin, *Hombre-Dios, Religion y Politica en el Mundo Nahuatl* (Mexico City: Universidad Nacional Autonoma de Mexico, 1972), 106; and Nigel Davies, *The Toltecs Until the Fall of Tula* (Norman: University of Oklahoma Press, 1977), 292–93, each use this same example to somewhat different ends.

46. Johanna Broda, "Astronomy, Cosmovision, and Ideology in Pre-Hispanic Mesoamerica," in *Ethnoastronomy and Archaeoastronomy in the American Tropics*, ed. Anthony F. Aveni and Gary Urton (New York: New York Academy of Sciences, 1982), 101.

47. Joyce Marcus, "Archaeology and Religion: A Comparison of the Zapotec and Maya," in *Ancient Mesoamerica: Selected Readings*, ed. John A. Graham (Palo Alto: Peek Publications, 1981), 299, 311, explains that this arrangement of a "highly sacred inner room" and a "less sacred outer room" is characteristic of the Maya as well as the Zapotecs. Similar floor plans abound throughout Mesoamerica.

48. Landa, *Relación de las Cosas de Yucatán,* 62; quoted and discussed by Tozzer, *Chichén Itzá and its Cenote of Sacrifice*, 73, 83. Subsequent settlement pattern studies have challenged the archaeological viability of Landa's ideas of Mayapan planning and particularly their overgeneralization to other Maya sites; see, for

instance, Diane Z. Chase, "Ganned but not Forgotten: Late Postclassic Archaeology and Ritual at Santa Rita Corozal, Belize," in *The Lowland Maya Postclassic*, ed. Arlen F. Chase and Prudence M. Rice (Austin: University of Texas Press, 1985), 104–25.

49. Carmack, *The Quiché Maya of Utatlán*, 159–64.

50. See, for instance, James Early, *The Colonial Architecture of Mexico* (Albuquerque: University of New Mexico Press, 1994), 122–24.

51. Jacques Maquet, *The Aesthetic Experience: An Anthropologist Looks at the Visual Arts* (New Haven, Conn.: Yale University Press, 1986), 165–66.

52. Harold Osborne, quoted by Maquet, *The Aesthetic Experience*, 165–66.

53. Ibid., 166. The phrase "insight-oriented processes" is also borrowed from Maquet, ibid.

54. See Jones, *Hermeneutics of Sacred Architecture*, II:215.

55. Freedberg, *The Power of Images*, 162. Actually, all of chapter 8 in Freedberg's book is exceptionally relevant and helpful for this discussion of the contemplation mode.

56. See Jones, *Hermeneutics of Sacred Architecture*, II:219–21.

57. Nadar Ardalan and Laleh Bakhtiar, *The Sense of Unity: The Sufi Tradition in Persian Architecture* (Chicago: University of Chicago Press, 1973), 31, write: "As the Manifest is a spatial externalization, so man begin his intellectual search by relating to space. This relation must of necessity be structured so that the intellect may function and not dissipate. The mandala as a symbol of emanation and reabsorption provides this structure." The most specific example of Islamic "mandala-aided" contemplation that Ardalan and Bakhtiar provide comes from Edward Granville Browne, *A Year among the Persians* (London: Adam and Charles Black, 1950), 161, wherein Brown recounts a conversation with a "philosopher" who explains his regime of forty days of solitary meditation: "[This philosopher] spends the greater part of this time in incantation in the Arabic language, which he recites within the area of the mandal[a] or geometric figure, which he must describe in a certain way upon the ground … the operator must not … above all, quit the mandal[a] else he will lose the result of his pain." See Ardalan and Bakhtiar, *The Sense of Unity*, 133–34n13.

58. Suger, *On the Abbey Church of St. Denis and Its Art Treasures*, ed. Panofsky. On the uniqueness of Abbot Suger's treatise, besides Panofsky's thorough introduction to Suger's treatise, see von Simson, *The Gothic Cathedral*, 102.

59. Suger, *On the Abbey Church of St. Denis and Its Art Treasures*; quoted by Erwin Panofsky on page 21 of his introduction to that treatise.

60. Note, for instance, that Hiram W. Woodward, "Borobudur and the Mirrorlike Mind," *Archaeology* 34 (November-December 1981), 47, hypothesizes that Borobudur may have had more gilded, "mirrorlike" surfaces than are typically acknowledged, and that these surfaces symbolized elements of existence that were "reflected" and without "real" existence.

61. Claude Lévi-Strauss, "The Effectiveness of Symbols," in *Structural Anthropology*, trans. Chris Jacobson and Brooke Grundfest Schoepf (New York: Basic Books, Inc., 1963), 186–205.

62. Regarding the elaborate liturgical objects and "altar furnishings that Suger added to or had embellished for Saint-Denis," see William D. Wixom, "For the Service of the Table of God," in *The Royal Abbey of Saint-Denis in the Time of Abbot Suger (1122–1151)*, ed. Sumner McKnight Crosby et al. (New York: The Metropolitan Museum of Art, 1981), 101–18.

63. Panofsky's introduction to Abbot Suger, *On the Abbey Church of St. Denis and Its Art Treasures*, ed. Panofsky, 21.

64. Joan Gadol, *Leon Battista Alberti: Universal Man of the Early Renaissance* (Chicago: University of Chicago Press, 1969), 101.

65. Von Simson, *The Gothic Cathedral*, 38–39, 109.

66. Abbot Suger, quoted in Panofsky's commentary on Suger's *On the Abbey Church of St. Denis and Its Art Treasures*, ed. Panofsky, 203.

67. I. W. Mabbett, "The Symbolism of Mount Meru," *History of Religions* 23 (August 1983), 77–78, for instance, notes the sense in which both Mount Meru and Borobudur have been interpreted as mandalas.

68. Giuseppe Tucci, *The Theory and Practice of the Mandala*, trans. Alan Houghton Brodrick (London: Rider and Co., 1961), vii. Even the two-dimensional mandala paintings that Tucci describes are replete with explicitly architectural imagery; the Tantric Mandala of rDorjeac'an, the Holder of the Diamond, is, for instance, described as a "palace" (Vimana, in Tibetan, *zal yas k'ang*) and a "walled city." Ibid., 39–43.

69. Romi Khosla, "Architecture and Symbolism in Tibetan Monasteries," in *Shelter, Sign, and Symbol: An Exploratory Work on Vernacular Architecture*, ed. Paul Oliver (Woodstock, N.Y.: Overlook Press, 1975), 76.

70. Ibid. Romi Khosla, *Buddhist Monasteries in the Western Himalayas* (Kathmandu, Nepal: Ratna Pustak Bhander, 1979), also explains that in the early

period in Tibet, whole monastery complexes were laid out according to mandala plans, and even where the layout of the monastery was forced to conform to the lay of the land—as at Hemis, for instance—the mandala model was preserved in the individual temple rooms. Also see Jack Finegan, *Tibet: A Dreamt of Image* (New Delhi: Tibet House, 1986).

71. S. F. G. Brandon, *Man and God in Art and Ritual: A Study of Iconography, Architecture and Ritual Action as Primary Evidence of Religious Belief and Practice* (New York: Charles Scribner's Sons, 1975), 57.

72. Khosla, "Architecture and Symbolism in Tibetan Monasteries," 78.

73. Woodward, "Borobudur and the Mirrorlike Mind," 45.

74. Ibid.

75. Woodward, ibid., 43–46, argues that Borobudur needs to be interpreted in an international Buddhist context and that there is actually a historical connection between Borobudur and Kukai, the founder of Japanese Shingon Buddhism.

76. Ibid., 45.

77. The description of the liberating transformation facilitated by concentration on Japanese mandalas provided by Alan G. Grapard, "Flying Mountains and Walkers of Emptiness: Towards a Definition of Sacred Space in Japanese Religion," *History of Religions* 20 (February 1982): 209, is likewise relevant to the pilgrim's experience of ascending Borobudur: "A practitioner of Esoteric Buddhism 'enters' a mandala through its gate, invokes the divinities which are represented, and identifies with them one after the other until reaching the center, in which there is a representation of the cosmic Buddha from which all other Buddhas and their lands emanate. The practitioner goes from the manifestation to the source, from the form to the essence, and finally reaches the realization that form and essence are two-but-not-two."

78. Frank Waters, *Mexico Mystique: The Coming Sixth World of Consciousness* (Chicago: Swallow Press, 1975), 140–42, discusses Seler's allusions to mandala-like symbolism in his commentary on the Codex Borgia, which was first published in German, 1904–1909.

79. For instance, J. Eric S. Thompson, *The Rise and Fall of Maya Civilization* (Norman: University of Oklahoma Press, 1973), 74–75.

80. See, for instance, Laurette Séjourné, *Burning Water: Thought and Religion in Ancient Mexico*, trans. Irene Nicholson (Berkeley: Shambhala Press, 1976), 89–96; Irene Nicholson, *Mexican and Central Amer-*

ican Mythology (London: Paul Hamyln, 1976); and Waters, *Mexico Mystique*, 141–42, 180–81, who speaks about pre-Columbian "mandala symbols" that "evoke a psychic effect from all [their] imparted meanings."

81. Though this chapter is not the place to engage this large body of popular writing on Mesoamerican wisdoms, a handful of exemplars includes José Argüelles, *The Mayan Factor: Path Beyond Technology* (Rochester, Vt.: Inner Traditions/Bear & Company, 1987); Hunbatz Men, *Secrets of Mayan Science/Religion* (Rochester, Vt.: Bear & Company, 1990); and Adalberto A. Rivera, *The Mysteries of Chichén Itzá: The First Guide to the Esoteric Function of the Temples and Pyramids of Ancient Chichén Itzá* (Panama: Universal Image Enterprise Inc., 1995).

82. Jones, *Hermeneutics of Sacred Architecture*, vol. II, chapter 22, provides examples of the contemplation mode in all of these contexts.

83. Panofsky, introduction to Suger, *On the Abbey Church of St. Denis and Its Art Treasures*, ed. Panofsky, provides a very useful account of the tenuous relationship between Suger and Bernard. Also see, for instance, Louis J. Lakai, *The Cistercians: Ideals and Reality* (Kent, Ohio: Kent State University Press, 1977), 263.

84. Lakai, *The Cistercians: Ideals and Reality*, provides these useful quotations from St. Bernard. Regarding the persistence of the same ambivalence toward art among twentieth-century Cistercians, particularly Trappists, Thomas Merton, *Seeds of Contemplation* (New York: New Directions, 1949), 163, explains that the elaborate iconography in the basilica of the Trappist monastery of Gethesemani in Kentucky, along with the Stations of the Cross and other statuary on the grounds, are all designed as aids to contemplation and are, moreover, very useful in that respect. But, contrary to Suger's reliance on such artistic devices, Merton is emphatic that these works of art under no circumstances should be confused with what he terms "the sanctity or with the pure love which is the substance of true contemplation" (163). For Merton, while art may assist in contemplative meditation, it is certainly not indispensable.

85. On the romanticization of Asian "mysticism," see Richard King, *Orientalism and Religion: Post-Colonial Theory, India and "The Mystic East"* (London: Routledge, 1999).

86. For a rigorously skeptical assessment of the "market forces" that may account for the "rebranding" of "religion" as "spirituality," see, for instance, Jeremy Carrette and Richard King, *Selling Spirituality: The*

Silent Takeover of Religion (New York: Routledge, 2005).

87. Harold Osborne, quoted by Maquet, *The Aesthetic Experience*, 165–66.

88. On the ever-widening range of creative and interested "revalorations" of pre-Columbian ruins, see Lindsay Jones, "Revalorizing Mircea Eliade's Notion of Revalorization: Reflections on the Present-day Reuses of Mesoamerica's Pre-Columbian Sites and Architectures," *Archaevs: Studies in the History of Religions* XV (special issue on the theme "Remembering/Rethinking/Revalorizing Mircea Eliade") (2011): 119–60.

89. Regarding the diverse, creative, and interested experience of Mesoamerican archaeological tourist sites, see Lindsay Jones, "Zapotec Sacred Places, Enduring and/or Ephemeral: Reverence, Realignment and Commodification at an Archaeological-Tourist Site in Southern Mexico," *Culture and Religion* 11, no. 4 (December 2010): 345–93.

90. Stephanie South, *Biography of a Time Traveler: The Journey of José Argüelles* (Franklin Lakes, N.J.: New Page Books, 2009), back cover.

91. The film *Apocalypto*, directed by Mel Gibson (2006), provides, in other words, a popularized vision of the ancient Maya that is, for all its historical flaws, actually more consistent with contemporary academic views insofar as it depicts the Yucatec Maya as highly aggressive political actors whose architectural configurations are, therefore, much stronger exemplifications of what I term the "theatric mode" than the "contemplation mode."

92. Anthony Aveni, *The End of Time: The Maya Mystery of 2012* (Niwot: University Press of Colorado, 2009), for example, devotes a whole book to the thoughtfully critical assessment of the "New Age" enthusiasms for the Maya, a set of ideas and practices that he considers to be more informing about present-day preoccupations with "the end of time" than pre-Columbian calendrics. Relative specifically to José Argüelles, Aveni writes, "Although I have spent years studying Mesoamerican calendars, I must confess that I cannot understand even one of Argüelles's complicated-looking diagrams. Nor can I follow his explanations, which, like the McKenna brothers' and so many other 2012 narratives, is punctuated with scientific jargon incomprehensible even to scientists" (8).

93. See Lewis Hanke, *All Mankind Is One: A Study of the Disputation between Bartolomé de Las Casas and Juan Ginés Sepúlveda in 1550 on the Religious and Intellectual Capacity of the American Indians* (DeKalb, Ill.: Northern Illinois University Press, 1994).

94. In other words, though the shifting trends in Mesoamerican scholarship are too complex to discuss here, it is worth noting that the prevailing view among the most prominent Mayanists of the 1940s through the 1970s, notably Sylvanus Morley and Eric Thompson, depicted the Classic Maya as apolitical, peace-loving, nature-worshipping "mystics," a characterization that opens the way to attributing to them nuanced exercises of the contemplation mode. That romanticizing view persists, and has actually been much amplified, *by popular writers.* But, since the 1980s, *mainstream Mayanists* have vehemently rejected that stance in favor of characterizing the Classic Maya as exceptionally violent, political, worldly, and so forth, an (over) correction that, among other things, largely eliminated serious consideration of the possibility that ancient Maya architects were indeed committed to "contemplative" priorities. For a seminal account of that drastic scholarly reassessment of Classic Maya priorities, see the introduction to Linda Schele and Mary Ellen Miller, *The Blood of Kings: Dynasty and Ritual in Maya Art* (Fort Worth: Kimbell Art Museum, 1986), 9–32.

95. Following through with this line of questioning would be the subject of a different chapter. But, for now, I simply note in staccato three of the most viable contenders for the pre-Columbian exercise of the so-termed contemplative mode: First, there are, to be sure, numerous pyramidal structures that show all the signs of being conceived, and thus presumably experienced at least by some, as architectural mandalas. Besides the paramount exemplar of Chichén Itzá's Castillo, the similarly symmetrical Pyramid E-VII-sub at Uaxactun in Guatemala and the Pyramid of the Niches at El Tajín in Veracruz are only two among countless constructions that seem very clearly to be microcosmic replicas of the universe. Second, Eric Thompson's passing reference decades ago (see Thompson, *The Rise and Fall of Maya Civilization*, 74–75) to the intentionally circuitous routes raises a promising, if still neglected, possibility of ambulatory pathways that recall the pilgrim's choreographed ascent of Borobudur. The compulsory indirectness required to climb up the multitiered site of Xochicalco, along with the convoluted routes through several Maya cities, provide especially strong candidates in that respect. And third, the famously elaborate geometric facades, most notably at Mitla and in the Maya Puuc region, even now in their faded disrepair, can work very effectively as props to the sort of "anagogical illumination" about which Abbot Suger waxes—though virtually no professional Mesoamericanists have pursued that interpretive possibility.

13. TRANSCENDING AESTHETICS

1. Karsten Harries, "Untimely Meditations on the Need for Sacred Architecture," in *Constructing the Ineffable: Contemporary Sacred Architecture*, ed. Karla Cavarra Britton (New Haven, Conn.: Yale School of Architecture and Yale University Press, 2011), 48–65.

2. Peter Hawel, "Aspekte zur Sakralkunst," in *Sakralität und Moderne*, ed. Hanna-Barbara Gerl-Falkovitz (Dorfen: Hawel Verlag, 2010), 13–74.

3. Walter Benjamin, "The Work of Art in the Age of Mechanical Reproduction," in *Illuminations*, trans. Harry Zohn (New York: Schocken, 1968), 217–51.

4. Ibid., 242.

5. Benjamin, "The Work of Art in the Age of Mechanical Reproduction," 222–23.

6. Ibid., 222.

7. Walter Benjamin, "On Some Motifs in Baudelaire," in *Illuminations*, trans. Harry Zohn (New York: Schocken, 1968), 188, 200.

8. Edward Bullough, "'Psychical Distance' as a Factor in Art and as an Aesthetic Principle," *British Journal of Psychology* 5, no. 4 (1912): 87–117.

9. Jacques Maritain, *Art and Scholasticism and the Frontiers of Poetry*, trans. Joseph W. Evans (New York: Scribner's, 1962), 24.

10. Theodor Adorno, *Beethoven: The Philosophy of Music*, ed. Rolf Tiedmann, trans. Edmund Jephcott (Stanford, Calif.: Stanford University Press, 1998), 78. Cited in Rajeev S. Patke, "Benjamin's Aura, Stevens's Description without Place," in *Benjamin's Blindspot: Walter Benjamin and the Premature Death of Aura*, ed. Lise Patt (Topanga, Calif.: Institute of Cultural Inquiry, 2001), 81–98.

11. Karl Marx, "Contribution to the Critique Hegel's Philosophy of Right," in *Deutsch-Französische Jahrbücher*, February, 1844, 1; *Karl Marx: Early Writings*, trans. and ed. T. B. Bottomore (New York: McGraw Hill, 1964), 43–44.

12. Cf. Michael Fried, "Art and Objecthood," in *Minimal Art: A Critical Anthology*, ed. Gregory Battcock (New York: E. P. Dutton, 1968), 147: "Presenteness is grace."

13. Benjamin, "The Work of Art in the Age of Mechanical Reproduction," 223.

14. Ibid., 220.

15. Marcel Duchamp, "Painting … at the Service of the Mind," in *Theories of Modern Art: A Source Book by Artists and Critics*, ed. Herschel B. Chipp (Berkeley: University of California Press, 1969), 393–94.

16. Benjamin, "The Work of Art in the Age of Mechanical Reproduction," 223.

17. Ibid., 223–24.

18. Heidegger, "The Origin of the Work of Art," 43–44.

19. Benjamin, "The Work of Art in the Age of Mechanical Reproduction," 224.

20. Ibid., 244.

21. Heidegger, "The Origin of the Work of Art," 46–47.

22. Benjamin, "The Work of Art in the Age of Mechanical Reproduction," 223.

23. Ibid., 61.

24. Benjamin, "The Work of Art in the Age of Mechanical Reproduction," 226.

25. Benjamin, "On Some Motifs in Baudelaire," 188.

26. Ibid.

27. Ibid.

28. Jean Baudrillard, *Simulacra and Simulation*, trans. Sheila Faria Glaser (Ann Arbor: University of Michigan Press, 1994), 1.

29. Ibid., 6.

30. Immanuel Kant, *Kritik der Urteilskraft*, par. 42, A170–171/B172–173; trans. Werner S. Pluhar, *Critique of Judgment* (Indianapolis: Hackett, 1987), 169.

31. Ibid. 165–68.

32. Hegel, *Vorlesungen*, vol. 12, 20; trans., 4.

14. CALLING FORTH THE NUMINOUS IN ARCHITECTURE

1. Rudolf Otto, *The Idea of the Holy* (London: Oxford University Press, 1958), 6.

2. Wikipedia, "Numen," http://en.wikipedia.org/wiki/Numen#cite_note-0 (accessed April 9, 2013).

3. Ibid.

4. Wikipedia, "Noumenon," http://en.wikipedia.org/wiki/Noumenon (accessed April 9, 2013).

5. Otto, *The Idea of the Holy*, 7.

6. Ibid., 11.

7. Ibid., 7.

8. Ibid., 12.

9. Ibid.

10. Ibid.

11. Ibid.

12. Ibid.

13. Ibid.

14. Ibid.

15. Ibid., 13.

16. Ibid., 14.
17. Ibid., 20.
18. Ibid.
19. Ibid., 26.
20. Ibid.
21. Ibid., 31.
22. Ibid., 66.
23. Ibid., 67.
24. Ibid., 68.
25. Ibid.

26. Ibid., 69.
27. Julio Bermudez, "Amazing Grace: New Research into 'Extraordinary Architectural Experiences' Reveals the Central Role of Sacred Places," *Faith & Form* 42, no. 2 (2009): 8–11.
28. Ibid., 10.
29. Brick Lane Jamme Masjid website, http://www.bricklanejammemasjid.co.uk/about.html (accessed April 9, 2013).

15. ELEMENTAL SIMPLICITY

1. Jan Butterfield, *The Art of Light and Space* (New York: Abbeville Press, 1993), 68.

16. TRANSCENDENCE, WHERE HAST THOU GONE?

1. For Anders Sövik, the house of God was never intended by the early church. He replaces the idea of a holy place with a multipurpose building that should not be seen as an exclusive place of worship.
2. Mark Allen Torgerson, "Edward Anders Sövik and His Return to the 'Non-Church'" (PhD dissertation, University of Notre Dame, 1996). See also by the same author *An Architecture of Immanence: Architecture for Worship and Ministry Today* (Grand Rapids, Mich.: Wm. B. Eerdmans Publishing Company, 2007).
3. Genesis 28:17: "And he was afraid, and said,

'How awesome is this place! This is none other than the house of God, and this is the gate of heaven.'"
4. Comment made by Pope John Paul II after his parochial visit to San Mattia in Rome on March 14, 1999.
5. For one interpretation of a major architect's philosophy regarding absence, see Jin Baek, *Nothingness: Tadao Ando's Christian Sacred Space* (New York: Routledge, 2009). Another is Michael Arad's statement on his winning design for the World Trade Center Memorial titled "Reflecting Absence."

17. ARCHITECTURAL QUESTS INTO THE NUMINOUS

1. Travis Price, *The Mythic Modern: Architectural Expeditions into the Spirit of Place* (China: Oro Edition, 2012).
2. This poem was composed by Travis Price and inspired by various poems written by his students in

the Spirit of Place course that built the structure in Finland.
3. Ibid.
4. Written by architect Travis Price to describe his house design.

18. REACHING FOR THE NUMINOUS

1. Genesis 28:10-19.
2. Annie Dillard, *Pilgrim at Tinker Creek* (New York: Harper, 1974).
3. Alastair Macaulay, "The Fluid Human Dance That Is Grand Central," *The New York Times*, August 31, 2011, http://www.nytimes.com/2011/09/01/arts/

dance/art-of-summer-grand-centrals-fluid-human-dance.html (accessed June 8, 2013).
4. "U.S. Religious Landscape Survey," The Pew Forum on Religion and Public Life, http://religions.pewforum.org/reports (accessed March 27, 2012).

BIBLIOGRAPHY

Abell, John. "On 'That Oceanic Feeling': Architectural Formlessness, Otherness and Being Everything." *Quarterly Architectural Essays Journal* 3, no. 1 (Fall 2007).

Abramovitz, Anita. *People and Spaces: A View of History through Architecture*. New York: Viking Press, 1979.

Adorno, Theodor. *Beethoven: The Philosophy of Music*. Edited by Rolf Tiedmann, translated by Edmund Jephcott. Stanford, Calif.: Stanford University Press, 1998.

Aguirre, Rafael. "Early Christian House Churches." *Theological Digest* 12 (Summer 1985): 151–55.

Alexander, Christopher, Sara Ishikawa, and Murray Silverstein. *A Pattern Language: Towns, Buildings, Construction*. New York: Oxford University Press, 1977.

Almquist, Julka, and Julia Lupton. "Affording Meaning: Design-Oriented Research from the Humanities and Social Sciences." *Design Issues* 26, no. 1 (2010): 3–14.

American Community Gardening Association. http://communitygarden.org/learn/ (accessed December 5, 2011).

Anderson, Linnea M. "'The Playground of Today is the Republic of Tomorrow': Social Reform and Organized Recreation in the USA, 1890–1930s." 2007. http://www.infed.org/playwork/organized_recreation_and_playwork_1890-1930s.htm (accessed March 8, 2013).

Ando, Tadao. "Tadao Ando on Le Corbusier." In *Architects on Architects*, edited by Susan Gray, 11–17. New York: McGraw-Hill, 2002.

Andrews I. V., and E. Wyllys. *Balankanche: Throne of the Tiger Priest*. Publication 32. New Orleans: Middle American Research Institute, 1970.

Angrosino, Michael V. *The Culture of the Sacred: Exploring the Anthropology of Religion*. Longrove, Ill.: Waveland Press, 2004.

Anthes, Emily. "Building Around the Mind." *Scientific American Mind* 20, no. 4 (2009): 52–59.

Ardalan, Nadar, and Laleh Bakhtiar. *The Sense of Unity: The Sufi Tradition in Persian Architecture*. Chicago: University of Chicago Press, 1973.

Argüelles, José. *The Mayan Factor: Path beyond Technology*. Santa Fe: Inner Traditions/Bear & Company, 1987.

Arkoun, Mohammed. "Spirituality and Architecture." In *Architecture beyond Architecture: Creativity and Social Transformations in Islamic Cultures*, edited by Cynthia Davidson and Ismail Serageldin, 16–19. London: Academy Editions, 1995.

Austin, Alfredo López. *Hombre-Dios, Religion Y Politica En El Mundo Nahuatl*. Mexico City: Universidad Nacional Autonoma de Mexico, 1972.

Aveni, Anthony. *The End of Time: The Maya Mystery of 2012*. Boulder: University Press of Colorado, 2009.

Bachelard, Gaston. *The Poetics of Space*. Boston: Beacon Press, 1969.

———. *The Flame of a Candle*. Dallas, Tex.: Dallas Institute, 1988.

Baek, Jin. *Nothingness: Tadao Ando's Christian Sacred Space*. New York: Routledge, 2009.

Baker, Geoffrey H. *Le Corbusier—The Creative Search*. New York: Van Nostrand Reinhold, 1996.

Banerjee, Mahasweta M., and Edward R. Canda. "Comparing Rawlsian Justice and the Capabilities Approach to Justice from a Spiritually Sensitive Social Work Perspective." *Journal of Religion & Spirituality in Social Work: Social Thought* 31, nos. 1–2 (2012): 9–31.

Barracund, Marianne. "The Garden as a Reflection of Paradise." In *Islamic Art and Architecture*, edited by Markus Hattstein and Peter Delius, 490–94. Potsdam, Germany: H. F. Ullmann, 2004.

Barragán, Luis. "1980 Laureate Acceptance Speech." Pritzker Architecture Prize. www.pritzkerprize.com/1980/ceremony (accessed May 15, 2013).

———. "Acceptance Speech of the 1980 Pritzker Architecture Prize." Pritzker Architecture Prize. http://www.pritzkerprize.com/1980/ceremony_speech1 (accessed May 15, 2013).

Barrie, Thomas. *Spiritual Path, Sacred Place: Myth, Ritual, and Meaning in Architecture*. Boston: Shambhala, 1996.

———. *The Sacred In-between: The Mediating Roles of Architecture*. New York: Routledge, 2010.

Bassie-Sweet, Karen. *At the Edge of the World: Caves and Late Classic Maya World View*. Norman: University of Oklahoma Press, 1996.

Baudrillard, Jean. *Simulacra and Simulation*. Translated by Sheila Faria Glaser. Ann Arbor: Michigan University Press, 1994.

Beatley, Timothy. *Biophilic Cities: Integrating Nature into Urban Design and Planning*. Washington, D.C.: Island Press, 2011.

Bellow, Anne C., Katherine Brown, and Jac Smit. "Health Benefits of Urban Agriculture." Community Food Security Coalition. http://www.foodsecurity.org/UAHealthArticle.pdf (accessed December 5, 2011).

Benedikt, Michael. *Cyberspace, First Steps*. Cambridge, Mass.: The MIT Press, 1992.

———. *God Is the Good We Do: Theology of Theopraxy*. New York: Bottino Books, 2007.

———. *God, Creativity, and Evolution: The Argument from Design(ers)*. Austin, Tex.: Centerline Books, 2008.

Benjamin, Walter. "On Some Motifs in Baudelaire." In *Illuminations*, translated by Harry Zohn, 155–200. New York: Schocken, 1968.

———. "The Work of Art in the Age of Mechanical Reproduction." In *Illuminations*, translated by Harry Zohn, 217–51. New York: Schocken, 1968.

Bermudez, Julio. "Mapping the Phenomenological Territory of Profound Architectural Atmospheres: Results of a Large Survey." *Electronic Proceedings of the International Symposium "Creating an Atmosphere."* 2008. http://www.cresson.archi.fr/PUBLI/pubCOLLOQUE/AMB8-1Bermudez.pdf (accessed March 15, 2012).

———. "Amazing Grace: New Research into 'Extraordinary Architectural Experiences' Reveals the Central Role of Sacred Places." *Faith & Form* 42, no. 2 (June 2009): 8–13.

———. "The Extraordinary in Architecture." *2A Architecture and Art* Autumn Quarter, no. 12 (2009): 46–49.

———. "Non-Ordinary Architectural Phenomenologies: Non Dualist Experiences and Husserl's Reduction." *Environmental & Architectural Phenomenology (EAP)* 21, no. 2 (2010): 11–15.

———. "Empirical Aesthetics: The Body and Emotion in Extraordinary Architectural Experiences." In *Proceedings of the 2011 Architectural Research Centers Consortium: "Considering Research,"* edited by Philip Plowright and Bryce Gamper, 369–80. Detroit, Mich.: Lawrence Tech University, 2011.

———. "Profound Experiences of Architecture—the Role of 'Distancing' in the Ineffable." *2A Architecture and Art*, Spring Quarter, no. 17 (2011): 20–25.

———. "Transcending Architecture: Aesthetics & Ethics of the Numinous." School of Architecture and Planning, The Catholic University of America. 2011. http://www.sacred-space.net/symposium/ (accessed August 3, 2011).

Bermudez, Julio, and Brandon Ro. "Extraordinary Architectural Experiences: Comparative Study of Three Paradigmatic Cases of Sacred Space." In *Proceedings of the 2nd International Congress on Ambiances*, edited by J. P. Thibaud and D. Siret, 689–94. Montreal, Canada, 2012. http://halshs.archives-ouvertes.fr/docs/00/74/55/45/PDF/ambiances2012_bermudez_ro.pdf (accessed April 23, 2013).

———. "Memory, Social Interaction and Communicability in Extraordinary Experiences of Architecture." In *Proceedings of the 2013 Architectural Research Centers Consortium*, edited by C. Jarrett, K.-H. Kim, and N. Senske, 677–84. University of North Carolina–Charlotte: ARCC, 2013. http://arccweb.org/conferences/proceedings/ARCC2013_UNCC%20Conference%20Proceedings.pdf (accessed May 15, 2013).

"Bernard Tschumi." In *Studio Talk: Interview with 15 Architects*, edited by Yoshio Futagawa, 512–41. Tokyo: A.D.A. EDITA, 2002.

Biema, David Van. "Mother Teresa's Crisis of Faith." *Time Magazine*, August 23, 2007.

Birksted, J. K. *Le Corbusier and the Occult*. Cambridge, Mass.: The MIT Press, 2009.

Blunt, Anthony, ed. *Baroque and Rococo Architecture and Decoration*. New York: Harper & Row, 1978.

Bond, F. *Screens and Galleries*. Oxford: Oxford University Press, 1908.

Bonvillain, Nancy. *Cultural Anthropology*. 2nd edition. Boston: Prentice Hall, 2010.

Borgmann, Albert. *Crossing the Postmodern Divide*. Chicago: University of Chicago Press, 1992.

Bottomore, T. B., trans. and ed. *Karl Marx: Early Writings*. New York: McGraw Hill, 1964.

Bouyer, Louis. *Liturgical Piety*. Notre Dame: University of Notre Dame Press, 1954.

Boyer, M. Christine. *Le Corbusier, Homme De Lettres*. New York: Princeton Architectural Press, 2011.

Brandon, S. F. G. *Man and God in Art and Ritual: A Study of Iconography, Architecture and Ritual Action as Primary Evidence of Religious Belief and Practice*. New York: Charles Scribner's Sons, 1975.

Braunfels, Wolfgang. *Monasteries of Western Europe: The Architecture of the Orders*. Princeton, N.J.: Princeton University Press, 1972.

Brendler, Thomas, and Henry Carey. "'Community Forestry, Defined,' from What Is Community Forestry and Why Does It Matter?" National Community Forestry Center. http://www.yellowwood.org/what.pdf (accessed December 5, 2011).

Brereton, Joel P. "Sacred Space." In *The Encyclopedia of Religion*, edited by Mircea Eliade, 9:526–35. New York: Macmillan, 1995.

"Brick Lane Jamme Masjid." http://www.bricklanejammemasjid.co.uk/about.html (accessed April 9, 2013).

Britton, Karla. *Constructing the Ineffable: Contemporary Sacred Architecture*. New Haven, Conn.: Yale School of Architecture, 2011.

Broda, Johanna. "Astronomy, Cosmovision, and Ideology in Pre-Hispanic Mesoamerica." In *Ethnoastronomy and Archaeoastronomy in the American Tropics*, edited by Anthony F. Aveni and Gary Urton, 81–110. New York: New York Academy of Sciences, 1982.

———. "Templo Mayor as Ritual Space." In *The Great Temple of Tenochtitlán: Center and Periphery in the Aztec World*, edited by Johanna Broda, Davíd Carrasco, and Eduardo Matos Moctezuma, 61–123. Berkeley: University of California Press, 1987.

Brooks, H. Allen, ed. *Le Corbusier: The Garland Essays*. New York: Garland Publishing, 1987.

———. "Le Corbusier's Formative Years at La Chaux-De-Fonds." In *Le Corbusier: The Garland Essays*, edited by H. Allen Brooks, 27–45. New York: Garland Publishing, 1987.

———. *Le Corbusier's Formative Years*. Chicago: University of Chicago Press, 1996.

Browne, Edward Granville. *A Year among the Persians*. London: Adam and Charles Black, 1950.

Brunner Foundation. "2009 Rudy Brunner Award: Silver Medal Winner Hunts Point Riverside Park." 2009. http://brunerfoundation.org/rba/pdfs/2009/Hunts%20Point.FINAL.pdf (accessed March 8, 2013).

Bullough, Edward. "'Psychical Distance' as a Factor in Art and as an Aesthetic Principle." *British Journal of Psychology* 5, no. 4 (1912): 87–117.

Burke, Peter. *The Italian Renaissance: Culture and Society in Italy*. Princeton, N.J.: Princeton University Press, 1986.

Burtynsky, Edward. *Manufactured Landscapes*. New Haven, Conn.: Yale University Press, 2003.

Butterfield, Jan. *The Art of Light and Space*. New York: Abbeville Press, 1993.

Campbell, Joseph. *The Power of Myth*. With Bill Moyers. Edited by Betty Sue Flowers. New York: Anchor Books, 1988.

Campo Baeza, Alberto. *Principia Architectonica*. Madrid: Mairea Libros, 2012.

Canadian Conference of Catholic Bishops. *Our Place of Worship*. Ottawa: Publications Service, Canadian Conference of Catholic Bishops, 1999.

Canda, Edward R., and Leola D. Furman. *Spiritual Diversity in Social Work Practice: The Heart of Helping*. 2nd edition. New York: Oxford University Press, 2010.

Carmack, Robert M. *The Quiché Maya of Utatlán: The Evolution of a Highland Guatemala Kingdom*. Norman: University of Oklahoma Press, 1981.

Carpelan, Bo. *Homecoming*. Translated by David McDuff. Manchester: Carcanet, 1993.

Carr, Christopher, and D. Troy Case, eds. *Gathering Hopewell: Society, Ritual, and Ritual Interaction*. New York: Springer, 2006.

Carr, Mike. *Bioregionalism and Civil Society: Democratic Challenges to Corporate Globalism*. Vancouver: UBC Press, 2005.

Carrasco, Davíd. "Templo Mayor: The Aztec Vision of Place." *Religion* 2 (1981): 275–97.

———. *Quetzalcoatl and the Irony of Empire: Myths and Prophesies in the Aztec Tradition*. Chicago: University of Chicago Press, 1982.

Carré, M. H. *Realists and Nominalists*. Oxford: Oxford University Press, 1946.

Carrette, Jeremy, and Richard King. *Selling Spirituality: The Silent Takeover of Religion*. New York: Routledge, 2005.

Catherwood, Frederick. *The Views of Ancient Monuments of Central America, Chiapas and Yucatan*. London: Owen Jones, 1844. Reprint, Victor Wolfgang von Hagen, *Frederick Catherwood, Archt* (New York: Oxford University Press, 1950), 126–29.

Chambers, David J. *The Character of Consciousness*. New York: Oxford University Press, 2010.

Chase, Diane Z. "Ganned but Not Forgotten: Late Postclassic Archaeology and Ritual at Santa Rita Corozal, Belize." In *The Lowland Maya Postclassic*, edited by Arlen F. Chase and Prudence M. Rice, 104–215. Austin: University of Texas Press, 1985.

Cleage Jr., Albert B. *Black Christian Nationalism: New Directions for the Black Church*. New York: William Morrow and Company, 1972.

Clemmer, Richard, O. "'The Legal Effect of the Judgment': Indian Land Claims, Ecological Anthropology, Social Impact Assessment and the Public Domain." *Human Organization* 63, no. 3 (2004): 334–45.

Clendinnen, Inga. *Ambivalent Conquests: Maya and Spaniard in Yucatan, 1517–1570*. Cambridge: Cambridge University Press, 1987.

Cohen, Jean-Louis, ed. *Le Corbusier, Le Grand*. New York: Phaidon Press, 2008.

Cohn, Robert L. "Mountains in the Biblical Cosmos." In *The Shape of Sacred Space*, 25–41. Chico: Scholars Press, 1981.

———. *The Shape of Sacred Space: Four Biblical Studies*. Chico: Scholars Press, 1981.

Cole, Raymond J. 2011. "Regenerative Design and Development: Current Theory and Practice." *Building Research & Information* 40, no. 1 (2011): 1–6.

Colguhoun, Alan. "The Significance of Le Corbusier." In *Le Corbusier: The Garland Essays*, edited by H. Allen Brooks, 17–26. New York: Garland Publishing, 1987.

Conant, Kenneth J. *Carolingian and Romanesque Architecture*. Baltimore: Penguin Books, 1959.

Congar, Yves. *The Mystery of the Temple*. London: Burns & Oates, 1962.

Council on Social Work Education. *Educational Policy and Accreditation Standards*. Washington, D.C.: Council on Social Work Education, 2008.

Crosbie, Michael. "The 'S' Word." *Faith & Form* 45, no. 1 (2012): 4.

Crowe, Norman. *Nature and the Idea of a Man-Made World: An Investigation into the Evolutionary Roots of Form and Order in the Built Environment*. Cambridge, Mass.: The MIT Press, 1995.

Crowley, Eileen D. *Liturgical Art for a Media Culture*. Collegeville: Liturgical Press, 2007.

Csikszentmihalyi, Mihaly. *Flow: The Psychology of Optimal Experience*. New York: Harper & Row, 1990.

Cumes, David. "Nature as Medicine: The Healing Power of the Wilderness." *Alternative Therapies* 4 (1998): 79–86.

Curtis, William J. *Le Corbusier: Ideas and Forms*. London: Phaidon, 1986.

Daniélou, Jean. *Le Signe du temple ou de la présence de Dieu*. Paris: Gallimard, 1942.

Dannefeldt, Karl H., ed. *The Renaissance: Basic Interpretations*. Lexington: Heath, 1974.

Danto, Arthur C. *The Abuse of Beauty*. Peru, Ill.: Carus Publishing, 2006.

Davies, J. G. *Temples, Churches and Mosques: A Guide to the Appreciation of Religious Architecture*. Oxford: Basil Blackwell, 1982.

———. "Architecture." In *Encyclopedia of Religion*, edited by Lindsay Jones, I: 462–63. Detroit: Macmillan Reference, 2005.

Davies, Nigel. *The Toltecs until the Fall of Tula*. Norman: University of Oklahoma Press, 1977.

Dean, Andrea Oppenheimer, and Timothy Hursley. *Rural Studio: Samuel Mockbee and an Architecture of Decency*. New York: Princeton Architectural Press, 2002.

DeBona, Gueric, James Wallace, and Robert Waznak. *Lift Up Your Hearts*. New York: Paulist Press, 2004.

Debord, Guy. *The Society of the Spectacle*. New York: Zone Books, 1994.

"Dedication of an Altar." *The Rites of the Catholic Church as Revised by the Second Vatican Ecumenical Council*, 2:250–73. New York: Pueblo Publishing Company, 1980.

Desmet, Pieter. *Designing Emotions*. Delft: Delft University Press, 2002.

Dewey, John. *Art as Experience*. New York: Wideview/Perigee Book, 1934.

Dillard, Annie. *Pilgrim at Tinker Creek*. New York: Harper, 1974.

Doorly, Moyra. *No Place for God: The Denial of the Transcendent in Modern Church Architecture*. San Francisco: Ignatius Press, 2007.

Dripps, R. D. *The First House: Myth, Paradigm, and the Task of Architecture*. Cambridge, Mass.: The MIT Press, 1997.

Duchamp, Marcel. "Painting … at the Service of the Mind." In *Theories of Modern Art: A Source Book by Artists and Critics*, edited by Herschel B. Chipp, 392–95. Berkeley: University of California Press, 1969.

Dura-Europos: Crossroads of Antiquity. Boston: McMillan Museum of Art, 2011.

Durkheim, Emile. *The Elementary Forms of the Religious Life*. Trans. Joseph Ward Swain. New York: The Free Press, 1965[1912].

Early, James. *The Colonial Architecture of Mexico*. Albuquerque: University of New Mexico Press, 1994.

Eck, Diana. "Sacred Mountains." In *Encyclopedia of Religion*, edited by Mircea Eliade, 9:130–34. New York: Macmillan, 1985.

Eliade, Mircea. *Patterns in Comparative Religion*. New York: Sheed & Ward, 1958.

———. *The Sacred and the Profane: The Nature of Religion*. New York: Harper & Row, 1959.

———. *Images and Symbols: Studies in Religious Symbolism*. Princeton, N.J.: Princeton University Press, 1991.

Elkins, James. *Pictures and Tears*. New York: Routledge, 2001.

Eller, Jack David. *Cruel Creeds, Virtuous Violence: Religious Violence across Culture and History*. Amherst, N.Y.: Prometheus Books, 2010.

Etlin, Richard A. "Le Corbusier, Choisy, and French Hellenism: The Search for a New Architecture." *The Art Bulletin* 69, no. 2 (June 1987): 264–78.

———. "The Parthenon in the Modern Era." In *The Parthenon: From Antiquity to the Present*, edited by Jenifer Neils, 362–95. New York: Cambridge University Press, 2005.

Faber Taylor, Andrea, and France E. Kuo. "Is Contact with Nature Important for Healthy Child Development? State of Evidence." In *Children and Their Environments: Learning, Using and Designing Spaces*, edited by Christopher Spencer and Mark Blades, 124–40. Cambridge: Cambridge University Press, 2006.

Féret, H.-M. "Le temple du Dieu vivant." In *Prêtre et Apôtre*. Paris: Bonne Presse, 1947.

Figueira-McDonough, Josephine. "Policy Practice: The Neglected Side of Social Work Intervention." *Social Work* 38, no. 2 (1993): 179–87.

Fine, Steven. *This Holy Place: On the Sanctity of the Synagogue during the Greco-Roman Period*. Notre Dame: University of Notre Dame Press, 1997.

Finegan, Jack. *Tibet: A Dreamt of Image*. New Delhi: Tibet House, 1986.

Finney, Paul Corby. *The Invisible God: The Earliest Christians on Art*. New York: Oxford University Press, 1994.

"Forest Bathing." Healthy Parks Healthy People Central. http://www.hphpcentral.com/article/forest-bathing (accessed December 5, 2011).

Foucault, Michel. "Space, Knowledge, and Power." In *The Foucault Reader*, edited by Paul Rabinow, 239–56. New York: Pantheon Books, 1984.

Frampton, Kenneth. *Le Corbusier*. New York: Thames & Hudson, 2001.

Francis, Mark, and Ray Lorenzo. "Seven Realms of Children's Participation." *Journal of Environmental Psychology* 22 (2002): 157–69.

"Frank O. Gehry." In *Studio Talk: Interview with 15 Architects*, edited by Yoshio Futagawa, 6–57. Tokyo: A.D.A. EDITA, 2002.

Frascati-Lochhead, Marta. *Kenosis and Feminist Theology: The Challenge of Gianni Vattimo*. Albany: State University of New York Press, 1998.

Frazer, Sir James. *The Golden Bough: A Study in Magic and Religion*. Hertfordshire: Wordsworth Editions, Ltd. [Original one-vol. abridgement in 1922], 1993 [1911–1915].

Freedberg, David. *The Power of Images: Studies in the History and Theory of Response*. Chicago: University of Chicago Press, 1989.

Freud, Sigmund. "A Disturbance of Memory on the Acropolis." In *The Standard Edition of the Complete Psychological Works of Sigmund Freud*, edited by James Strachey, Anna Freud, and Angela Richards. London: Hogarth Press, 1966.

Fried, Michael. "Art and Objecthood." In *Minimal Art: A Critical Anthology*, edited by Gregory Battcock, 116–47. New York: E. P. Dutton, 1968.

Fromm, Erich. *Pako Vapaudesta* [Escape from Freedom]. Kirjayhtymä: Helsinki, 1976.

Gadamer, Hans-Georg. *The Relevance of the Beautiful and Other Essays*. Translated by Nicholas Walker. New York: Cambridge University Press, 1986.

Gadol, Joan. *Leon Battista Alberti: Universal Man of the Early Renaissance*. Chicago: University of Chicago Press, 1969.

Gaillardetz, Richard R. *Ecclesiology for a Global Church: A People Called and Sent*. Maryknoll: Orbis Books, 2008.

Geertz, Clifford. *The Interpretation of Cultures*. New York: Basic Books, 1973.

Gendrop, Paul. "Dragon-Mouth Entrances: Zoomorphic Portals in the Architecture of Central Yucatan." In *Third Palenque Round Table, 1978, Part 2*, edited by Merle Greene Robertson, 138–50. Austin: University of Texas Press, 1980.

Gibelman, Margaret. "The Search for Identity: Defining Social Work—Past, Present, Future." *Social Work* 44, no. 4 (1999): 298–310.

Gibson, Mel. "Apocalypto." 139 min. USA: Icon Entertainment International, 2006.

Giedion, Sigfried. *The Eternal Present*. New York: Bollingen Foundation, 1962.

Goodwin, Barbara, and Keith Taylor. *The Politics of Utopia: A Study in Theory and Practice*. Bern: Peter Lang AG, 2009.

Gordon, Bruce. *The Swiss Reformation*. New York: Manchester University Press, 2002.

Graburn, Nelson H. H. "Secular Ritual: A General Theory of Tourism." In *Tourists and Tourism: A Reader*, edited by Sharon Bohn Gmelch, 23–34. Long Grove, Ill.: Waveland Press, 2004.

Grapard, Alan G. "Flying Mountains and Walkers of Emptiness: Towards a Definition of Sacred Space in Japanese Religion." *History of Religions* 20 (February 1982): 195–221.

"Green Exercise Research Findings." University of Essex. http://www.greenexercise.org/Research_Findings.html (accessed December 5, 2011).

Gruber, Karl. *Bilder Zur Entwicklungsgeschichte Einer Deutschen Stadt*. Munich: F. Bruckmann, 1914.

Gunn, Giles. *The Culture of Criticism and the Criticism of Culture*. New York: Oxford University Press, 1987.

Habermas, Jürgen. "The Resurgence of Religion: A Challenge to the Secular Self-Interpretation of Modernity." *Castle Lectures*, Yale University (October 2008).

Habgood, John. "The Sacramentality of the Natural World." In *The Sense of the Sacramental: Movement and Measure in Art and Music, Place and Time*, edited by David Brown and Ann Loades. London: SPCK, 1995.

Hamma, Robert M. *Earth's Echo: Sacred Encounters with Nature*. Notre Dame: Sorin Books, 2002.

Hanke, Lewis. *All Mankind Is One: A Study of the Disputation between Bartolomé De Las Casas and Juan Ginés Sepúlveda in 1550 on the Religious and Intellectual Capacity of the American Indians*. DeKalb: Northern Illinois University Press, 1994.

Harman, Graham. *Prince of Networks: Bruno Latour and Metaphysics*. Melbourne, Australia: re.press, 2009.

"Harmony between Man and Architecture." In *Louis K. Kahn Writings, Lectures, Interviews*, edited by Alessandra Latour. New York: Rizzoli International Publications, 1991.

Harries, Karsten. "Building and the Terror of Time." *Perspecta: The Yale Architecture Journal* 19 (1982): 59–69.

———. *The Ethical Function of Architecture*. Cambridge, Mass.: The MIT Press, 1997.

———. "The Ethical Significance of Environmental Beauty." In *Architecture, Ethics, and the Personhood of Place*, edited by Gregory Caicco, 134–50. Lebanon, N.H.: University Press of New England, 2007.

———. "Untimely Meditations on the Need for Sacred Architecture." In *Constructing the Ineffable: Contemporary Sacred Architecture*, edited by Karla Cavarra Britton, 48–65. New Haven, Conn.: Yale School of Architecture and Yale University Press, 2011.

Harrison, Robert Pogue. *Forests: The Shadow of Civilization*. Chicago: University of Chicago Press, 1992.

———. *Gardens: An Essay on the Human Condition*. Chicago: University of Chicago Press, 2008.

Haughton, Rosemary. *Images for Change: The Transformation of Society*. New York: Paulist Press, 1997.

Hawel, Peter. "Aspekte zur Sakralkunst." In *Sakralität und Moderne*, edited by Hanna-Barbara Gerl-Falkovitz, 13–74. Dorfen: Hawel Verlag, 2010.

Hawthorne, Christopher. "Coming Clean in the Inner City: A Downtown Arts Center Signals Constancy and Community." *Los Angeles Times*, December 15, 2008. http://www.latimes.com/entertainment/news/arts/la-et-inner-city-arts15-2008dec15,0,3937956.story (accessed March 8, 2013).

Hegel, Georg Wilhelm Friedrich. "Vorlesungen über die Aesthetik." In *Jubiläumsausgabe*, edited by Hermann Glockner, vol. 12, 20. Stuttgart: Fromann, 1937. Translation: *Introductory Lectures on Aesthetics*, translated by Bernard Bosanquet, edited by Michael Inwood. Harmondsworth: Penguin, 1993.

Heidegger, Martin. "Building Dwelling Thinking." In *Poetry, Language, Thought*, translated by Alfred Hofstadter, 141–61. New York: HarperCollins, 1971.

———. "The Origin of the Work of Art." In *Poetry, Language, Thought*, translated by Albert Hofstadter, 15–86. New York: Harper and Row, 1971.

———. *Poetry, Language, Thought*. Translated by Albert Hofstadter. New York: Harper & Row, 1971.

Hejduk, Renata, and Jim Williamson. *The Religious Imagination in Modern and Contemporary Architecture: A Reader*. New York: Routledge, 2011.

Hermann, Heinrich. "On the Transcendent in Landscapes of Contemplation." In *Contemporary Landscapes of Contemplation*, edited by Rebecca Krinke. London: Routledge, 2005.

Heyden, Doris. "An Interpretation of the Cave underneath the Pyramid of the Sun in Teotihuacan, Mexico." *American Antiquity* 40 (April 1975): 131–47.

———. "Caves, Gods and Myths: World-View and Planning in Teotihuacan." In *Mesoamerican Sites and World-Views*, edited by Elizabeth P. Benson, 1–35. Washington, D.C.: Dumbarton Oaks Research Library and Collections, 1981.

Hicks, David. *Ritual and Belief: Readings in the Anthropology of Religion*. 3rd edition. Lanham, Md.: AltaMira Press, 2010.

Hirsch, Eric. "Introduction." In *The Anthropology of Landscape: Perspectives on Place and Space*, edited by E. Hirsch and M. O'Hanlon, 1–30. Oxford: Clarendon Press, 1995.

Holl, Steven. "Archetypal Experiences of Architecture." *A+U: Questions of Perception* (1994): 121–35.

———. *The Chapel of St. Ignatius*. New York: Princeton Architectural Press, 1999.

———. *Architecture Spoken*. New York: Rizzoli International Publications, 2007.

Holmes, William Henry. *Archaeological Studies among the Ancient Cities of Mexico*. Chicago: Field Columbian Museum, 1895–97.

Hoppe, Leslie J. *The Synagogue and Churches of Ancient Palestine*. Collegeville: Liturgical Press, 1994.

Hubert, Henri, and Marcel Mauss. *Sacrifice: Its Nature and Functions*. Translated by W. D. Halls. London: Cohen & West, 1898 [1964].

Huebner, Dwayne. "Education and Spirituality." *Journal of Curriculum Theorizing* 11, no. 2 (1995): 13–34.

Hugo, Victor Marie. *Notre Dame De Paris*. Vol. XII. New York: P. F. Collier & Son, 1917. Reprint, Bartleby.com, 2000.

"Hunts Point Riverside Park." http://www.majoracartergroup.com/services/case-histories/hunts-point-riverside-park/ (accessed March 8, 2013).

Imre, Roberta W. "The Nature of Knowledge in Social Work." *Social Work* 29, no. 1 (1984): 41–45.

"The Inside Story: A Guide to Indoor Air Quality." United States Environmental Protection Agency. http://www.epa.gov/iaq/pubs/insidestory.html (accessed December 5, 2011).

The International Positive Psychology Association. http://www.ippanetwork.org/ (accessed June 1, 2013).

Irish Episcopal Commission for Liturgy. *The Place of Worship*. Dublin: Veritas, 1994.

James, William. *Varieties of Religious Experiences*. New York: Touchstone, 2004.

Jenkins, Philip. *The Coming of Global Christianity*. 3rd edition. New York: Oxford University Press, 2011.

Johnson, Mark. *The Meaning of the Body*. Chicago: University of Chicago Press, 2007.

Jones, Cheslyn, et al. *The Study of the Liturgy*. Rev. ed. London: SPCK, 1992.

Jones, Lindsay. *The Hermeneutics of Sacred Architecture: Experience, Interpretation, Comparison*. 2 vols. Cambridge, Mass.: Harvard University Press, 2000.

———. "Zapotec Sacred Places, Enduring and/or Ephemeral: Reverence, Realignment and Commodification at an Archaeological-Tourist Site in Southern Mexico." *Culture and Religion* 11, no. 4 (December 2010): 345–93.

———. "Revalorizing Mircea Eliade's Notion of Revalorization: Reflections on the Present-Day Reuses of Mesoamerica's Pre-Columbian Sites and Architectures." *Archaevs: Studies in the History of Religions* XV (2011): 119–60.

Joye, Yannick. "Architectural Lessons from Environmental Psychology: The Case of Biophilic Architecture." *Review of General Psychology* 11, no. 4 (2007): 305–28.

Jungmann, J. A. "The Defensive Battle against Teutonic Arianism and its Immediate Reaction." In *Pastoral Liturgy*, 23–32. New York: Herder and Herder, 1962.

Kallendorf, Craig, ed. *Humanist Educational Treatises*. Cambridge, Mass.: The Tatti Renaissance Library, 2002.

Kandinsky, Wassily. *Concerning the Spiritual in Art*. Translated by M. T. H. Sadler. New York: Dover Publications, 1977.

Kant, Immanuel. *Kritik der Urteilskraft* (*Critique of Judgment*). Translated by Werner S. Pluhar. Indianapolis: Hackett, 1987.

Kaplan, Rachel, and Stephen Kaplan. *The Experience of Nature: A Psychological Perspective*. Cambridge: Cambridge University Press, 1989.

Kaplan, Stephen. "The Restorative Benefits of Nature: Toward an Integrative Framework." *Journal of Environmental Psychology* 15 (1995): 169–82.

Keating, Thomas. *Open Mind, Open Heart*. New York: Continuum, 2009.

Keene, Donald. *Anthology of Japanese Literature: From the Earliest Era to the Mid-Nineteenth Century*. New York: Grove Press, 1955.

Kelemen, Pal. *Medieval American Art*. New York: Macmillan, 1943.

Kellert, Stephen, and Edward Wilson, eds. *The Biophilia Hypothesis*. Washington, D.C.: Island Press, 1993.

Khosla, Romi. "Architecture and Symbolism in Tibetan Monasteries." In *Shelter, Sign, and Symbol: An Exploratory Work on Vernacular Architecture*, 71–83. Woodstock, N.Y.: Overlook Press, 1975.

———. *Buddhist Monasteries in the Western Himalayas*. Kathmandu, Nepal: Ratna Pustak Bhander, 1979.

Kim, Annette, and Phil Thompson. "God's Plan: A Podcast on Faith and City Planning." Polis: A Collaborative Blog about Cities. 2010. http://www.thepolisblog.org/2012/01/gods-plan-podcast-on-faith-and-city.html (accessed on January 10, 2012).

Kinder, Terryl N. *Architecture of Silence: Cistercian Abbeys of France*. New York: Harry N. Abrams, 2002.

———. *Cistercian Europe: Architecture of Contemplation*. Grand Rapids, Mich.: Eerdmans, 2002.

King, Richard. *Orientalism and Religion: Post-Colonial Theory, India and "the Mystic East."* London: Routledge, 1999.

Klein, Josephine. *Jacob's Ladder: Essays on Experiences of the Ineffable in the Context of Contemporary Psychotherapy*. New York: Karnac Books/Other Press, 2003.

Knott, Kim. "Spatial Theory and the Study of Religion." *Religion Compass* 2, no. 6 (2008): 1102–16.

Kostof, Spiro. *A History of Architecture, Settings and Rituals*. 2nd edition. New York and Oxford: Oxford University Press, 1995.

Kottak, Conrad Phillip. *Cultural Anthropology: Appreciating Cultural Diversity*. 14th edition. New York: McGraw Hill, 2011.

Krautheimer, Richard. *Early Christian and Byzantine Architecture*. New Haven, Conn.: Yale University Press, 1992.

Krinke, Rebecca. *Contemporary Landscapes of Contemplation*. New York: Routledge, 2005.

Kubicki, Judith. *The Presence of Christ in the Gathered Assembly*. New York: Continuum, 2006.

Kubler, George. "The Design of Space in Maya Architecture." In *Miscellanea Paul Rivet, Octogenario Dicata*, 515–31. Mexico: Universidad Nacional Autónoma de México, 1958.

———. *The Art and Architecture of Ancient America*. 3rd edition. New York: Penguin Books, 1984.

Kuspit, Donald B. *Modernin Ulottuvuuksia* [*Dimensions of the Modern*]. Edited by Jaakko Lintinen. Helsinki: Taide, 1989.

Lacoste, Jean-Yves. *Expérience et Absolu: Questions disputes sur la humanité de l'homme*. Paris: Presses Universitaires de France, 1994.

———. "Presence and Parousia." In *The Blackwell Companion to Postmodern Theology*, edited by Graham Ward, 394–98. Oxford: Blackwell Publishing, 2006.

Landa, Diego de. *Relación De Las Cosas De Yucatán*. Edited and translated by Alfred M. Tozzer. Cambridge, Mass.: Harvard University Press, 1941.

Lang, Andrew. *Myth, Ritual, and Religion*. London: Longmans, Green and Company, 1901.

Lasker, David. "International and Regional—Tales of Two Architects." *Canadian Interiors* 36, no. 3, 2–11.

Lathrop, Gordon W., and Timothy J. Wengert. *Christian Assembly: Marks of the Church in a Pluralistic Age*. Minneapolis: Fortress Press, 2004.

Le Corbusier. "L'espace Indicible." *L'Architecture d'Aujourd'hui* numero hors serie "Art" (January 1946): 9–10.

———. "Ineffable Space." In *New World of Space*, 7–9. New York, 1948.

———. *New World of Space*. New York: Reynal & Hitchcock, 1948.

———. *Creation Is a Patient Search*. Translated by James Palmes. New York: Frederick Praeger, 1960.

———. *Journey to the East*. Translated by Ivan Zaknic. Edited by Ivan Zaknic. Cambridge, Mass.: The MIT Press, 1987.

———. "The Parthenon." In *Journey to the East*, edited by Ivan Zaknic. Cambridge, Mass.: The MIT Press, 1987.

———. "Ineffable Space." In *Architecture Culture 1943–1968*, edited by Joan Ockman, 64–68. New York: Columbia University Graduate School of Architecture, Planning and Preservation, 1993.

———. *El Viaje De Oriente*. 2nd edition. Valencia, Spain: Artes Graficas Soler S.A., 1993.

———. *Voyage D'orient. Carnets*. Translated by Mayra Munson and Mege Shore. Milano: Mondadori Electa spa, 2002.

———. *Toward a New Architecture*. Translated by John Goodman. 2nd ed. Los Angeles: Getty Research Institute, 2007.

Le Corbusier, and Pierre Jeanneret. *Oeuvre Complète 1910–1929*. Switzerland: Les Editions d'Architecture, 1964.

Lee, Dorothy. "Religious Perspectives in Anthropology." In *Magic, Witchcraft, and Religion: A Reader in the Anthropology of Religion*, 8th edition, edited by Pamela A. Moro and James E. Myers, 20–27. New York: McGraw-Hill, 2010 [1952].

Leijssen, Lambert J. *With the Silent Glimmer of God's Spirit: A Postmodern Look at the Sacraments*. New York: Paulist Press, 2006.

Lekai, Louis J. *The Cistercians: Ideals and Reality*. Kent, Ohio: Kent State University Press, 1977.

Lessa, William A., and Evon Z. Vogt. *Reader in Comparative Religion: An Anthropological Approach*. 3rd edition. New York: Harper & Row, 1975 [1958].

Levi, Anthony. *Renaissance and Reformation*. New Haven, Conn.: Yale University Press, 2002.

Levin, David Michael. "Introduction." In *Modernity and the Hegemony of Vision*, edited by David Michael Levin. Berkeley: University of California Press, 1993.

Lévi-Strauss, Claude. "The Effectiveness of Symbols." In *Structural Anthropology*, 186–205. New York: Basic Books, 1963.

———. *Myth and Meaning: Cracking the Code of Culture*. New York: Schocken Books, 1995 [1978].

Lillich, Meredith Parsons, ed. *Studies in Cistercian Art and Architecture*. 4 vols. Kalamazoo, Mich.: Cistercian Publications, 1980, 1984, 1987, 1993.

Lindquist, Galina, and Don Handelman, eds. *Religion, Politics & Globalization: Anthropological Approaches*. New York: Berghahn Books, 2011.

Lindsay, Kenneth C., and Peter Vergo, eds. *Kandinsky: Complete Writings on Art*. New York: Da Capo Press, 1994.

Lobell, John. *Between Silence and Light: Spirit in the Architecture of Louis I. Kahn*. Boston: Shambala, 1985.

Loewenberg, Frank M. *Religion and Social Work Practice in Contemporary American Society.* New York: Columbia University Press, 1988.

Louv, Richard. *Last Child in the Woods: Saving our Children from Nature Deficit Disorder.* Chapel Hill, N.C.: Algonquin Press, 2005.

———. *The Nature Principle: Human Restoration and the End of Nature Deficit Disorder.* Chapel Hill, N.C.: Algonquin Books, 2011.

Louvel, François. "Le mystère de nos églises." *La Maison-Dieu* 63 (1960): 5–23.

Low, Setha M., and Denise Lawrence-Zúñiga, eds. *The Anthropology of Space and Place: Locating Culture.* Malden, Mass.: Blackwell Publishing, 2005.

Maathai, Wangari. *Replenishing the Earth: Spiritual Values for Healing Ourselves and the World.* New York: Doubleday, 2010.

Mabbett, I. W. "The Symbolism of Mount Meru." *History of Religions* 23 (August 1983): 64–83.

Macaulay, Alastair. "The Fluid Human Dance That Is Grand Central." *The New York Times*, August 31, 2011. http://www.nytimes.com/2011/09/01/arts/dance/art-of-summer-grand-centrals-fluid-human-dance.html (accessed June 8, 2013).

MacCannell, Dean. "Sightseeing and Social Structure: The Moral Integration of Modernity." In *Tourists and Tourism: A Reader*, edited by Sharon Bohn Gmelch, 55–70. Long Grove, Ill.: Waveland Press, 2004.

Mace, Ronald L. *Universal Design: Housing for the Lifespan of All People.* Rockville, Md.: U.S. Department of Housing and Urban Development, 1988.

MacLean, H. "Sacred Colors and Shamanic Vision among the Huichol Indians of Mexico." *Journal of Anthropological Research*, no. 57 (2001): 305–25.

Malinowski, Bronislaw. *Magic, Science and Religion, and Other Essays.* Boston: Beacon Press, 1948.

"Map of Memory, an Interview: Michael Singer with Rebecca Krinke." In *Contemporary Landscapes of Contemplation*, edited by Rebecca Krinke. London: Routledge, 2005.

Maquet, Jacques. *The Aesthetic Experience: An Anthropologist Looks at the Visual Arts.* New Haven, Conn.: Yale University Press, 1986.

Marcus, Joyce. "Archaeology and Religion: A Comparison of the Zapotec and Maya." In *Ancient Mesoamerica: Selected Readings*, edited by John A. Graham, 172–91. Palo Alto: Peek Publications, 1981.

Marcuse, Herbert. *The Aesthetic Dimension: Towards a Critique of Marxist Aesthetics.* Boston: Beacon Press, 1978.

Maritain, Jacques. *Art and Scholasticism and the Frontiers of Poetry.* Translated by Joseph W. Evans. New York: Scribner's, 1962.

Marx, Karl. "Contribution to the Critique Hegel's Philosophy of Right." *Deutsch-Französische Jahrbücher* (February, 1844).

Maybury-Lewis, David. *Millennium: Tribal Wisdom and the Modern World.* New York: Viking, 1992.

———. *Altars and Icons: Sacred Spaces in Everyday Life.* San Francisco: Chronicle Books, 1998.

Mayer, A. L. "Renaissance, Humanism und Liturgie." *Jahrbuch für Liturgiewissenschaft* 14 (1934): 123–70.

Mays, Vernon. "The New Rural Studio." *Architect*, November 2, 2007. http://www.architectmagazine.com/educational-projects/the-new-rural-studio.aspx (accessed March 8, 2013).

McGillchrist, Iain. *The Master and His Emissary: The Divided Brain and the Making of the Western World.* New Haven, Conn.: Yale University Press, 2009.

McKim, Donald K., ed. *The Cambridge Companion to Martin Luther.* New York: Cambridge University Press, 2003.

McLeman, Robert. "Impacts of Population Change on Vulnerability and the Capacity to Adapt to Climate Change and Variability: A Typology Based on Lessons from a Hard Country." *Population and Environment* 31, no. 5 (2010): 286–316.

McMann, Jean. *Altars and Icons: Sacred Spaces in Everyday Life.* San Francisco: Chronicle Books, 1998.

Men, Hunbatz. *Secrets of Mayan Science/Religion.* Santa Fe: Bear & Company, 1989.

Merton, Thomas. *Seeds of Contemplation.* New York: New Directions, 1949.

———. "Transcendent Experience." In *Zen and the Birds of Appetite.* New York: A New Direction Book, 1968.

———. *The Waters of Siloe.* San Diego: Harcourt Brace & Company, 1979.

Mezger, Marcel. *History of the Liturgy: The Major Stages.* Collegeville: Liturgical Press, 1997.

Michell, George. *The Hindu Temple: An Introduction to Its Meaning and Forms.* Chicago: University of Chicago Press, 1977.

Mikul, Chris. *The Cult Files: True Stories from the Extreme Edges of Religious Beliefs.* New York: Metro Books, 2010.

Miles, Margaret. *Images as Insight: Visual Understanding in Western Christianity and Secular Culture.* Boston: Beacon Press, 1985.

Mill, John Stuart. *Utilitarianism.* London: Parker, Son, and Bourn, West Strand, 1863.

Mirsky, Jeanette. *Houses of God.* Chicago: University of Chicago Press, 1965.

Moneo, Rafael. "Architecture as a Vehicle for Religious Experience: The Los Angeles Cathedral." In *Constructing the Ineffable: Contemporary Sacred Architecture,* edited by Karla Britton, 158–70. New Haven, Conn.: Yale School of Architecture, 2011.

Moore, Thomas. *The Re-Enchantment of Everyday Life.* New York: HarperCollins Publishers, 1996.

Moro, Pamela A., and James E. Myers. *Magic, Witchcraft, and Religion: A Reader in the Anthropology of Religion.* 8th edition. New York: McGraw Hill, 2010.

Morris, Patricia M. "The Capabilities Perspective: A Framework for Social Justice. Families in Society." *A Journal for Contemporary Human Services* 83, no. 4 (2002): 365–73.

Mostafavi, Mohsen, and David Leatherbarrow. *On Weathering, the Life of Buildings in Time.* Cambridge, Mass.: The MIT Press, 1993.

Mugerauer, Robert. "Eliade: Restoring the Possibilities of Place." In *Interpretations on Behalf of Place: Environmental Displacements and Alternative Responses,* 52–64. Albany: State University of New York Press, 1994.

Müller, Frederick Max. *Anthropological Religion: The Gifford Lectures Delivered Before the University of Glasgow in 1891.* London: Longmans, Green, and Company, 1892.

Mullins, Edwin. *Cluny: In Search of God's Lost Empire.* New York: Blue Bridge, 2006.

Murray, Peter. *The Architecture of the Italian Renaissance.* New York: Schocken Books, 1963.

Nabokov, Peter, and Robert Easton. *Native American Architecture.* Oxford: Oxford University Press, 1989.

Naegele, Daniel. "Object, Image, Aura: Le Corbusier and the Architecture of Photography." *Harvard Design Magazine* (Fall 1998): 37–41.

Naess, Arne. "The Shallow and the Deep, Long-Range Ecology Movement: A Summary." *Inquiry* 16, no. 1 (1973): 95–100.

———. *Ecology, Community, and Lifestyle: Outline of an Ecosophy.* Translated and edited by David Rothenberg. Cambridge: Cambridge University Press, 1990.

Nas, Peter J. M., and Annemarie Samuels. *Hypercity: The Symbolic Side of Urbanism.* London: Routledge, 2006.

National Association of Social Workers. *Code of Ethics.* Washington, D.C.: NASW, 2008.

"Negative Ions." Iris Wellbeing. http://www.iriswellbeing.com/negative_ions.html (accessed December 5, 2011).

Nehamas, Alexander. *Only a Promise of Happiness.* Princeton, N.J.: Princeton University Press, 2007.

Neumeyer, Fritz. *The Artless Word: Mies Van Der Rohe on the Building Art.* Cambridge, Mass.: The MIT Press, 1991.

Nicholson, Irene. *Mexican and Central American Mythology.* London: Paul Hamlyn, 1976.

Norberg-Schulz, Christian. *Meaning in Western Architecture.* New York: Praeger Publishers, 1975.

Novak, Marcos. "Trans Terra Firma: After Territory." *Sites,* no. 26 (1995): 34–53.

———. "Transmitting Architecture." *Architects in Cyberspace* (*AD Profile #18*), 1996, 42–47.

Nussbaum, Martha C. "Women and Equality: The Capabilities Approach," *International Labor Review* 138, no. 3 (1999): 227–51.

———. *Creating Capabilities: The Human Development Approach.* Cambridge, Mass.: The Belknap Press of Harvard University Press, 2011.

Occhipinti, Frank, D. "American Indian Sacred Sites and the National Historic Preservation Act: The Enola Hill Case." *Journal of Northwest Anthropology* 36, no. 1 (2002): 3–50.

O'Malley, John W., Thomas M. Izbicki, and Gerald Christianson, eds. *Humanity and Divinity in Renaissance and Reformation.* New York: Brill, 1993.

Otto, Rudolf. *The Idea of the Holy: An Inquiry into the Non-Rational Factor in the Idea of the Divine and Its Relation to the Rational.* New York: Oxford University Press, 1970.

Pallasmaa, Juhani. *Encounters: Architectural Essays.* Edited by Peter MacKeith. Helsinki, Finland: Rakennustieto Oy, 2008.

———. "The Aura of the Sacred." In *The Religious Imagination in Modern and Contemporary Architecture: A Reader*, edited by Renata Hejduk and Jim Williamson, 235–41. New York: Routledge, 2011.

Panofsky, Erwin. *Gothic Architecture and Scholasticism*. New York: Meridian Books, 1957.

Papapetros, Spyros. "Le Corbusier and Freud on the Acropolis: Notes on a Parallel Itinerary." In *Architects' Journeys: Building, Traveling, Thinking*, edited by Craig Buckley and Pollyanna Rhee, 136–71. New York: GSAPP Books, 2011.

Parker, T. H. L. *Calvin: An Introduction to His Thought*. New York: Continuum, 2002.

Passanti, Francesco. "Architecture: Proportion, Classicism and Other Issues." In *Le Corbusier before Le Corbusier*, edited by Stanislaus von Moos and Arthur Rüegg. New Haven, Conn.: Yale University Press, 2002.

Patke, Rajeev S. "Benjamin's Aura, Stevens's Description without Place." In *Benjamin's Blindspot: Walter Benjamin & the Premature Death of Aura*, edited by Lise Patt, 81–98. Topanga, Calif.: Institute of Cultural Inquiry, 2001.

Pearson, Clifford A. "Inner-City Arts: Phase III." *Architectural Record*, February, 2009. http://archrecord.construction.com/projects/portfolio/archives/0902innercity-1.asp (accessed March 8, 2013).

Pennebaker, James W. *Opening Up: The Healing Power of Expressing Emotions*. New York: Guilford Press, 1997.

Pérez-Gómez, Alberto. *Architecture and the Crisis of Modern Science*. Cambridge, Mass.: The MIT Press, 1985.

———. *Polyphilo or the Dark Forest Revisited: An Erotic Epiphany of Architecture*. Cambridge, Mass.: The MIT Press, 1994.

———. *Built Upon Love: Architectural Longing after Ethics and Aesthetics*. Cambridge, Mass.: The MIT Press, 2006.

Petruccioli, Attilio. "Nature in Islamic Urbanism." In *Islam and Ecology*, edited by Richard C. Foltz, Frederick. M. Denny, and Azizan Baharuddin, 499–510. Cambridge, Mass.: Harvard University Press, 2003.

Picard, Max. *The World of Silence (1948)*. Washington, D.C.: Gateway Editions, 1988.

Pickstock, Catherine. "Justice and Prudence: Principles of Order in the Platonic City." In *The Blackwell Companion to Postmodern Theology*, edited by Graham Ward, 162–76. Oxford: Blackwell Publishing, 2006.

Pollock, H. E. D. "Architecture of the Maya Lowlands." In *Handbook of Middle American Indians*, vol. 2, 378–440. Austin: University of Texas Press, 1965.

Popple, Philip R., and Leslie Leighninger. *Social Work, Social Welfare, and American Society*. Boston: Allyn & Bacon, 2005.

Post, Paul. "Dura Europos Revisited: Rediscovering Sacred Space." *Worship* 86 (May 2012): 254–70.

Predock, Antoine. "Antoine Predock on the Alhambra." In *Architects on Architects*, edited by Susan Gray, 146–53. New York: McGraw-Hill, 2002.

Price, Travis. *The Mythic Modern. Architectural Expeditions into the Spirit of Place*. China: Oro Edition, 2012.

Pugin, Augustus Welby. *Contrasts: Or, a Parallel between the Noble Edifices of the Middle Ages, and Corresponding Buildings of the Present Day, Shewing the Present Decay of Taste*. London: Charles Dolman, 1841.

Pyles, Loretta. "The Capabilities Approach and Violence against Women: Implications for Social Development." *International Social Work* 51, no. 1 (2008): 25–36.

Pyles, Loretta, and Mahasweta M. Banerjee. "Work Experiences of Women Survivors: Insights from the Capabilities Approach." *Affilia* 25, no. 1 (2010): 43–55.

Rahner, Karl. *The Church and the Sacraments*. London: Burns & Oates, 1963.

Rappaport, Roy A. "Ritual Regulation of Environmental Relations among a New Guinea People." *Ethnology* 6, no. 1 (1967): 17–30.

———. *Pigs for the Ancestors*. New Haven, Conn.: Yale University Press, 1968.

Rattenbury, J. Ernest. "Methodist Spirituality." In *Protestant Spiritual Traditions*, edited by Frank C. Senn, 217–73. New York: Paulist Press, 1986.

Rawls, John. *A Theory of Justice*. Cambridge, Mass.: Harvard University, 1971.

———. *A Theory of Justice*, rev. ed. Cambridge, Mass.: The Belknap Press of Harvard University Press, 1999.

———. *Justice as Fairness: A Restatement*. Cambridge, Mass.: The Belknap Press of Harvard University Press, 2001.

Rees, William. "Human Nature, Eco-Footprints and Environmental Injustice." *Local Environment* 13, no. 8 (2008): 685–701.

———. "The Ecological Crisis and Self-Delusion: Implications for the Building Sector." *Building Research & Information* 37, no. 3 (2009): 300–11.

Reisch, Michael. "Defining Social Justice in a Socially Unjust World." *Families in Society: The Journal of Contemporary Human Services* 83, no. 4 (2002): 343–54.

Renan, Ernest. *Recollection of My Youth*. London: Chapman and Hall Limited, 1897.

Richards, Simon. *Le Corbusier and the Concept of Self*. New Haven, Conn.: Yale University Press, 2003.

Richter, Gottfried. *Art and Human Consciousness*. Translated by Burley Channer and Margaret Frohlich. Spring Valley, N.Y.: Anthroposophic Press, 1985.

Rilke, Rainer Maria. *Letters to a Young Poet*. New York: Random House, 1986.

Rivera A., Adalberto. *The Mysteries of Chichén Itzá: The First Guide to the Esoteric Function of the Temples and Pyramids of Ancient Chichén Itzá*. Universal Image Enterprise, 1995.

Romain, William F. *Mysteries of the Hopewell: Astronomers, Geometers, and Magicians of the Eastern Woodlands*. Akron, Ohio: The University of Akron Press, 2000.

Rudolph, Conrad. *The "Things of Greater Importance": Bernard of Clairvaux's Apologia and the Medieval Attitude toward Art*. Philadelphia: University of Pennsylvania Press, 1990.

Russel, Robin. "Spirituality and Religion in Graduate Social Work Education." *Social Thought* 18, no. 2 (1998): 15–29.

Rykwert, Joseph. *On Adam's House in Paradise*. New York: The Museum of Modern Art, 1972.

———. *The Idea of a Town*. Princeton, N.J.: Princeton University Press, 1976.

Sacred Congregation for Divine Worship. *General Instruction of the Roman Missal*. Translated by ICEL. Liturgy Documents Series 2. Washington, D.C.: United States Conference of Catholic Bishops, 2003.

Sandercock, Leonie, and Maged Senbel. "Spirituality, Urban Life and Urban Professions." In *Postsecular Cities: Space, Theory and Practice*, edited by Justin Beamont and Christopher Baker, 87–103. London: Continuum, 2011.

Sartre, Jean-Paul. *What Is Literature?* Gloucester, Mass.: Peter Smith, 1978.

———. "What Is Literature?" In *Jean-Paul Sartre: Basic Writings,* edited by Stephen Priest. London: Routledge, 2001.

Schaab, Gloria L. "Environment, Ecology, and Creation Theology: Visions and Revisions in the Christian Tradition." *Liturgical Ministry* 20 (Spring 2011): 57–67.

Schele, Linda, and Mary Ellen Miller. *The Blood of Kings: Dynasty and Ritual in Maya Art*. Fort Worth: Kimbell Art Museum, 1986.

Schmemann, Alexander. *The World as Sacrament*. London: Longman, Darton & Todd, 1965.

School of Architecture and Planning, the Catholic University of America. *Transcending Architecture: Aesthetics and Ethics of the Numinous*. Brochure. Washington, D.C.: The Catholic University of America, 2011.

Schwarz, Rudolf. *Vom Bau Der Kirche*. Heidelberg: Schneider, 1938.

———. *The Church Incarnate*. Translated by Cynthia Harris. Chicago: H. Regnery Co., 1958.

Scruton, Roger. *Beauty: A Very Short Introduction*. New York: Oxford University Press, 2011.

Scully, Vincent. *The Earth, the Temple, and the Gods: Greek Sacred Architecture*. New Haven, Conn.: Yale University Press, 1962.

———. "The Earth, the Temple, and Today." In *Constructing the Ineffable: Contemporary Sacred Architecture*, edited by Karla Britton, 26–48. New Haven, Conn.: Yale School of Architecture, 2011.

Seasoltz, R. Kevin. "Liturgical Movement." In *The Encyclopedia of Christianity*, edited by Erwin Fahlbusch et al., 5 vols., 3:314–19. Grand Rapids, Mich.: Eerdmans Publishing Company, 2003.

———. *A Sense of the Sacred: Theological Foundations of Christian Architecture and Art*. New York: Continuum, 2005.

———. *God's Gift Giving: In Christ and through the Spirit*. New York: Continuum, 2007.

Second Vatican Ecumenical Council. "Constitution on the Liturgy." In *Decrees of the Ecumenical Councils, Vol. II Trent to Vatican II*. English ed. Norman P. Tanner, SJ, 849–900. Washington, D.C.: Sheed and Ward and Georgetown University Press, 1990.

Segel, Robert A. *Myth: A Very Short Introduction*. Oxford: Oxford University Press, 2004.

Séjourné, Laurette. *Burning Water: Thought and Religion in Ancient Mexico*. Translated by Irene Nicholson. Berkeley: Shambhala Press, 1976.

Seligman, Martin E. P. *Authentic Happiness: Using the New Positive Psychology to Realize Your Potential for Lasting Fulfillment*. New York: Atria Books, 2003.

Seligman, Martin E. P., and M. Csikszentmihalyi. "Positive Psychology: An Introduction." *American Psychologist* 55, no. 1 (2000): 5–14.

Sen, Amartya K. *Commodities and Capabilities*. Amsterdam: Elsevier Science Publisher, 1985.

———. *Inequality Reexamined*. New York: Russell Sage Foundation, 1992.

———. *The Idea of Justice*. Cambridge, Mass.: The Belknap Press of Harvard University Press, 2009.

Senbel, Maged. "Ecology and Spirituality in Cities: Towards a Spirit Enriching Urban Environment." *2A: Architecture and Art* 12 (2009): 68–70.

Senbel, Maged, Timothy McDaniels, and Hadi Dowlatabadi. "The Ecological Footprint: A Non-Monetary Metric of Human Consumption Applied to North America." *Global Environmental Change* 13, no. 2 (2003): 83–100.

Senn, Frank C. *Christian Liturgy: Catholic and Evangelical*. Minneapolis: Fortress Press, 1997.

Shanes, Eric. *Constantin Brancusi*. New York: Abbeville Press, 1989.

Shear, Jonathan. *Explaining Consciousness: The Hard Problem*. Cambridge, Mass.: The MIT Press, 1999.

Sheridan, Michael J. "The Spiritual Person." In *Dimensions of Human Behavior: Person and Environment*, edited by Elizabeth D. Hutchison, 163–208. Thousand Oaks, Calif.: Sage, 2011.

Shildt, Cöran. *Alvar Aalto a Life's Work—Architecture, Design and Art*. Helsinki: Otava Publishing, 1994.

Short, Ernst. *A History of Religious Architecture*, 3rd revised edition. New York: W. W. Norton, 1951.

Silvestrin, Claudio. *Ad (Architectural Design): Aspects of Minimal Architecture Ii*. Waltham, Mass.: Academy Press, 1999.

———. *Claudio Silvestrin*. Basel, Switzerland: Birkhaüser, 1999.

Simson, Otto von. *The Gothic Cathedral*. Princeton, N.J.: Princeton University Press, 1956.

Siporin, Max. "Contribution of Religious Values to Social Work and the Law." *Social Thought* 12, no. 4 (1986): 35–50.

Skinner, Burrhus Frederic. *Walden II*. Indianapolis: Hackett, 1948.

Smith, E. Baldwin. *Egyptian Architecture as Cultural Expression*. New York: D. Appleton-Century Company, 1938.

———. *The Dome: A Study in the History of Ideas*. Princeton, N.J.: Princeton University Press, 1950.

Smith, Jonathan Z. *To Take Place: Toward Theory in Ritual*. Chicago: University of Chicago Press, 1987.

Snyder, S. R., Shane J. Lopez, and Jennifer Teramoto Pedrotti. *Positive Psychology: The Scientific and Practical Explorations of Human Strengths*. Thousand Oaks, Calif.: Sage, 2011.

South, Stephanie. *Biography of a Time Traveler: The Journey of José Argüelles*. Franklin Lakes, N.J.: New Page Books, 2009.

Spector, Tom. "Codes of Ethics and Coercion." In *Architecture and Its Ethical Dilemmas*, edited by Nicholas Ray, 101–12. New York: Taylor and Francis, 2005.

Spinden, Herbert J. *A Study of Maya Art: Its Subject Matter and Historical Development*. New York: Dover Publications, 1975.

Spriggs, N. Gerlach, R. E. Kaufman, and S. B. Warner Jr. *Restorative Gardens: The Healing Landscape*. New Haven, Conn.: Yale University Press, 1998.

Stalley, Roger. *Early Medieval Architecture*. New York: Oxford University Press, 1999.

Stephens, John L. *Incidents of Travel in Yucatan*. New York: Dover Publications, 1846.

———. *Incidents of Travel in Central America, Chiapas and Yucatan*. New York: Dover Publications, 1969.

Sternberg, Esther M. *Healing Spaces: The Science of Place and Well-Being*. Cambridge, Mass.: The Belknap Press of Harvard University Press, 2009.

Sternberg, Esther, M., and Matthew A. Wilson. "Neuroscience and Architecture: Seeking Common Ground." *Cell* 127 (2006): 239–42.

Stoddard, Whitney S. *Art and Architecture in Medieval France*. New York: Harper and Row, 1972.

Story, Molly F., James L. Mueller, and Ronald L. Mace. *The Universal Design File: Design for People of All Ages and Disabilities*, rev. ed. Raleigh: The Center for Universal Design, North Carolina State University, 1998.

Stump, Roger W. *The Geography of Religion: Faith, Place, and Space.* Lanham, Md.: Rowman and Little-field Publishers, 2008.

Sturken, Marita. *Tourist of History: Memory, Kitsch, and Consumerism from Oklahoma City to Ground Zero.* Durham, N.C.: Duke University Press, 2007.

Suger, Abbot. *On the Abbey Church of Saint Denis and Its Art Treasures.* Edited and translated by Erwin Panofsky. Princeton, N.J.: Princeton University Press, 1979.

Swanson, Guy E. *The Birth of the Gods: Origin of Primitive Beliefs.* Ann Arbor: University of Michigan Press, 1964.

Swenson, Carol R. "Clinical Social Work's Contribution to a Social Justice Perspective." *Social Work* 43, no. 6 (1998): 527–37.

Taut, Bruno. *Houses and People of Japan.* Tokyo: The Sanseido Co., 1937.

Taylor, Bron. "Earth and Nature-Based Spirituality (Part II): From Earth First! and Bioregionalism to Scientific Paganism and the New Age." *Religion* 31, no. 3 (2001): 225–45.

Taylor, Mark. "The Nonabsent Absence of the Holy." In *Tears.* Albany: State University of New York Press, 1990.

Taylor, Sue Ann. "Mental Health and Successful Coping among Aged Black Women." In *Minority Aging: Sociological and Social Psychological Issues*, edited by Ron C. Manuel, 95–100. Westport, Conn.: Greenwood Press, 1982.

———. "Religion as a Coping Mechanism for Older Black Women." *Quarterly Contact* 5, no. 4 (1982): 2–3.

———. "At or Near: An Analysis of Proximity." In *Vietnam Veterans Memorial Center: Site Selection Study*, edited by James Cummings, appendix F, 1–15. Washington, D.C.: Vietnam Veterans Memorial Fund, 2005.

———. "Public Commemoration and Private Remembrance." *Anthropology News.* September 2011. http://www.anthropology-news.org/index.php/toc/an-table-of-contents-september-2011-526/ (accessed March 27, 2012).

Thacker, Christopher. *The History of Gardens.* Berkeley: University of California Press, 1979.

Thiry, Paul, Richard M. Bennett, and Henry L. Kamphoefner. *Churches and Temples.* New York: Reinhold Publishing Corp., 1953.

Thompson, J. Eric S. *Maya History and Religion.* Norman: University of Oklahoma Press, 1970.

———. *The Rise and Fall of Maya Civilization.* Norman: University of Oklahoma Press, 1973.

Thompson, Robert Farris. *Flash of the Spirit: African & Afro-American Art & Philosophy.* New York: Vintage Books, 1984.

Thoreau, Henry David. *Walden.* Boston: Houghton, Mifflin and Company, 1894.

———. *Walden.* Roslyn, N.Y.: Walter J. Black, Inc., 1942.

Tiberghein, Gilles A. *Land Art.* Princeton, N.J.: Princeton University Press, 1995.

Tierney, Brian. *Foundations of the Conciliar Theory.* Cambridge: Cambridge University Press, 1955.

Toman, Rolf, ed. *Romanesque: Architecture, Sculpture, Painting.* Cologne: Könemann, 1970.

———, ed. *The Art of Gothic: Architecture, Sculpture, Painting.* Cologne: Könemann, 1999.

Torgerson, Mark Allen. "Edward Anders Sovik and His Return to the 'Non-Church.'" Ph.D. dissertation, University of Notre Dame, 1996.

———. *An Architecture of Immanence: Architecture for Worship and Ministry Today.* Grand Rapids, Mich.: Wm. B. Eerdmans Publishing Company, 2007.

Townsend, Richard F. "The Mt. Tlaloc Project." In *To Change Place: Aztec Ceremonial Landscapes*, edited by Davíd Carrasco, 26–30. Niwot, Colo.: University Press of Colorado, 1991.

Tozzer, Alfred M. *Chichén Itzá and Its Cenote of Sacrifice: A Comparative Study of Contemporaneous Maya and Toltec.* Cambridge, Mass.: Harvard University, 1956.

Tuan, Yi-Fu. *Space and Place: The Perspective of Experience.* Minneapolis: University of Minnesota Press, 1977.

Tucci, Giuseppe. *The Theory and Practice of the Mandala.* Translated by Alan Houghton Brodrick. London: Rider and Co., 1961.

Turner, Paul V. *The Education of Le Corbusier.* New York: Garland Publishing, 1977.

Turner, Victor W. *The Ritual Process: Structure and Anti-Structure.* Chicago: Aldine Publishing Company, 1969.

Turner, Victor, and Edith Turner. *Image and Pilgrimage in Christian Culture.* New York: Columbia University Press, 1978.

Turrell, James. *The Thingness of Light*. Edited by Scott Poole. Blacksburg, Va.: Architecture Editions, 2000.

Twombly, Robert, ed. *Louis Kahn: Essential Texts*. New York: W. W. Norton & Company, 2003.

Tylor, Edward B. *Primitive Culture*. London: J. Murray, 1871.

U.S. Bishops' Committee on the Liturgy. *Environment and Art in Catholic Worship*. Washington, D.C.: National Conference of Catholic Bishops, 1978.

———. *Built of Living Stones: Art, Architecture, and Worship*. Washington, D.C.: United States Catholic Conference, 2000.

"U.S. Religious Landscape Survey." The Pew Forum on Religion and Public Life. http://religions.pewforum.org/reports (accessed March 27, 2012).

"U.S.A. National Symposium on Environment and Art." *Notitiae* 160 (November 1979).

Valéry, Paul. "Euphalinos, or the Architect." In *Dialogues*. New York: Pantheon Books, 1956.

van der Leeuw, Gerardus. *Sacred and Profane Beauty: The Holy in Art*. Translated by David E. Green. New York: Holt, Rinehart and Winston, 1963.

van der Rohe, Ludwig Mies. "Wir Stehen in Der Wende Der Zeit." *Innendekoration* 39 (1928): 262.

van Gennep, Arnold. *The Rites of Passage*. Translated by Monika B. Vizedom and Gabrielle L. Caffee. Chicago: University of Chicago Press, 1960 [1908].

Vattimo, Gianni. *Etica Dell'interpretazione*. Turin: Rosenberg & Sellier, 1989.

———. *Credere Di Credere*. Milan: Garzanti Libri, 1998.

———. *Belief*. Stanford, Calif: Stanford University Press, 1999.

Veilleux, Armand. "Monasticism and Culture-Encounter." *Tjuringa* (May 1975): 43–48.

Venturi, Robert, Denise Scott Brown, and Steven Izenour. *Learning from Las Vegas: The Forgotten Symbolism of Architectural Form*. Cambridge, Mass.: The MIT Press, 1977.

Vidler, Anthony. "Framing Infinity: Le Corbusier, Ayn Rand, and the Idea of 'Ineffable Space.'" In *Warped Space: Art, Architecture and Modern Culture*, 51–64. Cambridge, Mass.: The MIT Press, 1999.

Vogt, Adolf Max. *Le Corbusier: The Noble Savage*. Translated by Radka Donnell. Cambridge, Mass.: The MIT Press, 1998.

von Moos, Stanislaus. *Le Corbusier: Elements of a Synthesis*. Cambridge, Mass.: The MIT Press, 1980.

von Moos, Stanislaus, and Arthur Rüegg. *Le Corbusier before Le Corbusier*. New Haven, Conn.: Yale University Press, 2002.

von Simson, Otto. *The Gothic Cathedral: Origins of the Medieval Concept of Order*. Princeton, N.J.: Princeton University Press, 1956.

Vosko, Richard S. "Liturgical Technology, Social Media, and the Green Church." *Liturgical Ministry* 20 (Spring 2011): 87–92.

Wackernagel, Mathis, and William Rees. *Our Ecological Footprint*. Gabriola Island, BC: New Society Publishers, 1996.

Wakefield, Jerome C. "Psychotherapy, Distributive Justice, and Social Work Part I: Distributive Justice as a Conceptual Framework for Social Work." *Social Service Review* 62, no. 2 (1988): 187–210.

Wallace, Anthony F. C. "Revitalization Movements." *American Anthropologists* 58, no. 2 (1956): 264–81.

———. *Religion: An Anthropological View*. New York: Random House, 1966.

Ward, Graham. "Introduction, or, A Guide to Theological Thinking in Cyberspace." In *The Postmodern God: A Theological Reader*, edited by Graham Ward, xv–xlvii. Oxford: Blackwell Publishing, 1997.

———, ed. *The Postmodern God: A Theological Reader*. Oxford: Blackwell Publishing, 1997.

Warms, Richard, James Garber, and R. Jon McGee, eds. *Sacred Realms: Readings in the Anthropology of Religion*. 2nd edition. London: Oxford University Press, 2008.

Waters, Frank. *Mexico Mystique: The Coming Sixth World of Consciousness*. Chicago: Swallow Press, 1975.

Weber, Nicholas Fox. *Le Corbusier, a Life*. New York: Alfred A. Knopf, 2008.

Wedig, Mark E. "Edifice and Image: Reform of the Roman Catholic Worship Environment." *New Theology Review* 15, no. 3 (August 2002): 5–15.

———. "No Neutral Zones: Hermeneutics and the Interpretation of Liturgical Space." *Liturgical Ministry* 14 (Winter 2005): 1–7.

Weinstein, Netta, Andrew K. Przybylski, and Richard M. Ryan. "Can Nature Make Us More Caring? Effects of Immersion in Nature on Intrinsic Aspirations and Generosity." *Personality and Social Psychology Bulletin* 35, no. 10 (2009): 1315–1529.

Weller, Charles Frederick. "Needy Families in their Homes." In *Proceedings of the National Conference of Charities and Corrections*, edited by Isabel C. Barrows, 265–77. Boston: George H. Ellis Company, 1902.

Wheeler-Barclay, Marjorie. *The Science of Religion in Britain, 1860–1915*. Charlottesville: University of Virginia Press, 2010.

White, James. *Protestant Worship: Traditions in Transition*. Louisville: Westminster John Knox, 1989.

———. *Catholic Worship: Trent to Today*. Collegeville: Liturgical Press, 2003.

White, L. M. *Social Origins of Christian Architecture*, vol. 1, *Building God's House in the Roman World: Architectural Adaptation among Pagans, Jews, and Christians*. Valley Forge: Trinity Press International, 1990.

Wilber, Ken. *Integral Psychology*. Boston: Shambala, 2000.

———. *Integral Spirituality*. Boston: Shambala, 2006.

Wilken, Robert. *The Land Called Holy: Palestine in Church History and Thought*. New Haven, Conn.: Yale University Press, 1992.

Wilson, Edward O. *Biophilia: The Human Bond with Other Species*. Cambridge, Mass.: Harvard University Press, 1984.

———. "Biophilia and the Conservation Ethic." In *Evolutionary Perspectives on Environmental Problems*, edited by Dustin J. Penn and Iver Mysterud, 249–57. New Brunswick, N.J.: Transaction Publishers, 2007.

Witcombe, Christopher. "Sacred Places." http://witcombe.sbc.edu/sacredplaces/ise.html (accessed on December 5, 2011).

Wittkower, Rudolf. *Architectural Principles in the Age of Humanism*. London: Warburg Institute, 1949.

Wixom, William D. "For the Service of the Table of God." In *The Royal Abbey of Saint-Denis in the Time of Abbot Suger (1122–1151)*, edited by Sumner McKnight Crosby et al. New York: The Metropolitan Museum of Art, 1981.

Wogensky, André. *Le Corbusier's Hands*. Translated by Martina Millá Bernad. Cambridge, Mass.: The MIT Press, 2006.

Woodward, Hiram W. "Borobudur and the Mirrorlike Mind." *Archaeology* 34 (November–December 1981).

Yablon, Marcia. "Property Rights and Sacred Sites: Federal Regulatory Responses to American Indian Religious Claims on Public Land." *Yale Law Journal* 113 (2004): 1623–62.

Zagzebski, Linda, and Timothy D. Miller, eds. *Readings in Philosophy of Religion: Ancient to Contemporary*. Chichester: Wiley-Blackwell, 2009.

Zajonc, Arthur. *Catching the Light: The Entwined History of Light and Mind*. New York: Oxford University Press, 1995.

Zaknic, Ivan. *The Final Testament of Père Corbu: A Translation and Interpretation of Mise Au Point by Ivan Zaknic*. New Haven, Conn.: Yale University Press, 1997.

Zarka, Yves Charles. "The Meaning of Utopia." *The New York Times, Opinionator*. August 28, 2011. http://opinionator.blogs.nytimes.com/2011/08/28/the-meaning-of-utopia/ (accessed on April 15, 2013).

Zarnecki, George. *Romanesque*. New York: Universe Books, 1971.

Zeisel, John. *Inquiry by Design: Environment/Behavior/Neuroscience in Architecture, Interiors, Landscape, and Planning*, rev. ed. New York: Norton, 2006.

Zevi, Bruno. *Architecture as Space: How to Look at Architecture*. Translated by Milton Gendel. Edited by Joseph A. Barry. Revised edition. New York: Horizon Press, 1974.

CONTRIBUTORS

THOMAS BARRIE, AIA, is professor of architecture at North Carolina State University, where he served as school director from 2002–7. He is an award-winning architect and the author of *The Sacred In-Between: The Mediating Roles of Architecture* (*2010*) and *Spiritual Path, Sacred Place: Myth Ritual and Meaning in Architecture* (*1996*). Barrie is a founding member of the Forum for Architecture, Culture and Spirituality.

JULIO BERMUDEZ is an associate professor and directs the sacred space and cultural studies graduate concentration at the Catholic University of America School of Architecture and Planning. Bermudez co-founded and, since 2007, co-directs the Forum for Architecture, Culture and Spirituality, an international group with over three hundred and fifty members. He has received the 1998

AIA Education Honors Award, the 2004–5 ACSA Creative Achievement Award, the 2005 Montagu Creative Career Prize by SiGraDi (a Latin American organization), the 2006 ACADIA Award for Teaching Excellence, and the 2010 Sasada Award (conferred by CAADRIA, Asia).

KARLA CAVARRA BRITTON's academic work focuses on the modern architect's engagement with tradition in twentieth-century architecture and urbanism. Her teaching has emphasized the intersection of classicism and modernization and the evolution of modern ecclesiastical building. Her books include the monograph *Auguste Perret* (*2001*), the prize-winning *Hawaiian Modern* (*2008*), and the interdisciplinary *Constructing the Ineffable* (*2011*).

MICHAEL J. CROSBIE, FAIA, has made significant contributions in architectural journalism, research, teaching, and practice. He has served as an editor at *Architecture: The AIA Journal, Progressive Architecture* and *ArchitectureWeek.com*. Since 2001 he has been the editor-in-chief of *Faith & Form*, a quarterly journal on interfaith religious art and architecture. He is a frequent contributor to *Oculus* magazine, *Architectural Record*, and the *Hartford Courant*. He is the author of more than fifteen books on architecture, including five books for children. Crosbie is chair of the department of Architecture at the University of Hartford and has served as an adjunct professor at Roger Williams University and the Catholic University of America.

KARSTEN HARRIES is the Howard H. Newman Professor of Philosophy at Yale University. He has published and lectured widely on Heidegger, early modern philosophy, and the philosophy of art and architecture. He is the author of more than two hundred articles and reviews and of nine books, including *The Ethical Function of Architecture* (1997), winner of the AIA 8th Annual International Architecture Book Award for Criticism; *Infinity and Perspective* (2001); and *Art Matters: A Critical Commentary on Heidegger's The Origin of the Work of Art* (2009). With Christoph Jamme, he has edited *Martin Heidegger: Kunst, Politik, Technik* (1992), which appeared in an English version as *Martin Heidegger: Politics, Art, and Technology* (1994).

LINDSAY JONES is a professor in the Department of Comparative Studies and the director of the Center for the Study of Religion at Ohio State University. Jones combines long-term interests in architecture and comparative religion, concentrating on sacred architecture and ritual studies. He is author of *Twin City Tales: A Hermeneutical Reassessment of Tula and Chichén Itzá* (1995) and *The Hermeneutics of Sacred Architecture: Experience, Interpretation, Comparison* (*2000*), two volumes. Jones also served as editor-in-chief of the revised second edition of Mircea Eliade's 16-volume *Encyclopedia of Religion* (2005).

REBECCA KRINKE is professor of landscape architecture at the University of Minnesota and a multimedia artist and designer working in sculpture, installations, and site art. Krinke's published works address the trauma-recovery dialectic and include *Contemporary Landscapes of Contemplation* (editor) and chapters in *Manufactured Sites: Rethinking the Post-Industrial Landscape*. Krinke disseminates her work through gallery shows and temporary and permanent public works, which include the *Great Island Memorial Garden* (West Yarmouthport, Mass., with Randall Imai, architect) and *Site Index/West Garden* (University of Minnesota, with John Roloff, public artist). Recent interior installations are the *Present Moment Project* (with Henry Emmons, M.D., and Diane Willow, artist) and *The Table for Contemplation and Action*.

JUHANI PALLASMAA, Finnish architect and honorary FAIA, is one of the most lucid architectural theoreticians and practitioners in the world today. His many books, writings, exhibitions, and buildings are internationally renowned. His *The Eyes of the Skin* (1996) has become a classic book of architectural theory all over the world, and his exhibitions of

Finnish architecture have been displayed in more than thirty countries. He has published several other books, including *The Architecture of Image* (2001), *Encounters, Architectural Essays* (edited by Peter MacKeith, 2006), *The Thinking Hand* (2009), and *Understanding Architecture* (2012). He has been an acting jury member of the Pritzker Prize since 2009, the most prestigious architectural award in the world.

TRAVIS PRICE, FAIA, is registered in ten states, including New York and the District of Columbia. Besides his award-winning architectural practice, he directs the Spirit of Place program in the sacred space and cultural studies graduate concentration at the Catholic University of America School of Architecture and Planning. He is a regular international lecturer at colleges of architecture, environmental forums, the National AIA, the Smithsonian Institution, and the National Geographic Society.

SUZANE REATIG is the recipient of numerous national and international awards. *New York Times* critic Herbert Muschamp described her Metropolitan Community Church, the first newly constructed church for a gay congregation in America, as a "prodigy of the Washington cityscape, a building that recalls Maya Lin's Vietnam Memorial in its enlargement of emotional impact through a reduction of formal means.... Ms. Reatig has made a place for sorting out feelings shattered almost beyond repair. It is a public space for private grief." Addressing the needs of nonprofit groups and individual artist clients that often build in disadvantaged neighborhoods, her work demonstrates that modest budgets and big dreams can support

an architecture of remarkable character and high quality.

FATHER KEVIN SEASOLTZ was a Benedictine monk of Saint John's Abbey in Collegeville, Minnesota. He was on the faculty of the Catholic University of America for twenty-five years. He then became the rector of the Diocesan Seminary in Collegeville and a professor in the School of Theology at Saint John's University in Collegeville. His most recent books are *A Sense of the Sacred: Theological Foundations of Sacred Architecture and Art* (which was awarded first place in the liturgical division by the Catholic Press Association) and *God's Gift Giving: In Christ and through the Spirit*. He was working on a manuscript titled *Virtue Morality, a Virtuous Church and Virtuous Worship* at the time of his passing on April 27, 2013.

MAGED SENBEL, CIP, is a planner, urban designer, and educator. He is an assistant professor of urban design at the School of Community and Regional Planning at the University of British Columbia. His current research is on social mobilization and reflective practice for climate change planning through visualization media and social media. Senbel has numerous publications in the areas of public engagement in local neighborhood planning, particularly as it relates to environmental issues, sustainability, and climate change.

MICHAEL J. SHERIDAN has more than eighteen years of experience as a social work practitioner and administrator in health, mental health, juvenile and criminal justice, and family service settings. She is currently on the faculty of the National Catholic School of Social Service at the Catholic

University of America, where she teaches courses in transpersonal theory and spirituality, diversity and social justice, international social development, conflict resolution and peace-building, and human behavior theory. Sheridan has made numerous scholarly contributions in the area of spirituality and social work that have been used by other researchers of spirituality in various parts of the world. She serves as director of the Center for Spirituality and Social Work at NCSSS and was a founding member of the Society for Spirituality and Social Work.

Well known for his ecclesiastical buildings, **DUNCAN G. STROIK**'s portfolio includes cathedrals, parish churches, shrines, and university chapels across the United States, as well as residential, commercial, and educational buildings. Professor Stroik is the editor of the semi-annual journal *Sacred Architecture*, which he established in 1998. He has co-edited the monograph *Reconquering Sacred Space 2000: The Church in the City of the Third Millennium* and is currently working on a book with Liturgy Training Publications titled *Beauty, Transcendence, and the Eternal*.

SUE ANN TAYLOR is a public anthropologist- in-residence in the Department of Anthropology at American University and an independent consultant in urban anthropology. Recently, she completed an oral history project for the National Park Service and served as a consultant to the Vietnam Veterans Memorial Fund's on-site selection for the Vietnam Veterans Education Center. Among her many publications are *Conserving Place: Prince William Forest Park 1900–1945* (with Arvilla Payne-Jackson) and *Prince William Forest Park: The African American Experience*.

RICHARD S. VOSKO, Hon. AIA, a Catholic priest from the Diocese of Albany, New York, has been a sacred space planner for Christian and Jewish congregations throughout North America since 1970. His portfolio contains award-winning projects like Central Synagogue (New York) and the Cathedral of Our Lady of the Angels (Los Angeles). His many personal honors include the Elbert M. Conover Award from AIA IFRAA, the Georgetown University Center for Liturgy Award, and the Berakah Award for scholarship and practice in liturgical design. He is the author of *God's House Is Our House: Re-Imagining the Environment for Worship* and is currently writing a compendium on all the Roman Catholic cathedrals in the United States.

THOMAS WALTON's twenty-five-year career in teaching at the Catholic University of America's School of Architecture and Planning focused on design as an expression of social and cultural values and the rich layers of meaning embedded in architecture. For the past twenty-one years, he has been editor of the Design Management Institute's *Design Management Review*. He has lectured for the American Institute of Architects and the Smithsonian Institution and served as a consultant to the National Endowment for the Arts.

MARK E. WEDIG is associate dean for graduate studies in the College of Arts and Sciences, chair of the Department of Theology and Philosophy, and professor of theology at Barry University. He is a Dominican friar of the province of St. Martin de Porres. His publications include "The Arrangement and Furnishing of Churches for the Celebration of the Eucharist: De

Ecclesiarum Dispositione et Ornatu ad
Eucharistiam Celebrandam" (with Richard
Vosko), "No Neutral Zones: Hermeneutics
and the Interpretation of Liturgical Space,"
"Edifice and Image: Reform of the Roman
Catholic Worship Environment," and "The
Visual Hermeneutics of Hispanic/Latino
Popular Religion and the Recovery of the
Image in Christian Praxis."

INDEX

nontheistic, 160–61

Norberg-Schulz, Christian, 121, 284n19

nothingness, xv, 13, 133, 226, 228, 297n5

numinous, 3–4, 10, 15–16, 19–20, 33, 39, 47, 49, 53, 56, 61–62, 88–90, 92, 95, 96, 102–5, 150, 158, 162, 169–70, 208–9, 225–30, 239, 243, 247–49, 252–54, 256–57, 259, 261, 276nn1–2, 276n6, 280n57, 281n71–72, 287n36; architectural, 12, 254; consciousness, 226; dimension, 108; experience, 73, 90–91, 105, 107, 209, 229, 257–59, 276n2; space, 50

Nussbaum, Martha, 149–53, 287n31, 287n35

Old Testament, 114–16

oneness, 103, 238

openness, 22, 215, 218–20, 226, 238

original sin, 114

Osborne, Harold, 192, 293n52

other-worldly, 28, 105, 226

Other, 69, 80, 88, 105, 114, 282n75

Otto, Rudolf, 3, 15, 88, 96, 103, 105, 107, 162, 169, 193, 225–37, 228–30, 239, 269n1, 272n12, 276n1–2, 281n68, 281n72

pagan, 121, 176, 239

paganism, 71, 274n17, 284n14

Palenque, 172, 292n41

Pallasmaa, Juhani, 11, 14–16, 89, 231, 263–65, 269n2, 271n19, 272n33, 272n36

Panofsky, Erwin, 75, 193, 275n3, 291n35, 293nn58–59, 293n66, 294n83

Pantheon, Rome, 5, 263, 276n6

paradise, 11, 37, 72, 106, 185, 211, 218, 259, 272n11, 272n17, 274n18

paradisus claustralis, 185

Pärt, Arvo, 32

Parthenon, 12, 90–94, 96–103, 105–8, 270n17, 276n9, 277n17, 278n23, 278n25, 278n28, 279n30, 279n39, 280n64, 281n71, 282n89, 282n92, 283n95

Pattern Language, 67, 274n8

pedagogic, 16, 194, 278n17

Pentecostal, 127

Pérez-Gómez, Alberto, 4, 42, 89, 95, 269n4, 272n19, 273n40, 276n5, 272n7, 276n8, 279n35

performance, 16, 66, 103, 155, 165, 172, 187, 190, 214

Perrault, Dominique, 49–50

Perret, Auguste, 82, 97

phenomenology, 8, 10, 13, 15, 88, 90–91, 133, 135, 162, 277n10, 280n61, 282n75, 282n92

Piano, Renzo, 26

Picard, Max, 28–30, 271n17,

Pickstock, Catherine, 138, 286n14

Piero della Francesca, 29

pietas, 86–87

pilgrim, 131, 135–36, 138, 140, 142, 194–96, 205, 260, 294n77, 295n95, 297n2

pilgrimage, xv, 35, 38, 100, 114, 165, 243, 264, 292n35

plan, basilican, 176, 290n8

plan, Latin, 176

Plato, 88, 95, 249, 269n3

pluralism, 69, 74, 86, 168

poetic, 12, 16, 38, 42, 67, 73, 94, 107, 247, 276n7–8

poetics, 248–49, 273n42

poetry, 29, 38, 70, 100–101, 201, 211, 214, 275n23, 282n74, 296n9

Pollock, Jackson, 217, 292n41

pollution, 64

polytheist, 144

positivism, 131, 203; rational, 205

postmodern, 13–14, 89, 91, 110, 130–33, 135, 138–42, 218, 269n3, 283n6, 285n1, 285n5, 285n11, 286n14; postmodernity, 6, 131–33, 142

postmodernism, 132, 135, 142; postmodernist, 86, 132, 140

postsecular age, 76, 82

poststructuralism, 7, 163

poverty, 13, 160, 131, 133, 148, 185

Power, Nancy Goslee, and Associates, 157

powerlessness, 13, 133, 226, 230

practice: architectural, 4, 7, 9, 75; contemplative, 48, 199; meditative, 191; religious, 8, 164–65, 169, 201

prayer, 13, 58, 69, 116–17, 119, 138, 141, 163–65, 183–85, 201, 246, 265, 278n16, 281n67

pre-Columbian, 14–15, 172–74, 177–78, 181–82, 186, 189–90, 192, 196–99, 202–5, 248, 264–65, 290n2, 294n80, 295n88, 295n92, 295n95

premodernity, 7

presence, 3, 13, 19, 19, 23, 26, 71, 79, 87, 100, 103, 105, 107–8, 113, 116, 118, 120, 123, 126–28, 132, 136, 211, 213, 215, 217, 225–28, 263–64, 281n66, 282n83, 283n7, 283n95, 285n11; divine, 114–16, 132, 138, 150, 170, 209; God's, 122, 126, 128, 133, 258, 284n11; sacramental, 136

primitive hut, 34, 37–39, 43, 261

procession, 16, 123, 125–26, 174, 176, 178, 181, 239, 261, 264, 290n8

profane, 39, 70, 73, 162–63, 166, 170, 189, 215, 226, 246–47, 256, 283n4, 291n25, 291n27, 292n35; outside, 182–83; space, 162, 248

Promised Land, 115

Protestant church, 122, 127, 270n14

Protestantism, 14, 121–25, 127, 171, 190, 198–99, 201, 205, 284n36, 285n43

Protestant Reformation, 121–23

Provensal, Henry, 96–97, 108

psychical distance, 211, 296n8

Pueblo people, 248

Pugin, Augustus Welby, 75, 275n4

purpose, 8–9, 14–15, 19, 20, 22, 56, 94, 138, 144–45, 159, 175, 189, 191, 220, 257–58, 281n70; devotional, 19, 21; of life, 74, 163; religious, 133

Rappaport, Roy, 162

rapture, 94, 105, 107–8

rationalism, 97, 124

rationality, xiv, 77, 89, 276n8

Rawls, John, 146–48, 150, 286n18, 287n16

realization, xiv, 8, 11, 28, 71, 107, 120, 132, 226, 294n77

Reatig, Nooni, 233–35

Transcending Architecture: Contemporary Views on Sacred Space was designed in Garamond Premier Pro with Hypatia display and typeset by Kachergis Book Design of Pittsboro, North Carolina. It was printed on 70-pound Huron Matte and bound by Thomson-Shore of Dexter, Michigan.